Management Accounting For Business Decisions

First Edition

Insert within front cover of book

MANAGEMENT ACCOUNTING FOR BUSINESS DECISIONS

Will Seal

London Boston Burr Ridge, IL Dubuque, IA Madison, WI New York San Francisco
St. Louis Bangkok Bogotá Caracas Kuala Lumpur Lisbon Madrid Mexico City Milan
Montreal New Delhi Santiago Seoul Singapore Sydney Taipei Toronto

Management Accounting for Business Decisions
Will Seal
ISBN-13 9780077126728
ISBN-10 0077126726

Published by McGraw-Hill Education
Shoppenhangers Road
Maidenhead
Berkshire
SL6 2QL
Telephone: 44 (0) 1628 502 500
Fax: 44 (0) 1628 770 224
Website: www.mheducation.co.uk

British Library Cataloguing in Publication Data
A catalogue record for this book is available from the British Library

Library of Congress Cataloguing in Publication Data
The Library of Congress data for this book has been applied for from the Library of Congress

Acquisitions Editor: Leiah Batchelor
Development Editor: Emma Ramirez Gain
Head of Production: Beverley Shields
Marketing Manager: Alexis Thomas

Text design by Hard Lines
Cover design by Adam Renvoize
Typesetting by S R Nova Pvt Ltd., Bangalore, India
Printed and bound in the UK by Ashford Colour Press

ISBN-13 9780077126728
ISBN-10 0077126726

This book is dedicated to my family

Will Seal

① Production budget : closing inventory − Opening inventory + Sales.

Chapter 13:

① Number of units (WIP) to be processed = time available / cycle time.

② Little's law: Throughput ~~rate~~ time (time available) = WIP X cycle time.

③ Throughput rate = $\frac{\text{WIP}}{\text{Cycle time}}$.

④ Throughput efficiency = $\frac{\text{work content}}{\text{throughput time}}$ X 100%

⑤ Utilisation = $\frac{\text{time activated}}{\text{time available}}$

⑥ Throughput efficiency = $\frac{\text{work content}}{\text{throughput time}}$ X 100%.

⑦ Process velocity (throughput ratio) = $\frac{\text{throughput time}}{\text{Value-added time}}$ (增值时间)

⑧ Efficiency = $\frac{\text{actual output}}{\text{Standard output}}$

⑨ Productivity = $\frac{\text{output}}{\text{Input}}$

① Total annual cost of holding inventory of the Component = {[Buffer inventory + (EOQ ÷ 2)] X Annual holding cost per Component}

Operations Process.

— multi-stage Processes.

① Buffering. 0 → 1/2 → 1.

② Blocking 1 → 2/2 → 1

③ Starving 1 → 0/2 → 0

④ Bottleneck 3 units/hr → 5 units/hr → 2 units/hr (Longest cycle time. Smallest throughput rate)

Brief table of contents

① Reorder Point (ROP)
ROP = DD X L under certainty
ROP = (DD X RC) + SS. under uncertainty
where DD = periodic demand
L = length of replenishment cycle
SS = safety stock.

② Inventory turnover
= (Cost goods sold) (av. value Inventory)
Formula = $\frac{D}{Q/2 + SS}$

Detailed table of contents

Preface

Aim and approach

Building on the success of *Management Accounting*, which is soon to be in its 4th edition, I created this new text with the aim of offering a streamlined and balanced introduction to management accounting and practice. This text is written to cover the core topics in introductory management accounting in a less technical way. It is primarily intended as an introductory text for students taking a degree in accounting, or business studies with a substantial element of accounting, and is ideal for students who have no prior management accounting knowledge. It is informed by ongoing academic research and my concern to place management accounting in its organizational and institutional context.

Content

McGraw-Hill undertook extensive market research to identify which key topics are required on introductory management accounting modules throughout the UK and Europe, and I believe the contents of this book are closely aligned to those topics. The result is a focused and concise textbook, which gets to the very heart of the subject in a simple and effective manner. This book has a strong focus on material for decision makers rather than for specialist preparers of management accounts. The key content features are outlined below:

- The book is useful for students who are not required to learn the more advanced topics found in detailed management accounting textbooks. For example, this book does not include coverage of process costing and has very little on profit reporting issues. The material on variance analysis and budgeting material have also been simplified.
- The content is not too technical and the numerical material has been kept to a minimum without losing the essence of the subject. For example, it seeks to avoid complex calculations, such as multiple regression, which can sometimes overwhelm students.
- The book has a clear real-world focus. Due to the reduced technical material, the multiple examples from the real world take on more prominence.

Learning features

As with my other textbook, I have aimed to maintain a clear and succinct writing style that students find accessible and engaging. I also believe in practice as a method of learning and, for this reason, I have included the following:

- Pedagogical features such as *Focus on Business Practice* boxes and the chapter-opening vignettes (*Concepts in Context*), which provide current real-world examples to support students in the application of key concepts. This was something that was requested by reviewers, so I hope the readers of this text will find these examples both interesting and insightful. After all, the aim of this text is to provide future decision makers with the knowledge, skills and tools that they will need to implement management accounting theory in the real world.
- Today's economy is increasingly dependent on the services industry and it is likely that most students will enter into careers in this sector. With the aim of reflecting the current economic climate, this book features balanced coverage of both manufacturing and services, with examples from a wide range of industries. The service examples focus on areas such as human resources, waste management, healthcare and hospitality.

More details on the book's excellent pedagogy can be found in the *Guided tour* on pages xiv–xv.

Resources

A wealth of online resources provide support for students, including tests, quizzes and practice exercises. For instructors, solutions and teaching resources ensure the book is as easy to use as possible. An exciting addition to the support package for this book is *Connect*™ *Plus* Accounting. This excellent online assignment and assessment platform provides opportunities for additional interaction between students and instructors, allowing instructors to continually assess each student's individual progress through practice and assessment. More information on this can be found in the technology section on pages xvi–xx.

Guided tour

LO Learning **objectives**

After studying Chapter 1, you should be able to:

1. Describe what managers do and why they need accounting information
2. Appreciate the key characteristics of management accounting information
3. Review the impact on business of organizational and technological change, managing for value, the sustainability agenda and corporate governance
4. Appreciate that management accounting principles can be useful irrespective of who applies them or where they are located in an organization

Learning objectives

Each chapter opens with a set of learning objectives, summarizing what you should learn from each chapter. There are also Learning Objective icons to indicate where in the chapter each objective is accomplished.

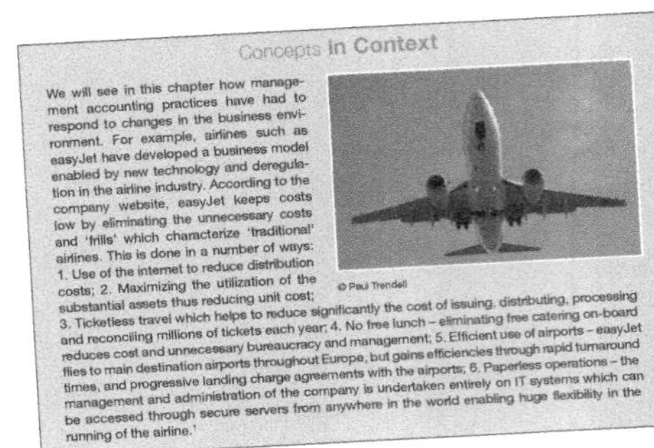

Concepts **in Context**

We will see in this chapter how management accounting practices have had to respond to changes in the business environment. For example, airlines such as easyJet have developed a business model enabled by new technology and deregulation in the airline industry. According to the company website, easyJet keeps costs low by eliminating the unnecessary costs and 'frills' which characterize 'traditional' airlines. This is done in a number of ways: 1. Use of the internet to reduce distribution costs; 2. Maximizing the utilization of the substantial assets thus reducing unit cost; 3. Ticketless travel which helps to reduce significantly the cost of issuing, distributing, processing and reconciling millions of tickets each year; 4. No free lunch – eliminating free catering on-board reduces cost and unnecessary bureaucracy and management; 5. Efficient use of airports – easyJet flies to main destination airports throughout Europe, but gains efficiencies through rapid turnaround times, and progressive landing charge agreements with the airports; 6. Paperless operations – the management and administration of the company is undertaken entirely on IT systems which can be accessed through secure servers from anywhere in the world enabling huge flexibility in the running of the airline.'

© Paul Trendell

Concepts in Context

These chapter-opening vignettes introduce you to the topics to follow and ground the chapter concepts in real-life terms.

Focus on Business Practice

Business planning: Eco-hotel

© Sashi Ono

James has a proposal to build an 'Eco-hotel' on an island in the Red Sea. The project involves renovating a historic site using local labour and materials and the latest 'green' sustainable technologies. In order to attract investors, James has produced a prospectus which includes detailed forecasts of revenues, costs and profits for the next ten years. In the prospectus, he has also explained what assumptions he has made about likely visitor numbers and possible competitors for the main recreational activity in the area, which is scuba diving in the warm and spectacular waters of the Red Sea.

James has produced a business *plan* but this plan can also form the basis of a *control model*. Once the project is under way, James can check whether his plans are being realized – are the costs over-running? Are the visitor numbers coming through? Are there any actions that need to be taken to keep the project on track? Or maybe the plans have to be modified?

Exercise: Refer to Exhibit 1.1 and see how the hotel project matches up to the planning and control features of the model in the exhibit.

Focus on Business Practice

These lively mini real-world examples illustrate precisely how management accounting theory affects well-known companies, using examples of management accounting in a variety of industry sectors.

Exhibits

Each chapter includes four-colour exhibits, illustrating the concepts you need to know and the techniques you need to learn.

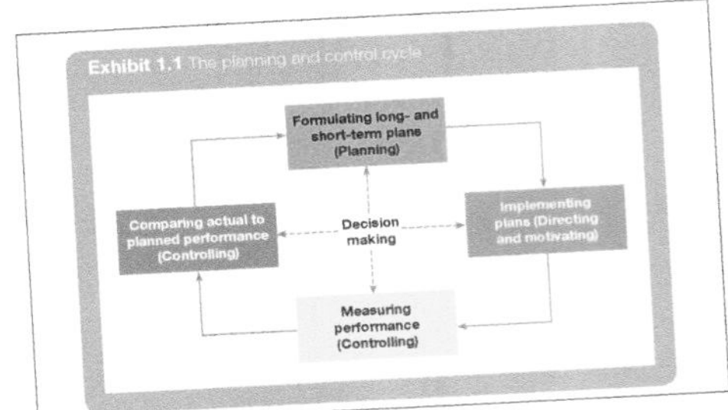

Key terms

Avoidable cost Any cost that can be eliminated (in whole or in part) by choosing one alternative over another in a decision-making situation. In managerial accounting, this term is synonymous with relevant cost and differential cost (p. 76).

Bottleneck A machine or process that limits total output because it is operating at capacity (p. 89).

Constraint A limitation under which a company must operate, such as limited machine time available or limited raw materials available that restricts the company's ability to satisfy demand (p. 88)

Make or buy decision A decision as to whether an item should be produced internally or purchased from an outside supplier (p. 85).

Relevant cost A cost that differs between alternatives in a particular decision. In managerial accounting, this term is synonymous with avoidable cost and differential cost (p. 76).

Special order A one-time order that is not considered part of the company's normal ongoing business (p. 87).

Vertical integration The involvement by a company in more than one of the steps from production of basic raw materials to the manufacture and distribution of a finished product (p. 85).

Key terms

These are highlighted throughout the chapter, and definitions and page references are provided in a useful end-of-chapter list.

Summary

This briefly reviews and reinforces the main topics you will have covered in each chapter to ensure you have acquired a solid understanding of key topics.

Summary

- A standard is a benchmark or 'norm' for measuring performance. In business organizations, standards are set for both the cost and the quantity of inputs needed to manufacture goods or to provide services. Quantity standards indicate how much of a cost element, such as labour time or raw materials, should be used in manufacturing a unit of product or in providing a unit of service. Cost standards indicate what the cost of the time or the materials should be.
- Standards are normally practical in nature, meaning that they can be attained by reasonable, though highly efficient, efforts. Such standards are generally felt to have a favourable motivational impact on employees.
- When standards are compared to actual performance, the difference is referred to as a variance. Variances are computed and reported to management on a regular basis for both the price and the quantity elements of materials, labour and overhead. Price and rate variances for inputs are computed by taking the difference between the actual and standard prices of the inputs and multiplying the result by the amount of input purchased. Quantity and efficiency variances are computed by taking the difference between the actual amount of the input used and the amount of input that is allowed for the actual output, and then multiplying the result by the standard price of the input.

Assessment

Questions

[Instructors note: these are non-technical exercises that might be used for either individual or group work]

connect

1-1 Preparing a business plan

Imagine that you are a newly qualified chef and that you want to set up your own restaurant. You need to raise some funds from the bank. Draw up a list of the financial and non-financial information that you would need in order to present a credible business case to the bank.

1-2 Ethics on the job

Ethical standards are very important in business, but they are not always followed. If you have ever held a job – even a summer job – describe the ethical climate in the organization where you worked. Did employees work a full day or did they arrive late and leave early? Did employees honestly report the hours they worked? Did employees use their employer's resources for their own purposes? Did managers set a good example? Did the organization have a code of ethics and were employees made aware of its existence? If the ethical climate in the organization you worked for was poor, what problems, if any, did it create?

End of chapter assessment material

Each chapter has a wealth of assessment material designed to make learning and self-testing easy and fun. You will find the following features in all chapters:

- Questions
- Exercises
- Problems

Technology to enhance learning and teaching

STUDENTS...

Want to get **better grades**? *(Who doesn't?)*

Prefer to do your **homework online**? *(After all, you are online anyway.)*

With McGraw-Hill's *Connect™ Plus Accounting,*

STUDENTS GET:

- **Easy online access** to homework, tests and quizzes assigned by your instructor.
- **Immediate feedback** on how you're doing. (No more wishing you could call your instructor at 1 a.m.)
- Also **Quick access** to eBook (The material you need to be successful is right at your fingertips.)

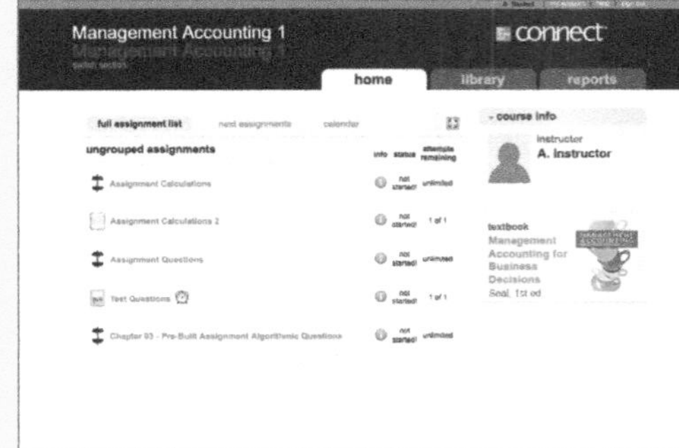

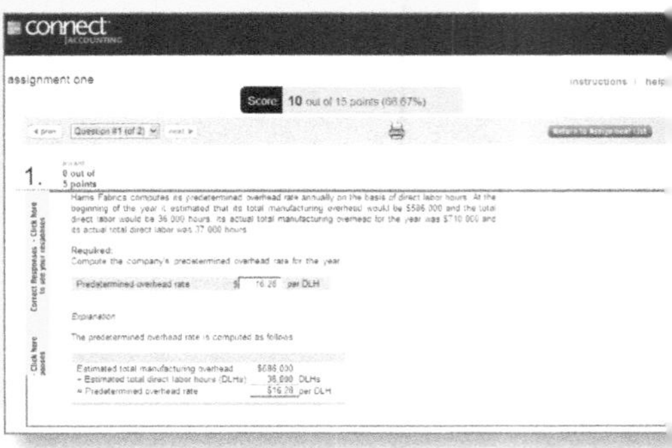

Less managing. More teaching. Greater learning.

INSTRUCTORS...

Would you like your **students** to show up for class **more prepared**?
(Let's face it, class is much more fun if everyone is engaged and prepared...)

Want an **easy way to assign** homework online and track student **progress**?
(Less time grading means more time teaching...)

Want an **instant view** of student or class performance?
(No more wondering if students understand...)

Need to **collect data and generate reports** required for administration or accreditation? *(Say goodbye to manually tracking student learning outcomes...)*

Want to **record and post your lectures** for students to view online?

With *McGraw-Hill's Connect™ Plus Accounting,*

INSTRUCTORS GET:

- Simple **assignment management,** allowing you to spend more time teaching.
- **Auto-graded** assignments, quizzes and tests.
- **Detailed Visual Reporting** where student and section results can be viewed and analysed.
- Sophisticated **online testing** capability.
- A **filtering and reporting** function that allows you to easily assign and report on materials that are correlated to learning outcomes, and level of difficulty.
- An easy-to-use **lecture capture** tool.
- The option to **upload course documents** for student access.

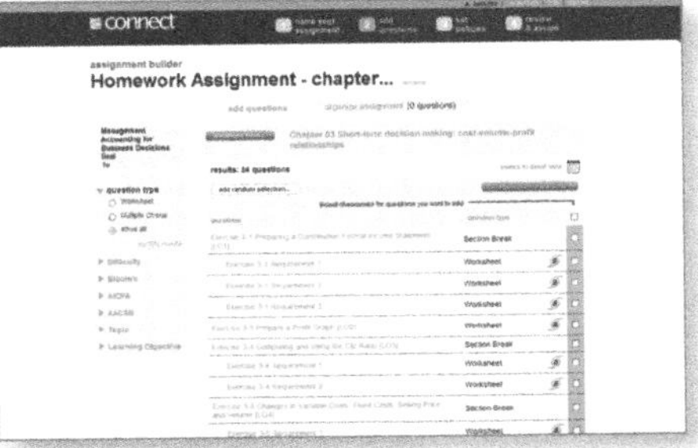

Want an online, **searchable version** of your textbook?

Wish your textbook could be **available online** while you're doing your assignments?

Connect™ Plus Accounting eBook

If you choose to use *Connect™ Plus Accounting*, you have an affordable and searchable online version of your book integrated with your other online tools.

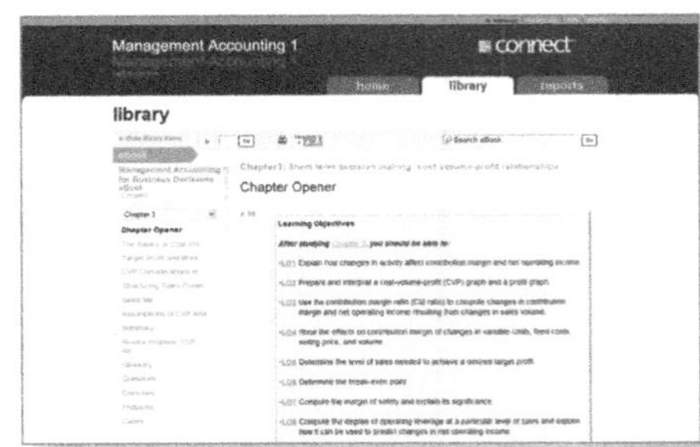

Connect™ Plus Accounting eBook offers features like:

- Topic search
- Direct links from assignments
- Adjustable text size
- Jump to page number
- Print by section

Visit **http://connect.mcgraw-hill.com** today!

Visit **www.mheducation.co.uk/textbooks/sealmabd1** today!

Online Learning Centre (OLC)

For students

The Online Learning Centre (OLC) is your gateway to the following activities designed to accompany the book:

- Self test questions provide immediate feedback on your understanding
- Internet exercises
- Excel-based exercises and questions
- Glossary

For lecturers

This collection of resources has been put together to help lecturers adopting this text save time when preparing their teaching, and to help them engage and challenge their students so that they get more out of their course.

- PowerPoint slides covering the main concepts in each chapter
- Lecturer manual
- Solutions to exercises from the book
- Case studies and solutions
- Group exercises
- Testbank
- Excel-based questions and solutions

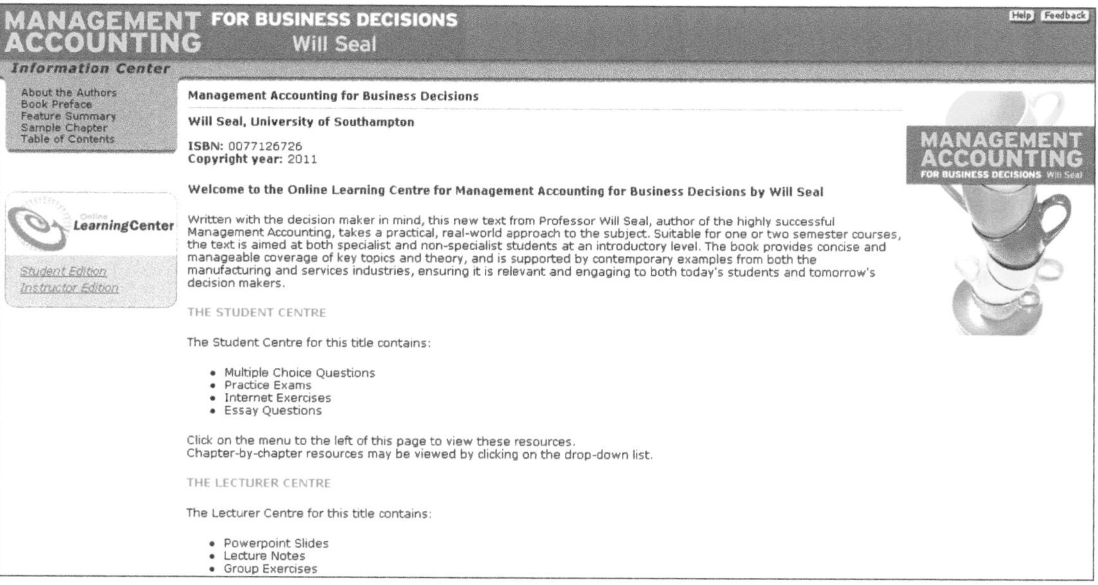

Test Bank available in McGraw-Hill EZ Test Online

A test bank of hundreds of questions is available to lecturers adopting this book for their module. A range of questions is provided for each chapter including multiple choice, true or false, and short answer or essay questions. The questions are identified by type, difficulty and topic to help you to select questions that best suit your needs and are accessible through an easy-to-use online testing tool, **McGraw-Hill EZ Test Online**.

McGraw-Hill EZ Test Online is accessible to busy academics virtually anywhere – in their office, at home or while travelling – and eliminates the need for software installation. Lecturers can choose from question banks associated with their adopted textbook or easily create their own questions. They also have access to hundreds of banks and thousands of questions created for other McGraw-Hill titles. Multiple versions of tests can be saved for delivery on paper or online through WebCT, Blackboard and other course management systems. When created and delivered though EZ Test Online, students' tests can be immediately marked, saving lecturers time and providing prompt results to students.

To register for this FREE resource, visit www.eztestonline.com

Custom publishing solutions: *Let us help make our content your solution!*

At McGraw-Hill Education our aim is to help lecturers to find the most suitable content for their needs delivered to their students in the most appropriate way. Our **custom publishing solutions** offer the ideal combination of content delivered in the way which best suits lecturer and students.

Our custom publishing programme offers lecturers the opportunity to select just the chapters or sections of material they wish to deliver to their students from a database called CREATE™ at

http://create.mheducation.com/uk/

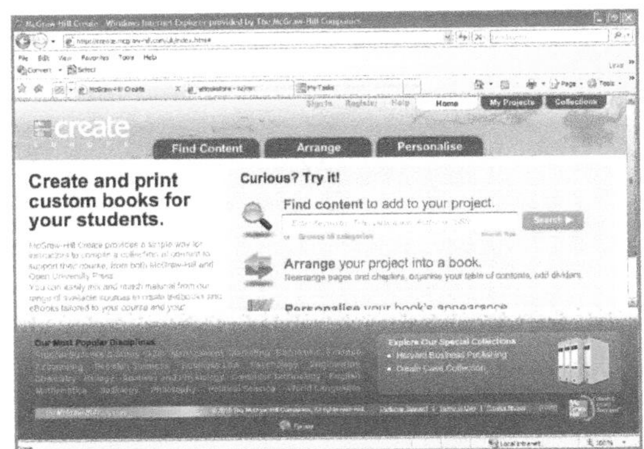

CREATE™ contains over two million pages of content from:

- Textbooks
- Professional books
- Case books – Harvard Articles, Insead, Ivey, Darden, Thunderbird and BusinessWeek
- Taking Sides – debate materials

across the following imprints:

- McGraw-Hill Education
- Open University Press
- Harvard Business Publishing
- US and European material

There is also the option to include additional material authored by lecturers in the custom product – this does not necessarily have to be in English.

We will take care of everything from start to finish in the process of developing and delivering a custom product to ensure that lecturers and students receive exactly the material needed in the most suitable way.

With a Custom Publishing Solution, students enjoy the best selection of material deemed to be the most suitable for learning everything they need for their courses – something of real value to support their learning. Teachers are able to use exactly the material they want, in the way they want, to support their teaching on the course.

Please contact your local McGraw-Hill representative with any questions.

Make the grade!

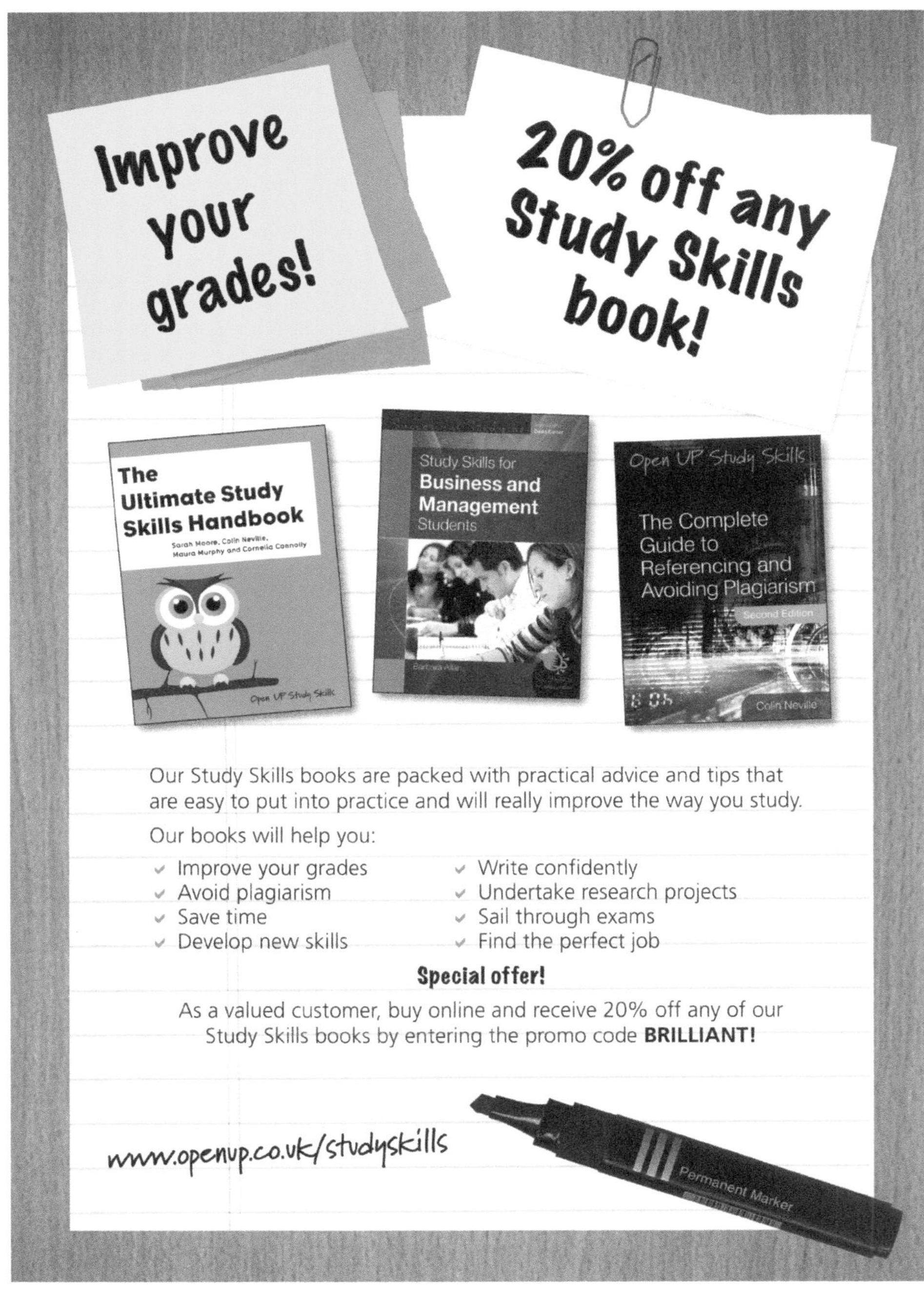

Acknowledgements

Publishers' acknowledgements

Our thanks go to the following people for their feedback at various stages in the text's development:

Rachel Baskerville, University of Exeter
Tongyu Cao, University College Cork
Helen Doyle, University of Manchester
Sandra Einig, Oxford Brookes University
Maria Gee, University of Reading
Samuel Idowu, London Metropolitan University
Tracy Jones, University of Gloucestershire
Wondimu Mekonnen, University of Buckingham
Julinda Nuri, University of Surrey
Martin Quinn, Dublin City University
Zulfiqar Shar, University of Warwick
Bruce Sharman, Regents College London
Helen Smith, University of Abertay Dundee
Petar Sudar, University of Westminster
Rennie Tjerkstra, University of Kent (Canterbury)
Hassan Yazdifar, University of Sheffield

We would also like to extend our thanks to Martin Quinn for his contribution to the *Focus on Business Practice* boxes throughout the text.

Every effort has been made to trace and acknowledge ownership of copyright and to clear permission for material reproduced in this book. The publishers would be pleased to make suitable arrangements to clear permission with any copyright holders whom it has not been possible to contact.

About the author

Will Seal is Professor of Accounting at the University of Southampton, having previously held Chairs at the Universities of Essex, Birmingham and Loughborough. He has also previously lectured at the Universities of Nottingham, Bath, Nottingham Trent and Sheffield Hallam.

Professor Seal is a current and active research academic as well as a lecturer. His research interests include accounting for hotels and hospitality, supply chains and relational contracting; management accounting in local government; management control in shared service centres; management control and corporate governance. He has published in many leading journals including *Accounting, Organizations and Society; Management Accounting Research; British Accounting Review; European Accounting Review; Critical Perspectives on Accounting; Accounting, Accountability and Auditing Journal; Financial Accountability and Management;* and *Cambridge Journal of Economics*. His most recent research paper includes: 'Managerial discourse and the link between theory and practice: From ROI to value-based management', *Management Accounting Research*, 21, 2010, pp. 95–109. Currently Professor Seal also serves as a member on editorial boards for *Management Accounting Research; Financial Accountability and Management* and *Qualitative Research in Accounting and Management.*

He is currently working on updating the fourth edition of his well known textbook, *Management Accounting* (with R. Garrison and E. Noreen), also published by McGraw-Hill.

Part I

An introduction to management accounting

Chapter 1
Accounting and decision making in business

LO Learning objectives

After studying Chapter 1, you should be able to:

1 Describe what managers do and why they need accounting information
2 Appreciate the key characteristics of management accounting information
3 Review the impact on business of organizational and technological change, managing for value, the sustainability agenda and corporate governance
4 Appreciate that management accounting principles can be useful irrespective of who applies them or where they are located in an organization

Concepts in Context

© Paul Trendell

We will see in this chapter how management accounting practices have had to respond to changes in the business environment. For example, airlines such as easyJet have developed a business model enabled by new technology and deregulation in the airline industry. According to the company website, easyJet keeps costs low by eliminating the unnecessary costs and 'frills' which characterize 'traditional' airlines. This is done in a number of ways: 1. Use of the internet to reduce distribution costs; 2. Maximizing the utilization of the substantial assets thus reducing unit cost; 3. Ticketless travel which helps to reduce significantly the cost of issuing, distributing, processing and reconciling millions of tickets each year; 4. No free lunch – eliminating free catering on-board reduces cost and unnecessary bureaucracy and management; 5. Efficient use of airports – easyJet flies to main destination airports throughout Europe, but gains efficiencies through rapid turnaround times, and progressive landing charge agreements with the airports; 6. Paperless operations – the management and administration of the company is undertaken entirely on IT systems which can be accessed through secure servers from anywhere in the world enabling huge flexibility in the running of the airline.[1]

What is management accounting?

Planning

LO 1 In simple terms, **management accounting** provides information that may be used to plan, direct, motivate and control an organization. Although it is predominantly used by managers in an organization, management accounting information might also be the basis of a business plan that can be presented to outside interested parties such as banks or potential private investors. Among other data, potential investors look at the *sales volumes*, *profit margins* and *costs*. They will also consider the *cash* needs of the business. Going forward, the plan should indicate not just long-term projections of profit but suggest a way of co-ordinating and controlling the business so that it is 'kept on track'.

The plans of management are often expressed formally in **budgets**, and the term budgeting is applied generally to describe this part of the planning process. Typically, budgets are prepared annually and represent management's plans in specific, quantitative terms. These data will be collected, analysed and summarized for management use in the form of budgets. Although they may be prepared annually, ever cheaper and more powerful computer packages now mean that actual outturns can be checked against the planned budget with great frequency and with a high level of detail, with data that can be 'sliced and diced'.

Directing and motivating

In addition to planning for the future, managers must oversee day-to-day activities and keep the organization functioning smoothly. This requires the ability to motivate and effectively direct people. Managers assign tasks to employees, arbitrate disputes, answer questions, solve on-the-spot problems, and make many small decisions that affect customers and employees. In effect, directing is that part of the managers' work that deals with the routine and the here and now. Management accounting data, such as daily sales reports, are often used in this type of day-to-day decision making.

Controlling

In carrying out the **control** function, managers seek to ensure that the plan is being followed. **Feedback** which signals whether operations are on track, is the key to effective control. In sophisticated organizations this feedback is provided by detailed reports of various types. One of these reports, which compares budgeted to actual results, is called a **performance report**. Performance reports suggest where operations are

Exhibit 1.1 The planning and control cycle

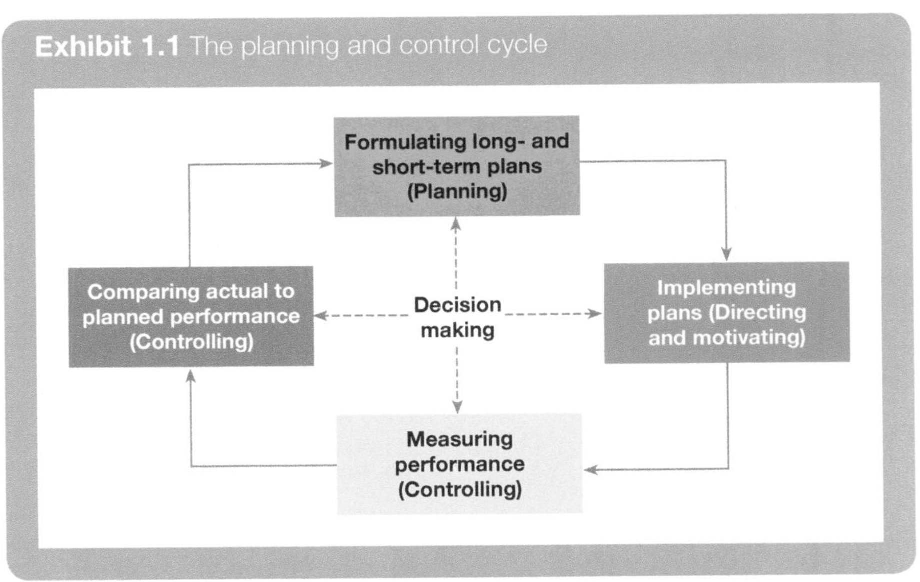

Focus on Business Practice

Business planning: Eco-hotel

© Sashi Ono

James has a proposal to build an 'Eco-hotel' on an island in the Red Sea. The project involves renovating a historic site using local labour and materials and the latest 'green' sustainable technologies. In order to attract investors, James has produced a prospectus which includes detailed forecasts of revenues, costs and profits for the next ten years. In the prospectus, he has also explained what assumptions he has made about likely visitor numbers and possible competitors for the main recreational activity in the area, which is scuba diving in the warm and spectacular waters of the Red Sea.

James has produced a business *plan* but this plan can also form the basis of a *control model*. Once the project is under way, James can check whether his plans are being realized – are the costs over-running? Are the visitor numbers coming through? Are there any actions that need to be taken to keep the project on track? Or maybe the plans have to be modified?

Exercise: Refer to Exhibit 1.1 and see how the hotel project matches up to the planning and control features of the model in the exhibit.

not proceeding as planned and where some parts of the organization may require additional attention. As we shall see in following chapters, providing this kind of feedback to managers is one of the central purposes of management accounting.

The planning and control cycle

The work of management can be summarized in a model such as the one shown in Exhibit 1.1. The model, which depicts the **planning and control cycle**, illustrates the smooth flow of management activities from planning through directing and motivating, controlling, and then back to planning again. All of these activities involve *decision making*, so it is depicted as the hub around which the other activities revolve.

An overview of management accounting principles

LO 2

Financial accounting is mandatory; that is, it must be done. Various outside parties such as the Stock Exchange regulators and the tax authorities require periodic financial statements. Management accounting, on the other hand, is not mandatory. A company is completely free to do as much or as little as it wishes. Since management accounting is completely optional, the important question is always, 'Is the information useful?' rather than, 'Is the information required?' With these criteria in mind, management accounting is characterized by:

- **An emphasis on the future.** Since planning is such an important part of the manager's job, management accounting has a strong future orientation. In contrast, financial accounting primarily provides

summaries of past financial transactions. Changes are constantly taking place in economic conditions, customer needs and desires, competitive conditions and so on.

- **Relevance and flexibility of data.** Managers want information that is relevant even if it is not completely objective or verifiable. By relevant, we mean appropriate for the problem at hand. The management accounting information system should be flexible enough to provide whatever data are relevant for a particular decision.
- **Emphasis on timeliness rather than precision.** Timeliness is often more important than precision to managers. If a decision must be made, a manager would much rather have a good estimate now than wait a week for a more precise answer. A decision involving tens of millions of pounds does not have to be based on estimates that are precise down to the penny, or even to the pound. Management accounting increasingly places considerable weight on non-monetary data. For example, information about customer satisfaction is of tremendous importance even though it would be difficult to express such data in a monetary form. If customers are dissatisfied then the future revenues and profits of the organization might be at risk.
- **Focus on the segments of an organization.** Financial accounting is primarily concerned with reporting for the company as a whole. By contrast, management accounting focuses much more on the parts, or segments, of a company. These segments may be product lines, sales territories, divisions, departments, or any other categorization of the company's activities that management finds useful.

Focus on Business Practice

Accounting in human resources

© Andresr

Human resources (HR) professionals often say 'people are our greatest asset', but might not understand what an asset is, or forget to look at the profit and loss account to see what payroll and related costs are. According to a recent article in *People Management*, not many HR professionals have sufficient basic accounting knowledge to understand basic accounting principles. They need to be familiar with the basic financial statements – the profit and loss account (income statement), balance sheet and cash flow statement – as well as understand costs. The article suggests accounting is a communication medium, a language indeed, that not everyone understands. While HR professionals may not think they require fluency in accounting, they do need to make business decisions which are underpinned by sound financial information, for example hiring someone, or approving redundancy packages. Having an understanding of accounting information (rather than just accepting it from accountants) would benefit HR managers and staff. Certainly, management accountants within an organization could provide some help by training HR staff in the basics of accounting and costs.[2]

Exercise: Can you think of how other sections of an organization (like product design, for example) might use accounting information?

Management accounting: responding to challenges in the business environment

LO 3

New business processes and technologies

The last three decades have been a period of tremendous ferment and change in the business environment. Competition in many industries has become worldwide in scope, and the pace of innovation in products and services has accelerated. This has been good news for consumers, since intensified competition has generally led to lower prices, higher quality and more choices. However, the last two decades have been a period of wrenching change for many businesses and their employees. Many managers have learned that cherished ways of doing business do not work any more and that major changes must be made in how organizations are managed and in how work gets done.

Another significant influence on management accounting is new and ever-changing technology, especially in computers and telecommunications. These technologies have not just resulted in the automation of existing manual management accounting systems but have enabled the restructuring of whole industries and economies. Even if some of the hype surrounding the internet has died down a little since the heady days of the late 1990s, the internet has, and is, changing the way business is done. Production philosophies pioneered in manufacturing such as lean production are now applied in service as well as manufacturing activities.

Enterprise resource planning systems

Some technological changes have not just affected the environment of management accounting but have had a direct impact on the collection and dissemination of management information.[3] The increasing use of sophisticated real time information systems known as enterprise resource planning (ERP) provided by companies such as SAP, Oracle, J.D. Edwards and Baan, has changed the nature of management accounting work and the role of the finance function.[4] One of the emerging implications for the management accountant is that there is more emphasis on business support rather than routine information gathering. Furthermore, not only is there a greater dispersion of finance personnel into process areas, but accounting information itself has become more dispersed throughout the organization as it becomes more accessible to non-accounting personnel.

More emphasis on business ethics

If ethical standards in business were not generally adhered to, there would be undesirable consequences for everyone. Essentially, abandoning ethical standards would lead to a lower standard of living with lower-quality goods and services, less to choose from, and higher prices. In short, following ethical rules is not just a matter of being 'nice'; it is absolutely essential for the smooth functioning of an advanced market economy. The single-minded emphasis placed on short-term profits in some companies may make it seem as if the only way to get ahead is to act unethically. When top managers say, in effect, that they will only be satisfied with bottom-line results and will accept no excuses, they are asking for trouble, as recent collapses in the banking sector illustrate.

The increased importance of service sector management

Management accounting has expanded its influence from its traditional base in manufacturing to service sectors, which themselves have become increasing sources of employment and income in many economies. Many traditional management accounting approaches to issues such as costing were developed with manufacturing industry in mind. In comparison with traditional manufacturing where the product is easy to see and touch, products in service industries are less tangible. A bank may offer a number of different 'products' such as types of account or loans which are defined by dimensions such as accessibility or repaymen terms, secured or unsecured and so on. Services cannot be stored in inventory so that managers in bank and other service industries may be less interested in *product* cost but, rather, which *customers* are profitabl and which customers are not. Service industries provide new challenges and opportunities for managemen accounting information, particularly as competitive success is especially dependent on intangible assets suc as employee expertise and customer relations.

Not only are service activities becoming more important relative to manufacturing but they are increasingly subject to reorganization in both public and private sectors.[5] In particular, we have seen the emergenc of shared service centres where the support services of an entire corporation are concentrated in a singl geographical location. Other companies have gone a stage further by sub-contracting them to independen companies in a practice known as outsourcing.[6]

Management accounting's spread into the public sector is driven by government demands for new measures of performance and new delivery systems. Although its precise form and motivation varies in differen countries, this phenomenon, often referred to as the 'New Public Management',[7] may be seen as a globa movement.[8] These developments are not without controversy, especially where there is an attempt to apply in the not-for-profit, public sector organizations, the same management philosophies and techniques tha were originally developed for private, profit-making organizations.

Managing for value

Traditionally, accountants were portrayed as 'bean-counters' or 'corporate policemen' with an emphasis o past performance and organizational control. While these functions are still part of an accountant's role, th trend recently has been to emphasize the creation and management of value. Pressures from corporate raiders and new sources of capital, such as private equity, mean that managers have to be increasingly aware o shareholder value. There are challenges both to *measure* shareholder value and to discover how to *create* i through the adoption and implementation of corporate strategies. Managers are also aware of the importanc of *customer value* and its relationship to shareholder value. Managing for value has to balance the possibl

Focus on Business Practice

New IT and business analysis

© Greg Nicholas

Rachel has trained as a management accountant and is now director of divisional finance in a large restaurant and public house chain. The company has an advanced accounting system in which transactions recording and reporting has been automated. Freed up from routine data gathering, Rachel liaises between the regional operational managers and the company's board as she and her team of analysts monitor and manage the financial performance of the many restaurant and pub brands that make up the business.

Exercise: Note how advances in IT have automated the 'score-keeping' aspects of accounting and enabled managers not only to have more up-to-the-minute business intelligence but also freeing up their time for value creation.

gains to short-run profitability arising from cost-cutting exercises to possible long-run damage to shareholder value as costs may be cut at the expense of customer satisfaction. For the management accountant the challenge is not just to devise appropriate financial and non-financial metrics to measure value but to try and understand cause-and-effect relationships.[9]

Managing for environmental sustainability

While concern about the environment has been around for some decades, the threat of rapid man-induced climate change has raised the profile of a whole range of environmental sustainability issues. Even managers focusing on shareholder value may be concerned about the environment for three main reasons. First, there is a compliance motive – companies may find that they are forced through regulation and green taxes to manage environmental resources more carefully. Second, eco-efficiency not only may save the planet but reduce business costs. Finally, there may be strategic reasons – companies may have customers who demand green business policies and who are increasingly suspicious of 'environmental window dressing' through environmental reporting. **Environmental management accounting** is not just about reporting but collecting and analysing *physical* information on flows of energy, water and other materials as well as *monetary* information on environmental costs and benefits in order to make environmentally sensitive decisions.[10]

The practice of management accounting

LO 4

Management accounting principles may be useful for non-specialists as well as specialists

Although management accounting has traditionally been practised by professionals in a specialized finance function, one of the results of the changes discussed above in technology and organizational processes, has meant that it is not just finance workers but other-finance specialists (such as engineers, doctors and many other professionals) who have become more 'finance literate' and aware of the importance of management accounting data. The spread of management accounting practices to non-accounting managers has been influenced by the changes such as privatization. New information technology has also played a part by 'de-centring' accounting knowledge. Some academics have coined the term 'hybrid accountants' to describe individuals who 'may be accountants (but are) ... more likely people from other functions who are financially literate'.[11] The result is that management accounting practices are not simply located in a specialist finance function but are dispersed throughout all levels in many functional areas of the organization.[12]

The sources of business knowledge

The practice and principles of management accounting have been developed over many decades, even centuries. In the early days the main source of practice was practitioners such as early industrialists at Josiah Wedgewood's potteries or at Alfred Sloan's General Motors. More recently other inputs have come from business schools, management consultants and even management gurus.[13] In the particular case of accounting other contributors to managerial knowledge production include professional bodies. Managerial and business knowledge may be visualized as being produced via a circulation of ideas and practices as shown in Exhibit 1.2.

Yet the processes that impact on the production and circulation of managerial knowledge should not be seen as infallible. Academic theories may be rejected by practitioners on the grounds of 'irrelevance' and practices may develop that weaken rather than enhance long-run business performance.[14] The latest practices may not really be 'best practice' but rather introduced because of managerial fashions and fads. One of the aims of this book is to enable the reader to develop a *critical* understanding of the principles behind management accounting so that faulty practices may be recognized even if they cannot always be changed in a particular organizational setting.

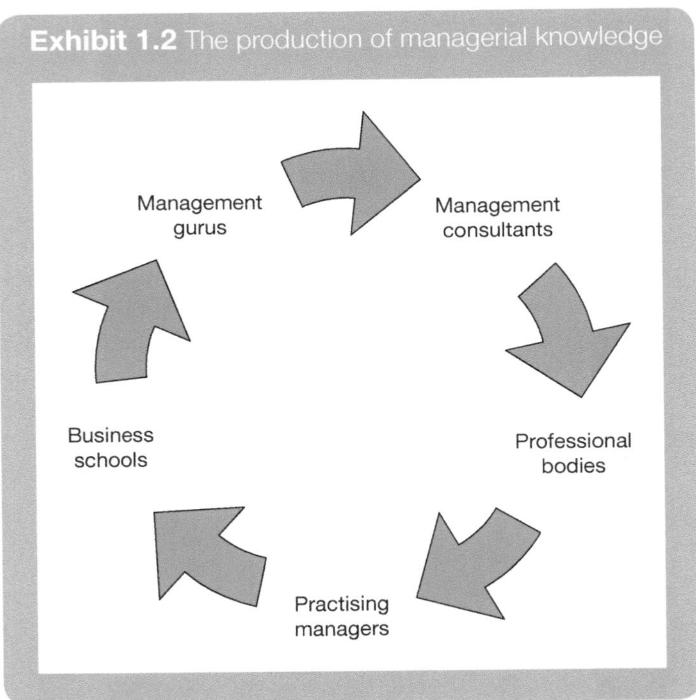

Summary

- Management accounting assists managers in carrying out their responsibilities, which include planning, directing and motivating, and controlling.
- Since management accounting is geared to the needs of the manager rather than to the needs of outsiders, it differs substantially from financial accounting. Management accounting is oriented more towards the future, places less emphasis on precision, emphasizes segments of an organization (rather than the organization as a whole), is not governed by generally accepted accounting principles, and is not mandatory.
- Most organizations are decentralized to some degree. Accountants perform a staff function – they support and provide assistance to others inside the organization.
- The business environment in recent years has been characterized by increasing competition and a relentless drive for continuous improvement. Organizations have also restructured with outsourcing and relocation of company activities. Reformed public sectors are increasingly applying management accounting techniques.
- Management accounting principles and practices may be useful for non-finance specialists and may be useful in many parts of the organization outside the finance function.

Key terms

At the end of each chapter, a list of key terms for review is given, along with the definition of each term. (These terms are highlighted in colour.) Carefully study each term to be sure you understand its meaning, since these terms are used repeatedly in the chapters that follow. The list for Chapter 1 follows.

Budget A detailed plan for the future, usually expressed in formal quantitative terms (p. 4).

Control The process of instituting procedures and then obtaining feedback to ensure that all parts of the organization are functioning effectively and moving towards overall company goals (p. 4).

Environmental management accounting is the collection and analysis of physical and monetary information on environmental costs and benefits in order to make environmentally sensitive decisions (p. 9).

Feedback Accountii managers monitor on problems and/or otherwise go unnoticed

Management accounting Th accounting concerned with information to managers for and controlling operations and making (p. 4).

Performance report A detailed report comparing budgeted data to actual data (p. 4).

Planning and control cycle The flow of management activities through planning, directing and motivating, and controlling, and then back to planning again (p. 5).

Endnotes

1 Adapted from the easyJet company website, 24 March 2005.

2 *People Management*, July 2009.

3 See Scapens, Ezzamel, Burns and Baldvinsdottir (2003).

4 See May (2002).

5 See, e.g., Bain and Taylor (2000).

6 Hayward (2002); CIMA Technical Briefing (2001a).

7 Hood (1995).

8 Olson, Guthrie and Humphrey (1998).

9 For a historical view on value based management see Ittner and Larcker (2001). For a very recent attempt to analyse the cost of customer satisfaction see Cugini, Caru and Zerbini (2007).

10 See IFAC (2005).

11 Burns and Scapens (2000).

12 May (2002).

13 Thrift (2005).

14 Johnson and Kaplan (1987) and Seal (2010).

connect

When you have read this chapter, log on to the Online Learning Centre for *Management Accounting for Business Decisions* at **www.mheducation.co.uk/textbooks/sealmabd1**, where you'll find multiple choice questions, practice exams and extra study tools for management accounting.

Assessment

Questions

connect™

[Instructors note: these are non-technical exercises that might be used for either individual or group work]

1-1 Preparing a business plan

Imagine that you are a newly qualified chef and that you want to set up your own restaurant. You need to raise some funds from the bank. Draw up a list of the financial and non-financial information that you would need in order to present a credible business case to the bank.

1-2 Ethics on the job

Ethical standards are very important in business, but they are not always followed. If you have ever held a job – even a summer job – describe the ethical climate in the organization where you worked. Did employees work a full day or did they arrive late and leave early? Did employees honestly report the hours they worked? Did employees use their employer's resources for their own purposes? Did managers set a good example? Did the organization have a code of ethics and were employees made aware of its existence? If the ethical climate in the organization you worked for was poor, what problems, if any, did it create?

1-3 Relevance of management accounting principles

Imagine that you are:

1. A medical doctor
2. An engineer
3. A lawyer
4. An accountant in professional practice
5. A head teacher
6. A local government manager
7. A manager in a job centre
8. A film producer

In each case suggest when and why management accounting concepts and practices may impact on some aspects of your work.

Part II

Cost and revenues for decision making

Chapter 2
Cost terms and concepts

LO Learning objectives

After studying Chapter 2, you should be able to:

1. Understand the need for costing for external financial reporting
2. Identify each of the three basic cost elements involved in the manufacture of a product
3. Distinguish between product costs and period costs and give examples of each
4. Understand the basics of cost behaviour
5. Identify and give examples of variable costs and fixed costs
6. Define cost classifications used in making decisions: differential costs, opportunity costs and sunk costs

Concepts in Context

This chapter introduces issues concerned with the classification of costs. These issues may be controversial. For example, the British Broadcasting Corporation (BBC) has been accused of concealing the true costs of its individual channels by reporting the cost of items such as news gathering, marketing and publicity under separate headings instead of allocating them as overheads to each channel. It was alleged that the corporation wished to reduce the apparent costs both of expanding into digital broadcasting and the budget of BBC1, the channel that competes with the main commercial broadcasters. The BBC responded by claiming that the new format reflected the corporation's internal reporting system and that the new format was 'more transparent'.[1]

© Anthony Baggett

In introductory financial accounting, you learn that firms prepare periodic financial reports for creditors shareholders and others to show the financial condition of the firm and the firm's earnings performance ove some specified interval. Since firms are generally legally obliged to produce financial statements, many orga nizations may only produce cost data for such *financial reporting* purposes. The financial accounting concept of cost classification will concern us in the first part of the chapter.

Later in this chapter, we will also consider other ways of looking at costs. For example, how do cost *behave* especially with changes in the level of activity? Which costs are fixed and which are variable and ove what range of activity level?

Finally, we will explore different concepts of costs classified according to the principle of 'decision relevance'. The decision-relevance approach may suggest that the costs collected for finance reportin purposes may not be either appropriate or sufficient for decision-making purposes.[2]

LO 1

Costing for financial reporting purposes: an example from manufacturing

Manufacturing costs

Costs are associated with all types of organizations – business, non-business, manufacturing, retail and ser vice. Generally, the kinds of costs incurred and the way in which these costs are classified depends on th type of organization involved. Management accounting is as applicable to one type of organization as t another. The focus in this chapter is on manufacturing companies, since their basic activities include mos of the activities found in other types of business organizations. Manufacturing companies are involved i acquiring raw materials, producing finished goods, marketing, distributing, billing and almost every othe business activity. Therefore, an understanding of costs in a manufacturing company can be very helpful i understanding costs in other types of organizations. Most manufacturing companies divide manufacturin costs into three broad categories: **direct materials**, **direct labour**, and **manufacturing overhead**. A discus sion of each of these categories follows.

LO 2

Direct materials

The materials that go into the final product are called **raw materials**. This term is somewhat misleading since it seems to imply unprocessed natural resources like wood pulp or iron ore. Actually, raw materi als refer to any materials that are used in the final product; and the finished product of one company ca become the raw materials of another company. Direct materials are those materials that become an inte gral part of the finished product and that can be physically and conveniently traced to it. Sometimes i isn't worth the effort to trace the costs of relatively insignificant materials to the end products. Such mino items would include the solder used to make electrical connections in a TV. Materials such as solder an glue are called **indirect materials** and are included as part of manufacturing overhead, which is discusse later in this section.

Direct labour

The term direct labour is reserved for those labour costs that can easily (i.e., physically and conveniently) b traced to individual units of product. Direct labour is sometimes called *touch labour*, since direct labour work ers typically touch the product while it is being made. The labour costs of assembly-line workers, for example would be direct labour costs, as would the labour costs of carpenters, bricklayers and machine operators.

Labour costs that cannot be physically traced to the creation of products, or that can be traced only a great cost and inconvenience, are termed **indirect labour** and treated as part of manufacturing overhead along with indirect materials. Indirect labour includes the labour costs of caretakers, supervisors, materi als handlers and night security guards. Although the efforts of these workers are essential to production, would either be impractical or impossible accurately to trace their costs to specific units of product. Hence, such labour costs are treated as indirect labour.

Manufacturing overhead

Manufacturing overhead, the third element of manufacturing cost, includes all costs of manufacturing except direct materials and direct labour. Manufacturing overhead includes items such as indirect materials; indirect labour; maintenance and repairs on production equipment; and heat and light, property taxes, depreciation and insurance on manufacturing facilities. A company also incurs costs for heat and light, property taxes, insurance, depreciation and so forth, associated with its selling and administrative functions, but these costs are not included as part of manufacturing overhead. Only those costs associated with *operating the factory* are included in the manufacturing overhead category.

Various names are used for manufacturing overhead, such as *indirect manufacturing cost, factory overhead,* and *factory burden*. All of these terms are synonymous with *manufacturing overhead*.

Manufacturing overhead combined with direct labour is called **conversion cost**. This term stems from the fact that direct labour costs and overhead costs are incurred in the conversion of materials into finished products. Direct labour combined with direct materials is called **prime cost**.

Non-manufacturing costs

Generally, non-manufacturing costs are subclassified into two categories:

1. Marketing or selling costs
2. Administrative costs

Marketing or selling costs include all costs necessary to secure customer orders and get the finished product or service into the hands of the customer. These costs are often called *order-getting* and *order-filling costs*. Examples of marketing costs include advertising, shipping, sales travel, sales commissions, sales salaries and costs of finished goods warehouses.

Administrative costs include all executive, organizational and clerical costs associated with the *general management* of an organization rather than with manufacturing, marketing or selling. Examples of administrative costs include executive compensation, general accounting, secretarial, public relations and similar costs involved in the overall general administration of the organization *as a whole*.

Product costs versus period costs

LO 3

In addition to the distinction between manufacturing and non-manufacturing costs, there are other ways to look at costs. For instance, they can also be classified as either **product costs** or **period costs**. To understand the difference between product costs and period costs, we must first refresh our understanding of the matching principle from financial accounting.

Generally, costs are recognized as expenses on the *profit and loss account* (sometimes alternatively known as the *income statement*)[3] in the period that benefits from the cost. For example, if a company pays for liability insurance in advance for two years, the entire amount is not considered an expense of the year in which the payment is made. Instead, half of the cost would be recognized as an expense each year. This is because both years – not just the first – benefit from the insurance payment. The unexpensed portion of the insurance payment is carried on the balance sheet as an asset called prepaid insurance. You should be familiar with this type of *accrual* from your financial accounting course.

The *matching principle* is based on the accrual concept and states that *costs incurred to generate a particular revenue should be recognized as expenses in the same period that the revenue is recognized*. This means that if a cost is incurred to acquire or make something that will eventually be sold, then the cost should be recognized as an expense only when the sale takes place – that is, when the benefit occurs. Such costs are called *product costs*.

Product costs

For financial accounting purposes, product costs include all the costs that are involved in acqu
making a product. In the case of manufactured goods, these costs consist of direct materials, di
and manufacturing overhead. Product costs are viewed as 'attaching' to units of product as

purchased or manufactured, and they remain attached as the goods go into stock awaiting sale. So, initially, product costs are assigned to a stock account on the balance sheet. When the goods are sold, the costs are released from stock as expenses (typically called cost of goods sold) and matched against sales revenue. Since product costs are initially assigned to stocks, they are also known as *stock-related costs*.

We want to emphasize that product costs are not necessarily treated as expenses in the period in which they are incurred. Rather, as explained above, they are treated as expenses in the period in which the related products *are sold*. This means that a product cost such as direct materials or direct labour might be incurred during one period but not treated as an expense until a following period when the completed product is sold.

Period costs

Period costs are all the costs that are not included in product costs. These costs are expensed on the profit and loss account in the period in which they are incurred, using the usual rules of accrual accounting you have already learned in financial accounting. Period costs are not included as part of the cost of either purchased or manufactured goods. Sales commissions and office rent are good examples of the kind of costs we are talking about. Neither commissions nor office rent are included as part of the cost of purchased or manufactured goods. Rather, both items are treated as expenses on the profit and loss account in the period in which they are incurred. Thus, they are said to be period costs.

As suggested above, *all selling and administrative expenses are considered to be period costs*. Therefore, advertising, executive salaries, sales commissions, public relations, and other non-manufacturing costs discussed

Exhibit 2.1 Summary of cost terms

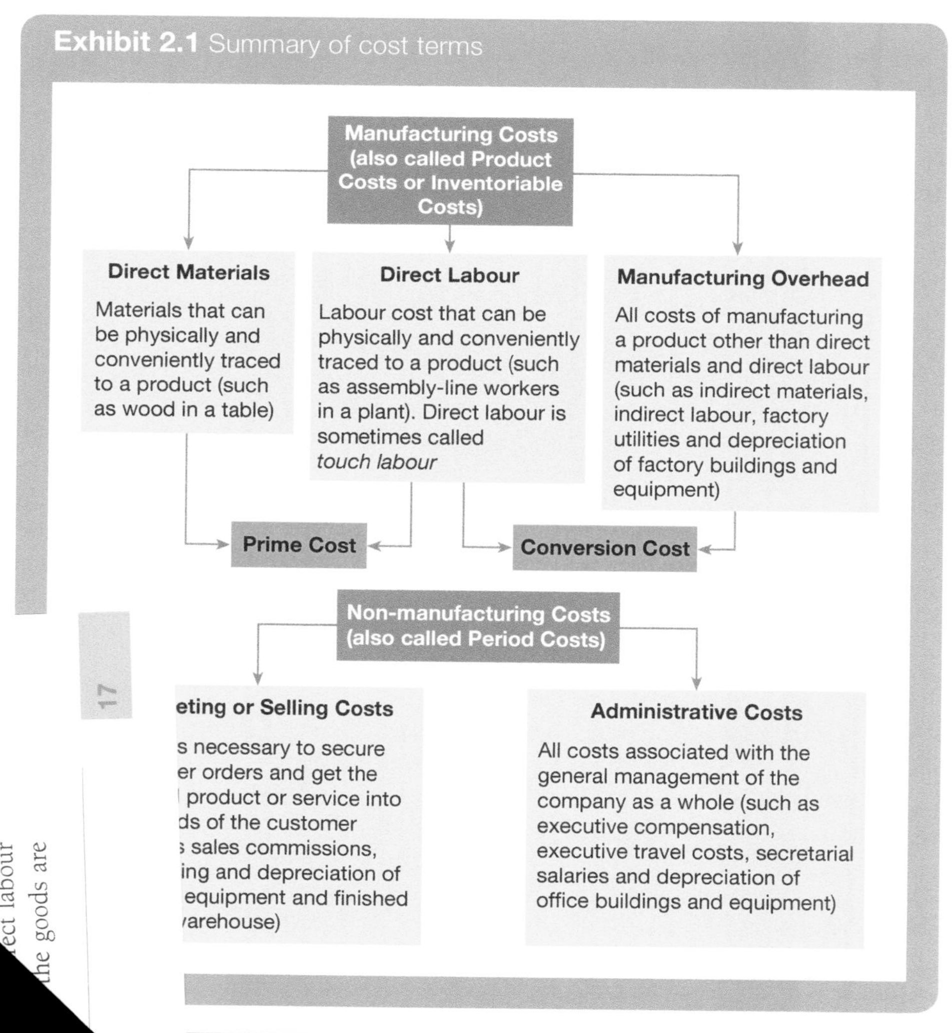

Manufacturing Costs (also called Product Costs or Inventoriable Costs)
Direct Materials
Materials that can be physically and conveniently traced to a product (such as wood in a table)
Direct Labour
Labour cost that can be physically and conveniently traced to a product (such as assembly-line workers in a plant). Direct labour is sometimes called *touch labour*
Manufacturing Overhead
All costs of manufacturing a product other than direct materials and direct labour (such as indirect materials, indirect labour, factory utilities and depreciation of factory buildings and equipment)
Prime Cost
Conversion Cost
Non-manufacturing Costs (also called Period Costs)
eting or Selling Costs
s necessary to secure
er orders and get the
product or service into
ds of the customer
sales commissions,
ing and depreciation of
equipment and finished
arehouse)
Administrative Costs
All costs associated with the general management of the company as a whole (such as executive compensation, executive travel costs, secretarial salaries and depreciation of office buildings and equipment)

earlier would all be period costs. They will appear on the profit and loss account as expenses in the period in which they are incurred.

Exhibit 2.1 contains a summary of the cost terms that we have introduced so far.

Product costs – a closer look

To understand product costs more fully, it will be helpful at this point to look briefly at the flow of costs in a manufacturing company. By doing so, we will be able to see how product costs move through the various accounts and affect the balance sheet and the profit and loss account in the course of producing and selling products.

Exhibit 2.2 illustrates the flow of costs in a manufacturing company. Raw materials purchases are recorded in the Raw Materials inventory account. When raw materials are used in production, their costs are transferred to the Work in Progress inventory account as direct materials. Notice that direct labour cost and manufacturing overhead cost are added directly to Work in Progress. Work in Progress can be viewed most simply as an assembly line where workers are stationed and where products slowly take shape as they move from one end of the assembly line to the other. The direct materials, direct labour and manufacturing overhead costs added to Work in Progress in Exhibit 2.2 are the costs needed to complete these products as they move along this assembly line.

Notice from the exhibit that as goods are completed, their cost is transferred from Work in Progress into Finished Goods. Here the goods await sale to a customer. As goods are sold, their cost is then transferred from Finished Goods into Cost of Goods Sold. It is at this point that the various material, labour and overhead costs that are required to make the product are finally treated as expenses.

Stock/inventory-related costs

As stated earlier, product costs are often called stock-related (or inventoriable[+]) costs. The reason is that these costs go directly into inventory accounts as they are incurred (first into Work in Progress and then into Finished Goods), rather than going into expense accounts. Thus, they are termed **stock-related costs**. *This is a key concept in management accounting, since such costs can end up on the balance sheet as assets if goods are only*

Exhibit 2.2 Cost flows and classifications in a manufacturing company

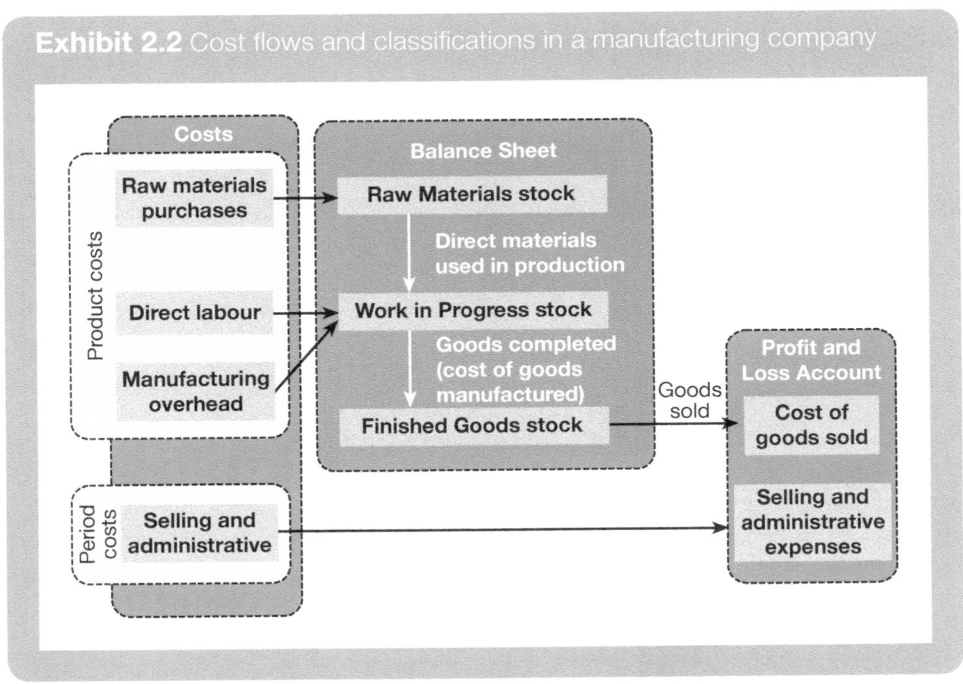

partially completed or are unsold at the end of a period. At the end of the period, the materials, labour and overhead costs that are associated with the units in the Work in Progress and Finished Goods stock accounts will appear on the balance sheet as part of the company's assets. As explained earlier, these costs will not become expenses until later when the goods are completed and sold.

Focus on Business Practice

The full cost of the 2010 Gulf of Mexico oil spill

© M

When management accountants talk about the full costs of a product or service this usually means that all costs – materials, labour and a portion of overhead – are included in the cost of the product/service. In more basic terms, this means that whatever the cost object is, accountants ensure that the cost calculated includes as many costs as possible (if not all). Consider for a moment an event like the oil spill from a BP-owned well in the Gulf of Mexico in 2010. How could an accountant begin to work out the full cost of this environmental disaster? The first thing to do would be to try to think of all the costs which might arise. Prior to this oil spill, the Exxon Valdez tanker leak off Alaska in 1989 was the biggest oil spill in the US. The full cost of the clean up then was $4 billion, more than 600 times what the oil lost was worth at the time. In the Gulf of Mexico case, which at the time of writing is still ongoing, a picture of the full costs of the disaster is beginning to emerge. The first cost is the cost of the 3 million or so litres of oil per day being lost. The clean-up and containment costs are in the order of $5–10 million per day. As of early June 2010, BP themselves had incurred costs of $1.43 billion in clean-up, claims and other costs. Lawsuits to the tune of $25 billion have been filed against BP and related companies. Lost tourism and fishing in and around the Gulf area accounts for $8–12 billion in cost. In addition to the mentioned costs, the costs of extra personnel and administrative staff involved might also be included. While this example does not portray a product or service, it does highlight the difficulties faced by management accountants in calculating any full cost. This does not mean they abandon efforts, however, as in most cases a reasonably accurate full cost figure can be determined.[5]

Exercise: Look up other examples of cases where large-scale damage has been caused by an industrial or environmental type accident/disaster. Try to find out the full costs to the company and/or the community/environment.

As shown in Exhibit 2.2, selling and administrative expenses are not involved in the manufacture of a product. For this reason, they are not treated as product costs but rather as period costs that go directly into expense accounts as they are incurred.

Thus far, we have been mainly concerned with classifications of manufacturing costs for the purpose of determining inventory valuations on the balance sheet and cost of goods sold on the profit and loss account of external financial reports. There are, however, many other purposes for which costs are used, and each

Exhibit 2.3 Summary of cost classifications

Purpose of cost classification	Cost classifications
Preparing external financial statements	• Product costs (inventoriable) • Direct materials • Direct labour • Manufacturing overheads • Period costs (expensed) • Non-manufacturing costs • Marketing or selling costs • Administrative costs
Predicting cost behaviour in response to changes in activity	• Variable cost (proportional to activity) • Fixed cost (constant in total)
Assigning costs to cost objects such as departments or products	• Direct cost (can easily be traced) • Indirect cost (cannot easily be traced; must be allocated)
Making decisions	• Differential cost (differs between alternatives) • Sunk cost (past cost not affected by a decision) • Opportunity cost (forgone benefit)

purpose requires a different classification of costs. We will consider several different purposes for cost classifications in the remaining sections of this chapter. These purposes and the corresponding cost classifications are summarized in Exhibit 2.3. To maintain focus, we suggest that you refer back to this exhibit frequently as you progress through the rest of this chapter.

Cost classifications for predicting cost behaviour

LO 4

Quite frequently, it is necessary to predict how a certain cost will behave in response to a change in activity. **Cost behaviour** means how a cost will react or respond to changes in the level of business activity. As the activity level rises and falls, a particular cost may rise and fall as well – or it may remain constant. For planning purposes, a manager must be able to anticipate which of these will happen; and if a cost can be expected to change, the manager must know by how much it will change. To help make such distinctions, costs are often categorized as variable or fixed.

Variable cost

LO 5

A **variable cost** is a cost that varies, in total, in direct proportion to changes in the level of activity. The activity can be expressed in many ways, such as units produced, units sold, miles driven, beds occupied, lines of print, hours worked, and so forth. A good example of a variable cost is direct materials. The cost of direct materials used during a period will vary, in total, in direct proportion to the number of units that are produced. To illustrate this idea, consider the example of a car factory. Each car requires one battery. As the output of cars increases and decreases, the number of batteries used will increase and decrease proportionately. If car production goes up 10%, then the number of batteries used will also go up 10%. The concept of a variable cost is shown in graphic form in Exhibit 2.4.

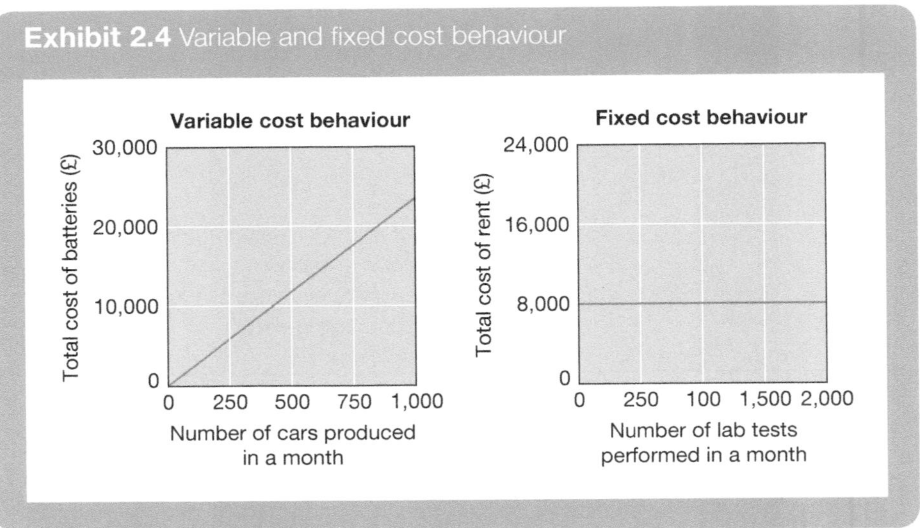

It is important to note that when we speak of a cost as being variable, we mean the *total* cost rises and falls as the activity level rises and falls. This idea is presented below, assuming that a battery costs £24:

Number of cars produced	Cost per battery	Total variable cost-batteries
1	£24	£24
500	24	12,000
1,000	24	24,000

One interesting aspect of variable cost behaviour is that a variable cost is constant if expressed on a *per unit* basis. Observe from the tabulation above that the per unit cost of batteries remains constant at £24 even though the total amount of cost involved increases and decreases with activity.

There are many examples of costs that are variable with respect to the products and services provided by a company. In a manufacturing company, variable costs include items such as direct materials and some elements of manufacturing overhead such as lubricants, shipping costs and sales commissions. For the present we will also assume that direct labour is a variable cost, although as we shall see later, direct labour may act more like a fixed cost in many situations. In a merchandising company, variable costs include items such as cost of goods sold, commissions to salespersons and billing costs. In a hospital, the variable costs of providing healthcare services to patients would include the costs of the supplies, drugs, meals and, perhaps, nursing services.

The activity causing changes in a variable cost need not be how much output is produced or sold. For example, the wages paid to employees at a video outlet will depend on the number of hours the shop is open and not strictly on the number of videos rented. In this case, we would say that wage costs are variable with respect to the hours of operation. Nevertheless, when we say that a cost is variable, we ordinarily mean it is variable with respect to the volume of revenue-generating output – in other words, how many units are produced and sold, how many videos are rented, how many patients are treated and so on.

Fixed cost

A **fixed cost** is a cost that remains constant, in total, regardless of changes in the level of activity. Unlike variable costs, fixed costs are not affected by changes in activity. Consequently, as the activity level rises and falls, the fixed costs remain constant in total amount unless influenced by some outside force, such as price changes. Rent is a good example of a fixed cost. Suppose a hospital rents a machine for £8,000 per month that tests blood samples for the presence of leukaemia cells. The £8,000 monthly rental cost will be sustained regardless of the number of tests that may be performed during the month. The concept of a fixed cost is shown in graphic form in Exhibit 2.4.

Very few costs are completely fixed. Most will change if there is a large enough change in activity. For example, suppose that the capacity of the leukaemia diagnostic machine at the hospital is 2,000 tests per month. If the clinic wishes to perform more than 2,000 tests in a month, it would be necessary to rent an additional machine, which would cause a jump in the fixed costs. When we say a cost is fixed, we mean it is fixed within some *relevant range*. The **relevant range** is the range of activity within which the assumptions about variable and fixed costs are valid. For example, the assumption that the rent for diagnostic machines is £8,000 per month is valid within the relevant range of 0 to 2,000 tests per month.

Fixed costs can create difficulties if it becomes necessary to express the costs on a per unit basis. This is because if fixed costs are expressed on a per unit basis, they will react inversely with changes in activity. In the hospital, for example, the average cost per test will fall as the number of tests performed increases. This is because the £8,000 rental cost will be spread over more tests. Conversely, as the number of tests performed in the clinic declines, the average cost per test will rise as the £8,000 rental cost is spread over fewer tests. This concept is illustrated in the table below:

Monthly rental cost	Number of tests performed	Average cost per test
£8,000	10	£800
8,000	500	16
8,000	2,000	4

Note that if the hospital performs only ten tests each month, the rental cost of the equipment will average £800 per test. But if 2,000 tests are performed each month, the average cost will drop to only £4 per test. More will be said later about the problems created for both the accountant and the manager by this variation in unit costs.

Examples of fixed costs include straight-line depreciation, insurance, property taxes, rent, supervisory salaries, administrative salaries and advertising.

A summary of both variable and fixed cost behaviour is presented in Exhibit 2.5.

Exhibit 2.5 Summary of variable and fixed cost behaviour

	Behaviour of the cost (within the relevant range)	
Cost	**In total**	**Per unit**
Variable cost	Total variable cost increases and decreases in proportion to changes in the activity level.	Variable costs remain constant per unit.
Fixed cost	Total fixed cost is not affected by changes in the activity level within the relevant range.	Fixed costs decrease per unit as the activity level rises and increases per unit as the activity level falls.

Focus on Business Practice

The cost of phone calls

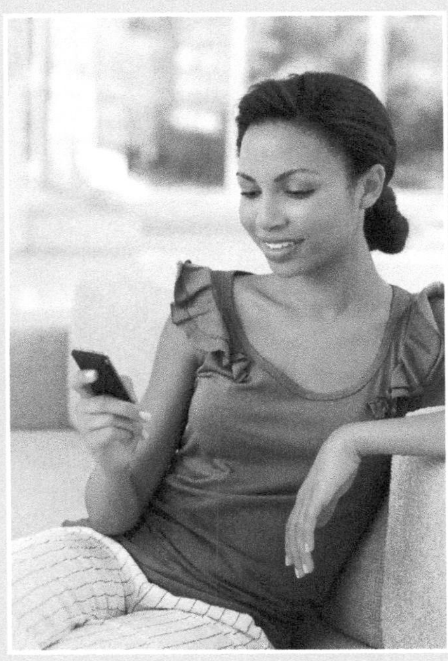
© Neustockimages

Because of national and European regulation of the telecommunications industry, considerable research has been published on calculating the cost of providing telecommunications such as phone, text and other forms of communication. In a recent report, the UK regulator discussed the way that these costs have been calculated using many of the terms used in this and subsequent chapters (direct cost, variable cost, common cost allocation, overheads, avoidable costs, and so on...). As Exhibit 2.6 shows, they have estimated cost behaviour for different types of calls and networks. The exhibit shows how the cost structure varies between different types of traffic and networks. Much of the debate between the regulators and providers concerns the *allocation* of 'common costs' rather than direct costs which may be estimated using economic cost models.

Exercise: Note how the discussions of fair phone tariffs combine the *technological character* of telecommunications, which helps to explain cost behaviour, with *commercial* decisions based on marketing and accounting issues.

Exhibit 2.6 Cost structures in the phone industry

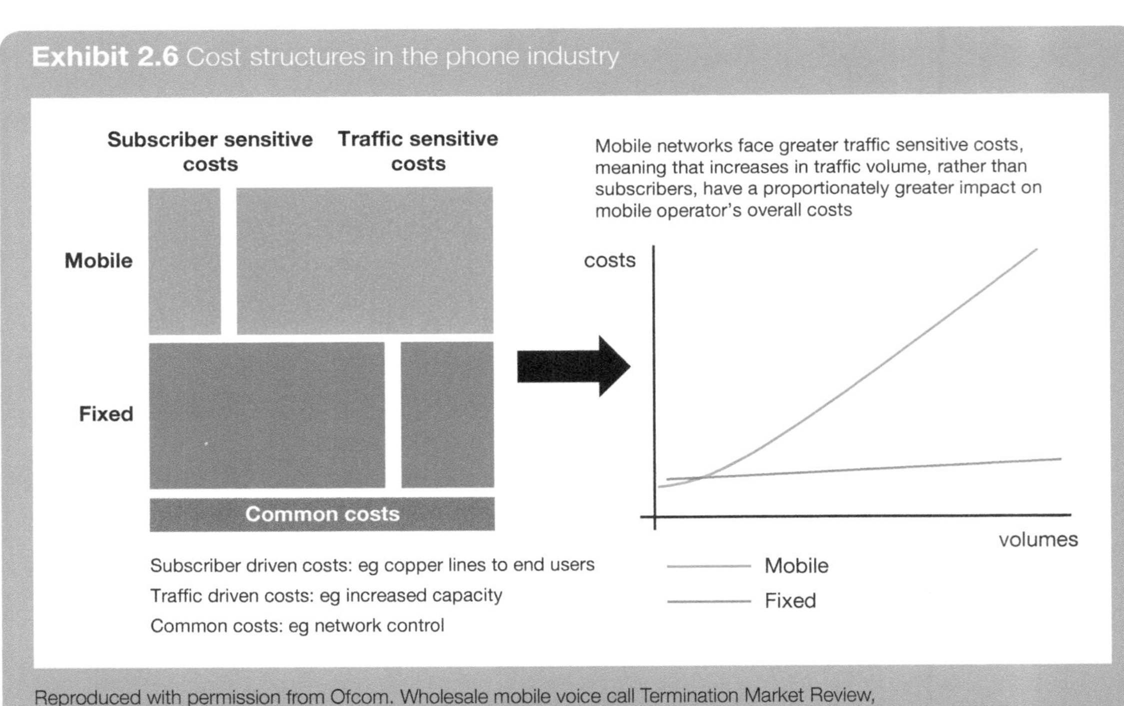

Reproduced with permission from Ofcom. Wholesale mobile voice call Termination Market Review, *Volume 2 – Main consultation,* 1/04/10.

The contribution format

Once the manager has separated costs into fixed and variable elements, what is done with the data? We have already answered this question somewhat by showing how a cost formula can be used to predict costs. To answer this question more fully would require most of the remainder of this text, since much of what the manager does rests in some way on an understanding of cost behaviour. One immediate and very significant application of the ideas we have developed, however, is found in a new profit statement format known as the **contribution approach**. The unique thing about the contribution approach is that it provides the manager with a profit statement geared directly to cost behaviour.

Why a new profit and loss statement format?

The *traditional approach* to the profit and loss statement is not organized in terms of cost behaviour. Rather, it is organized in a 'functional' format – emphasizing the functions of production, administration and sales in the classification and presentation of cost data. No attempt is made to distinguish between the behaviour of costs included under each functional heading. Under the heading 'Administrative expense', for example, one can expect to find both variable and fixed costs lumped together.

Although a profit and loss statement prepared in the functional format may be useful for external reporting purposes, it has serious limitations when used for internal purposes. Internally, the manager needs cost data organized in a format that will facilitate planning, control and decision making. These tasks are much easier when cost data are available in a fixed and variable format. The contribution approach to the profit and loss statement has been developed in response to this need.

The contribution approach

Exhibit 2.7 illustrates the contribution approach to the profit and loss statement with a simple example, along with the traditional approach discussed above.

Notice that the contribution approach separates costs into fixed and variable categories, first deducting variable expenses from sales to obtain what is known as the *contribution margin*. The **contribution margin** is

Exhibit 2.7 Comparison of the contribution profit statement with the traditional profit statement

Traditional approach (costs organized by function)			Contribution approach (costs organized by behaviour)		
Sales		£12,000	Sales		£12,000
Less cost of goods sold		6,000*	Less variable expenses:		
Gross margin		6,000	Variable production	£2,000	
Less operating expenses:			Variable selling	600	
Selling	£3,100*		Variable administrative	400	3,000
Administrative	1,900*	5,000	Contribution margin		9,000
Net profit		£1,000	Less fixed expenses:		
			Fixed production	4,000	
			Fixed selling	2,500	
			Fixed administrative	1,500	8,000
			Net profit		£1,000

*Contains both variable and fixed expenses. This is the profit statement for a manufacturing company; thus, when the profit statement is placed in the contribution format, the 'cost of goods sold' figure is divided between variable production costs and fixed production costs. If this were the profit statement for a *merchandising* company (which simply purchases completed goods from a supplier), then the cost of goods sold would *all* be variable.

the amount remaining from sales revenues after variable expenses have been deducted. This amount *contributes* towards covering fixed expenses and then towards profits for the period.

The contribution approach to the profit and loss statement is used as an internal planning and decision-making tool. Its emphasis on costs by behaviour facilitates cost–volume–profit analysis, which we will tackle in Chapter 3. The approach is also very useful in appraising management performance, in segmented reporting of profit data, and in budgeting. Moreover, the contribution approach helps managers organize data pertinent to all kinds of special decisions such as product-line analysis, pricing, use of scarce resources, and make or buy analysis. All of these topics are covered in later chapters.

Managers use costs organized by behaviour as a basis for many decisions. To facilitate this use, the profit statement can be prepared in a contribution format. The contribution format classifies costs on the profit and loss statement by cost behaviour (i.e., variable versus fixed) rather than by the functions of production, administration, and sales.

LO 6

Cost classifications for decision-relevance

Costs are an important feature of many business decisions. In making decisions, it is essential to have a firm grasp of the concepts *differential cost, opportunity cost* and *sunk cost*.

Differential cost and revenue

Decisions involve choosing between alternatives. In business decisions, each alternative will have certain costs and benefits that must be compared to the costs and benefits of the other available alternatives. A difference in costs between any two alternatives is known as a **differential cost**. A difference in revenues between any two alternatives is known as **differential revenue**.

A differential cost is also known as an **incremental cost**, although technically an incremental cost should refer only to an increase in cost from one alternative to another; decreases in cost should be referred to as *decremental costs*. Differential cost is a broader term, encompassing both cost increases (incremental costs) and cost decreases (decremental costs) between alternatives.

The accountant's differential cost concept can be compared to the economist's marginal cost concept. In speaking of changes in cost and revenue, the economist employs the terms *marginal cost* and *marginal revenue*. The revenue that can be obtained from selling one more unit of product is called marginal revenue, and the cost involved in producing one more unit of product is called marginal cost. The economist's marginal concept is basically the same as the accountant's differential concept applied to a single unit of output.

Differential costs can be either fixed or variable. To illustrate, assume that Nature Way Cosmetics is thinking about changing its marketing method from distribution through retailers to distribution by door-to-door direct sale. Present costs and revenues are compared to projected costs and revenues in the following table:

	Retailer distribution (present)	Direct sale distribution (proposed)	Differential costs and revenues
Revenues (V)	£700,000	£800,000	£100,000
Cost of goods sold (V)	350,000	400,000	50,000
Advertising (F)	80,000	45,000	(35,000)
Commissions (V)	0	40,000	40,000
Warehouse depreciation (F)	50,000	80,000	30,000
Other expenses (F)	60,000	60,000	0
Total	540,000	625,000	85,000
Profit	£160,000	£175,000	£15,000

V = Variable; F = Fixed

According to the above analysis, the differential revenue is £100,000 and the differential costs total £85,000, leaving a positive differential profit of £15,000 under the proposed marketing plan.

The decision of whether Nature Way Cosmetics should stay with the present retail distribution or switch to door-to-door direct selling could be made on the basis of the profits of the two alternatives. As we see in the above analysis, the profit under the present distribution method is £160,000, whereas the profit under door-to-door direct selling is estimated to be £175,000. Therefore, the door-to-door direct distribution method is preferred, since it would result in £15,000 higher profit. Note that we would have arrived at exactly the same conclusion by simply focusing on the differential revenues, differential costs and differential profit, which also show a £15,000 advantage for the direct selling method.

In general, only the differences between alternatives are relevant in decisions. Those items that are the same under all alternatives and that are not affected by the decision can be ignored. For example, in the Nature Way Cosmetics example above, the 'Other expenses' category, which is £60,000 under both alternatives, can be ignored, since it has no effect on the decision. If it were removed from the calculations, the door-to-door direct selling method would still be preferred by £15,000.

Opportunity cost

Opportunity cost is the potential benefit that is given up when one alternative is selected over another. To illustrate this important concept, consider the following examples:

Example 1

Vicki has a part-time job that pays her £100 per week while attending college. She would like to spend a week at the beach during spring break, and her employer has agreed to give her the time off, but without pay. The £100 in lost wages would be an opportunity cost of taking the week off to be at the beach.

Example 2

Suppose that Tesco is considering investing a large sum of money in land that may be a site for a future shop. Rather than invest the funds in land, the company could invest the funds in high-grade securities. If the land is acquired, the opportunity cost will be the investment income that could have been realized if the securities had been purchased instead.

Example 3

Steve is employed with a company that pays him a salary of £20,000 per year. He is thinking about leaving the company and going to university. Since going to university would require that he give up his £20,000 salary, the forgone salary would be an opportunity cost of seeking further education.

Opportunity cost is not usually entered in the accounting records of an organization, but it is a cost that must be explicitly considered in every decision a manager makes. Virtually every alternative has some opportunity cost attached to it. In Example 3 above, for instance, if Steve decides to stay at his job, there still is an opportunity cost involved: it is the greater income that could be realized in future years as a result of returning to university.

Sunk cost

A **sunk cost** is a cost *that has already been incurred* and that cannot be changed by any decision made now or in the future. Since sunk costs cannot be changed by any decision, they are not differential costs. Therefore, they can and should be ignored when making a decision.

To illustrate a sunk cost, assume that a company paid £50,000 several years ago for a special-purpose machine. The machine was used to make a product that is now obsolete and is no longer being sold. Even though in hindsight the purchase of the machine may have been unwise, no amount of regret can undo that decision. And it would be folly to continue making the obsolete product in a misguided attempt to 'recover' the original cost of the machine. In short, the £50,000 originally paid for the machine has already been incurred and cannot be a differential cost in any future decisions. For this reason, such costs are said to be sunk and should be ignored in decisions.

We will explore some applications of relevant cost principles further in Chapter 4 when making a number of important business decisions such as replacing equipment, make-or-buy, special orders and dealing with capacity constraints.

Focus on Business Practice

Cost considerations at a retail florist

© Catherine Yeulet

Terri, the owner of a retail florist shop, has been trying to decide for some time whether she should continue to use a local courier service to deliver flowers to customers or buy a delivery van and use one of her employees to make the deliveries. At a recent family dinner, she brought up the subject of the delivery van with her brother-in-law, who fancies himself as an expert on all management subjects. He grabbed this opportunity to impress on Terri his understanding of costs.

In rapid-fire succession, Terri's brother-in-law told her that the fees paid to the courier to deliver flowers are a variable cost and a period cost, but the costs of the flowers are product costs rather than period costs, even though the flower costs are also variable costs. On the other hand, the depreciation of the delivery van would be a fixed cost and a period cost. And while the fuel for the truck would be a variable cost and a differential cost, the wages of the person making the deliveries would be a fixed cost, not a differential cost, and would involve an opportunity cost. At this point, Terri excused herself, pleading that she had to help in the kitchen. Terri felt that her brother-in-law's comments were more confusing than helpful, but she knew that she could no longer put off the decision about the delivery van.

Exercise: Referring to Exhibit 2.3, which costs *should* be considered in this decision?

Focus on Business Practice

Hotel accounting and costs

© Elena Elisseeva

In a recent project, an author was undertaking research into management accounting in the hospitality industry. He noted that many hotels saw room costs in terms of servicing the room and the ongoing expense of maintaining the fixtures and fittings. They did not have an operational measure of the biggest fixed cost of all – the cost of the land and buildings. In the short run, this approach seemed logical as the managers could reduce some of the costs of servicing the rooms through better labour scheduling but they could not (in the short-term) *avoid* the fixed costs of the building itself.

Exercise: In what sense are room servicing costs *variable* in that they vary with activity levels? What other room-related costs are also variable?

Summary

- In this chapter, we have looked at some of the ways in which managers classify costs. How the costs will be used – for preparing external reports, predicting cost behaviour, assigning costs to cost objects, or decision making – will dictate how the costs will be classified.
- For purposes of valuing stocks and determining expenses for the balance sheet and profit and loss account, costs are classified as either product costs or period costs. Product costs are assigned to stocks and are considered assets until the products are sold. At the point of sale, product costs become costs of goods sold on the profit and loss account. In contrast, following the usual accrual practices, period costs are taken directly to the profit and loss account as expenses in the period in which they are incurred.
- For purposes of predicting cost behaviour – how costs will react to changes in activity – managers commonly classify costs into two categories – variable and fixed. Variable costs, in total, are strictly proportional to activity. Thus, the variable cost per unit is constant. Fixed costs, in total, remain at the same level for changes in activity that occur within the relevant range. Thus, the average fixed cost per unit decreases as the number of units increases.
- For purposes of assigning costs to cost objects such as products or departments, costs are classified as direct or indirect. Direct costs can conveniently be traced to the cost objects. Indirect costs cannot conveniently be traced to cost objects.
- For purposes of making decisions, the concepts of differential costs and revenue, opportunity cost and sunk cost are of vital importance. Differential cost and revenue are the cost and revenue items that differ between alternatives. Opportunity cost is the benefit that is forgone when one alternative is selected over another. Sunk cost is a cost that occurred in the past and cannot be altered. Differential cost and opportunity cost should be considered carefully in decisions. Sunk cost is always irrelevant in decisions and should be ignored.
- These various cost classifications are *different* ways of looking at costs. A particular cost, such as the cost of cheese in a cheese burger, could be a manufacturing cost, a product cost, a variable cost, a direct cost, and a differential cost – all at the same time.

Key terms

Administrative costs All executive, organizational and clerical costs associated with the general management of an organization rather than with manufacturing, marketing or selling (p. 17).

Contribution approach A profit statement format that is geared to cost behaviour in that costs are separated into variable and fixed categories rather than being separated according to the functions of production, sales and administration (p. 25).

Contribution margin The amount remaining from sales revenue after all variable expenses have been deducted (p. 25).

Conversion cost Direct labour cost plus manufacturing overhead cost (p. 17).

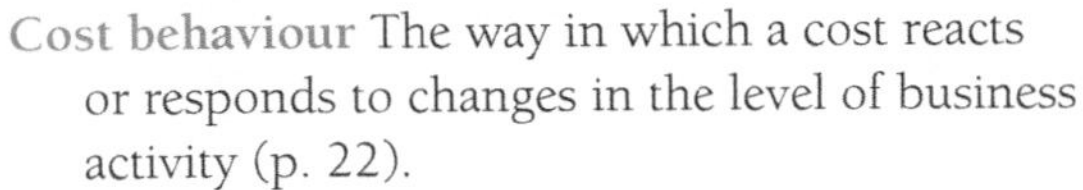

Cost behaviour The way in which a cost reacts or responds to changes in the level of business activity (p. 22).

Differential cost Any cost that differs between alternatives in a decision-making situation. In managerial accounting, this term is synonymous with avoidable cost and relevant cost. Also see Incremental cost (p. 26).

Differential revenue The difference in revenue between any two alternatives (p. 26).

Direct labour Those factory labour costs that can easily be traced to individual units of product. Also called touch labour (p. 16).

Direct materials Those materials that become an integral part of a finished product and can conveniently be traced into it (p. 16).

Fixed cost A cost that remains constant, in total, regardless of changes in the level of activity within the relevant range. If a fixed cost is expressed on a per unit basis, it varies inversely with the level of activity (p. 23).

Incremental cost An increase in cost between two alternatives. Also see Differential cost (p. 26).

Indirect labour The labour costs of caretakers, supervisors, materials handlers, and other factory workers that cannot conveniently be traced directly to particular products (p. 16).

Indirect materials Small items of material such as glue and nails. These items may become an integral part of a finished product but are traceable to the product only at great cost or inconvenience (p. 16).

Manufacturing overhead All costs associated with manufacturing except direct materials and direct labour (p. 16).

Marketing or selling costs All costs necessary to secure customer orders and get the finished product or service into the hands of the customer (p. 17).

Opportunity cost The potential benefit that is given up when one alternative is selected over another (p. 27).

Period costs Those costs that are taken directly to the profit and loss account as expenses in the period in which they are incurred or accrued; such costs consist of selling (marketing) and administrative expenses (p. 17).

Prime cost Direct materials cost plus direct labour cost (p. 17).

Product costs All costs that are involved in the purchase or manufacture of goods. In the case of manufactured goods, these costs consist of direct materials, direct labour, and manufacturing overhead. Also see Stock-related costs (p. 17).

Raw materials Any materials that go into the final product (p. 16).

Relevant range The range of activity within which assumptions about variable and fixed cost behaviour are valid (p. 23).

Stock-related costs (also known as inventoriable costs) Synonym for product costs (p. 19).

Sunk cost Any cost that has already been incurred and that cannot be changed by any decision made now or in the future (p. 27).

Variable cost A cost that varies, in total, in direct proportion to changes in the level of activity. A variable cost is constant per unit (p. 21).

Endnotes

1 *Financial Management*, September 2003, p. 4.

2 These issues are discussed thoroughly in Johnson and Kaplan (1987).

3 See note 4.

4 In many countries, such as the US, 'stock' is known as 'inventory'. With globalization of capital markets and accounting, terms such as *stock* and *inventory* are increasingly used interchangeably. Other examples of interchangeable terms are *profit* (UK) = *net income* (US), *debtors* (UK) = *accounts receivable* (US) and *creditors* (UK) = *accounts payable* (US), *work in progress* (UK) = *work in process* (US).

5 http://moneymorning.com/2010/05/10/gulf-oil-spill-2/; http://news.bbc.co.uk/2/hi/americas/8666276.stm; http://www.rte.ie/business/2010/0610/bp.html

connect™

When you have read this chapter, log on to the Online Learning Centre for *Management Accounting for Business Decisions* at **www.mheducation.co.uk/textbooks/sealmabd1**, where you'll find multiple choice questions, practice exams and extra study tools for management accounting.

Assessment

Questions

connect

2–1 What are the three major elements of product costs in a manufacturing company?

2–2 Distinguish between the following: (a) direct materials, (b) indirect materials, (c) direct labour, (d) indirect labour, and (e) manufacturing overhead.

2–3 Explain the difference between a product cost and a period cost.

2–4 Why are product costs sometimes called stock-related costs? Describe the flow of such costs in a manufacturing company from the point of incurrence until they finally become expenses on the profit and loss account.

2–5 What is meant by the term *cost behaviour*?

2–6 'A variable cost is a cost that varies per unit of product, whereas a fixed cost is constant per unit of product.' Do you agree? Explain.

2–7 How do fixed costs create difficulties in costing units of product?

2–8 Why is manufacturing overhead considered an indirect cost of a unit of product?

2–9 Define the following terms: differential cost, opportunity cost, and sunk cost.

2–10 Only variable costs can be differential costs. Do you agree? Explain.

Exercises

connect

E2–1 Time allowed: 15 minutes

The following are a number of cost terms introduced in the chapter:

Variable cost	Product cost
Fixed cost	Sunk cost
Prime cost	Conversion cost
Opportunity cost	Period cost

Choose the term or terms above that most appropriately describe the cost identified in each of the following situations. A cost term can be used more than once.

1 Lake Company produces a bag that is very popular with college students. The cloth going into the manufacture of the bag would be called direct materials and classified as a ________ cost. In terms of cost behaviour, the cloth could also be described as a ________ cost.

2 The direct labour cost required to produce the bags, combined with the manufacturing overhead cost involved, would be known as ________ cost.

3 The company could have taken the funds that it has invested in production equipment and invested them in interest-bearing securities instead. The interest forgone on the securities would be called ________ cost.

4 Taken together, the direct materials cost and the direct labour cost required to produce bags would be called ________ cost.

5 The company used to produce a smaller bag that was not very popular. Some three hundred of these smaller bags are stored in one of the company's warehouses. The amount invested in these bags would be called a ________ cost.
6 The bags are sold through agents who are paid a commission on each bag sold. These commissions would be classified by Lake Company as a ________ cost. In terms of cost behaviour, commissions would be classified as a ________ cost.
7 Depreciation on the equipment used to produce the bags would be classified by Lake Company as a ________ cost. However, depreciation on any equipment used by the company in selling and administrative activities would be classified as ________ cost. In terms of cost behaviour, depreciation would probably be classified as a ________ cost.
8 A ________ cost is also known as a stock-related cost, since such costs go into the Work in Progress stock account and then into the Finished Goods stock account before appearing on the profit and loss account as part of cost of goods sold.
9 The salary of Lake Company's managing director would be classified as a ________ cost, since the salary will appear on the profit and loss account as an expense in the time period in which it is incurred.
10 Costs can often be classified in several ways. For example, Lake Company pays £5,000 rent each month on its factory building. The rent would be part of manufacturing overhead. In terms of cost behaviour, it would be classified as a ________ cost. The rent can also be classified as a ________ cost and as part of ________ cost.

E2–2 Time allowed: 10 minutes

A product cost is also known as a stock-related cost. Classify the following costs as either product (stock-related) costs or period (non-stock-related) costs in a manufacturing company:

1 Depreciation on salespersons' cars
2 Rent on equipment used in the factory
3 Lubricants used for maintenance of machines
4 Salaries of finished goods warehouse personnel
5 Soap and paper towels used by factory workers at the end of a shift
6 Factory supervisors' salaries
7 Heat, water and power consumed in the factory
8 Materials used in boxing units of finished product for shipment overseas (units are not normally boxed)
9 Advertising outlays
10 Workers' compensation insurance on factory employees
11 Depreciation on chairs and tables in the factory lunchroom
12 The salary of the switchboard operator for the company
13 Depreciation on a Lear Jet used by the company's executives
14 Rent on rooms at a West Country resort for holding of the annual sales conference
15 Attractively designed box for packaging breakfast cereal.

E2–3 Time allowed: 10 minutes

Below are a number of costs that are incurred in a variety of organizations:

1 X-ray film used in the radiology lab at Queens Medical Centre in Nottingham
2 The costs of advertising a Madonna rock concert in London
3 Depreciation on the Planet Hollywood restaurant building in Hong Kong
4 The electrical costs of running a roller-coaster at Blackpool
5 Property taxes on a local cinema
6 Commissions paid to salespersons at McGraw-Hill
7 Property insurance on a Coca-Cola bottling plant
8 The costs of synthetic materials used to make Nike running shoes
9 The costs of shipping Panasonic televisions to retail shops
10 The cost of leasing an ultra-scan diagnostic machine at St Thomas's hospital in London.

Required

Classify each cost as being variable or fixed with respect to the number of units of product or services sold by the organization. Set out your answers as below.

	Cost behaviour	
Cost Item	**Variable**	**Fixed**

Place an X in the appropriate column for each cost to indicate whether the cost involved would be variable or fixed with respect to the number of units of products or services sold by the organization.

E2–4 Time allowed: 20 minutes

The following cost and stock data are taken from the accounting records of Mason Company for the year just completed:

Costs incurred:		
Direct labour cost		£70,000
Purchases of raw materials		118,000
Indirect labour		30,000
Maintenance, factory equipment		6,000
Advertising expense		90,000
Insurance, factory equipment		800
Sales salaries		50,000
Rent, factory facilities		20,000
Supplies		4,200
Depreciation, office equipment		3,000
Depreciation, factory equipment		19,000
	Beginning of the Year	**End of the Year**
Stocks:		
Raw materials	£7,000	£15,000
Work in progress	10,000	5,000
Finished goods	20,000	35,000

Required

1. Prepare a schedule of cost of goods manufactured in good form
2. Prepare the cost of goods sold section of Mason Company's profit and loss account for the year

E2–5 Time allowed: 15 minutes

Below are listed various costs that are found in organizations:

1. Hamburger buns in a McDonald's outlet
2. Advertising by a dental office
3. Apples processed and canned by Del Monte Corporation
4. Shipping canned apples from a Del Monte plant to customers
5. Insurance on a Bausch & Lomb factory producing contact lenses
6. Insurance on IBM's corporate headquarters
7. Salary of a supervisor overseeing production of circuit boards at Hewlett-Packard
8. Commissions paid to *Encyclopaedia Britannica* salespersons
9. Depreciation of factory lunchroom facilities at an ICI plant
10. Steering wheels installed in BMWs.

Required

Classify each cost as being either variable or fixed with respect to the number of units sold. Also classify each cost as either a selling and administrative cost or a product cost. Prepare your answer sheet as shown below.

Cost item	Cost behaviour		Selling and administrative cost	Product cost
	Variable	Fixed cost		

Place an X in the appropriate columns to show the proper classification of each cost.

Problems

P2–6 Cost identification

Time allowed: 30 minutes

Wollongong Group Ltd of New South Wales, Australia, acquired its factory building about ten years ago. For several years the company has rented out a small annex attached to the rear of the building. The company has received a rental income of £30,000 per year on this space. The renter's lease will expire soon and, rather than renewing the lease, the company has decided to use the space itself to manufacture a new product.

Direct materials cost for the new product will total £80 per unit. To have a place to sell finished units of product, the company will rent a small warehouse nearby. The rental cost will be £500 per month. In addition, the company must rent equipment for use in producing the new product; the rental cost will be £4,000 per month. Workers will be hired to manufacture the new product, with direct labour cost amounting to £60 per unit. The space in the annex will continue to be depreciated on a straight-line basis, as in prior years. This depreciation is £8,000 per year.

Advertising costs for the new product will total £50,000 per year. A supervisor will be hired to oversee production; her salary will be £1,500 per month. Electricity for operating machines will be £1.20 per unit. Costs of shipping the new product to customers will be £9 per unit.

To provide funds to purchase materials, meet payrolls and so forth, the company will have to liquidate some temporary investments. These investments are presently yielding a return of about £3,000 per year.

Required

Prepare an answer sheet with the following column headings:

Name of the cost	Variable cost	Fixed cost	Product cost: Direct materials	Product cost: Direct labour	Product cost: Manufacturing overhead	Period (selling and administrative) cost	Opportunity cost	Sunk cost

List the different costs associated with the new product decision down the extreme left column (under Name of the cost). Then place an X under each heading that helps to describe the type of cost involved. There may be Xs under several column headings for a single cost (for example, a cost may be a fixed cost, a period cost and a sunk cost; you would place an X under each of these column headings opposite the cost).

P2–7 Supply missing production and cost data

Time allowed: 30 minutes

Supply the missing data in the following cases. Each case is independent of the others.

	Case 1	Case 2	Case 3	Case 4
Direct materials	£4,500	£6,000	£5,000	£3,000
Direct labour	?	3,000	7,000	4,000
Manufacturing overhead	5,000	4,000	?	9,000
Total manufacturing costs	18,500	?	£20,000	?
Beginning work in progress stock	2,500	?	3,000	?
Ending work in progress stock	?	1,000	4,000	3,000
Cost of goods manufactured	£18,000	£14,000	£?	£?
Sales	£30,000	£21,000	£36,000	£40,000
Beginning finished goods stock	1,000	2,500	?	2,000
Cost of goods manufactured	?	?	?	17,500
Goods available for sale	?	?	?	?

(continued)

Ending finished goods stock	?	1,500	4,000	3,500
Cost of goods sold	17,000	?	18,500	?
Gross margin	13,000	?	17,500	?
Operating expenses	?	3,500	?	?
Profit	£4,000	£ ?	£5,000	£9,000

P2–8 Cost classification

Time allowed: 20 minutes

Various costs associated with the operation of a factory are given below:

1. Electricity used in operating machines
2. Rent on a factory building
3. Cloth used in drapery production
4. Production superintendent's salary
5. Cost of labourers assembling a product
6. Depreciation of air purification equipment used in furniture production
7. Caretaker salaries
8. Peaches used in canning fruit
9. Lubricants needed for machines
10. Sugar used in soft-drink production
11. Property taxes on the factory
12. Cost of workers painting a product
13. Depreciation on cafeteria equipment
14. Insurance on a building used in producing TV sets
15. Picture tubes used in TV sets.

Required

Classify each cost as being either variable or fixed with respect to the number of units produced and sold. Also indicate whether each cost would typically be treated as a direct cost or an indirect cost with respect to units of product. Prepare your answer sheet as shown below:

	Cost behaviour		To units of product	
Cost Item	**Variable**	**Fixed**	**Direct**	**Indirect**
Example: Factory insurance		X		X

P2–9 Cost identification

Time allowed: 40 minutes

The Dorilane Company specializes in producing a set of wooden patio furniture consisting of a table and four chairs. The set enjoys great popularity, and the

company has ample orders to keep production going at its full capacity of 2,000 sets per year. Annual cost data at full capacity follow:

To units of product	Product cost
Factory labour, direct	£118,000
Advertising	50,000
Factory supervision	40,000
Property taxes, factory building	3,500
Sales commissions	80,000
Insurance, factory	2,500
Depreciation, office equipment	4,000
Lease cost, factory equipment	12,000
Indirect materials, factory	6,000
Depreciation, factory building	10,000
General office supplies (billing)	3,000
General office salaries	60,000
Direct materials used (wood, bolts, etc.)	94,000
Utilities, factory	20,000

Required

1 Prepare an answer sheet with the column headings shown below. Enter each cost item on your answer sheet, placing the pound amount under the appropriate headings. As examples, this has been done already for the first two items in the list above. Note that each cost item is classified in two ways: first, as variable or fixed, with respect to the number of units produced and sold; and second, as a selling and administrative cost or a product cost. (If the item is a product cost, it should be classified as being either direct or indirect as shown.)

2 Total the pound amounts in each of the columns in 1 above. Compute the cost to produce one patio set.

3 Assume that production drops to only 1,000 sets annually. Would you expect the cost per set to increase, decrease, or remain unchanged? Explain. No computations are necessary.

4 Refer to the original data. The managing director's brother-in-law has considered making himself a patio set and has priced the necessary materials at a building supply shop. The brother-in-law has asked the managing director if he could purchase a patio set from the Dorilane Company 'at cost', and the managing director agreed to let him do so.
   (a) Would you expect any disagreement between the two men over the price the brother-in-law should pay? Explain. What price does the managing director probably have in mind? The brother-in-law?
   (b) Since the company is operating at full capacity, what cost term used in the chapter might be justification for the managing director to charge the full, regular price to the brother-in-law and still be selling 'at cost'?

Cost item	Cost behaviour		Selling or administrative cost	Product cost	
	Variable	Fixed		Direct	Indirect*
Factory labour, direct	£118,000			£118,000	
Advertising		£50,000	£50,000		

*To units of product.

P2–10 Cost classification

Time allowed: 25 minutes

Listed below are a number of costs typically found in organizations:

1. Property taxes, factory
2. Boxes used for packaging detergent
3. Salespersons' commissions
4. Supervisor's salary, factory
5. Depreciation, executive cars
6. Workers assembling computers
7. Packing supplies for shipments
8. Insurance, finished goods warehouses
9. Lubricants for machines
10. Advertising costs
11. 'Chips' used in producing calculators
12. Shipping costs on merchandise sold
13. Magazine subscriptions, factory lunchroom
14. Thread in a garment factory
15. Billing costs
16. Executive life insurance
17. Ink used in textbook production
18. Fringe benefits, assembly-line workers
19. Yarn used in sweater production
20. Receptionist, executive offices.

Required

Prepare an answer sheet with column headings as shown below. For each cost item, indicate whether it would be variable or fixed with respect to the number of units produced and sold; and then whether it would be a selling cost, an administrative cost, or a manufacturing cost. If it is a manufacturing cost, indicate whether it would typically be treated as a direct cost or an indirect cost with respect to units of product. Three sample answers are provided for illustration.

Cost Item	Variable or fixed	Selling cost	Administrative cost	Manufacturing (product) cost Direct	Indirect
Direct labour	V			X	
Executive salaries	F		X		
Factory rent	F				X

P2–11 Cost identification

Time allowed: 20 minutes

Tracy Beckham began dabbling in pottery several years ago as a hobby. Her work is quite creative, and it has been so popular with friends and others that she has decided to quit her job with an aerospace firm and manufacture pottery full time. The salary from Tracy's aerospace job is £2,500 per month.

Tracy will rent a small building near her home to use as a place for manufacturing the pottery. The rent will be £500 per month. She estimates that the cost of clay and glaze will be £2 for each finished piece of pottery. She will hire workers to produce the pottery at a labour rate of £8 per pot. To sell her pots, Tracy feels that she must advertise heavily in the local area. An advertising agency states that it will handle all advertising for a fee of £600 per month. Tracy's brother will sell the pots; he will be paid a commission of £4 for each pot sold. Equipment needed to manufacture the pots will be rented at a cost of £300 per month.

Tracy has already paid some start-up fees associated with her business. These fees amounted to £500. A small room has been located in a tourist area that Tracy will use as a sales office. The rent will be £250 per month. A phone installed in the room for taking orders will cost £40 per month. In addition, a recording device will be attached to the phone for taking after-hours messages

Tracy has some money in savings that is earning interest of £1,200 per year. These savings will be withdrawn and used to get the business going. For the time being, Tracy does not intend to draw any salary from the new company.

Required

1 Prepare an answer sheet with the following column headings:

Name of the cost	Variable cost	Fixed cost	Product cost: Direct materials	Direct labour	Manufacturing overhead	Period (selling and administrative) cost	Opportunity cost	Sunk cost

List the different costs associated with the new company down the extreme left column (under Name of cost). Then place an X under each heading that helps to describe the type of cost involved. There may be Xs under several column headings for a single cost. (That is, a cost may be a fixed cost, a period cost, and a sunk cost; you would place an X under each of these column headings opposite the cost.)
Under the Variable cost column, list only those costs that would be variable with respect to the number of units of pottery that are produced and sold.

2 All the costs you have listed above, except one, would be differential costs between the alternatives of Tracy producing pottery or staying with the aerospace firm. Which cost is not differential? Explain.

P2–12 Cost behaviour; manufacturing statement; unit costs

Time allowed: 40 minutes

Visic Company, a manufacturing firm, produces a single product. The following information has been taken from the company's production, sales, and cost records for the just completed year.

Production in units		29,000
Sales in units		?
Ending finished goods stock in units		?
Sales in pounds		£1,300,000
Costs:		
Advertising		105,000
Entertainment and travel		40,000
Direct labour		90,000
Indirect labour		85,000
Raw materials purchased		480,000
Building rent (production uses 80% of the space administrative and sales offices use the rest)		40,000
Utilities, factory		108,000
Royalty paid for use of production patent, £1.50 per unit produced		?
Maintenance, factory		9,000
Rent for special production equipment, per year		£7,000
plus £0.30 per unit produced		?
Selling and administrative salaries		210,000
Other factory overhead costs		6,800
Other selling and administrative expenses		17,000
	Beginning of year	**End of year**
Stocks:		
Raw materials	£20,000	£30,000
Work in progress	50,000	40,000
Finished goods	0	?

The finished-goods stock is being carried at the average unit production cost for the year. The selling price of the product is £50 per unit.

Required

1 Prepare a schedule of goods manufactured for the year.
2 Compute the following:
   (a) The number of units in the finished goods stock at the end of the year
   (b) The cost of the units in the finished goods stock at the end of the year.
3 Prepare a profit and loss account for the year.

Chapter 3 Short-term decision making: cost–volume–profit relationships

Learning objectives

After studying Chapter 3, you should be able to:

1. Explain how changes in activity affect contribution margin and profit
2. Compute the contribution margin ratio (CM ratio) and use it to compute changes in contribution margin and profit
3. Show the effects on contribution margin of changes in variable costs, fixed costs, selling price and volume
4. Compute the break-even point by both the equation method and the contribution margin method
5. Prepare a cost–volume–profit (CVP) graph and explain the significance of each of its components
6. Use the CVP formulas to determine the activity level needed to achieve a desired target profit
7. Compute the margin of safety and explain its significance
8. Compute the degree of operating leverage at a particular level of sales and explain how the degree of operating leverage can be used to predict changes in profit
9. Compute the break-even point for a multiple product company and explain the effects of shifts in the sales mix on contribution margin and the break-even point.

Concepts in Context

© Getty Images

Since CVP analysis shows that levels of activity can have a big effect on profits, choices on the best way of compensating salespersons must be chosen with a great deal of care. Digital Equipment Corporation's founder, Kenneth Olsen, believed that salespersons should never sell customers something they do not need and, accordingly, Digital paid them salaries rather than sales commissions. This approach worked fine for many years because 'Digital's products were the hottest alternative to expensive mainframe computers, and because they were cheaper, they almost sold themselves. But when competition arrived, the Digital sales staff was hopelessly outclassed.' When commissions were introduced in an attempt to stem the tide, the new system backfired. 'Some salesmen sold product at little or no profit to pump up volume – and their commission.'[1]

Cost–volume–profit (CVP) analysis is one of the most powerful tools that managers have at their command. It helps them understand the interrelationship between cost, volume and profit in an organization by focusing on interactions between the following five elements:

1. Prices of products
2. Volume or level of activity
3. Per unit variable costs
4. Total fixed costs
5. Mix of products sold.

Because CVP analysis helps managers understand the interrelationship between cost, volume and profit, it is a vital tool in many business decisions. These decisions include, for example, what products to manufacture or sell, what pricing policy to follow, what marketing strategy to employ, and what type of productive facilities to acquire.

The basics of cost–volume–profit (CVP) analysis

Recall the discussion on cost behaviour in Chapter 2 and how we showed that the contribution profit and loss account emphasizes the behaviour of costs and therefore is extremely helpful to a manager in judging the impact on profits of changes in selling price, cost or volume. Let us consider the case of Acoustic Concepts which has the following contribution profit and loss account:

Acoustic Concepts Ltd
Contribution profit and loss account
For the month of June

	Total	Per unit
Sales (400 speakers)	£100,000	£250
Less variable expenses	60,000	150
Contribution margin	40,000	£100
Less fixed expenses	35,000	
Profit	£5,000	

Notice that sales, variable expenses and contribution margin are expressed on a per unit basis as well as in total. This is commonly done on profit and loss accounts prepared for management's own use, since, as we shall see, it facilitates profitability analysis.

LO 1 Contribution margin

Contribution margin is the amount remaining from sales revenue after variable expenses have been deducted. Thus, it is the amount available to cover fixed expenses and then to provide profits for the period. Notice the sequence here – contribution margin is used *first* to cover the fixed expenses, and then whatever remains goes towards profits. If the contribution margin is not sufficient to cover the fixed expenses, then a loss occurs for the period. To illustrate with an extreme example, assume that by the middle of a particular month Acoustic Concepts has been able to sell only one speaker. At that point, the company's profit and loss account will appear as follows:

	Total	Per unit
Sales (1 speaker)	£250	£250
Less variable expenses	150	150
Contribution margin	100	£100
Less fixed expenses	35,000	
Net loss	£(34,900)	

For each additional speaker that the company is able to sell during the month, £100 more in contribution margin will become available to help cover the fixed expenses. If a second speaker is sold, for example, then the total contribution margin will increase by £100 (to a total of £200) and the company's loss will decrease by £100, to £34,800:

	Total	Per unit
Sales (2 speakers)	£500	£250
Less variable expenses	300	150
Contribution margin	200	£100
Less fixed expenses	35,000	
Net loss	£(34,800)	

If enough speakers can be sold to generate £35,000 in contribution margin, then all of the fixed costs will be covered and the company will have managed to at least *break even* for the month – that is, to show neither profit nor loss but just cover all of its costs. To reach the break-even point, the company will have to sell 350 speakers in a month, since each speaker sold yields £100 in contribution margin:

	Total	Per unit
Sales (350 speakers)	£87,500	£250
Less variable expenses	52,500	150
Contribution margin	35,000	£100
Less fixed expenses	35,000	
Profit	£0	

Computation of the **break-even point** is discussed in detail later in the chapter; for the moment, note that the break-even point can be defined as the level of sales at which profit is zero.

Once the break-even point has been reached, profit will increase by the unit contribution margin for each additional unit sold. If 351 speakers are sold in a month, for example, then we can expect that the profit for the month will be £100, since the company will have sold one speaker more than the number needed to break even:

	Total	Per unit
Sales (351 speakers)	£87,750	£250
Less variable expenses	52,650	150
Contribution margin	35,100	£100
Less fixed expenses	35,000	
Profit	£100	

If 352 speakers are sold (2 speakers above the break-even point), then we can expect that the profit for the month will be £200, and so forth. To know what the profits will be at various levels of activity, therefore, it is not necessary for a manager to prepare a whole series of profit and loss accounts. The manager can simply take the number of units to be sold over the break-even point and multiply that number by the unit contribution margin. The result represents the anticipated profits for the period. Or, to estimate the effect of a planned increase in sales on profits, the manager can simply multiply the increase in units sold by the unit contribution margin. The result will be the expected increase in profits. To illustrate, if Acoustic Concepts is currently selling 400 speakers per month and plans to increase sales to 425 speakers per month, the anticipated impact on profits can be computed as follows:

Increased number of speakers to be sold		25
Contribution margin per speaker	×	£100
increase in profit		£2,500

These calculations can be verified as follows:

	Sales volume			
	400 speakers	425 speakers	Difference 25 speakers	Per unit
Sales	£100,000	£106,250	£6,250	£250
Less variable expenses	60,000	63,750	3,750	150
Contribution margin	40,000	42,500	2,500	£100
Less fixed expenses	35,000	35,000	0	
Profit	£5,000	£7,500	£2,500	

To summarize the series of examples given above, if there were no sales, the company's loss would equal its fixed expenses. Each unit that is sold reduces the loss by the amount of the unit contribution margin. Once the break-even point has been reached, each additional unit sold increases the company's profit by the amount of the unit contribution margin.

Focus on Business Practice

Green regulation and fixed costs

© AFP/Getty Images

The recent alliance between Renault/Nissan and Daimler was driven by the high fixed costs of developing new low emission technology and rules about average carbon emissions within car groups: '"these technologies are utterly expensive and almost impossible to shoulder alone for carmakers like Daimler or BMW," said Gregor Matthies, partner with the consultancy Bain & Co.'[2] Clearly the strategy for carmakers is to spread the higher fixed costs of new technology over higher volumes of cars.

Exercise: What might be a strategic risk for Daimler in this sort of deal?

Contribution margin ratio (CM ratio)

LO 2

In addition to being expressed on a per unit basis, sales revenues, variable expenses, and contribution margin for Acoustic Concepts can also be expressed as a percentage of sales:

	Total	Per unit	Percentage of sales
Sales (400 speakers)	£100,000	£250	100
Less variable expenses	60,000	150	60
Contribution margin	40,000	£100	40
Less fixed expenses	35,000		
Profit	£5,000		

The contribution margin as a percentage of total sales is referred to as the **contribution margin ratio (CM ratio)**. This ratio is computed as follows:

$$\text{CM ratio} = \frac{\text{Contribution margin}}{\text{Sales}}$$

For Acoustic Concepts, the computations are as follows:

$$\frac{\text{Total contribution margin, £40,000}}{\text{Total sales, £100,000}} = 40\%$$

or

$$\frac{\text{Per unit contribution margin, £100}}{\text{Per unit sales, £250}} = 40\%$$

The CM ratio is extremely useful since it shows how the contribution margin will be affected by a change in total sales. To illustrate, notice that Acoustic Concepts has a CM ratio of 40%. This means that for each pound increase in sales, total contribution margin will increase by 40 pence (£1 sales × CM ratio of 40%). Profit will also increase by 40 pence, assuming that there are no changes in fixed costs.

As this illustration suggests, *the impact on profit of any given pound change in total sales can be computed in seconds by simply applying the CM ratio to the pound change.* If Acoustic Concepts plans a £30,000 increase in sales during the coming month, for example, management can expect contribution margin to increase by £12,000 (£30,000 increased sales × CM ratio of 40%). As we noted above, profit will also increase by £12,000 if fixed costs do not change.

This is verified by the following table:

	Sales volume			
	Present	Expected	Increase	Percentage of sales
Sales	£100,000	£130,000	£30,000	100
Less variable expenses	60,000	78,000*	18,000	60
Contribution margin	40,000	52,000	12,000	40
Less fixed expenses	35,000	35,000	0	
Profit	£5,000	£17,000	£12,000	

*£130,000 expected sales/£250 per unit = 520 units. 520 units × £150 per unit = £78,000.

Some managers prefer to work with the CM ratio rather than the unit contribution margin figure. The CM ratio is particularly valuable in those situations where the manager must make trade-offs between more pound sales of one product versus more pound sales of another. Generally speaking, when trying to increase sales, products that yield the greatest amount of contribution margin per pound of sales should be emphasized.

LO 3

Some applications of CVP concepts

If we want to see how the concepts developed on the preceding pages of this text can be used in planning and decision making, we can use the following basic data:

	Per unit	Percentage of sales
Sales price	£250	100
Less variable expenses	150	60
Contribution margin	£100	40

Recall that fixed expenses are £35,000 per month, these data can show the effects of changes in variable costs fixed costs, sales price and sales volume on the company's profitability.

Change in fixed cost and sales volume

Acoustic Concepts is currently selling 400 speakers per month (monthly sales of £100,000). The sales manager feels that a £10,000 increase in the monthly advertising budget would increase monthly sales by £30,000. Should the advertising budget be increased?

The following table shows the effect of the proposed change in monthly advertising budget:

	Current sales	Advertising budget	Sales with additional difference	Percentage of sales
Sales	£100,000	£130,000	£30,000	100
Less variable expenses	60,000	78,000	18,000	60
Contribution margin	40,000	52,000	12,000	40
Less fixed expenses	35,000	45,000*	10,000	
Profit	£5,000	£7,000	£2,000	

*£35,000 plus additional £10,000 monthly advertising budget = £45,000.

Assuming there are no other factors to be considered, the increase in the advertising budget should be approved since it would lead to an increase in profit of £2,000. There are two shorter ways to present this solution. The first alternative solution follows:

Expected total contribution margin:	
£130,000 × 40% CM ratio	£52,000
Present total contribution margin:	
£100,000 × 40% CM ratio	40,000
Incremental contribution margin	12,000
Change in fixed costs:	
Less incremental advertising expense	10,000
Increased profit	£2,000

Since, in this case, only the fixed costs and the sales volume change, the solution can be presented in an even shorter format, as follows:

Incremental contribution margin:	
£30,000 × 40% CM ratio	£12,000
Less incremental advertising expense	10,000
Increased profit	£2,000

Notice that this approach does not depend on a knowledge of previous sales. Also notice that it is unnecessary under either shorter approach to prepare a profit and loss account. Both of the solutions above involve an **incremental analysis** in that they consider only those items of revenue, cost and volume that will change if the new programme is implemented. Although in each case a new profit and loss account could have been prepared, most managers would prefer the incremental approach. The reason is that it is simpler and more direct, and it permits the decision maker to focus attention on the specific items involved in the decision.

Change in variable costs and sales volume

Refer to the original data. Recall that Acoustic Concepts is currently selling 400 speakers per month. Management is contemplating the use of higher-quality components, which would increase variable costs (and thereby reduce the contribution margin) by £10 per speaker. However, the sales manager predicts that the higher overall quality would increase sales to 480 speakers per month. Should the higher-quality components be used?

The £10 increase in variable costs will cause the unit contribution margin to decrease from £100 to £90. So the solution is:

Expected total contribution margin with higher-quality components:	
480 speakers × £90	£43,200
Present total contribution margin:	
400 speakers × £100	40,000
Increase in total contribution margin	£3,200

Yes, based on the information above, the higher-quality components should be used. Since fixed costs will not change, profit should increase by the £3,200 increase in contribution margin shown above.

Change in fixed cost, sales price and sales volume

Refer to the original data and recall again that the company is currently selling 400 speakers per month. To increase sales, the sales manager would like to cut the selling price by £20 per speaker and increase the advertising budget by £15,000 per month.

The sales manager argues that if these two steps are taken, unit sales will increase by 50% to 600 speakers per month. Should the changes be made?

A decrease of £20 per speaker in the selling price will cause the unit contribution margin to decrease from £100 to £80. The solution is:

Expected total contribution margin with lower selling price:	
600 speakers × £80	£48,000
Present total contribution margin:	
400 speakers × £100	40,000
Incremental contribution margin	8,000
Change in fixed costs:	
Less incremental advertising expense	15,000
Reduction in profit	£(7,000)

No, based on the information above, the changes should not be made. The same solution can be obtained by preparing comparative profit and loss accounts:

	Present 400 speakers per month		Expected 600 speakers per month		
	Total	Per unit	Total	Per unit	Difference
Sales	£100,000	£250	£138,000	£230	£38,000
Less variable expenses	60,000	150	90,000	£150	30,000
Contribution margin	40,000	£100	48,000	£80	8,000
Less fixed expenses	35,000		50,000*		15,000
Profit (loss)	£5,000		£(2,000)		£(7,000)

*£35,000 + Additional monthly advertising budget of £15,000 = £50,000.

Notice that the effect on profit is the same as that obtained by the incremental analysis above.

Change in variable cost, fixed cost and sales volume

Refer to the original data. As before, the company is currently selling 400 speakers per month. The sales manager would like to place the sales staff on a commission basis of £15 per speaker sold, rather than on flat salaries that now total £6,000 per month. The sales manager is confident that the change will increase monthly sales by 15% to 460 speakers per month. Should the change be made?

Changing the sales staff from a salaried basis to a commission basis will affect both fixed and variable costs. Fixed costs will decrease by £6,000, from £35,000 to £29,000. Variable costs will increase by £15, from £150 to £165, and the unit contribution margin will decrease from £100 to £85.

Expected total contribution margin with sales staff on commissions:	
460 speakers × £85	£39,100
Present total contribution margin:	
400 speakers × £100	40,000
Decrease in total contribution margin	(900)
Change in fixed costs:	
Add salaries avoided if a commission is paid	6,000
Increase in profit	£5,100

Yes, based on the information above, the changes should be made. Again, the same answer can be obtained by preparing comparative profit and loss accounts:

	Present 400 speakers per month		Expected 600 speakers per month		
	Total	Per unit	Total	Per unit	Difference: increase or (decrease) in profit
Sales	£100,000	£250	£115,000	£250	£15,000
Less variable expenses	60,000	150	75,900	165	(15,900)
Contribution margin	40,000	£100	39,100	£85	(900)
Less fixed expenses	35,000		29,000		6,000
Profit	£5,000		£10,100		£5,100

Change in regular sales price

Refer to the original data where Acoustic Concepts is currently selling 400 speakers per month. The company has an opportunity to make a bulk sale of 150 speakers to a wholesaler if an acceptable price can be worked out. This sale would not disturb the company's regular sales. What price per speaker should be quoted to the wholesaler if Acoustic Concepts wants to increase its monthly profits by £3,000? The solution is:

Variable cost per speaker	£150
Desired profit per speaker:	
£3,000/150 speakers	20
Quoted price per speaker	£170

Notice that no element of fixed cost is included in the computation. This is because fixed costs are not affected by the bulk sale, so all additional revenue in excess of variable costs goes to increasing the profits of the company.

Importance of the contribution margin

As stated in the introduction to the chapter, CVP analysis seeks the most profitable combination of variable costs, fixed costs, selling price and sales volume. The above examples show that the effect on the contribution margin is a major consideration in deciding on the most profitable combination of these factors. We have seen that profits can sometimes be improved by reducing the contribution margin if fixed costs can be reduced by a greater amount. More commonly, however, we have seen that the way to improve profits is to increase the total contribution margin figure. Sometimes this can be done by reducing the selling price and thereby increasing volume; sometimes it can be done by increasing the fixed costs (such as advertising) and thereby increasing volume; and sometimes it can be done by trading off variable and fixed costs with appropriate changes in volume. Many other combinations of factors are possible.

The size of the unit contribution margin figure (and the size of the CM ratio) will have a heavy influence on what steps a company is willing to take to improve profits. For example, the greater the unit contribution margin for a product, the greater is the amount that a company will be willing to spend in order to increase unit sales of the product by a given percentage. This explains in part why companies with high unit contribution margins (such as car manufacturers) advertise so heavily, while companies with low unit contribution margins (such as dishware manufacturers) tend to spend much less for advertising.

In short, the effect on the contribution margin holds the key to many decisions.

Break-even analysis

CVP analysis is sometimes referred to simply as break-even analysis. This is unfortunate because break-even analysis is only one element of CVP analysis – although an important element. Break-even analysis is designed to answer questions concerning how far sales could drop before the company begins to lose money.

Break-even computations

LO 4

Earlier in the chapter we defined the break-even point to be the level of sales at which the company's profit is zero. The break-even point can be computed using the *contribution margin method.*

The contribution margin method

The **contribution margin method** centres on the idea discussed earlier that each unit sold provides a certain amount of contribution margin that goes towards covering fixed costs. To find how many units must be sold to break even, divide the total fixed costs by the unit contribution margin:

$$\text{Break-even point in units sold} = \frac{\text{Fixed expenses}}{\text{Unit contribution margin}}$$

Each speaker generates a contribution margin of £100 (£250 selling price, less £150 variable expenses). Since the total fixed expenses are £35,000, the break-even point is as follows:

$$\frac{\text{Fixed expenses}}{\text{Unit contribution margin}} = \frac{£35{,}000}{£100} = 350 \text{ speakers}$$

A variation of this method uses the CM ratio instead of the unit contribution margin. The result is the break-even point in total sales in pounds rather than in total units sold.

$$\text{Break-even point in total sales} = \frac{\text{Fixed expenses}}{\text{CM ratio}}$$

In the Acoustic Concepts example, the calculations are as follows:

$$\frac{\text{Fixed expenses}}{\text{CM ratio}} = \frac{£35{,}000}{40\%} = £87{,}500$$

This approach, based on the CM ratio, is particularly useful in those situations where a company has multiple product lines and wishes to compute a single break-even point for the company as a whole. More is said on this point in a later section on the concept of sales mix.

Focus on Business Practice

Costing in event management

© Digital Hallway

Laura is the manager of a company that specialises in events organizing. She is in a very competitive industry and usually sets the price per person for an event with reference to market rates. Each event has some fixed costs and she must try to work out how many tickets must be sold before these costs are covered. She can spend more money on publicity and advertising but this will push up the fixed costs of the event. Will the extra revenue from more delegates justify the increased expenditure on promotion?

Exercise: Is advertising a fixed or variable cost?

LO 5 CVP relationships in graphic form

The relationships among revenue, cost, profit and volume can be expressed graphically by preparing **cost–volume–profit (CVP) graph**. A CVP graph highlights CVP relationships over wide ranges of activit and can give managers a perspective that can be obtained in no other way. We can prepare a CVP graph fo Acoustic Concepts.

Preparing the CVP graph

Preparing a CVP graph (sometimes called a *break-even chart*) involves three steps. These steps are keyed to the graph in Exhibit 3.1:

1. Draw a line parallel to the volume axis to represent total fixed expenses. For Acoustic Concepts, total fixed expenses are £35,000.
2. Choose some volume of sales and plot the point representing total expenses (fixed and variable) at the activity level you have selected. In Exhibit 3.1, at a volume of 600 speakers, the total expenses at that activity level would be as follows:

Fixed expenses	£35,000
Variable expenses (600 speakers × £150)	90,000
Total expenses	£125,000

   After the point has been plotted, draw a line through it back to the point where the fixed expenses line intersects the pounds axis.
3. Choose some volume of sales and plot the point representing total sales pounds at the activity level you have selected. In Exhibit 3.1, at a volume of 600 speakers, sales at that activity level total £150,000 (600 speakers × £250). Draw a line through this point back to the origin.

The interpretation of the completed CVP graph is given in Exhibit 3.2. The anticipated profit or loss at any given level of sales is measured by the vertical distance between the total revenue line (sales) and the total expenses line (variable expenses plus fixed expenses).

The break-even point is where the total revenue and total expenses lines cross. The break-even point of 350 speakers in Exhibit 3.2 agrees with the break-even point obtained for Acoustic Concepts in earlier computations.

Exhibit 3.1 Preparing the CVP graph

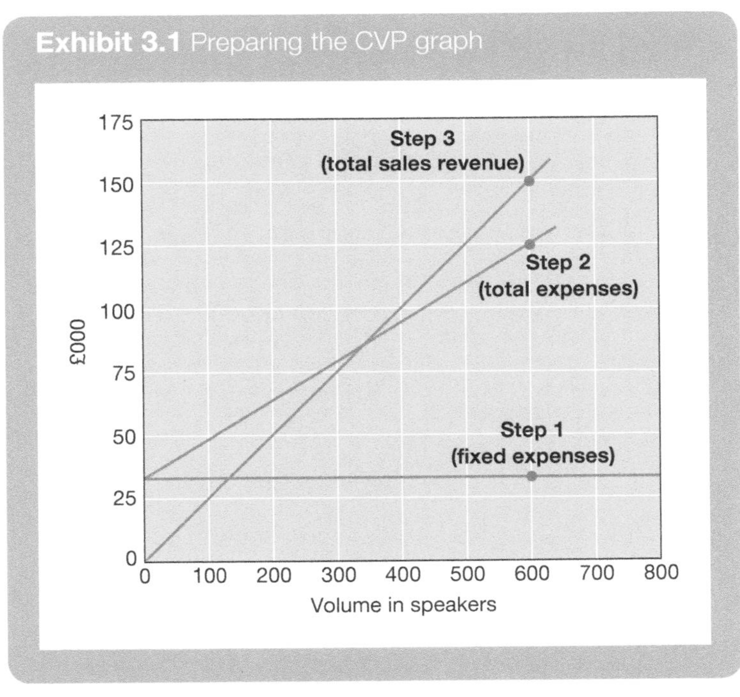

Exhibit 3.2 The completed CVP graph

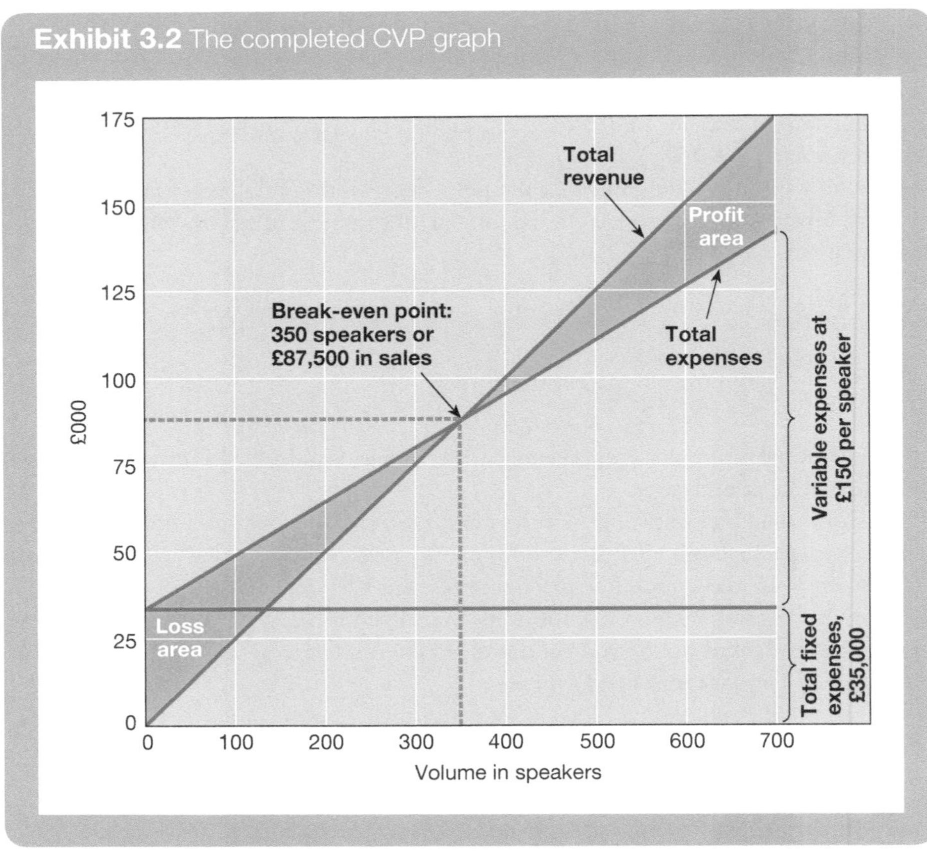

LO 6 Target profit analysis

CVP formulas can be used to determine the sales volume needed to achieve a target profit. Suppose that Acoustic Concepts would like to earn a target profit of £40,000 per month. How many speakers would have to be sold?

We may expand the contribution margin formula to include the target profit:

$$\text{Units sold to attain the target profit} = \frac{\text{Fixed expenses} + \text{Target profit}}{\text{Unit contribution margin}}$$

$$= \frac{\text{£35,000 fixed expenses} + \text{£40,000 target profit}}{\text{£100 contribution margin per speaker}} = 750 \text{ speakers}$$

LO 7 The margin of safety

The **margin of safety** is the excess of budgeted (or actual) sales over the break-even volume of sales. It states the amount by which sales can drop before losses begin to be incurred. The formula for its calculation is as follows:

Margin of safety = Total budgeted (or actual) sales − Break-even sales

The margin of safety can also be expressed in percentage form. This percentage is obtained by dividing the margin of safety in pound terms by total sales:

$$\text{Margin of safety percentage} = \frac{\text{Margin of safety in pounds}}{\text{Total budgeted (or actual) sales}}$$

The calculations for the margin of safety for Acoustic Concepts are as follows:

Sales (at the current volume of 400 speakers) (a)	£100,000
Break-even sales (at 350 speakers)	87,500
Margin of safety (in pounds) (b)	£12,500
Margin of safety as a percentage of sales,(b)/(a)	12.5%

This margin of safety means that at the current level of sales and with the company's current prices and cost structure, a reduction in sales of £12,500, or 12.5%, would result in just breaking even.

In a single-product firm like Acoustic Concepts, the margin of safety can also be expressed in terms of the number of units sold by dividing the margin of safety in pounds by the selling price per unit. In this case, the margin of safety is 50 units (£12,500/£250 per unit = 50 units).

CVP considerations in choosing a cost structure

We stated in the preceding chapter that *cost structure* refers to the relative proportion of fixed and variable costs in an organization. We also stated that an organization often has some latitude in trading off between fixed and variable costs. Such a trade-off is possible, for example, by automating facilities rather than using direct labour workers. In this section, we discuss various considerations involved in choosing a cost structure.

We look first at the matter of cost structure and profit stability, and then we discuss an important concept known as *operating leverage*.

Cost structure and profit stability

When a manager has some latitude in trading off between fixed and variable costs, which cost structure is better – high variable costs and low fixed costs, or the opposite? No categorical answer to this question is possible; there may be advantages either way, depending on the specific circumstances. To show what we mean by this statement, refer to the profit and loss accounts given below for two blackberry farms. Bogside Farm depends on migrant workers to pick its berries by hand, whereas Sterling Farm has invested in expensive berry-picking machines. Consequently, Bogside Farm has higher variable costs, but Sterling Farm has higher fixed costs:

	Bogside Farm		Sterling Farm	
	Amount	%	Amount	%
Sales	£100,000	100	£100,000	100
Less variable expenses	60,000	60	30,000	30
Contribution margin	40,000	40	70,000	70
Less fixed expenses	30,000		60,000	
Profit	£10,000		£10,000	

The question as to which farm has the better cost structure depends on many factors, including the long-run trend in sales, year-to-year fluctuations in the level of sales, and the attitude of the owners toward risk. If sales are expected to be above £100,000 in the future, then Sterling Farm probably has the better cost structure. The reason is that its CM ratio is higher, and its profits will therefore increase more rapidly as sales increase. To illustrate, assume that each farm experiences a 10% increase in sales without any increase in fixed costs. The new profit and loss accounts would be as follows:

	Bogside Farm		Sterling Farm	
	Amount	%	Amount	%
Sales	£110,000	100	£110,000	100
Less variable expenses	66,000	60	33,000	30
Contribution margin	44,000	40	77,000	70
Less fixed expenses	30,000		60,000	
Profit	£14,000		£17,000	

Sterling Farm has experienced a greater increase in profit due to its higher CM ratio even though the increase in sales was the same for both farms.

What if sales drop below £100,000 from time to time? What are the break-even points of the two farms? What are their margins of safety? The computations needed to answer these questions are carried out below using the contribution margin method:

	Bogside Farm	Sterling Farm
Fixed expenses	£30,000	£60,000
Contribution margin ratio	÷40%	÷70%
Break-even in total sales pounds	£75,000	£85,714
Total current sales (a)	£100,000	£100,000
Break-even sales	75,000	85,714
Margin of safety in sales pounds (b)	£25,000	£14,286
Margin of safety as a percentage of sales,(b)/(a)	25.0%	14.3%

This analysis makes it clear that Bogside Farm is less vulnerable to downturns than Sterling Farm. We can identify two reasons why it is less vulnerable. First, due to its lower fixed expenses, Bogside Farm has a lower break-even point and a higher margin of safety, as shown by the computations above. Therefore, it will not incur losses as quickly as Sterling Farm in periods of sharply declining sales. Secondly, due to its lower CM ratio, Bogside Farm will not lose contribution margin as rapidly as Sterling Farm when sales fall off. Thus Bogside Farm's profit will be less volatile. We saw earlier that this is a drawback when sales increase, but it provides more protection when sales drop.

To summarize, without knowing the future, it is not obvious which cost structure is better. Both have advantages and disadvantages. Sterling Farm, with its higher fixed costs and lower variable costs, will experience wider swings in profit as changes take place in sales, with greater profits in good years and greater losses in bad years. Bogside Farm, with its lower fixed costs and higher variable costs, will enjoy greater stability in profit and will be more protected from losses during bad years, but at the cost of lower profit in good years.

Operating leverage

LO 8

A lever is a tool for multiplying force. Using a lever, a massive object can be moved with only a modest amount of force. In business, *operating leverage* serves a similar purpose. **Operating leverage** is a measure of how sensitive profit is to percentage changes in sales. Operating leverage acts as a multiplier. If operating leverage is high, a small percentage increase in sales can produce a much larger percentage increase in profit.

Operating leverage can be illustrated by returning to the data given above for the two blackberry farms. We previously showed that a 10% increase in sales (from £100,000 to £110,000 in each farm) results in a 70% increase in the profit of Sterling Farm (from £10,000 to £17,000) and only a 40% increase in the profit of Bogside Farm (from £10,000 to £14,000). Thus, for a 10% increase in sales, Sterling Farm experiences a much greater percentage increase in profits than does Bogside Farm. Therefore, Sterling Farm has greater operating leverage than Bogside Farm.

The **degree of operating leverage** at a given level of sales is computed by the following formula:

$$\text{Degree of operating leverage} = \frac{\text{Contribution margin}}{\text{Profit}}$$

The degree of operating leverage is a measure, at a given level of sales, of how a percentage change in sales volume will affect profits. To illustrate, the degree of operating leverage for the two farms at a £100,000 sales level would be as follows:

$$\text{Bogside Farm: } \frac{£40{,}000}{£10{,}000} = 4$$

$$\text{Sterling Farm: } \frac{£70{,}000}{£10{,}000} = 7$$

Since the degree of operating leverage for Bogside Farm is four, the farm's profit grows four times as fast as its sales. Similarly, Sterling Farm's profit grows seven times as fast as its sales. Thus, if sales increase by 10%, then we can expect the profit of Bogside Farm to increase by four times this amount, or by 40%, and the profit of Sterling Farm to increase by seven times this amount, or by 70%.

	1 Percentage increase in sales	2 Degree of operating leverage	3 Percentage increase in profit (1 × 2)
Bogside Farm	10	4	40
Sterling Farm	10	7	70

What is responsible for the higher operating leverage at Sterling Farm? The only difference between the two farms is their cost structure. If two companies have the same total revenue and same total expense but different cost structures, then the company with the higher proportion of fixed costs in its cost structure will have higher operating leverage. Referring back to the original example on page 55, when both farms have sales of £100,000 and total expenses of £90,000, one-third of Bogside Farm's costs are fixed but two-thirds of Sterling Farm's costs are fixed. As a consequence, Sterling's degree of operating leverage is higher than Bogside's.[3]

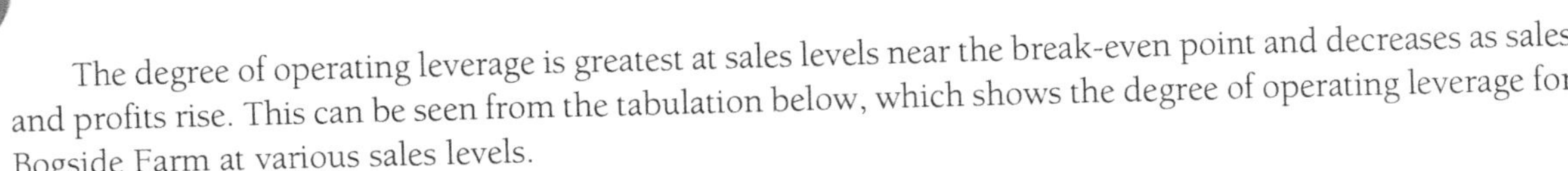

The degree of operating leverage is greatest at sales levels near the break-even point and decreases as sales and profits rise. This can be seen from the tabulation below, which shows the degree of operating leverage for Bogside Farm at various sales levels.

Sales	£75,000	£80,000	£100,000	£150,000	£225,000
Less variable expenses	45,000	48,000	60,000	90,000	135,000
Contribution margin (a)	30,000	32,000	40,000	60,000	90,000
Less fixed expenses	30,000	30,000	30,000	30,000	30,000
Profit (b)	£0	£2,000	£10,000	£30,000	£60,000
Degree of operating leverage, (a)/(b)	∞	16	4	2	1.5

Thus, a 10% increase in sales would increase profits by only 15% (10% × 1.5) if the company were operating at a £225,000 sales level, as compared to the 40% increase we computed earlier at the £100,000 sales level. The degree of operating leverage will continue to decrease the farther the company moves from its break-even point. At the break-even point, the degree of operating leverage will be infinitely large (£30,000 contribution margin/£0 profit = ∞).

A manager can use the degree of operating leverage quickly to estimate what impact various percentage changes in sales will have on profits, without the necessity of preparing detailed profit and loss accounts. As shown by our examples, the effects of operating leverage can be dramatic. If a company is near its break-even point, then even small percentage increases in sales can yield large percentage increases in profits.

This explains why management will often work very hard for only a small increase in sales volume. If the degree of operating leverage is five, then a 6% increase in sales would translate into a 30% increase in profits.

LO 9

The concept of sales mix

The preceding sections have given us some insights into the principles involved in CVP analysis, as well as some selected examples of how these principles are used by the manager. Before concluding our discussion, it will be helpful to consider one additional application of the ideas that we have developed – the use of CVP concepts in analysing sales mix.

The definition of sales mix

The term **sales mix** means the relative proportions in which a company's products are sold. Managers try to achieve the combination, or mix, that will yield the greatest amount of profits. Most companies have several products, and often these products are not equally profitable. Where this is true, profits will depend to some extent on the company's sales mix. Profits will be greater if high-margin rather than low-margin items make up a relatively large proportion of total sales.

Changes in the sales mix can cause interesting (and sometimes confusing) variations in a company's profits. A shift in the sales mix from high-margin items to low-margin items can cause total profits to decrease even though total sales may increase. Conversely, a shift in the sales mix from low-margin items to high-margin items can cause the reverse effect – total profits may increase even though total sales decrease. It is one thing to achieve a particular sales volume; it is quite a different thing to sell the most profitable mix of products.

Sales mix and break-even analysis

If a company sells more than one product, break-even analysis is somewhat more complex than discussed earlier in the chapter. The reason is that different products will have different selling prices, different costs and different contribution margins. Consequently, the break-even point will depend on the mix in which the various products are sold. To illustrate, consider Sound Unlimited, a small company that imports CD-ROMs from France for use in personal computers. At present, the company distributes the following to retail computer stores: the Le Louvre CD, a multimedia free-form tour of the famous art museum in Paris; and the Le Vin CD, which features the wines and wine-growing regions of France. Both multimedia products have sound, photos, video clips, and sophisticated software. The company's September sales, expenses and break-even point are shown in Exhibit 3.3.

As shown in the exhibit, the break-even point is £60,000 in sales. This is computed by dividing the fixed costs by the company's *overall* CM ratio of 45%. But £60,000 in sales represents the break-even point for the company only as long as the sales mix does not change. *If the sales mix changes, then the break-even point will also change.* This is illustrated by the results for October in which the sales mix shifted away from the more profitable Le Vin CD (which has a 50% CM ratio) towards the less profitable Le Louvre CD (which has only a 25% CM ratio). These results appear in Exhibit 3.4.

Although sales have remained unchanged at £100,000, the sales mix is exactly the reverse of what it was in Exhibit 3.3, with the bulk of the sales now coming from the less profitable Le Louvre CD. Notice that this shift in the sales mix has caused both the overall CM ratio and total profits to drop sharply from the prior month – the overall CM ratio has dropped from 45% in September to only 30% in October, and profit has dropped from £18,000 to only £3,000. In addition, with the drop in the overall CM ratio, the company's break-even point is no longer £60,000 in sales. Since the company is now realizing less average contribution margin per pound of sales, it takes more sales to cover the same amount of fixed costs. Thus, the break-even point has increased from £60,000 to £90,000 in sales per year.

In preparing a break-even analysis, some assumption must be made concerning the sales mix. Usually the assumption is that it will not change. However, if the manager knows that shifts in various factors (consumer tastes, market share and so forth) are causing shifts in the sales mix, then these factors must be explicitly considered in any CVP computations. Otherwise, the manager may make decisions on the basis of outmoded or faulty data.

Exhibit 3.3 Multiple-product break-even analysis

Sound Unlimited
Contribution profit statement
For the month of September

	Le Louvre CD		Le Vin CD		Total	
	Amount	**Per cent**	**Amount**	**Per cent**	**Amount**	**Per cent**
Sales	£20,000	100	£80,000	100	£100,000	100
Less variable expenses	15,000	75	40,000	50	55,000	55
Contribution margin	£5,000	25	£40,000	50	45,000	45
Less fixed expenses					27,000	
Profit					£18,000	

Computation of the break-even point:

$$\frac{\text{Fixed expenses, £27,000}}{\text{Overall CM ratio, 45\%}} = \text{£60,000}$$

Verification of the break-even:

	Le Louvre CD		Le Vin CD		Total	
	Amount	Per cent	Amount	Per cent	Amount	Per cent
Sales	£12,000	100	£48,000	100	£60,000	100
Less variable expenses	9,000	75	24,000	50	33,000	55
Contribution margin	£3,000	25	£24,000	50	27,000	45
Less fixed expenses					27,000	
Profit					£0	

Exhibit 3.4 Multiple-product break-even analysis: a shift in sales mix (see Exhibit 3.3)

Sound Unlimited
Contribution profit statement
For the month of October

	Le Louvre CD		Le Vin CD		Total	
	Amount	Per cent	Amount	Per cent	Amount	Per cent
Sales	£80,000	100	£20,000	100	£100,000	100
Less variable expenses	60,000	75	10,000	50	70,000	70
Contribution margin	£20,000	25	£10,000	50	30,000	30
Less fixed expenses					27,000	
Profit					£3,000	

Computation of the break-even point:

$$\frac{\text{Fixed expenses, £27,000}}{\text{Overall CM ratio, 30\%}} = £90,000$$

Focus on Business Practice

Making the labour force more flexible

© Mike Liu

Geoff is the general manager of a large resort hotel. Geoff has a sophisticated forecasting model which tells him what the balance of demand is likely to be for each holiday package. For example, a 'Motown' weekend will mean a lot of extra demand at the bar. He has trained his workforce to multi-task which makes his costs more flexible for the different mixes of demand that relate to the expected preferences of his guests.

Exercise: Are the hotel's labour costs now more variable with respect to total guest numbers or just more variable in respect of sales mix?

Assumptions of CVP analysis

A number of assumptions typically underlie CVP analysis:

1. Selling price is constant throughout the entire relevant range. The price of a product or service will not change as volume changes.
2. Costs are linear throughout the entire relevant range, and they can be accurately divided into variable and fixed elements. The variable element is constant per unit, and the fixed element is constant in total over the entire relevant range.
3. In multiproduct companies, the sales mix is constant.
4. In manufacturing companies, stocks do not change. The number of units produced equals the number of units sold.

While some of these assumptions may be technically violated, the violations are usually not serious enough to call into question the basic validity of CVP analysis. For example, in most multiproduct companies, the sales mix is constant enough for the results of CVP analysis to be reasonably valid.

Perhaps the greatest danger lies in relying on simple CVP analysis when a manager is contemplating a large change in volume that lies outside the relevant range. For example, a manager might contemplate increasing the level of sales far beyond what the company has ever experienced before. However, even in these situations a manager can adjust the model as we have done in this chapter to take into account anticipated changes in selling prices, fixed costs and the sales mix that would otherwise violate the assumptions. For example, in a decision that would affect fixed costs, the change in fixed costs can be explicitly taken into account as illustrated earlier in the chapter in the Acoustic Concepts example on page 48.

Separation of costs into fixed and variable elements: the high-low method

So far we have assumed that we can easily determine which are fixed and which are variable costs. But if we are given levels of activity and associated costs how can we separate these mixed costs into fixed and variable elements? One simple method is known as the *high-low* method. In the case of Brentline Hospital, we will use the following records of maintenance costs and patient-days for the first seven months of the year to estimate the fixed and variable elements of maintenance costs:

Month	Activity level: patient-days	Maintenance cost incurred
January	5,600	£7,900
February	7,100	8,500
March	5,000	7,400
April	6,500	8,200
May	7,300	9,100
June	8,000	9,800
July	6,200	7,800

The high-low method

To analyse mixed costs with the **high-low method**, one begins by identifying the period with the lowest level of activity and the period with the highest level of activity. The difference in cost observed at the two extremes is divided by the change in activity between the extremes in order to estimate the variable cost per unit of activity.

Since total maintenance cost at Brentline Hospital appears generally to increase as the activity level increases, it is likely that some variable cost element is present. Using the high-low method, we first identify the periods with the highest and lowest activity – in this case, June and March. We then use the activity and cost data from these two periods to estimate the variable cost component as follows:

	Patient-days	Maintenance cost incurred
High activity level (June)	8,000	£9,800
Low activity level (March)	5,000	7,400
Change	3,000	£2,400

$$\text{Variable cost} = \frac{\text{Change in cost}}{\text{Change in activity}} = \frac{£2400}{3000} = £0.80 \text{ per patient day}$$

Having determined that the variable rate for maintenance cost is 80 pence per patient-day, we can now determine the amount of fixed cost. This is done by taking total cost at *either* the high *or* the low activity level and

deducting the variable cost element. In the computation below, total cost at the high activity level is used in computing the fixed cost element:

Fixed cost element = Total cost − Variable cost element
= £9,800 − (£0.80 per patient-day × per 8,000 patient-days)
= £3,400

Both the variable and fixed cost elements have now been isolated. The cost of maintenance can be expressed as £3,400 per month plus 80 pence per patient-day.

The cost of maintenance can also be expressed in terms of the equation for a straight line as follows:

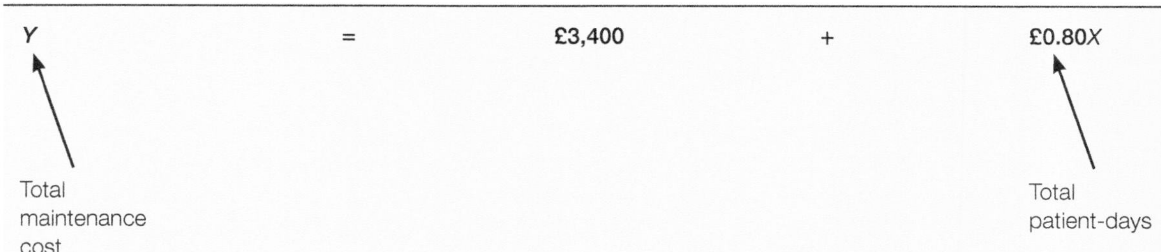

Although there are other more sophisticated ways of measuring cost functions, the high-low method is a quick and easy approach.

Summary

- CVP analysis involves finding the most favourable combination of variable costs, fixed costs, selling price, sales volume, and mix of products sold.
- Trade-offs are possible between types of costs, as well as between costs and selling price, and between selling price and sales volume.
- Sometimes these trade-offs are desirable, and sometimes they are not. CVP analysis provides the manager with a powerful tool for identifying those courses of action that will improve profitability.
- The concepts developed in this chapter represent *a way of thinking* rather than a mechanical set of procedures. That is, to put together the optimum combination of costs, selling price and sales volume, the manager must be trained to think in terms of the unit contribution margin, the break-even point, the CM ratio, the sales mix, and the other concepts developed in this chapter.
- These concepts are dynamic in that a change in one will trigger changes in others – changes that may not be obvious on the surface.

Key terms

Break-even point The level of sales at which profit is zero. The break-even point can also be defined as the point where total sales equals total expenses or as the point where total contribution margin equals total fixed expenses (p. 45).

Contribution margin method A method of computing the break-even point in which the fixed expenses are divided by the contribution margin per unit (p. 51).

Contribution margin ratio (CM ratio) The contribution margin as a percentage of total sales (p. 47).

Cost–volume–profit (CVP) graph The relations between revenues, costs and level of activity in an organization presented in graphic form (p. 52).

Degree of operating leverage A measure, at a given level of sales, of how a percentage change in sales volume will affect profits. The degree of operating leverage is computed by dividing contribution margin by profit (p. 57).

High-low method A technique for separating mixed costs into fixed and variable components (p. 61).

Incremental analysis An analytical approach that focuses only on those items of revenue, cost and volume that will change as a result of a decision (p. 49)

Margin of safety The excess of budgeted (or actual) sales over the break-even volume of sales (p. 54).

Operating leverage A measure of how sensitive profit is to a given percentage change in sales. It is computed by dividing the contribution margin by profit (p. 57).

Sales mix The relative proportions in which a company's products are sold. Sales mix is computed by expressing the sales of each product as a percentage of total sales (p. 58).

Endnotes

1 Wilke (1994).

2 Reed and Schafer (2010).

3 See Lord (1995) for an extensive discussion of the impact of cost structure on the degree of operating leverage.

connect

When you have read this chapter, log on to the Online Learning Centre for *Management Accounting for Business Decisions* at **www.mheducation.co.uk/textbooks/sealmabd1**, where you'll find multiple choice questions, practice exams and extra study tools for management accounting.

Assessment

Questions

connect™

3–1 What is meant by a product's CM ratio? How is this ratio useful in planning business operations?

3–2 Company A's cost structure includes costs that are mostly variable, whereas Company B's cost structure includes costs that are mostly fixed. In a time of increasing sales, which company will tend to realize the most rapid increase in profits? Explain.

3–3 What is meant by the term ***operating leverage***?

3–4 A 10 per cent decrease in the selling price of a product will have the same impact on profit as a 10 per cent increase in the variable expenses. Do you agree? Why or why not?

3–5 What is meant by the term ***break-even point***?

3–6 Name three approaches to break-even analysis. Briefly explain how each approach works.

3–7 In response to a request from your immediate supervisor, you have prepared a CVP graph portraying the cost and revenue characteristics of your company's product and operations. Explain how the lines on the graph and the break-even point would change if (a) the selling price per unit decreased, (b) fixed costs increased throughout the entire range of activity portrayed on the graph, and (c) variable costs per unit increased.

3–8 Al's Car Wash charges £4 to wash a car. The variable costs of washing a car are 15 per cent of sales. Fixed expenses total £1,700 monthly. How many cars must be washed each month for Al to break even?

3–9 What is meant by the margin of safety?

3–10 Companies X and Y are in the same industry. Company X is highly automated, whereas Company Y relies primarily on labour to make its products. If sales and total expenses in the two companies are about the same, which would you expect to have the lower margin of safety? Why?

3–11 What is meant by the term sales mix? What assumption is usually made concerning sales mix in CVP analysis?

3–12 Explain how a shift in the sales mix could result in both a higher break-even point and a lower profit.

Exercises

connect™

E3–1 Time allowed: 20 minutes

Menlo Company manufactures and sells a single product. The company's sales and expenses for the last quarter follow:

	Total	Per unit
Sales	£450,000	£30
Less variable expenses	180,000	12
Contribution margin	270,000	£18
Less fixed expenses	216,000	
Profit	£54,000	

Required

1. What is the quarterly break-even point in units sold and in sales pounds?
2. Without resorting to computations, what is the total contribution margin at the break-even point?
3. How many units would have to be sold each quarter to earn a target profit of £90,000? Use the unit contribution method. Verify your answer by preparing a contribution profit and loss account at the target level of sales.
4. Refer to the original data. Compute the company's margin of safety in both pound and percentage terms.
5. What is the company's CM ratio? If sales increase by £50,000 per quarter and there is no change in fixed expenses, by how much would you expect quarterly profit to increase? (Do not prepare a profit and loss account; use the CM ratio to compute your answer.)

E3–2 Time allowed: 20 minutes

Lindon Company is the exclusive distributor for an automotive product. The product sells for £40 per unit and has a CM ratio of 30%. The company's fixed expenses are £180,000 per year.

Required

1. What are the variable expenses per unit?
2. Using the equation method:
   (a) What is the break-even point in units and sales pounds?
   (b) What sales level in units and in sales pounds is required to earn an annual profit of £60,000?
   (c) Assume that by using a more efficient shipper, the company is able to reduce its variable expenses by £4 per unit. What is the company's new break-even point in units and sales pounds?
3. Repeat Question 2 above using the unit contribution method.

E3–3 Time allowed: 25 minutes

The Hartford Symphony Guild is planning its annual dinner-dance. The dinner-dance committee has assembled the following expected costs for the event:

Dinner (per person)	**£18**
Favours and programme (per person)	2
Band	2,800
Rental of ballroom	900
Professional entertainment during intermission	1,000
Tickets and advertising	1,300

The committee members would like to charge £35 per person for the evening's activities.

Required

1. Compute the break-even point for the dinner-dance (in terms of the number of persons that must attend).
2. Assume that last year only 300 persons attended the dinner-dance. If the same number attend this year, what price per ticket must be charged in order to break even?
3. Refer to the original data (£35 ticket price per person). Prepare a CVP graph for the dinner-dance from a zero level of activity up to 900 tickets sold. Number of persons should be placed on the horizontal (*x*) axis, and pounds should be placed on the vertical (*z*) axis.

E3–4 Time allowed: 15 minutes

Magic Realm Ltd has developed a new fantasy board game. The company sold 15,000 games last year at a selling price of £20 per game. Fixed costs associated with the game total £182,000 per year, and variable costs are £6 per game. Production of the game is entrusted to a printing contractor. Variable costs consist mostly of payments to this contractor.

Required

1 Prepare a profit and loss account for the game last year and compute the degree of operating leverage.
2 Management is confident that the company can sell 18,000 games next year (an increase of 3,000 games, or 20 per cent, over last year). Compute:
3 (a) The expected percentage increase in profit for next year.
(b) The expected total pound profit for next year. (Do not prepare a profit and loss account; use the degree of operating leverage to compute your answer.)

E3–5 Time allowed: 20 minutes

Miller Company's most recent profit and loss account is shown below:

	Total	Per unit
Sales (20,000 units)	£300,000	£15.00
Less variable expenses	180,000	9.00
Contribution margin	120,000	£6.00
Less fixed expenses	70,000	
Profit	£50,000	

Required

Prepare a new profit and loss account under each of the following conditions (consider each case independently):

1 The sales volume increases by 15%.
2 The selling price decreases by £1.50 per unit, and the sales volume increases by 25%.
3 The selling price increases by £1.50 per unit, fixed expenses increase by £20,000, and the sales volume decreases by 5%.
4 The selling price increases by 12%, variable expenses increase by 60 pence per unit, and the sales volume decreases by 10%.

E3–6 Time allowed: 20 minutes

Fill in the missing amounts in each of the eight case situations below. Each case is independent of the others. (*Hint*: One way to find the missing amounts would be to prepare a contribution profit and loss account for each case, enter the known data, and then compute the missing items.)

(a) Assume that only one product is being sold in each of the four following case situations:

Case	Units sold	Sales	Variable expenses	Contribution margin per unit	Fixed expenses	Net profit (loss)
1	15,000	£180,000	£120,000	£?	£50,000	£?
2	?	100,000	?	10	32,000	8,000
3	10,000	?	70,000	13	?	12,000
4	6,000	300,000	?	?	100,000	(10,000)

(b) Assume that more than one product is being sold in each of the four following case situations:

Case	Sales	Variable expenses	Contribution margin (per cent)	Average fixed expenses	Net profit (loss)
1	£500,000	£?	20	£?	£7,000
2	400,000	260,000	?	100,000	?
3	?	?	60	130,000	20,000
4	600,000	420,000	?	?	(5,000)

E3–7 Time allowed: 25 minutes

Olongapo Sports Corporation is the distributor in the Philippines of two premium golf balls – the Flight Dynamic and the Sure Shot. Monthly sales and the contribution margin ratios for the two products follow:

	Product		
	Flight Dynamic	Sure Shot	Total
Sales	P150,000	P250,000	P400,000
CM ratio	80%	36%	?

Fixed expenses total P183,750 per month (the currency in the Philippines is the peso, which is denoted by P).

Required

1 Prepare a profit and loss account for the company as a whole. Use the format shown in Exhibit 3.3 and carry computations to one decimal place.

2 Compute the break-even point for the company based on the current sales mix.

3 If sales increase by P100,000 a month, by how much would you expect profit to increase? What are your assumptions?

E3–8 Time allowed: 25 minutes

Outback Outfitters manufactures and sells recreational equipment. One of the company's products, a small camp stove, sells for £50 per unit. Variable expenses are £32 per stove, and fixed expenses associated with the stove total £108,000 per month.

Required

1 Compute the break-even point in number of stoves and in total sales pounds.

2 If the variable expenses per stove increase as a percentage of the selling price, will it result in a higher or a lower break-even point? Why? (Assume that the fixed expenses remain unchanged.)

3 At present, the company is selling 8,000 stoves per month. The sales manager is convinced that a 10 per cent reduction in the selling price would result in a 25% increase in monthly sales of stoves. Prepare two contribution profit and loss accounts, one under present operating conditions, and one as operations would appear after the proposed changes. Show both total and per unit data on your statements.

4 Refer to the data in Question 3 above. How many stoves would have to be sold at the new selling price to yield a minimum profit of £35,000 per month?

Problems

connect™

P3–9 Basic CVP analysis; graphing

Time allowed: 60 minutes

The Fashion Shoe Company operates a chain of women's shoe shops around the country. The shops carry many styles of shoes that are all sold at the same price. Sales personnel in the shops are paid a substantial commission on each pair of shoes sold (in addition to a small basic salary) in order to encourage them to be aggressive in their sales efforts.

The following cost and revenue data relate to Shop 48 and are typical of one of the company's many outlets:

	Per pair of shoes
Sales price	£30.00
Variable expenses:	
Invoice cost	£13.50
Sales commission	4.50
Total variable expenses	£18.00
	Annual
Fixed expenses:	
Advertising	£30,000
Rent	20,000
Salaries	100,000
Total fixed expenses	£150,000

Required

1. Calculate the annual break-even point in pound sales and in unit sales for Shop 48.
2. Prepare a CVP graph showing cost and revenue data for Shop 48 from a zero level of activity up to 20,000 pairs of shoes sold each year. Clearly indicate the break-even point on the graph.
3. If 12,000 pairs of shoes are sold in a year, what would be Shop 48's profit or loss?
4. The company is considering paying the store manager of Shop 48 an incentive commission of 75 pence per pair of shoes (in addition to the salesperson's commission). If this change is made, what will be the new break-even point in pound sales and in unit sales?
5. Refer to the original data. As an alternative to (4) above, the company is considering paying the store manager 50 pence commission on each pair of shoes sold in excess of the break-even point. If this change is made, what will be the shop's profit or loss if 15,000 pairs of shoes are sold?
6. Refer to the original data. The company is considering eliminating sales commissions entirely in its shops and increasing fixed salaries by £31,500 annually. If this change is made, what will be the new break-even point in pound sales and in unit sales for Shop 48? Would you recommend that the change be made? Explain.

P3–10 Basics of CVP analysis; cost structure

Time allowed: 60 minutes

Due to erratic sales of its sole product – a high-capacity battery for laptop computers – PEM Ltd has been experiencing difficulty for some time. The company's profit and loss account for the most recent month is given below:

Sales (19,500 units × £30)	£585,000
Less variable expenses	409,500
Contribution margin	175,500
Less fixed expenses	180,000
Net loss	£(4,500)

Required

1 Compute the company's CM ratio and its break-even point in both units and pounds.

2 The president believes that a £16,000 increase in the monthly advertising budget, combined with an intensified effort by the sales staff, will result in an £80,000 increase in monthly sales. If the president is right, what will be the effect on the company's monthly profit or loss? (Use the incremental approach in preparing your answer.)

3 Refer to the original data. The sales manager is convinced that a 10% reduction in the selling price, combined with an increase of £60,000 in the monthly advertising budget, will cause unit sales to double. What will the new profit and loss account look like if these changes are adopted?

4 Refer to the original data. The Marketing Department thinks that a fancy new package for the laptop computer battery would help sales. The new package would increase packaging costs by 75 pence per unit. Assuming no other changes, how many units would have to be sold each month to earn a profit of £9,750?

5 Refer to the original data. By automating certain operations, the company could reduce variable costs by £3 per unit. However, fixed costs would increase by £72,000 each month.

6 (a) Compute the new CM ratio and the new break-even point in both units and pounds.

(b) Assume that the company expects to sell 26,000 units next month. Prepare two profit and loss accounts, one assuming that operations are not automated and one assuming that they are. (Show data on a per unit and percentage basis, as well as in total, for each alternative.)

(c) Would you recommend that the company automate its operations? Explain.

P3–11 Sales mix assumptions; break-even analysis

Time allowed: 35 minutes

Gold Star Rice Ltd of Thailand, exports Thai rice throughout Asia. The company grows three varieties of rice – Fragrant, White and Loonzain. (The currency in Thailand is the baht, which is denoted by B.) Budgeted sales by product and in total for the coming month are shown below:

	Product							
	White		Fragrant		Loonzain		Total	
Percentage of total sales	20%		52%		28%		100%	
Percentage of sales	B150,000	100%	B390,000	100%	B210,000	100%	B750,000	100%
Less variable expenses	108,000	72%	78,000	20%	84,000	40%	270,000	36%
Contribution margin	B 42,000	28%	B312,000	80%	B126,000	60%	480,000	64%
Less fixed expenses							449,280	
Profit							B30,720	

$$\frac{\text{Break-even sales: Fixed Expenses, B449,280}}{\text{CM Ratio, 0.64}} = \text{B702,000}$$

As shown by these data, profit is budgeted at B30,720 for the month and break-even sales at B702,000.

Assume that actual sales for the month total B750,000 as planned. Actual sales by product are: White, B300,000; Fragrant, B180,000; and Loonzain, B270,000.

Required

1. Prepare a contribution profit and loss account for the month based on actual sales data. Present the profit and loss account in the format shown above.
2. Compute the break-even sales for the month based on your actual data.
3. Considering the fact that the company met its B750,000 sales budget for the month, the managing director is shocked at the results shown on your profit and loss account in Question 1 above. Prepare a brief memo for the MD explaining why both the operating results and break-even sales are different from what was budgeted.

P3–12 Basics of CVP analysis

Time allowed: 20 minutes

Feather Friends Ltd makes a high-quality wooden birdhouse that sells for £20 per unit. Variable costs are £8 per unit, and fixed costs total £180,000 per year.

Required

Answer the following independent questions:

1. What is the product's CM ratio?
2. Use the CM ratio to determine the break-even point in sales pounds.
3. Due to an increase in demand, the company estimates that sales will increase by £75,000 during the next year. By how much should profit increase (or net loss decrease) assuming that fixed costs do not change?
4. Assume that the operating results for last year were:

Sales	£400,000
Less variable expenses	160,000
Contribution margin	240,000
Less fixed expenses	180,000
Profit	£60,000

   (a) Compute the degree of operating leverage at the current level of sales.

   (b) The MD expects sales to increase by 20% next year. By what percentage should profit increase?

5. Refer to the original data. Assume that the company sold 18,000 units last year. The sales manager is convinced that a 10% reduction in the selling price, combined with a £30,000 increase in advertising, would cause annual sales in units to increase by one-third. Prepare two contribution profit and loss accounts, one showing the results of last year's operations and one showing the results of operations if these changes are made. Would you recommend that the company do as the sales manager suggests?
6. Refer to the original data. Assume again that the company sold 18,000 units last year. The president does not want to change the selling price. Instead, he wants to increase the sales commission by £1 per unit. He thinks that this move, combined with some increase in advertising, would increase annual sales by 25%. By how much could advertising be increased

with profits remaining unchanged? Do not prepare a profit and loss account; use the incremental analysis approach.

P3–13 The case of the elusive contribution margin

Time allowed: 30 minutes

The Shirt Works sells a large variety of tee shirts and sweat shirts. Steve Hooper, the owner, is thinking of expanding his sales by hiring local high school students, on a commission basis, to sell sweat shirts bearing the name and mascot of the local high school.

These sweat shirts would have to be ordered from the manufacturer six weeks in advance, and they could not be returned because of the unique printing required. The sweat shirts would cost Mr Hooper £8 each with a minimum order of 75 sweat shirts. Any additional sweat shirts would have to be ordered in increments of 75.

Since Mr Hooper's plan would not require any additional facilities, the only costs associated with the project would be the costs of the sweat shirts and the costs of the sales commissions. The selling price of the sweat shirts would be £13.50 each. Mr Hooper would pay the students a commission of £1.50 for each shirt sold.

Required

1 To make the project worth while, Mr Hooper would require a £1,200 profit for the first three months of the venture. What level of sales in units and in pounds would be required to reach this target profit? Show all computations.
2 Assume that the venture is undertaken and an order is placed for 75 sweat shirts. What would be Mr Hooper's break-even point in units and in sales pounds? Show computations and explain the reasoning behind your answer.

P3–14 Sensitivity analysis of profit; changes in volume

Time allowed: 30 minutes

Minden Company introduced a new product last year for which it is trying to find an optimal selling price. Marketing studies suggest that the company can increase sales by 5,000 units for each £2 reduction in the selling price. The company's present selling price is £70 per unit, and variable expenses are £40 per unit. Fixed expenses are £540,000 per year. The present annual sales volume (at the £70 selling price) is 15,000 units.

Required

1 What is the present yearly profit or loss?
2 What is the present break-even point in units and in pound sales?
3 Assuming that the marketing studies are correct, what is the maximum profit that the company can earn yearly? At how many units and at what selling price per unit would the company generate this profit?
4 What would be the break-even point in units and in pound sales using the selling price you determined in Question 3 above (e.g., the selling price at the level of maximum profits)? Why is this break-even point different from the break-even point you computed in Question 2 above?

P3–15 Graphing; incremental analysis; operating leverage

Time allowed: 60 minutes

Angie Silva has recently opened The Sandal Shop in Brisbane, Australia, a store that specializes in fashionable sandals. Angie has just received a degree in business and she is anxious to apply the principles she has learned to her business. In time, she hopes to open a chain of sandal shops. As a first step, she has prepared the following analysis for her new store:

Sales price per pair of sandals	£40
Variable expenses per pair of sandals	16
Contribution margin per pair of sandals	£24
Fixed expenses per year:	
Building rental	£15,000
Equipment depreciation	7,000
Selling	20,000
Administrative	18,000
Total fixed expenses	£60,000

Required

1 How many pairs of sandals must be sold each year to break even? What does this represent in total pound sales?

2 Angie has decided that she must earn at least £18,000 the first year to justify her time and effort. How many pairs of sandals must be sold to reach this target profit?

3 Angie now has two salespersons working in the store – one full time and one part time. It will cost her an additional £8,000 per year to convert the part-time position to a full-time position. Angie believes that the change would bring in an additional £25,000 in sales each year. Should she convert the position? Use the incremental approach (do not prepare a profit and loss account).

4 Refer to the original data. During the first year, the store sold only 3,000 pairs of sandals and reported the following operating results:

Sales (3,000 pairs)	£120,000
Less variable expenses	48,000
Contribution margin	72,000
Less fixed expenses	60,000
Profit	£12,000

5 (a) What is the store's degree of operating leverage?
(b) Angie is confident that with a more intense sales effort and with a more creative advertising programme she can increase sales by 50% next year. What would be the expected percentage increase in profit? Use the degree of operating leverage to compute your answer.

P3–16 Sales mix; commission structure; break-even point

Time allowed: 60 minutes

Carbex Ltd produces cutlery sets out of high-quality wood and steel. The company makes a standard cutlery set and a deluxe set and sells them to retail department stores throughout the country. The standard set sells for £60, and the deluxe set sells for £75.

The variable expenses associated with each set are given below (in cost per set):

	Standard	Deluxe
Production costs	£ 15.00	£30.00
Sales commissions (15% of sales price)	9.00	11.25
The company's fixed		
Advertising	£105,000	
Depreciation	21,700	
Administrative	63,000	

Salespersons are paid on a commission basis to encourage them to be aggressive in their sales efforts. Mary Parsons, the financial vice president, watches sales commissions carefully and has noted that they have risen steadily over the last year. For this reason, she was shocked to find that even though sales have increased, profits for the current month – May – are down substantially from April. Sales, in sets, for the last two months are given below:

	Standard	Deluxe	Total
April	4,000	2,000	6,000
May	1,000	5,000	6,000

Required

1 Prepare a profit and loss account for April and a profit and loss account for May. Use the contribution format, with the following headings:

	Standard		Deluxe		Total	
	Amount	Percentage	Amount	Percentage	Amount	Percentage
Sales etc.						

Place the fixed expenses only in the Total column. Carry percentage computations to one decimal place. Do not show percentages for the fixed expenses.

2 Explain why there is a difference in profit between the two months, even though the same total number of sets was sold in each month.

3 What can be done to the sales commissions to optimize the sales mix?

4 (a) Using April's figures, what was the break-even point for the month in sales pounds?

(b) Has May's break-even point gone up or down from that of April? Explain your answer without calculating the break-even point for May.

P3–17 Various CVP questions: break-even point; cost structure; target sales

Time allowed: 60 minutes

Northwood Company manufactures basketballs. The company has a standard ball that sells for £25. At present, the standard ball is manufactured in a small plant that relies heavily on direct labour workers. Thus, variable costs are high, totalling £15 per ball.

Last year, the company sold 30,000 standard balls, with the following results:

Sales (30,000 standard balls)	£750,000
Less variable expenses	450,000
Contribution margin	300,000
Less fixed expenses	210,000
Profit	£90,000

Required

1 Compute (a) the CM ratio and the break-even point in balls (b), and the degree of operating leverage at last year's level of sales.

2 Due to an increase in labour rates, the company estimates that variable costs will increase by £3 per ball next year. If this change takes place and the selling price per ball remains constant at £25, what will be the new CM ratio and break-even point in balls?

3 Refer to the data in Question 2 above. If the expected change in variable costs takes place, how many balls will have to be sold next year to earn the same profit (£90,000) as last year?
4 Refer again to the data in Question 2 above. The managing director feels that the company must raise the selling price on the standard balls. If Northwood Company wants to maintain the same CM ratio as last year, what selling price per ball must it charge next year to cover the increased labour costs?
5 Refer to the original data. The company is discussing the construction of a new, automated plant to manufacture the standard balls. The new plant would slash variable costs per ball by 40%, but it would cause fixed costs to double in amount per year. If the new plant is built, what would be the company's new CM ratio and new break-even point in balls?
6 Refer to the data in Question 5 above.
7 (a) If the new plant is built, how many balls will have to be sold next year to earn the same profit (£90,000) as last year?
   (b) Assume the new plant is built and that next year the company manufactures and sells 30,000 balls (the same number as sold last year). Prepare a contribution profit and loss account and compute the degree of operating leverage.
   (c) If you were a member of top management, would you have voted in favour of constructing the new plant? Explain.

P3–18 Changing levels of fixed and variable costs

Time allowed: 30 minutes

Neptune Company produces toys and other items for use in beach and resort areas. A small, inflatable toy has come onto the market that the company is anxious to produce and sell. Enough capacity exists in the company's plant to produce 16,000 units of the toy each month. Variable costs to manufacture and sell one unit would be £1.25, and fixed costs associated with the toy would total £35,000 per month.

The company's Marketing Department predicts that demand for the new toy will exceed the 16,000 units that the company is able to produce. Additional manufacturing space can be rented from another company at a fixed cost of £1,000 per month. Variable costs in the rented facility would total £1.40 per unit, due to somewhat less efficient operations than in the main plant. The new toy will sell for £3 per unit.

Required

1 Compute the monthly break-even point for the new toy in units and in total pound sales. Show all computations in good form.
2 How many units must be sold each month to make a monthly profit of £12,000?
3 If the sales manager receives a bonus of 10 pence for each unit sold in excess of the break-even point, how many units must be sold each month to earn a return of 25% on the monthly investment in fixed costs?

Chapter 4
Relevant costs for decision making

Learning objectives

After studying Chapter 4, you should be able to:
1. Distinguish between relevant and irrelevant costs in decisions
2. Prepare an analysis showing whether to keep or replace old equipment
3. Prepare an analysis showing whether a product line or other organizational segment should be dropped or retained
4. Prepare a make or buy analysis
5. Prepare an analysis showing whether a special order should be accepted
6. Determine the most profitable use of a constrained resource

Concepts in Context

© Damir Cudic

The costing used in routine accounting may be difficult to reconcile with costs that have been developed for decision making in *ad hoc* projects. Why? The main reason is that traditional accounting is period-oriented while project budgets are task- or decision-oriented. As Arthur[1] explains: 'Project managers and project planners tend to think in terms of tasks, task costs, and planning-based forecasts. They are used to being able to produce *ad hoc* reports at any time of the month and to being able to do extensive "what if?" analysis on the project plan. They are unaware of the data collection and reporting processes that underlie accounting reports, and tend to be unsympathetic to the restrictions these impose. ...' Accountants, on the other hand, tend to think in terms of time periods and cost types – they ask, 'What did we spend on labour in May?', rather than, 'What did it cost us to build module 4?' If accountants want to be relevant to project decision making, then they need to adjust the orientation of their accounting models.

Making decisions is one of the basic functions of a manager. Managers are constantly faced with problems of deciding what products to sell, what production methods to use, whether to make or buy component parts, what prices to charge, what channels of distribution to use, whether to accept special orders at special prices, and so forth. Decision making is often a difficult task that is complicated by the existence of numerous alternatives and massive amounts of data, only some of which may be relevant.

Every decision involves choosing from among at least two alternatives. In making a decision, the costs and benefits of one alternative must be compared to the costs and benefits of other alternatives. Costs that differ between alternatives are called **relevant costs.** Distinguishing between relevant and irrelevant cost and benefit data is critical for two reasons. First, irrelevant data can be ignored and need not be analysed. This can save decision makers tremendous amounts of time and effort. Second, bad decisions can easily result from erroneously including irrelevant cost and benefit data when analysing alternatives. To be successful in decision making, managers must be able to tell the difference between relevant and irrelevant data and must be able to correctly use the relevant data in analysing alternatives. The purpose of this chapter is to develop these skills by illustrating their use in a wide range of decision-making situations. We hasten to add that these decision-making skills are as important in your personal life as they are to managers. After completing your study of the material in this chapter, you should be able to think more clearly about decisions in all facets of your life.

Cost concepts for decision making

Four cost terms discussed in Chapter 2 are particularly applicable to this chapter. These terms are *differential costs, incremental costs, opportunity costs* and *sunk costs*. You may find it helpful to turn back to Chapter 2 and refresh your memory concerning these terms before reading on.

LO 1

Identifying relevant costs and benefits

Only those costs and benefits that differ in total between alternatives are relevant in a decision. If a cost will be the same regardless of the alternative selected, then the decision has no effect on the cost and it can be ignored. For example, if you are trying to decide whether to go to a film or to rent a DVD for the evening, the rent on your apartment is irrelevant. Whether you go to a film or rent a DVD, the rent on your apartment will be exactly the same and is therefore irrelevant in the decision. On the other hand, the cost of the film ticket and the cost of renting the DVD would be relevant in the decision since they are *avoidable* costs.

An **avoidable cost** is a cost that can be eliminated in whole or in part by choosing one alternative over another. By choosing the alternative of going to the film, the cost of renting the DVD can be avoided. By choosing the alternative of renting the DVD, the cost of the film ticket can be avoided. Therefore, the cost of the film ticket and the cost of renting the DVD are both avoidable costs. On the other hand, the rent on the apartment is not an avoidable cost of either alternative. You would continue to rent your apartment under either alternative. Avoidable costs are relevant costs. Unavoidable costs are irrelevant costs.

Two broad categories of costs are never relevant in decisions. These irrelevant costs are:

1. Sunk costs
2. Future costs that do not differ between the alternatives.

As we learned in Chapter 2, a sunk cost is a cost that has already been incurred and that cannot be avoided regardless of what a manager decides to do. Sunk costs are always the same, no matter what alternatives are being considered, and they are therefore always irrelevant and should be ignored. On the other hand, future costs that do differ between alternatives are relevant. For example, when deciding whether to go to a film or rent a DVD, the cost of buying a film ticket and the cost of renting a DVD have not yet been incurred. These are future costs that differ between alternatives when the decision is being made and therefore are relevant.

Along with sunk cost, the term differential cost was introduced in Chapter 2. In management accounting, the terms *avoidable cost, differential cost, incremental cost*, and *relevant cost* are often used interchangeably.

To identify the costs that are avoidable (differential) in a particular decision situation and are therefore relevant, these steps can be followed:

1. Eliminate costs and benefits that do not differ between alternatives. These irrelevant costs consist of (a) sunk costs and (b) future costs that do not differ between alternatives.
2. Use the remaining costs and benefits that do differ between alternatives in making the decision. The costs that remain are the differential, or avoidable, costs.

Different costs for different purposes

We need to recognize from the outset of our discussion that costs that are relevant in one decision situation are not necessarily relevant in another. Simply put, this means that *the manager needs different costs for different purposes*. For one purpose, a particular group of costs may be relevant; for another purpose, an entirely different group of costs may be relevant. Thus, in each decision situation the manager must examine the data at hand and isolate the relevant costs. Otherwise, the manager runs the risk of being misled by irrelevant data.

The concept of 'different costs for different purposes' is basic to managerial accounting; we shall see its application frequently in the pages that follow.

Sunk costs are not relevant costs

One of the most difficult conceptual lessons that managers have to learn is that sunk costs are never relevant in decisions. The temptation to include sunk costs in the analysis is especially strong in the case of book value of old equipment. We focus on book value of old equipment below, and then we consider other kinds of sunk costs in other parts of the chapter. We shall see that regardless of the kind of sunk cost involved, the conclusion is always the same – sunk costs are not avoidable, and therefore they should be ignored in decisions.

Book value of old equipment

LO 2

Let us consider the following data concerning the old machine and the proposed new machine:

Old machine		**Proposed new machine**	
Original cost	£175,000	List price new	£200,000
Remaining book value	140,000	Expected life	4 years
Remaining life	4 years	Disposal value in four years	£0
Disposal value now	£90,000	Annual variable expenses to operate	300,000
Disposal value in four years	£0	Annual revenue from sales	500,000
Annual variable expenses to operate	345,000		
Annual revenue from sales	500,000		

Should the old machine be disposed of and the new machine purchased? The first reaction may be to say 'no!', since disposal of the old machine would result in a 'loss' of £50,000:

Old machine	
Remaining book value	£140,000
Disposal value now	90,000
Loss if disposed of now	£50,000

Given this potential loss if the old machine is sold, a manager may reason, 'We've already made an investment in the old machine, so now we have no choice but to use it until our investment has been fully recovered.' A manager may tend to think this way even though the new machine is clearly more efficient than the old machine. An error made in the past cannot be corrected by simply using the machine. The investment that has been made in the old machine is a sunk cost. The portion of this investment that remains on the company's books (the book value of £140,000) should not be considered in a decision about whether to buy the new machine. But we may verify the irrelevance of the book value of the old machine by the following analysis:

	Total cost and revenues – four years		
	Keep old machine	Purchase new machine	Differential costs and benefits
Sales	£2,000,000	£2,000,000	£0
Variable expenses	(1,380,000)	(1,200,000)	180,000
Cost (depreciation) of the new machine	–	(200,000)	(200,000)
Depreciation of the old machine or book value write-off	(140,000)	(140,000)*	0
Disposal value of the old machine	–	90,000*	90,000
Total net operating profit over the four years	£480,000	£550,000	£70,000

*For external reporting purposes, the £140,000 remaining book value of the old machine and the £90,000 disposal value would be netted together and deducted as a single £50,000 'loss' figure.

Looking at all four years together, notice that the firm will be £70,000 better off by purchasing the new machine. Also notice that the £140,000 book value of the old machine had no effect on the outcome of the analysis. Since this book value is a sunk cost, it must be absorbed by the firm regardless of whether the old machine is kept and used or whether it is sold. If the old machine is kept and used, then the £140,000 book value is deducted in the form of depreciation. If the old machine is sold, then the £140,000 book value is deducted in the form of a lump-sum write-off. Either way, the company bears the same £140,000 cost and the differential cost is zero.

Focusing on relevant costs

What costs in the example above are relevant in the decision concerning the new machine? Looking at the original cost data, we should eliminate first the sunk costs and second the future costs and benefits that do not differ between the alternatives at hand.

1 The sunk costs:
   (a) The remaining book value of the old machine (£140,000).
2 The future costs and benefits that do not differ
   (a) The sales revenue (£500,000 per year)
   (b) The variable expenses (to the extent of £300,000 per year).

The costs and benefits that remain will form the basis for a decision. The analysis is as follows:

	Differential costs and benefits over four years
Reduction in variable expense promised by the new machine (£45,000* per year × 4 years)	£180,000
Cost of the new machine	(200,000)
Disposal value of the old machine	90,000
Net advantage of the new machine	£70,000

*£345,000 – £300,000 = £45,000

Note that the items above are the same as those in the last column of the earlier analysis and represent those costs and benefits that differ between the two alternatives.

Future costs that do not differ are not relevant costs

We stated above that people often have difficulty accepting the idea that sunk costs are never relevant in a decision. Some people also have difficulty accepting the principle that future costs that do not differ between alternatives are never relevant in a decision. An example will help illustrate how future costs *should* be handled in a decision.

An example of irrelevant future costs

A company is contemplating the purchase of a new labour-saving machine that will cost £30,000 and have a 10-year useful life. Data concerning the company's annual sales and costs with and without the new machine are shown below:

	Current situation	Situation with the new machine
Units produced and sold	5,000	5,000
Selling price per unit	£40	£40
Direct materials cost per unit	14	14
Direct labour cost per unit	8	5
Variable overhead cost per unit	2	2
Fixed costs, other	62,000	62,000
Fixed costs, new machine	–	3,000

The new machine promises a saving of £3 per unit in direct labour costs (£8 – £5 = £3), but it will increase fixed costs by £3,000 per year. All other costs, as well as the total number of units produced and sold, will remain the same. Following the steps outlined earlier, the analysis is as follows:

1. Eliminate the sunk costs. (No sunk costs are included in this example.)
2. Eliminate the future costs and benefits that do not differ between the alternatives:
   (a) The selling price per unit and the number of units sold do not differ between the alternatives. (Therefore, total future sales revenues will not differ.)
   (b) The direct materials cost per unit, the variable overhead cost per unit, and the number of units produced do not differ between the alternatives. (Therefore, total future direct materials costs and variable overhead costs will not differ.)
   (c) The 'Fixed costs, other' do not differ between the alternatives.

The remaining costs – direct labour costs and the fixed costs associated with the new machine – are the only relevant costs.

Savings in direct labour costs (£5,000 units at a cost saving of £3 per unit)	£15,000
Less increase in fixed costs	3,000
Net annual cost savings promised by the new machine	£12,000

This solution can be verified by looking at all of the cost data (both those that are relevant and those that are not) under the two alternatives. This is done in Exhibit 4.1. Notice from the exhibit that the net advantage in favour of buying the machine is £12,000 – the same answer we obtained by focusing on just the relevant costs. Thus, we can see that future costs that do not differ between alternatives are indeed irrelevant in the decision-making process and can safely be eliminated from the analysis.

Exhibit 4.1 Differential cost analysis

	5,000 units produced and sold		
	Present method	New machine	Differential costs and benefits
Sales	£200,000	£200,000	£0
Variable expenses:			
Direct materials	70,000	70,000	0
Direct labour	40,000	25,000	15,000
Variable overhead	10,000	10,000	0
Total variable expenses	120,000	105,000	
Contribution margin	80,000	95,000	
Less fixed expenses:			
Other	62,000	62,000	0
New machine	0	3,000	(3,000)
Total fixed expenses	62,000	65,000	
Net operating profit	£18,000	£30,000	£12,000

Why isolate relevant costs?

In the preceding example, we used two different approaches to analyse the alternatives. First, we considered only the relevant costs; and, second, we considered all costs, both those that were relevant and those that were not We obtained the same answer under both approaches. It would be natural to ask, 'Why bother to isolate relevant costs when total costs will do the job just as well?' Isolating relevant costs is desirable for at least two reasons.

First, only rarely will enough information be available to prepare a detailed profit statement for both alternatives such as we have done in the preceding examples. Assume, for example, that you are called on to make a decision relating to a single operation of a multidepartmental, multiproduct firm. Under these circumstances, it would be virtually impossible to prepare a profit statement of any type. You would have to rely on your ability to recognize which costs are relevant and which are not in order to assemble that data necessary to make a decision.

Second, mingling irrelevant costs with relevant costs may cause confusion and distract attention from the matters that are really critical. Furthermore, the danger always exists that an irrelevant piece of data may be used improperly, resulting in an incorrect decision. The best approach is to ignore irrelevant data and base the decision entirely on the relevant data.

Relevant cost analysis, combined with the contribution approach to the profit statement, provides a powerful tool for making decisions. We will investigate various uses of this tool in the remaining sections of this chapter.

Adding and dropping product lines and other segments

Decisions relating to whether old product lines or other segments of a company should be dropped and new ones added are among the most difficult that a manager has to make. In such decisions, many qualitative and quantitative factors must be considered. Ultimately, however, any final decision to drop an old segment or to add a new one is going to hinge primarily on the impact the decision will have on net profit. To assess this impact, it is necessary to make a careful analysis of the costs involved.

Exhibit 4.2 Discount Drug Company product lines

			Product line	
	Total	Drugs	Cosmetics	Housewares
Sales	£250,000	£125,000	£75,000	£50,000
Less variable expenses	105,000	50,000	25,000	30,000
Contribution margin	145,000	75,000	50,000	20,000
Less fixed expenses:				
Salaries	50,000	29,500	12,500	8,000
Advertising	15,000	1,000	7,500	6,500
Utilities	2,000	500	500	1,000
Depreciation – fixtures	5,000	1,000	2,000	2,000
Rent	20,000	10,000	6,000	4,000
Insurance	3,000	2,000	500	500
General administrative	30,000	15,000	9,000	6,000
Total fixed expenses	125,000	59,000	38,000	28,000
Net operating profit (loss)	£20,000	£16,000	£12,000	£(8,000)

An illustration of cost analysis

Consider the three major product lines of the Discount Drug Company – drugs, cosmetics and housewares. Sales and cost information for the preceding month for each separate product line and for the store in total are given in Exhibit 4.2.

What can be done to improve the company's overall performance? One product line – housewares – shows a net operating loss for the month. Perhaps dropping this line would cause profits in the company as a whole to improve. In deciding whether the line should be dropped, management should reason as follows:

If the housewares line is dropped, then the company will lose £20,000 per month in contribution margin. By dropping the line, however, it may be possible to avoid some fixed costs. It may be possible, for example, to discharge certain employees, or it may be possible to reduce advertising costs. If by dropping the housewares line the company is able to avoid more in fixed costs than it loses in contribution margin, then it will be better off if the line is eliminated, since overall profit should improve. On the other hand, if the company is not able to avoid as much in fixed costs as it loses in contribution margin, then the housewares line should be retained. In short, the manager should ask, 'What costs can I avoid if I drop this product line?'

As we have seen from our earlier discussion, not all costs are avoidable. For example, some of the costs associated with a product line may be sunk costs. Other costs may be allocated common costs that will not differ in total regardless of whether the product line is dropped or retained. To show how the manager should proceed in a product-line analysis, suppose that the management of the Discount Drug Company has analysed the costs being charged to the three product lines and has determined the following:

1. The salaries expense represents salaries paid to employees working directly in each product-line area. All the employees working in housewares would be discharged if the line is dropped.
2. The advertising expense represents direct advertising of each product line and is avoidable if the line is dropped.
3. The utilities expense represents utilities costs for the entire company. The amount charged to each product line is an allocation based on space occupied and is not avoidable if the product line is dropped.

4 The depreciation expense represents depreciation on fixtures used for display of the various product lines. Although the fixtures are nearly new, they are custom-built and will have little resale value if the housewares line is dropped.
5 The rent expense represents rent on the entire building housing the company; it is allocated to the product lines on the basis of sales. The monthly rent of £20,000 is fixed under a long-term lease agreement.
6 The insurance expense represents insurance carried on inventories within each of the three product-line areas.
7 The general administrative expense represents the costs of accounting, purchasing and general management, which are allocated to the product lines on the basis of sales. Total administrative costs will not change if the housewares line is dropped.

With this information, management can identify costs that can and cannot be avoided if the product line is dropped:

	Cost	Not avoidable*	Avoidable
Salaries	£8,000		£8,000
Advertising	6,500		6,500
Utilities	1,000	£1,000	
Depreciation – fixtures	2,000	2,000	
Rent	4,000	4,000	
Insurance	500		500
General administrative	6,000	6,000	
Total fixed expenses	£28,000	£13,000	£15,000

*These costs represent either (1) sunk costs or (2) future costs that will not change if the housewares line is retained or discontinued.

To determine how dropping the line will affect the overall profits of the company, we can compare the contribution margin that will be lost to the costs that can be avoided if the line is dropped:

Contribution margin lost if the housewares line is discontinued (see Exhibit 4.2)	£(20,000)
Less fixed costs that can be avoided if the housewares line is discontinued (see above)	15,000
Decrease in overall company net operating profit	£(5,000)

In this case, the fixed costs that can be avoided by dropping the product line are less than the contribution margin that will be lost. Therefore, based on the data given, the housewares line should not be discontinued unless a more profitable use can be found for the floor and counter space that it is occupying.

A comparative format

Some managers prefer to approach decisions of this type by preparing comparative profit statements showing the effects on the company as a whole of either keeping or dropping the product line in question. A comparative analysis of this type for the Discount Drug Company is shown in Exhibit 4.3.

Exhibit 4.3 A comparative format for product-line analysis

	Keep housewares	Drop housewares	Difference: profit increase or (decrease)
Sales	£50,000	£0	£(50,000)
Less variable expenses	30,000	0	30,000
Contribution margin	20,000	0	(20,000)
Less fixed expenses:			
Salaries	8,000	0	8,000
Advertising	6,500	0	6,500
Utilities	1,000	1,000	0
Depreciation – fixtures	2,000	2,000	0
Rent	4,000	4,000	0
Insurance	500	0	500
General administrative	6,000	6,000	0
Total fixed expenses	28,000	13,000	15,000
Net operating profit (loss)	£(8,000)	£(13,000)	£(5,000)

As shown by column 3 in the exhibit, overall company profit will decrease by £5,000 each period if the housewares line is dropped. This is the same answer, of course, as we obtained in our earlier analysis.

Beware of allocated fixed costs

Our conclusion that the housewares line should not be dropped seems to conflict with the data shown earlier in Exhibit 4.2. Recall from the exhibit that the housewares line is showing a loss rather than a profit. Why keep a line that is showing a loss? The explanation for this apparent inconsistency lies at least in part with the common fixed costs that are being allocated to the product lines. One of the great dangers in allocating ommon fixed costs is that such allocations can make a product line (or other segment of a business) look less profitable than it really is. By allocating the common fixed costs among all product lines, the housewares line has been made to look as if it were unprofitable, whereas, in fact, dropping the line would result in a decrease in overall company net operating profit. This point can be seen clearly if we recast the data in Exhibit 4.2 and eliminate the allocation of the common fixed costs. This recasting of data is shown in Exhibit 4.4.

Exhibit 4.4 gives us a much different perspective of the housewares line than does Exhibit 4.2. As shown in Exhibit 4.4, the housewares line is covering all of its own traceable fixed costs and is generating a £3,000 segment margin towards covering the common fixed costs of the company. Unless another product line can be found that will generate a greater segment margin than this, the company would be better off keeping the housewares line. By keeping the line, the company's overall profit will be higher than if the product line was ropped.

Additionally, we should note that managers may choose to retain an unprofitable product line if the line is necessary to the sale of other products or if it serves as a 'magnet' or 'loss-leader' to attract customers. Bread, for example, is not an especially profitable line in food stores, but customers expect it to be available, and many would undoubtedly shift their buying elsewhere if a particular store decided to stop carrying it.

Exhibit 4.4 Discount Drug Company product lines – recast in contribution format (from Exhibit 4.2)

	Total	Drugs	Cosmetics	Housewares
			Product line	
Sales	£250,000	£125,000	£75,000	£50,000
Less variable expenses	105,000	50,000	25,000	30,000
Contribution margin	145,000	75,000	50,000	20,000
Less traceable fixed expenses:				
Salaries	50,000	29,500	12,500	8,000
Advertising	15,000	1,000	7,500	6,500
Depreciation – fixtures	5,000	1,000	2,000	2,000
Insurance	3,000	2,000	500	500
Total	73,000	33,500	22,500	17,000
Product-line segment margin	72,000	£41,500	£27,500	£3,000*
Less common fixed expenses:				
Utilities	2,000			
Rent	20,000			
General administrative	30,000			
Total	52,000			
Net operating profit	£20,000			

*If the housewares line is dropped this £3,000 in segment margin will be lost to the company. In addition, we have seen that the £2,000 depreciation on the fixtures is a sunk cost that cannot be avoided. The sum of these two figures (£3,000 + £2,000 = £5,000) would be the decrease in the company's overall profits if the housewares line were discontinued.

Focus on Business Practice

The problem of 'common costs'

© Katarina Drpic

A bakery distributed its products through travelling salespersons, each of whom loaded a van with an assortment of products in the morning and spent the day calling on customers in an assigned territory. Believing that some items were more profitable than others, management asked for an analysis of product costs and sales. The accountants to whom the task was assigned allocated all manufacturing and marketing costs to products to obtain a net profit for each product. The resulting figures indicated that some of the products were being sold at a loss, and management discontinued these products. However, when this change was put into effect, the company's overall profit declined. It was then seen that by dropping some products, sales revenues had been reduced without commensurate reduction in costs because the common manufacturing costs and route sales costs had to be continued in order to make and sell the remaining products.

Exercise: But what are the factors driving 'common' costs? These issues are explored further in the concept of activity-based costing (see Chapter 6).

The make or buy decision

LO 4

A decision to produce a fabricated part internally, rather than to buy the part externally from a supplier, is called a **make or buy decision**. Actually, any decision relating to **vertical integration** is a make or buy decision, since the company is deciding whether to meet its own needs internally or to buy externally.

An example of make or buy

To provide an illustration of a make or buy decision, consider Mountain Goat Cycles. The company is now producing the heavy-duty gear shifters used in its most popular line of mountain bikes. The company's Accounting Department reports the following costs of producing the shifter internally:

	Per unit	8,000 units
Direct materials	£6	£48,000
Direct labour	4	32,000
Variable overhead	1	8,000
Supervisor's salary	3	24,000
Depreciation of special equipment	2	16,000
Allocated general overhead	5	40,000
Total cost	£21	£168,000

An outside supplier has offered to sell Mountain Goat Cycles 8,000 changers a year at a price of only £19 each. Should the company stop producing the shifters internally and start purchasing them from the outside supplier? To approach the decision from a financial point of view, the manager should again focus on the differential costs. As we have seen, the differential costs can be obtained by eliminating those costs that are not avoidable – that is, by eliminating first the sunk costs and second the future costs that will continue regardless of whether the shifters are produced internally or purchased outside. The costs that remain after making these eliminations are the costs that are avoidable to the company by purchasing outside. If these avoidable costs are less than the outside purchase price, then the company should continue to manufacture its own changers and reject the outside supplier's offer. That is, the company should purchase outside only if the outside purchase price is less than the costs that can be avoided internally as a result of stopping production of the changers.

Looking at the above data, note first that depreciation of special equipment is listed as one of the costs of producing the changers internally. Since the equipment has already been purchased, this depreciation is a sunk cost and is therefore irrelevant. If the equipment could be sold, its salvage value would be relevant. Or if the machine could be used to make other products, this could be relevant as well. However, we will assume that the equipment has no salvage value and that it has no other use except making the heavy-duty gear changers.

Also note that the company is allocating a portion of its general overhead costs to the changers. Any portion of this general overhead cost that would actually be eliminated if the gear changers were purchased rather than made would be relevant in the analysis. However, it is likely that the general overhead costs allocated to the gear changers are in fact common to all items produced in the factory and would continue unchanged even if the changers are purchased from the outside. Such allocated common costs are not differential costs (since they do not differ between the make or buy alternatives) and should be eliminated from the analysis along with the sunk costs.

The variable costs of producing the changers (materials, labour and variable overhead) are differential costs, since they can be avoided by buying the changers from the outside supplier. If the supervisor can be discharged and his or her salary avoided by buying the changers, then it too will be a differential cost and relevant to the decision. Assuming that both the variable costs and the supervisor's salary can be avoided by buying from the outside supplier, then the analysis takes the form shown in Exhibit 4.5.

Exhibit 4.5 Mountain Goat Cycles make or buy analysis

	Production 'cost' per unit	Per unit differential costs: Make	Per unit differential costs: Buy	Total differential costs – 8,000 units: Make	Total differential costs – 8,000 units: Buy
Direct materials	£6	£6		£48,000	
Direct labour	4	4		32,000	
Variable overhead	1	1		8,000	
Supervisor's salary	3	3		24,000	
Depreciation of special equipment	2	–		–	
Allocated general overhead	5	–		–	
Outside purchase price			£19		£152,000
Total cost	£21	£14	£19	£112,000	£152,000
Difference in favour of continuing to make		£5		£40,000	

Since it costs £5 less per unit to continue to make the changers, Mountain Goat Cycles should reject the outside supplier's offer. However, there is one additional factor that the company may wish to consider before coming to a final decision. This factor is the opportunity cost of the space now being used to produce the changers.

The matter of opportunity cost

If the space now being used to produce the changers *would otherwise be idle*, then Mountain Goat Cycles should continue to produce its own changers and the supplier's offer should be rejected, as stated above. Idle space that has no alternative use has an opportunity cost of zero.

But what if the space now being used to produce changers could be used for some other purpose? In that case, the space would have an opportunity cost that would have to be considered in assessing the desirability of the supplier's offer. What would this opportunity cost be? It would be the segment margin that could be derived from the best alternative use of the space.

To illustrate, assume that the space now being used to produce changers could be used to produce a new cross-country bike that would generate a segment margin of £60,000 per year. Under these conditions, Mountain Goat Cycles would be better off to accept the supplier's offer and to use the available space to produce the new product line:

	Make	Buy
Differential cost per unit (see prior example)	£14	£19
Number of units needed annually	× 8,000	× 8,000
Total annual cost	112,000	152,000
Opportunity cost–segment margin forgone on a potential new product line	60,000	
Total cost	£172,000	£152,000
Difference in favour of purchasing from the outside supplier	£20,000	

Opportunity costs are not recorded in accounts of an organization. They do not represent actual cash outlays. Rather, they represent economic benefits that are *forgone* as a result of pursuing some course of action. The opportunity costs of Mountain Goat Cycles are sufficiently large in this case to make continued production of the changers very costly from an economic point of view.

Focus on Business Practice

Asset stripping or realizing opportunity costs?

© Nikada

A writer in *Investing Strategy* stated that 'By selling off unwanted assets, the private equity asset-strippers are doing society a service. So why do they deny it?' The author added: 'Why should a company tie up capital in assets that it doesn't need: land, buildings, intellectual property or business units? If another business is willing to pay more for them than they're worth to you, why would you want to keep them? And if that other business is willing to pay more for them, then it's because they believe they can make better use of them, often through cost savings or synergies with their existing operations.'[2] Although many practices of the private equity industry may be difficult to justify (such as short-termism or tax evasion), perhaps the writer has a case here?

Exercise: Why might the current owners of the assets such as buildings fail to fully recognize the costs of their present usage? Check your understanding of the concept of *opportunity cost*.

Special orders

LO 5

Managers often must evaluate whether a special order should be accepted, and if the order is accepted, the price that should be charged. A **special order** is a one-time order that is not considered part of the company's normal ongoing business. To illustrate, Mountain Goat Cycles has just received a request from the Nottingham Police Department to produce 100 specially modified mountain bikes at a price of £179 each. The bikes would be used to patrol some of the more densely populated residential sections of the city. Mountain Goat Cycles can easily modify its City Cruiser model to fit the specifications of the Nottingham Police. The normal selling price of the City Cruiser bike is £249, and its unit product cost is £182 as shown below:

Direct materials	£86
Direct labour	45
Manufacturing overhead	51
Unit product cost	£182

The variable portion of the above manufacturing overhead is £6 per unit. The order would have no effect on the company's total fixed manufacturing overhead costs.

The modifications to the bikes consist of welded brackets to hold radios, handcuffs and other gear. These modifications would require £17 in incremental variable costs. In addition, the company would have to pay a graphics design studio £1,200 to design and cut stencils that would be used for spray painting the Nottingham Police Department's logo and other identifying marks on the bikes.

This order should have no effect on the company's other sales. The production manager says that she can handle the special order without disrupting any of the regular scheduled production.

What effect would accepting this order have on the company's profit?

Only the incremental costs and benefits are relevant. Since the existing fixed manufacturing overhead costs would not be affected by the order, they are not incremental costs and are therefore not relevant. The incremental profit can be computed as follows:

	Per unit	Total 100 bikes
Incremental revenue	£179	£17,900
Incremental costs:		
Variable costs:		
Direct materials	86	8,600
Direct labour	45	4,500
Variable manufacturing overhead	6	600
Special modifications	17	1,700
Total variable cost	£154	15,400
Fixed cost:		
Purchase of stencils		1,200
Total incremental cost		16,600
Incremental net operating profit		£1,300

Therefore, even though the price on the special order (£179) is below the normal unit product cost (£182) and the order would require incurring additional costs, the order would result in an increase in net operating profit. In general, a special order is profitable as long as the incremental revenue from the special order exceeds the incremental costs of the order. We must note, however, that it is important to make sure that there is indeed idle capacity and that the special order does not cut into normal sales. For example, if the company was operating at capacity, opportunity costs would have to be taken into account as well as the incremental costs that have already been detailed above.

LO 6

Utilization of a constrained resource

Managers are routinely faced with the problem of deciding how constrained resources are going to be utilized. A department store, for example, has a limited amount of floor space and therefore cannot stock every product that may be available. A manufacturing firm has a limited number of machine-hours and a limited number of direct labour-hours at its disposal. When a limited resource of some type restricts the company's ability to satisfy demand, the company is said to have a **constraint**. Because of the constrained resource, the company cannot fully satisfy demand, so the manager must decide how the constrained resource should be used. Fixed costs are usually unaffected by such choices, so the manager should select the course of action that will maximize the firm's total contribution margin.

Contribution in relation to a constrained resource

To maximize total contribution margin, a firm should not necessarily promote those products that have the highest *unit* contribution margins. Rather, total contribution margin will be maximized by promoting those products or accepting those orders that provide the highest unit contribution margin *in relation to the constrained resource*. To illustrate, Mountain Goat Cycles makes a line of panniers – a saddlebag for bicycles. There are two models of panniers – a touring model and a mountain model. Cost and revenue data for the two models of panniers are given below:

	Model	
	Mountain pannier	Touring pannier
Selling price per unit	£25	£30
Variable cost per unit	10	18
Contribution margin per unit	£15	£12
Contribution margin (CM) ratio	60%	40%

The mountain pannier appears to be much more profitable than the touring pannier. It has a £15 per unit contribution margin as compared to only £12 per unit for the touring model, and it has a 60% CM ratio as compared to only 40% for the touring model.

But now let us add one more piece of information – the plant that makes the panniers is operating at capacity. Ordinarily this does not mean that every machine and every person in the plant is working at the maximum possible rate. Because machines have different capacities, some machines will be operating at less than 100% of capacity. However, if the plant as a whole cannot produce any more units, some machine or process must be operating at capacity. The machine or process that is limiting overall output is called the **bottleneck** – it is the constraint.

At Mountain Goat Cycles, the bottleneck is a particular stitching machine. The mountain pannier requires two minutes of stitching time, and each unit of the touring pannier requires one minute of stitching time. Since this stitching machine already has more work than it can handle, something will have to be cut back. In this situation, which product is more profitable? To answer this question, the manager should look at the contribution margin per unit of the constrained resource. This figure is computed by dividing the contribution margin by the amount of the constrained resource a unit of product requires. These calculations are carried out below for the mountain and touring panniers.

	Model	
	Mountain pannier	Touring pannier
Contribution margin per unit (above) (a)	£15.00	£12.00
Time on the stitching machine required to produce one unit (b)	2 min.	1 min.
Contribution margin per unit of the constrained resource, (a)/(b)	£7.50/min.	£12.00/min.

It is now easy to decide which product is less profitable and should be de-emphasized. Each minute of processing time on the stitching machine that is devoted to the touring pannier results in an increase of £12 in contribution margin and profits. The comparable figure for the mountain pannier is only £7.50 per minute. Therefore, the touring model should be emphasized. Even though the mountain model has the larger per unit contribution margin and the larger CM ratio, the touring model provides the larger contribution margin in relation to the constrained resource.

To verify that the touring model is indeed the more profitable product, suppose an hour of additional stitching time is available and that there are unfilled orders for both products. The additional hour on the stitching machine could be used to make either 30 mountain panniers (60 minutes/2 minutes) or 60 touring panniers (60 minutes/1 minute), with the following consequences:

	Model	
	Mountain pannier	Touring pannier
Contribution margin per unit (above) (a)	£15	£12
Additional units that can be processed in one hour	× 30	× 60
Additional contribution margin	£450	£720

This example clearly shows that looking at unit contribution margins alone is not enough; the contribution margin must be viewed in relation to the amount of the constrained resource each product requires.

Summary

- All of the material in this chapter consists of applications of one simple but powerful idea. Only those costs and benefits that differ between alternatives are relevant in a decision. All other costs and benefits are irrelevant and can and should be ignored. In particular, sunk costs are irrelevant as are future costs that do not differ between alternatives.
- This simple idea was applied in a variety of situations including decisions that involve replacing equipment, making or buying a component, adding or dropping a product line, special orders and using a constrained resource.
- This list includes only a tiny sample of the possible applications of the relevant cost concept. Indeed, *any* decision involving costs hinges on the proper identification and analysis of the costs that are relevant.

Key terms

Avoidable cost Any cost that can be eliminated (in whole or in part) by choosing one alternative over another in a decision-making situation. In managerial accounting, this term is synonymous with relevant cost and differential cost (p. 76).

Bottleneck A machine or process that limits total output because it is operating at capacity (p. 89).

Constraint A limitation under which a company must operate, such as limited machine time available or limited raw materials available that restricts the company's ability to satisfy demand (p. 88).

Make or buy decision A decision as to whether an item should be produced internally or purchased from an outside supplier (p. 85).

Relevant cost A cost that differs between alternatives in a particular decision. In managerial accounting, this term is synonymous with avoidable cost and differential cost (p. 76).

Special order A one-time order that is not considered part of the company's normal ongoing business (p. 87).

Vertical integration The involvement by a company is more than one of the steps from production of basic raw materials to the manufacture and distribution of a finished product (p. 85).

Endnotes

1 Arthur (2000).

2 *Investing Strategy*, 14 June 2007.

connect

When you have read this chapter, log on to the Online Learning Centre for *Management Accounting for Business Decisions* at **www.mheducation.co.uk/textbooks/sealmabd1**, where you'll find multiple choice questions, practice exams and extra study tools for management accounting.

Assessment

Questions

connect

4–1 What is a relevant cost?

4–2 Define the following terms: *incremental cost, opportunity cost*, and *sunk cost.*

4–3 Are variable costs always relevant costs? Explain.

4–4 The book value of a machine (as shown on the balance sheet) is an asset to a company, but this same book value is irrelevant in decision making. Explain why this is so.

4–5 'Sunk costs are easy to spot – they're simply the fixed costs associated with a decision.' Do you agree? Explain.

4–6 'Variable costs and differential costs mean the same thing.' Do you agree? Explain.

4–7 'All future costs are relevant in decision making.' Do you agree? Why?

4–8 Prentice Company is considering dropping one of its product lines. What costs of the product line would be relevant to this decision? Irrelevant?

4–9 'If a product line is generating a loss, then that's pretty good evidence that the product line should be discontinued.' Do you agree? Explain.

4–10 How does opportunity cost enter into the make or buy decision?

4–11 Give four examples of possible constraints.

4–12 How will relating product contribution margins to the constrained resource they require help a company ensure that profits will be maximized?

Exercises

connect

E4–1 Time allowed: 15 minutes

Listed below are a number of costs that may be relevant in decisions faced by the management of Svahn, AB, a Swedish manufacturer of sailing yachts:

Item	Case 1		Case 2	
	Relevant	Not relevant	Relevant	Not relevant
(a) Sales revenue				
(b) Direct materials				
(c) Direct labour				
(d) Variable manufacturing overhead				
(e) Depreciation – Model B100 machine				
(f) Book value – Model B100 machine				
(g) Disposal value – Model B100 machine				
(h) Market value – Model B300 machine (cost)				
(i) Depreciation – Model B300 machine				
(j) Fixed manufacturing overhead (general)				
(k) Variable selling expense				
(l) Fixed selling expense				
(m) General administrative overhead.				

Required

Copy the information above onto your answer sheet and place an X in the appropriate column to indicate whether each item is relevant or not relevant in the following situations (requirement 1 relates to Case 1 above, and requirement 2 relates to Case 2):

1 Management is considering purchasing a Model B300 machine to use in addition to the company's present Model B100 machine. This will increase the company's production and sales. The increase in volume will be large enough to require increases in fixed selling expenses and in general administrative overhead, but not in the fixed manufacturing overhead.

2 Management is, instead, considering replacing its present Model B100 machine with a new Model B300 machine. The Model B100 machine would be sold.

This change will have no effect on production or sales, other than some savings in direct materials costs due to less waste.

E4–2 Time allowed: 20 minutes

Bill has just returned from a duck hunting trip. He has brought home eight ducks. Bill's friend, John, disapproves of duck hunting and, to discourage Bill from further hunting, John has presented him with the following cost estimate per duck:

Camper and equipment:	
Cost, £12,000; usable for eight seasons; 10 hunting trips per season	£150
Travel expense (pickup van):	
100 miles at £0.12 per mile (petrol, oil and tyres – £0.07 per mile: depreciation and insurance – £0.05 per mile)	12
Shotgun shells (two boxes)	20
Boat:	
Cost, £2,320, usable for eight seasons; 10 hunting trips per season	29
Hunting licence:	
Cost, £30 for the season; 10 hunting trips per season	3
Money lost playing poker:	
Loss, £18 (Bill plays poker every weekend)	18
A fifth of Old Grandad:	
Cost, £8 (used to ward off the cold)	8
Total cost	£240
Cost per duck (£240/8 ducks)	£30

Required

1 Assuming that the duck hunting trip Bill has just completed is typical, what costs are relevant to a decision as to whether Bill should go duck hunting again this season?

2 Suppose that Bill gets lucky on his next hunting trip and shoots 10 ducks in the amount of time it took him to shoot 8 ducks on his last trip. How much would it have cost him to shoot the last two ducks?

3 Which costs are relevant in a decision of whether Bill should give up hunting? Explain.

E4–3 Time allowed: 20 minutes

Thalassines Kataskeves SA of Greece makes marine equipment. The company has been experiencing losses on its bilge pump product line for several years. The most recent quarterly profit statement for the bilge pump product line is given below:

Thalassines Kataskeves SA Profit statement – bilge pump For the quarter ended 31 March		
Sales		€850,000
Less variable expenses:		
Variable manufacturing expenses	€330,000	
Sales commissions	42,000	
Shipping	18,000	
Total variable expenses		390,000
Contribution margin		460,000
Less fixed expenses:		
Advertising	270,000	
Depreciation of equipment (no resale value)	80,000	
General factory overhead	105,000*	
Salary of product-line manager	32,000	
Insurance on inventories	8,000	
Purchasing department expenses	45,000†	
Total fixed expenses		540,000†
Net loss		€(80,000)

*Common costs allocated on the basis of machine-hours.

†Common costs allocated on the basis of sales.

The discontinuance of the bilge pump product line would not affect sales of other product lines and would have no noticeable effect on the company's total general factory overhead or total Purchasing Department expenses.

Required

Would you recommend that the bilge pump product line be discontinued? Support your answer with appropriate computations.

E4–4 Time allowed: 20 minutes

Hollings Company sells office furniture. As part of its service, it delivers furniture to customers.

The costs associated with the acquisition and annual operation of a delivery van are given below:

Insurance	£1,600
Licences	250
Taxes (vehicle)	150
Garage rent for parking (per van)	1,200
Depreciation (£9,000/5 years)	1,800*
Petrol, oil, tyres, and repairs	0.07 per mile

*Based on obsolescence rather than on wear and tear.

Required

1. Assume that Hollings Company has purchased one van and that the van has been driven 50,000 miles during the first year. Compute the average cost per mile of owning and operating the van.
2. At the beginning of the second year, Hollings Company is unsure whether to use the van or leave it parked in the garage and have all hauling done commercially. (The state requires the payment of vehicle taxes even if the vehicle is not used.) What costs from the previous list are relevant to this decision? Explain.
3. Assume that the company decides to use the van during the second year. Near yearend an order is received from a customer over 1,000 miles away. What costs from the previous list are relevant in a decision between using the van to make the delivery and having the delivery done commercially? Explain.
4. Occasionally, the company could use two vans at the same time. For this reason, some thought is being given to purchasing a second van. The total miles driven would be the same as if only one van were owned. What costs from the previous list are relevant to a decision over whether to purchase the second van? Explain.

E4–5 Time allowed: 20 minutes

Barlow Company manufactures three products: A, B and C. The selling price, variable costs and contribution margin for one unit of each product follow:

	Product		
	A	B	C
Selling price	£180	£270	£240
Less variable expenses:			
Direct materials	24	72	32
Other variable expenses	102	90	148
Total variable expenses	126	162	180
Contribution margin	£54	£108	£60
Contribution margin ratio	30%	40%	25%

The same raw material is used in all three products. Barlow Company has only 5,000 kilos of material on hand and will not be able to obtain any more material for several weeks due to a strike in its supplier's plant. Management is trying to decide which product(s) to concentrate on next week in filling its backlog of orders. The material costs £8 per kilo.

Required

1. Compute the amount of contribution margin that will be obtained per kilo of material used in each product.
2. Which orders would you recommend that the company work on next week – the orders for product A, product B, or product C? Show computations.
3. A foreign supplier could furnish Barlow with additional stocks of the raw material at a substantial premium over the usual price. If there is unfilled demand for all three products, what is the highest price that Barlow Company should be willing to pay for an additional kilo of materials?

E4–6 Time allowed: 20 minutes

Troy Engines Ltd manufactures a variety of engines for use in heavy equipment. The company has always produced all of the necessary parts for its engines, including all of the carburettors. An outside supplier has offered to produce and sell one type of carburettor to Troy Engines for a cost of £35 per unit. To evaluate this offer, Troy Engines has gathered the following information relating to its own cost of producing the carburettor internally:

	Per unit	**15,000 units per year**
Direct materials	£14	£210,000
Direct labour	10	150,000
Variable manufacturing overhead	3	45,000
Fixed manufacturing overhead, traceable	6*	90,000
Fixed manufacturing overhead, allocated	9	135,000
Total cost	£42	£630,000

*One-third supervisory salaries; two-thirds depreciation of special equipment (no resale value).

Required

1 Assuming that the company has no alternative use for the facilities that are now being used to produce the carburettors, should the outside supplier's offer be accepted? Show all computations.

2 Suppose that, if the carburettors were purchased, Troy Engines, could use the freed capacity to launch a new product. The segment margin of the new product would be £150,000 per year. Should Troy Engines Ltd. accept the offer to buy the carburettors for £35 per unit? Show all computations.

E4–7 Time allowed: 10 minutes

Waukee Railroad is considering the purchase of a powerful, high-speed wheel grinder to replace a standard wheel grinder that is now in use. Selected information on the two machines is given below:

	Standard wheel grinder	**High-speed wheel grinder**
Original cost new	£20,000	£30,000
Accumulated depreciation to date	6,000	–
Current salvage value	9,000	–
Estimated cost per year to operate	15,000	7,000
Remaining years of useful life	5 years	5 years

Required

Prepare a computation covering the five-year period that will show the net advantage or disadvantage of purchasing the high-speed wheel grinder. Use only relevant costs in your analysis.

E4–8 Time allowed: 20 minutes

The Regal Cycle Company manufactures three types of bicycles – a dirt bike, a mountain bike and a racing bike. Data on sales and expenses for the past quarter follow:

	Total	Dirt bikes	Mountain bikes	Racing bikes
Sales	£300,000	£90,000	£150,000	£60,000
Less variable manufacturing and selling expenses	120,000	27,000	60,000	33,000
Contribution margin	180,000	63,000	90,000	27,000
Less fixed expenses:				
Advertising, traceable	30,000	10,000	14,000	6,000
Depreciation of special equipment	23,000	6,000	9,000	8,000
Salaries of product-line managers	35,000	12,000	13,000	10,000
Common allocated costs*	60,000	18,000	30,000	12,000
Total fixed expenses	148,000	46,000	66,000	36,000
Net operating income (loss)	£32,000	£17,000	£24,000	£(9,000)

*Allocated on the basis of sales.

Management is concerned about the continued losses shown by the racing bikes and wants a recommendation as to whether or not the line should be discontinued. The special equipment used to produce racing bikes has no resale value and does not wear out.

Required

1 Should production and sale of the racing bikes be discontinued? Show computations to support your answer.

2 Recast the above data in a format that would be more usable to management in assessing the long-run profitability of the various product lines.

E4–9 Special order

Time allowed: 10 minutes

Cosi Ltd produces and sells a single product, a fan called a tutte. Annual production capacity is 100,000 machine hours. Annual demand for tuttes is 80,000 fans. The selling price is expected to remain at £12 per fan. Cost data for producing and selling tuttes are as follows:

Variable costs (per unit)	**£**
Direct materials, labour and overhead	5.80
Selling costs	2.00
Fixed costs (per year)	**£000**
Fixed production costs	70,000
Fixed selling costs	40,000

Cosi Ltd has 2,000 tuttes in stock that were incorrectly painted. The company has two choices:

1 sell these lower quality fans through the normal distribution channels at a reduced price

or

2 scrap them at a net cost of zero.

Sales of these lower quality fans are not expected to affect regular sales of tuttes.

Determine and justify the minimum price per fan that would have to be received in order to make it worth while selling the lower quality fans rather than scrapping them.

(3 marks)

ICAEW Business Management, September 2001

P4–10 Relevant cost analysis; book value

Problems

Time allowed: 25 minutes

Murl Plastics Ltd purchased a new machine one year ago at a cost of £60,000. Although the machine operates well, the managing director (MD) wondered if the company should replace it with a new electronically operated machine that has just come on the market. The new machine would slash annual operating costs by two-thirds, as shown in the comparative data below:

		Proposed
	Present machine	New machine
Purchase cost new	£60,000	£90,000
Estimated useful life new	6 years	5 years
Annual operating costs	£42,000	£14,000
Annual straight-line depreciation	10,000	18,000
Remaining book value	50,000	–
Salvage value now	10,000	–
Salvage value in 5 years	0	0

In trying to decide whether to purchase the new machine, the MD has prepared the following analysis:

Book value of the old machine	£50,000
Less salvage value	10,000
Net loss from disposal	£40,000

'Even though the new machine looks good,' said the managing director, 'we can't get rid of the old one if it means taking a huge loss on it. We'll have to use it for at least a few more years.'

Sales are expected to be £200,000 per year, and selling and administrative expenses are expected to be £126,000 per year, regardless of which machine is used.

Required

1 Prepare a summary profit statement covering the next five years, assuming:
   (a) That the new machine is not purchased.
   (b) That the new machine is purchased.
2 Determine the desirability of purchasing the new machine using only relevant costs in your analysis.

P4–11 Dropping a flight; analysis of operating policy

Time allowed: 25 minutes

Profits have been decreasing for several years at Pegasus Airlines. In an effort to improve the company's performance, consideration is being given to dropping several flights that appear to be unprofitable.

A typical income statement for one such flight (flight 482) is given below (per flight):

Ticket revenue (175 seats × 40% occupancy × £200 ticket price)	£14,000	100.0%
Less variable expenses (£15 per person)	1,050	7.5%
Contribution margin	12,950	92.5%
Less flight expenses:		
Salaries, flight crew	1,800	
Flight promotion	750	
Depreciation of aircraft	1,550	
Fuel for aircraft	6,800	
Liability insurance	4,200	
Salaries, flight assistants	500	
Baggage loading and flight preparation	1,700	
Overnight costs for flight crew and assistants at destination	300	
Total flight expenses	17,600	
Net operating loss	£(4,650)	

The following additional information is available about flight 482:

(a) Members of the flight crew are paid fixed annual salaries, whereas the flight assistants are paid by the flight.
(b) One-third of the liability insurance is a special charge assessed against flight 482 because in the opinion of the insurance company, the destination of the flight is in a 'high-risk' area. The remaining two-thirds would be unaffected by a decision to drop flight 482.
(c) The baggage loading and flight preparation expense is an allocation of ground crews' salaries and depreciation of ground equipment. Dropping flight 482 would have no effect on the company's total baggage loading and flight preparation expenses.
(d) If flight 482 is dropped, Pegasus Airlines has no authorization at present to replace it with another flight.
(e) Depreciation of aircraft is due entirely to obsolescence. Depreciation due to wear and tear is negligible.
(f) Dropping flight 482 would not allow Pegasus Airlines to reduce the number of aircraft in its fleet or the number of flight crew on its payroll.

Required

1 Prepare an analysis showing what impact dropping flight 482 would have on the airline's profits.

2 The airline's scheduling officer has been criticized because only about 50% of the seats on Pegasus' flights are being filled compared to an average of 60% for the industry. The scheduling officer has explained that Pegasus' average seat occupancy could be improved considerably by eliminating about 10% of the flights, but that doing so would reduce profits. Explain how this could happen.

P4–12 Relevant cost potpourri

Time allowed: 60 minutes

Unless otherwise indicated, each of the following parts is independent. In all cases, show computations to support your answer.

1 A merchandising company has two departments, A and B. A recent monthly income statement for the company follows:

		Department	
	Total	**A**	**B**
Sales	£4,000,000	£3,000,000	£1,000,000
Less variable expenses	1,300,000	900,000	400,000
Contribution margin	2,700,000	2,100,000	600,000
Less fixed expenses	2,200,000	1,400,000	800,000
Net operating profit (loss)	£500,000	£700,000	£(200,000)

A study indicates that £340,000 of the fixed expenses being charged to Department B are sunk costs or allocated costs that will continue even if B is dropped. In addition, the elimination of Department B will result in a 10% decrease in the sales of Department A. If Department B is dropped, what will be the effect on the net operating profit of the company as a whole?

2 For many years Futura Company has purchased the starters that it installs in its standard line of farm tractors. Due to a reduction in output of certain of its products, the company has idle capacity that could be used for producing the starters. The chief engineer has recommended against this move, however, pointing out that the cost to produce the starters would be greater than the current £8.40 per unit purchase price:

	Per unit	**Total**
Direct materials	£3.10	
Direct labour	2.70	
Supervision	1.50	£60,000
Depreciation	1.00	40,000
Variable manufacturing overhead	0.60	
Rent	0.30	12,000
Total production cost	£9.20	

A supervisor would have to be hired to oversee production of the starters. However, the company has sufficient idle tools and machinery that no new equipment would have to be purchased. The rent charge above is based on space utilized in the plant. The total rent on the plant is £80,000 per period. Depreciation is due to obsolescence rather than wear and tear. Prepare computations to show the financial advantage or disadvantage per period of making the starters.

3 Wexpro Ltd produces several products from processing 1 ton of clypton, a rare mineral. Material and processing costs total £60,000 per ton, a quarter of which is allocated to product X. Seven thousand units of product X are produced from each ton of clypton. The units can either be sold at the split-off point for £9 each, or processed further at a total cost of £9,500 and then sold for £12 each. Should product X be processed further or sold at the split-off point?

4 Benoit Company produces three products, A, B and C. Data concerning the three products follows (per unit):

	Product		
	A	B	C
Selling price	£80	£56	£70
Less variable expenses:			
Direct materials	24	15	9
Other variable expenses	24	27	40
Total variable expenses	48	42	49
Contribution margin	£32	£14	£21
Contribution margin ratio	40%	25%	30%

Demand for the company's products is very strong, with far more orders each month than the company has raw materials available to produce. The same material is used in each product. The material costs £3 per kilo with a maximum of 5,000 kilos available each month. Which orders would you advise the company to accept first, those for A, for B, or for C? Which orders second? Third?

5 Delta Company produces a single product. The cost of producing and selling a single unit of this product at the company's normal activity level of 60,000 units per year is:

Direct materials	£5.10
Direct labour	3.80
Variable manufacturing overhead	1.00
Fixed manufacturing overhead	4.20
Variable selling and administrative expense	1.50
Fixed selling and administrative expense	2.40

The normal selling price is £21 per unit. The company's capacity is 75,000 units per year. An order has been received from a mail-order house for 15,000 units at a special price of £14 per unit. This order would not affect regular sales. If the order is accepted, by how much will annual profits be increased or decreased? (The order will not change the company's total fixed costs.)

6 Refer to the data in Question 5 above. Assume the company has 1,000 units of this product left over from last year that are vastly inferior to the current model. The units must be sold through regular channels at reduced prices. What unit cost figure is relevant for establishing a minimum selling price for these units? Explain.

P4–13 Make or buy analysis

Time allowed: 45 minutes

'In my opinion, we ought to stop making our own drums and accept that outside supplier's offer,' said Wim Niewindt, managing director of Antilles Refining NV of Aruba. 'At a price of 18 florins per drum, we would be paying 5 florins less than it costs us to manufacture the drums in our own plant. (The currency in Aruba is the florin, denoted below by fl.) Since we use 60,000 drums a year, that would be an annual cost saving of 300,000 florins.' Antilles Refining's present cost to manufacture one drum is given below (based on 60,000 drums per year)

Direct material	fl10.35
Direct labour	6.00
Variable overhead	1.50
Fixed overhead (fl2.80 general company overhead, fl1.60 depreciation and fl0.75 supervision)	5.15
Total cost per drum	fl23.00

A decision about whether to make or buy the drums is especially important at this time since the equipment being used to make the drums is completely worn out and must be replaced. The choices facing the company are:

Alternative 1	Purchase new equipment and continue to make the drums. The equipment would cost fl810,000; it would have a six-year useful life and no salvage value. The company uses straight-line depreciation.
Alternative 2	Purchase the drums from an outside supplier at fl18 per drum under a six-year contract.

The new equipment would be more efficient than the equipment that Antilles Refining has been using and, according to the manufacturer, would reduce direct labour and variable overhead costs by 30%. The old equipment has no resale value. Supervision cost (fl45,000 per year) and direct materials cost per drum would not be affected by the new equipment. The new equipment's capacity would be 90,000 drums per year. The company has no other use for the space being used to produce the drums.

The company's total general company overhead would be unaffected by this decision.

Required

1. To assist the managing director in making a decision, prepare an analysis showing what the total cost and the cost per drum would be under each of the alternatives given above. Assume that 60,000 drums are needed each year. Which course of action would you recommend to the managing director?
2. Would your recommendation in Question 1 above be the same if the company's needs were: (a) 75,000 drums per year or (b) 90,000 drums per year? Show computations to support your answer, with costs presented on both a total and a per unit basis.
3. What other factors would you recommend that the company consider before making a decision?

P4–14 Make or buy decision

Time allowed: 40 minutes

Silven Industries, which manufactures and sells a highly successful line of summer lotions and insect repellents, has decided to diversify in order to stabilize sales throughout the year. A natural area for the company to consider is the production of winter lotions and creams to prevent dry and chapped skin.

After considerable research, a winter products line has been developed. However, Silven's president has decided to introduce only one of the new products for this coming winter. If the product is a success, further expansion in future years will be initiated.

The product selected (called Chap-Off) is a lip balm that will be sold in a lipstick-type tube. The product will be sold to wholesalers in boxes of 24 tubes for £8 per box. Because of excess capacity, no additional fixed overhead costs will be incurred to produce the product. However, a £90,000 charge for fixed overhead will be absorbed by the product under the company's absorption costing system. Using the estimated sales and production of 100,000 boxes of Chap-Off, the Accounting Department has developed the following cost per box:

Direct material	£3.60
Direct labour	2.00
Manufacturing overhead	1.40
Total cost	£7.00

The costs above include costs for producing both the lip balm and the tube into which the lip balm is to be placed. As an alternative to making the tubes, Silven has approached a supplier to discuss the possibility of purchasing the tubes for Chap-Off. The purchase price of the empty tubes from the supplier would be £1.35 per box of 24 tubes. If Silven Industries accepts the purchase proposal, it is predicted that direct labour and variable manufacturing overhead costs per box of Chap-Off would be reduced by 10% and that direct materials costs would be reduced by 25%.

Required

1 Should Silven Industries make or buy the tubes? Show calculations to support your answer.
2 What would be the maximum purchase price acceptable to Silven Industries? Support your answer with an appropriate explanation.
3 Instead of sales of 100,000 boxes, revised estimates show sales volume at 120,000 boxes. At this new volume, additional equipment at an annual rental of £40,000 must be acquired to manufacture the tubes. Assuming that the outside supplier will not accept an order for less than 100,000 boxes, should Silven Industries make or buy the tubes? Show computations to support your answer.
4 Refer to the data in Question 3 above. Assume that the outside supplier will accept an order of any size for the tubes at £1.35 per box. How, if at all, would this change your answer? Show computations.
5 What qualitative factors should Silven Industries consider in determining whether they should make or buy the tubes?

(*CMA, heavily adapted*)

P4–15 Accept or reject special order

Time allowed: 30 minutes

Polaski Company manufactures and sells a single product called a Ret. Operating at capacity, the company can produce and sell 30,000 Rets per year. Costs associated with this level of production and sales are given below:

	Unit	Total
Direct materials	£15	£450,000
Direct labour	8	240,000
Variable manufacturing overhead	3	90,000
Fixed manufacturing overhead	9	270,000
Variable selling expense	4	120,000
Fixed selling expense	6	180,000
Total cost	£45	£1,350,000

The Rets normally sell for £50 each. Fixed manufacturing overhead is constant at £270,000 per year within the range of 25,000 through 30,000 Rets per year.

Required

1 Assume that due to a recession, Polaski Company expects to sell only 25,000 Rets through regular channels next year. A large retail chain has offered to purchase 5,000 Rets if Polaski is willing to accept a 16% discount off the regular price. There would be no sales commissions on this order; thus, variable selling expenses would be slashed by 75%. However, Polaski Company would have to purchase a special machine to engrave the retail chain's name on the 5,000 units. This machine would cost £10,000. Polaski Company has no assurance that the retail chain will

purchase additional units any time in the future. Determine the impact on profits next year if this special order is accepted.

2 Refer to the original data. Assume again that Polaski Company expects to sell only 25,000 Rets through regular channels next year. The US Army would like to make a one-time-only purchase of 5,000 Rets. The Army would pay a fixed fee of £1.80 per Ret, and in addition it would reimburse Polaski Company for all costs of production (variable and fixed) associated with the units. Since the army would pick up the Rets with its own vans, there would be no variable selling expenses of any type associated with this order. If Polaski Company accepts the order, by how much will profits be increased or decreased for the year?

3 Assume the same situation as that described in Question 2 above, except that the company expects to sell 30,000 Rets through regular channels next year. Thus, accepting the US Army's order would require giving up regular sales of 5,000 Rets. If the Army's order is accepted, by how much will profits be increased or decreased from what they would be if the 5,000 Rets were sold through regular channels?

Chapter 5
The principles of cost allocation: full costing

LO Learning objectives

After studying Chapter 5, you should be able to:

1 Understand the need for job-costing in a variety of industries
2 Compute predetermined overhead rates
3 Compute product cost in a simple manufacturing operation
4 Analyse the allocation of service department costs
5 Consider some pitfalls in the allocation of costs

POHR = Estimated Manufacturing Overhead Cost / Estimated Quantity of Allocation Base.

Concepts in Context

© AFP/Getty Images

In a film studio, each film produced by the studio is a 'job', and costs for direct materials (costumes, props, film, etc.) and direct labour (actors, directors and extras) are accounted for and charged to each film's job cost sheet. A share of the studio's overhead costs, such as utilities, depreciation of equipment, salaries of maintenance workers, and so forth, is also charged to each film. However, there is considerable controversy about the methods used by some studios to distribute overhead costs among films, and these controversies sometimes result in lawsuits. Some authors who have signed 'net profit' contracts may see virtually nothing from films that gross millions at the box office and millions more in merchandising. In the business, this is known as 'Hollywood Accounting'.[1]

We should keep in mind that the essential purpose of any managerial costing system should be to provide cost data to help managers plan, control, direct and make decisions. Nevertheless, external financial reporting and tax reporting requirements often heavily influence how costs are accumulated and summarized on managerial reports. This is true of product costing.

Recall from Chapter 2 with variable costing, only those costs of production that vary with output are treated as product costs. This would generally include direct materials, direct labour and the variable portion of manufacturing overhead. Fixed manufacturing overhead is not treated as a product cost under this method. Rather, fixed manufacturing overhead is treated as a period cost and, like selling and administrative expenses, it is charged off in its entirety against revenue each period. Consequently, the cost of a unit of product in stock or in cost of goods sold under the variable costing method contains no element of fixed overhead cost.

Variable costing is sometimes referred to as direct costing or marginal costing. The term *direct costing* was popular for many years, but is slowly disappearing from day-to-day use. The term *variable costing* is more descriptive of the way in which product costs are computed when a contribution profit and loss account is prepared.

In contrast, **absorption costing** assigns both variable and fixed costs to products – mingling them in a way that makes it difficult for managers to distinguish between them. In one form or another, most countries require absorption costing for both external financial reporting and for tax reporting. *In addition, the vast majority of companies throughout the world also use absorption costing for management accounting purposes.*

Focus on Business Practice

Full costing for municipal waste management

© Ben Blankenburg

Full costs are often used by public sector bodies as well as service/manufacturing concerns. In the United States, for example, the Environmental Protection Agency (EPA) has produced a handbook to help municipal authorities calculate the full cost of dealing with solid waste (i.e. household and commercial waste). The handbook states that full cost accounting for such waste 'takes into account past and future outlays, overhead (oversight and support service) costs, and operating costs'. With full costs on hand, municipal authorities can use the cost data to monitor service costs and improve efficiency. But what kind of overhead costs might be incurred in managing municipal waste? To give an example, the EPA manual lists four possible paths solid waste can take: disposal, recycling, waste-to-energy and composting. Thinking about each of these paths, it is easy to visualize administrative and support staff for each path. Other support type costs include education and outreach projects, legal costs, records management, facility services, supervision, and so on. By taking into account such support costs as well as operating costs, and then deducting revenues from sales of some recyclable materials and energy, a municipal authority can report figures like an average cost per household. If authorities can agree what is included in full cost, comparisons are also possible, a point which the EPA handbook views as good management practice.[2]

Exercise: In a related area, many countries charge households for water supply. Can you think of the full costs to a local authority of providing clean, treated water?

Absorption costing treats *all* costs of production as product costs, regardless of whether they are variable or fixed. The cost of a unit of product under the absorption costing method therefore consists of direct materials, direct labour, and both variable and fixed overhead. Thus, absorption costing *allocates* a portion of *fixed manufacturing overhead cost* to each unit of product, along with the variable manufacturing costs. Because absorption costing includes all costs of production as product costs, it is frequently referred to as the **full cost** method.

Record-keeping and cost assignment problems are more complex when a company sells many different products and services than when it has only a single product. Since the products are different, the costs are typically different. Consequently, cost records must be maintained for each distinct product or job. For example, a lawyer in a large criminal law practice would ordinarily keep separate records of the costs of advising and defending each of her clients.

Job-order costing: an overview

LO 1

A **job-order costing system** is used in situations where many *different* products are produced each period. In a job-order costing system, costs are traced and allocated to jobs and then the costs of the job are divided by the number of units in the job to arrive at an average cost per unit.

Recall from Chapter 2 that companies generally classify manufacturing costs into three broad categories: (1) direct materials, (2) direct labour, and (3) overhead. As the names imply, direct labour and direct costs are those costs that can be easily and directly traced to a particular job. The key issues in this chapter and in Chapter 6 are related to the issues of the allocation of overhead and other common costs that cannot easily be traced to a product of a department. In full costing, the convention adopted is to allocate costs by choosing an *overhead base*.

Job-order costing can be used in service organizations such as law firms, film studios, hospitals and repair shops, as well as in manufacturing companies. In a law firm, for example, each client represents a 'job', and the costs of that job are accumulated day by day on a job cost sheet as the client's case is handled by the firm. Legal forms and similar inputs represent the direct materials for the job; the time expended by lawyers represents the direct labour; and the costs of secretaries, clerks, rent, depreciation, and so forth, represent the overhead. An example of a job costing approach for a legal firm is shown in Exhibit 5.1.

Exhibit 5.1 Job costing in a service firm: a legal case handled by Sue Emall & Co

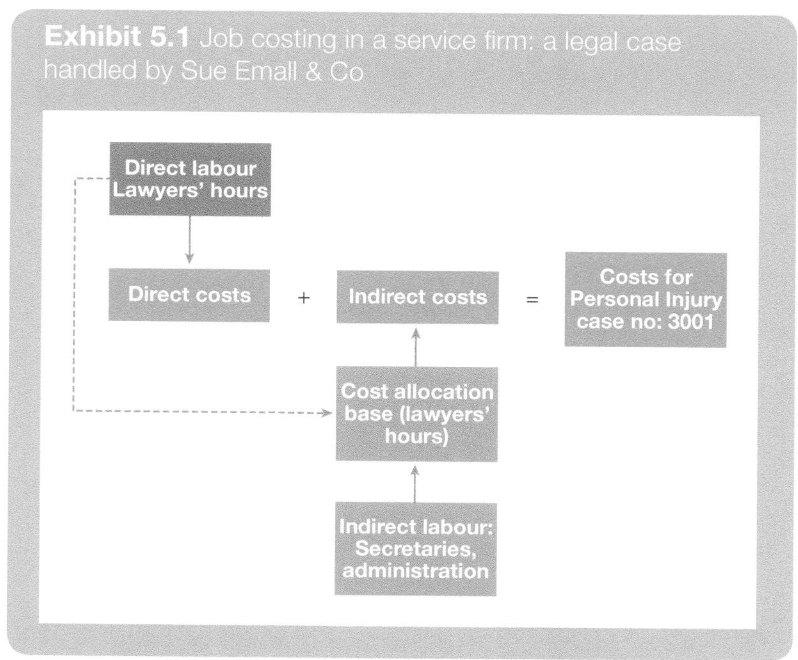

In total, the reader should be aware that job-order costing is a versatile and widely used costing method, and may be encountered in virtually any organization where there are diverse products or services.

LO 2 Choice of an allocation base for overhead cost

An **allocation base** should be used that is a *cost driver* of overhead cost. A **cost driver** is a factor, such as machine-hours, beds occupied, computer time, or flight-hours, that causes overhead costs. If a base is used to compute overhead rates that does not 'drive' overhead costs, then the result will be inaccurate overhead rates and distorted product costs. Overhead must be included with direct materials and direct labour on the job cost sheet since overhead is also a product cost. However, assigning overhead to units of product can be a difficult task. There are three reasons for this.

1. Overhead is an *indirect cost*. This means that it is either impossible or difficult to trace these costs to a particular product or job.
2. Overhead consists of many different items ranging from the grease used in machines to the annual salary of the senior managers.
3. Even though output may fluctuate due to seasonal or other factors, overhead costs tend to remain relatively constant due to the presence of fixed costs.

Given these problems, about the only way to assign overhead costs to products is to use an allocation process. This allocation of overhead costs is accomplished by selecting an *allocation base* that is common to all of the company's products and services. An allocation base is a measure such as direct labour-hours (DLH) or machine-hours (MH) that is used to assign overhead costs to products and services.

The most widely used allocation bases are direct labour-hours and direct labour cost, with machine-hours and even units of product (where a company has only a single product) also used to some extent.

The allocation base is used to compute the **predetermined overhead rate** in the following formula:

$$\text{Predetermined overhead rate} = \frac{\text{Estimated total overhead cost}}{\text{Estimated total units in the allocation base}}$$

Note that the predetermined overhead rate is based on *estimated* rather than actual figures. This is because the *predetermined* overhead rate is computed *before* the period begins and is used to apply overhead cost to jobs throughout the period. The process of assigning overhead cost to jobs is called **overhead application**. The formula for determining the amount of overhead cost to apply to a particular job is:

$$\text{Overhead applied to a particular job} = \text{Predetermined overhead rate} \times \text{Amount of allocation base incurred by the job}$$

So, for example, if the predetermined overhead rate is £8 per direct labour-hour, then £8 of overhead cost is *applied* to a job for each direct labour-hour incurred by the job. When the allocation base is direct labour-hours, the formula becomes:

$$\text{Overhead applied to a particular job} = \text{Predetermined overhead rate} \times \text{Actual direct labour hours charged to job}$$

LO 3 Job costing: an example

Classic Brass Ltd makes finely machined brass fittings for a variety of applications including stanchions, cleats and helms for luxury yachts. The company has decided to use machine-hours as the predetermined allocation base. The total estimated overheads of the company total £1,000,000 and the total number of estimated machine hours is 20,000. Therefore, the predetermined overhead rate per machine-hour is:

$$\frac{\text{Total manufacturing overhead, £1,000,000}}{\text{Total machine-hours, 20,000}} = \text{£50 per machine-hour}$$

Let us now consider the costing of two products: *Standard stanchions* and *Custom compass housing* which have the following design and cost characteristics:[3]

Standard stanchions

1. This is a standard design that does not require any new design resources.
2. Four hundred units were ordered during the year, comprising two separate orders.
3. Each stanchion required 0.5 machine-hours, for a total of 200 machine-hours.
4. Direct materials for 400 units totalled £2,110.
5. Direct labour for 400 units totalled £1,850.

Custom compass housing

1. This is a custom product that requires new design resources.
2. There was only one order for a single unit during the year.
3. The compass housing required 4 machine-hours.
4. Direct materials were £13.
5. Direct labour was £50.

From these data and using machine-hours as an overhead allocation base, we can determine the costs of different job-orders (400 standard stanchions and one custom compass housing) as shown in Exhibit 5.2.

Multiple predetermined overhead rates

In the above example, we have assumed that there is a single predetermined overhead rate for an entire factory called a **plantwide overhead rate**. This is, in fact, a common practice – particularly in smaller companies. In larger companies, multiple predetermined overhead rates are often used. In a **multiple predetermined overhead rate** system there is usually a different overhead rate for each production department. Such a system, while more complex, is considered to be more accurate, since it can reflect differences across departments in how overhead costs are incurred. We now consider the issue of how the overhead represented by *service department costs* may be allocated.

Service and operating departmental costing: selecting allocation bases

LO 4

Departments within an organization can be divided into two broad classes: (1) operating departments and (2) service departments. **Operating departments** include those departments or units where the central purposes of the organization are carried out. Examples of such departments or units would include the Surgery

Exhibit 5.2 Basic job-order costing using machine-hours as allocation base

Job 1: 400 standard stanchions	
Cost:	
Direct materials	£2,110
Direct labour	1,850
Manufacturing overhead (400 units × 0.5 machine-hours per unit × £50 per machine-hour*)	10,000
	13,960
Job 2: One custom compass housing	
Cost:	
Direct materials	13
Direct labour	50
Manufacturing overhead (1 unit × 4.0 machine-hours Per unit × £50 per machine-hour)	200
	263

Department in hospitals and producing departments such as Milling, Assembly, and Painting in manufacturing companies.

Service departments, by contrast, do not engage directly in operating activities. Rather, they provide services or assistance to the operating departments. Examples of service departments include Cafeteria, Internal Auditing, Personnel, Cost Accounting, and Purchasing. Although service departments do not engage directly in the operating activities of an organization, the costs that they incur are generally viewed as being part of the cost of the final product or service, the same as are materials, labour and overhead in a manufacturing company or medications in a hospital.

The major question we consider here is: How much of a service department's cost is to be allocated to each of the units that it serves? This is an important question, since the amount of service department cost allocated to a particular unit can have a significant impact on the computed cost of the goods or services that the unit is providing and can affect an operating unit's performance evaluation.

Many companies use a two-stage costing process. In the first stage, costs are assigned to the operating departments; in the second stage, costs are assigned from the operating departments to products and services. Costs are usually assigned from a service department to other departments using an allocation base, which is some measure of activity. The costs being allocated should be 'driven' by the allocation base. Ideally, the total cost of the service department should be proportional to the size of the allocation base. Managers also often argue that the allocation base should reflect as accurately as possible the benefits that the various departments receive from the services that are being provided. For example, most managers would argue that the square metres of building space occupied by each operating department should be used as the allocation base for janitorial services since both the benefits and costs of janitorial services tend to be proportional to the amount of space occupied by a department. Examples of allocation bases for some service departments are listed in Exhibit 5.3. A given service department's costs may be allocated using more than one base. For example, data processing costs may be allocated on the basis of CPU minutes for mainframe computers and on the basis of the number of personal computers used in each operating department.

Although the previous paragraph explains how to select an allocation base, another critical factor should not be overlooked. The allocations should be clear and straightforward and easily understood by the managers to whom the costs are being allocated.

Exhibit 5.3 Examples of bases used in allocating service department costs

Service Department	Bases (cost drivers) Involved
Laundry	Kilos of laundry
Airport Ground Services	Number of flights
Cafeteria	Number of employees; number of meals
Medical Facilities	Cases handled; number of employees; hours worked
Materials Handling	Hours of service; volume handled
Data Processing	CPU minutes; lines printed; disk storage used; number of personal computers
Custodial Services (building and grounds)	Square metres occupied
Cost Accounting	Labour-hours; clients or patients serviced
Power	KWh used; capacity of machines
Human Resources	Number of employees; employee turnover; training hours
Receiving, Shipping, and Stores	Units handled; number of requisitions; space occupied
Factory Administration	Total labour-hours
Maintenance	Machine-hours

The direct method

The **direct method** is the simplest cost allocation method. It ignores the services provided by a service department to other service departments and allocates all costs directly to operating departments. Even if a service department (such as Personnel) provides a large amount of service to another service department (such as the cafeteria), no allocations are made between the two departments. Rather, all costs are allocated directly to the operating departments. Hence the term *direct method*.

To provide an example of the direct method, assume that Mountain View Hospital has two service departments and two operating departments as shown below:

	Service department		Operating department		
	Hospital administration	Custodial services	Laboratory	Daily patient care	Total
Departmental costs before allocation	£360,000	£90,000	£261,000	£689,000	£1,400,000
Employee hours	12,000	6,000	18,000	30,000	66,000
Space occupied (square metres)	10,000	200	5,000	45,000	60,200

In the allocations that follow, Hospital Administration costs will be allocated on the basis of employee-hours and Custodial Services costs will be allocated on the basis of square metres occupied.

The direct method of allocating the hospital's service department costs to the operating departments is shown in Exhibit 5.4. Several things should be carefully noted in this exhibit. First, even though there are employee-hours in both the Hospital Administration Department itself and in the Custodial Services Department, these employee-hours are ignored when allocating service department costs using the direct method. *Under the direct method, any of the allocation base attributable to the service departments themselves is ignored; only the amount of the allocation base attributable to the operating departments is used in the allocation.* Note that the same rule is used when allocating the costs of the Custodial Services Department. Even though the Hospital Administration and Custodial Services departments occupy some space, this is ignored when the Custodial Services costs are allocated. Finally, note that after all allocations have been completed, all of the

Exhibit 5.4 Direct method of allocation

	Service department		Operating department		
	Hospital administration	Custodial services	Laboratory	Daily patient care	Total
Departmental costs before allocation	£360,000	£90,000	£261,000	£689,000	£1,400,000
Allocation:					
Hospital Administration costs ($^{18}/_{48}$, $^{30}/_{48}$)*	(360,000)		135,000	225,000	
Custodial Services costs ($^{5}/_{50}$, $^{45}/_{50}$)†		(90,000)	9,000	81,000	
Total costs after allocation	£ -0-	£ -0-	£405,000	£995,000	£1,400,000

*Based on the employee-hours in the two operating departments, which are 18,000 hours + 30,000 hours = 48,000 hours.
†Based on the space occupied by the two operating departments, which is 5,000 square metres + 45,000 square metres = 50,000 square metres.

departmental costs are contained in the two operating departments. These costs will form the basis for preparing overhead rates for purposes of costing products and services produced in the operating departments.

Some cautions in allocating service department costs

LO 5

Pitfalls in allocating fixed costs

Rather than allocate fixed costs in predetermined lump-sum amounts, some firms allocate them by use of a *variable* allocation base that fluctuates from period to period. This practice can distort decisions and create serious inequities between departments. The inequities will arise from the fact that the fixed costs allocated to one department will be heavily influenced by what happens in *other* departments or segments of the organization.

To illustrate, assume that Kolby Products has a car service centre that provides maintenance work on the fleet of cars used in the company's two sales territories. The car service centre costs are all fixed. Contrary to good practice, the company allocates these fixed costs to the sales territories on the basis of actual miles driven (a variable base). Selected cost data for the last two years follow:

	Year 1	Year 2
Car service centre costs (all fixed)	£120,000 (a)	£120,000 (a)
Western sales territory (miles driven)	1,500,000	1,500,000
Eastern sales territory (miles driven)	1,500,000	900,000
Total miles driven	3,000,000 (b)	2,400,000 (b)
Allocation rate per mile, (a)/(b)	£0.04	£0.05

Notice that the Western sales territory maintained an activity level of 1,500,000 miles driven in both years. On the other hand, the Eastern sales territory allowed its activity to drop off from 1,500,000 miles in Year 1 to only 900,000 miles in Year 2. The car service centre costs that would have been allocated to the two sales territories over the two-year span using actual miles driven as the allocation base are as follows:

Year 1:	
Western sales territory: 1,500,000 miles at £0.04	£60,000
Eastern sales territory: 1,500,000 miles at £0.04	60,000
Total cost allocated	£120,000
Year 2:	
Western sales territory: 1,500,000 miles at £0.05	£75,000
Eastern sales territory: 900,000 miles at £0.05	45,000
Total cost allocated	£120,000

In Year 1, the two sales territories share the service department costs equally. In Year 2, however, the bulk of the service department costs are allocated to the Western sales territory. This is not because of any increase in activity in the Western sales territory; rather, it is because of the decrease in activity in the Eastern sales territory. Even though the Western sales territory maintained the same level of activity in both years, the use of a variable allocation base has caused it to be penalized with a heavier cost allocation in Year 2 because of what has happened in another part of the company.

This kind of inequity is almost inevitable when a variable allocation base is used to allocate fixed costs. The manager of the Western sales territory undoubtedly will be upset about the inequity forced on his territory, but he will feel powerless to do anything about it. The result will be a loss of confidence in the system and considerable ill feeling.

Beware of sales as an allocation base

Over the years, sales have been a favourite allocation base for service department costs. One reason is that a sales base is simple, straightforward, and easy to work with. Another reason is that people tend to view sales as a measure of well-being, or 'ability to pay', and, hence, as a measure of how readily costs can be absorbed from other parts of the organization.

Unfortunately, sales are often a very poor allocation base, for the reason that sales vary from period to period, whereas the costs being allocated are often largely fixed in nature. As discussed earlier, if a variable base is used to allocate fixed costs, inequities can result between departments, since the costs being allocated to one department will depend in large part on what happens in *other* departments. For example, a let-up in sales effort in one department will shift allocated costs off that department and onto other, more productive departments. In effect, the departments putting forth the best sales efforts are penalized in the form of higher allocations, simply because of inefficiencies elsewhere that are beyond their control. The result is often bitterness and resentment on the part of the managers of the better departments.

Consider the following situation:

A large men's clothing store has Suits, Shoes and Accessories Departments. The Service costs total £60,000 and are allocated to the three sales departments according to monetary sales figures. A recent period showed the following allocation:

	Department			
	Suits	**Shoes**	**Accessories**	**Total**
Sales by department	£260,000	£40,000	£100,000	£400,000
Percentage of total sales	65%	10%	25%	100%
Allocation of service department costs, based on percentage of total sales	£39,000	£6,000	£15,000	£60,000

In a following period, the manager of the Suits Department launched a very successful programme to expand sales by £100,000 in his department. Sales in the other two departments remained unchanged. Total service department costs also remained unchanged, but the allocation of these costs changed substantially, as shown below:

	Department			
	Suits	**Shoes**	**Accessories**	**Total**
Sales by department	£360,000	£40,000	£100,000	£500,000
Percentage of total sales	72%	8%	20%	100%
Allocation of service department costs, based on percentage of total sales	£43,200	£4,800	£12,000	£60,000
Increase (or decrease) from prior allocation	4,200	(1,200)	(3,000)	–

The manager of the Suits Department complained that as a result of his successful effort to expand sales in his department, he was being forced to carry a larger share of the service department costs. On the other hand, the managers of the departments that showed no improvement in sales were relieved of a portion of the costs that they had been carrying. Yet there had been no change in the amount of services provided for any department.

The manager of the Suits Department viewed the increased service department cost allocation to his department as a penalty for his outstanding performance, and he wondered whether his efforts had really been worth while after all in the eyes of top management.

This example illustrates how sales should be used as an allocation base only in those cases where there is a direct causal relationship between sales and the service department costs being allocated.

Summary

- Job-order costing is used in situations where the organization offers many different products or services, such as in furniture manufacturing, hospitals, accounting and legal firms.
- Overhead costs are assigned to jobs through use of a predetermined overhead rate. The predetermined overhead rate is determined before the period begins by dividing the estimated total overhead cost for the period by the estimated total allocation base for the period.
- The most frequently used allocation bases are direct labour-hours and machine-hours. Overhead is applied to jobs by multiplying the predetermined overhead rate by the actual amount of the allocation base used by the job.
- In order to allocate the costs of service departments, many companies use a two-stage costing process. In the first stage, costs are assigned to the operating departments; in the second stage, costs are assigned from the operating departments to products and services.
- Costs are usually assigned from a service department to other departments using an allocation base, which is some measure of activity.

Key terms

Absorption costing A costing method that includes all manufacturing costs – direct materials, direct labour and both variable and fixed overhead – as part of the cost of a finished unit of product. This term is synonymous with full cost (p. 106).

Allocation base A measure of activity such as direct labour-hours or machine-hours that is used to assign costs to cost objects (p. 108).

Cost driver A factor, such as machine-hours, beds occupied, computer time, or flight-hours, that causes overhead costs (p. 108).

Direct method The allocation of all of a service department's costs directly to operating departments without recognizing services provided to other service departments (p. 111).

Full cost See Absorption costing (p. 107).

Job-order costing system A costing system used in situations where many different products, jobs or services are produced each period (p. 107)

Multiple predetermined overhead rates A costing system in which there are multiple overhead cost pools with a different predetermined rate for each cost pool, rather than a single predetermined overhead rate for the entire company. Frequently, each production department is treated as a separate overhead cost pool (p. 109).

Operating department A department or similar unit in an organization within which the central purposes of the organization are carried out (p. 109).

Overhead application The process of charging manufacturing overhead cost to job cost sheets and to the work in progress account (p. 108).

Plantwide overhead rate A single predetermined overhead rate that is used throughout a plant (p. 109).

Predetermined overhead rate A rate used to charge overhead cost to jobs in production; the rate is established in advance for each period by use of estimates of total manufacturing overhead cost and of the total allocation base for the period (p. 108).

Service department A department that provides support or assistance to operating departments and that does not engage directly in production or in other operating activities of an organization (p. 110).

Endnotes

1 Getlin (2008).

2 US Environmental Protection Agency (1997).

3 Note that the Classic Brass example will be used again in the next chapter to illustrate activity-based costing.

When you have read this chapter, log on to the Online Learning Centre for *Management Accounting for Business Decisions* at **www.mheducation.co.uk/textbooks/sealmabd1**, where you'll find multiple choice questions, practice exams and extra study tools for management accounting.

Assessment

Questions

connect™

5–1 Why are actual overhead costs not traced to jobs as are direct materials and direct labour costs?

5–2 What is a predetermined overhead rate, and how is it computed?

5–3 Explain why some production costs must be assigned to products through an allocation process. Name several such costs. Would such costs be classified as direct or as indirect costs?

5–4 Why do firms use predetermined overhead rates rather than actual manufacturing overhead costs in applying overhead to jobs?

5–5 What factors should be considered in selecting a base to be used in computing the predetermined overhead rate?

5–6 If a company fully allocates all of its overhead costs to jobs, does this guarantee that a profit will be earned for the period?

5–7 What is the difference between a service department and an operating department? Give several examples of service departments.

5–8 How are service department costs assigned to products and services?

Exercises

connect™

E5–1 Time allowed: 20 minutes

Kingsport Containers Ltd of Dublin experiences wide variation in demand for the 200-litre steel drums it fabricates. The leakproof, rustproof steel drums have a variety of uses from storing liquids and bulk materials to serving as makeshift musical instruments. The drums are made to order and are painted according to the customer's specifications – often in bright patterns and designs. The company is well known for the artwork that appears on its drums. Unit costs are computed on a quarterly basis by dividing each quarter's manufacturing costs (materials, labour and overhead) by the quarter's production in units. The company's estimated costs, by quarter, for the coming year follow:

	Quarter			
	First	Second	Third	Fourth
Direct materials	€240,000	€120,000	€60,000	€180,000
Direct labour	128,000	64,000	32,000	96,000
Manufacturing overhead	300,000	220,000	180,000	260,000
Total manufacturing costs	€668,000	€404,000	€272,000	€536,000
Number of units to be produced	80,000	40,000	20,000	60,000
Estimated cost per unit	€8.35	€10.10	€13.60	€8.93

Management finds the variation in unit costs to be confusing and difficult to work with. It has been suggested that the problem lies with manufacturing overhead, since it is the largest element of cost. Accordingly, you have been asked to find a more appropriate way of assigning manufacturing overhead cost to units of product. After some analysis, you have determined that the company's overhead costs are mostly fixed and therefore show little sensitivity to changes in the level of production.

Required

1 The company uses a job-order costing system. How would you recommend that manufacturing overhead cost be assigned to production? Be specific and show computations.

2 Recompute the company's unit costs in accordance with your recommendations in Question 1 above.

E5–2 Time allowed: 15 minutes

Estimated cost and operating data for three companies for the upcoming year follow:

	Company		
	X	Y	Z
Direct labour-hours	80,000	45,000	60,000
Machine-hours	30,000	70,000	21,000
Direct materials cost	£400,000	£290,000	£300,000
Manufacturing overhead cost	536,000	315,000	480,000

Predetermined overhead rates are computed using the following bases in the three companies:

Company	Overhead rate based on:
X	Direct labour-hours
Y	Machine-hours
Z	Direct materials cost

Required

Compute the predetermined overhead rate to be used in each company during the upcoming year.

E5–3 Time allowed: 25 minutes

The Ferre Publishing Company has three service departments and two operating departments. Selected data from a recent period on the five departments follow:

The company allocates service department costs by the direct method in the following order: A (number of employees), B (space occupied), and C (hours of press time). The company makes no distinction between variable and fixed service department costs.

	Service department			Operating department		
	A	B	C	1	2	Total
Overhead costs	£140,000	£105,000	£48,000	£275,000	£430,000	£998,000
Number of employees	60	35	140	315	210	760
Square metres of space occupied	15,000	10,000	20,000	40,000	100,000	185,000
Hours of press time	–	–	–	30,000	60,000	90,000

Required

Assuming that the company uses the direct method, how much overhead cost would be allocated to each operating department?

Problems

connect™

P5–4 Cost Allocation: Direct Method

Time allowed: 30 minutes

The Sendai Co. Ltd of Japan has budgeted costs in its various departments as follows for the coming year:

Factory administration	¥270,000,000
Custodial services	68,760,000
Personnel	28,840,000
Maintenance	45,200,000
Machining – overhead	376,300,000
Assembly – overhead	175,900,000
Total cost	¥965,000,000

The Japanese currency is the yen, denoted by ¥. The company allocates service department costs to other departments in the order listed below.

Department	Number of employees	Total labour-hours	Square metres of space occupied	Direct labour-hours	Machine-hours
Factory administration	12	–	5,000	–	–
Custodial services	4	3,000	2,000	–	–
Personnel	5	5,000	3,000	–	–
Maintenance	25	22,000	10,000	–	–
Machining	40	30,000	70,000	20,000	70,000
Assembly	60	90,000	20,000	80,000	10,000
	146	150,000	110,000	100,000	80,000

Machining and Assembly are operating departments; the other departments all act in a service capacity. The company does not make a distinction between fixed and variable service department costs. Factory administration is allocated on the basis of labour-hours; Custodial services on the basis of square metres occupied; Personnel on the basis of number of employees; and Maintenance on the basis of machine-hours.

Required

1 Allocate service department costs to departments using the direct method. Then compute predetermined overhead rates in the operating departments using a machine-hours basis in Machining and a direct labour-hours basis in Assembly.

2 Assume that the company does not want to bother with allocating service department costs but simply wants to compute a single plantwide overhead rate based on total overhead costs (both service department and operating department) divided by total direct labour-hours. Compute the overhead rate.

3 Suppose a job requires machine and labour time as follows:

	Machine-hours	Direct labour-hours
Machining department	190	25
Assembly department	10	75
Total hours	200	100

Using the overhead rates computed in (1) and (2), compute the amount of overhead cost that would be assigned to the job if the overhead rates were developed using the direct method and the plantwide method.

P5–5 Plantwide and Departmental Overhead Rates

Time allowed: 40 minutes

'Blast it!' said David Wilson, CEO of Teledex Company. 'We've just lost the bid on the Koopers job by €2,000. It seems we're either too high to get the job or too low to make any money on half the jobs we bid.'

Teledex Company manufactures products to customers' specifications and operates a job-order cost system. Manufacturing overhead cost is applied to jobs on the basis of direct labour cost. The following estimates were made at the beginning of the year:

	Department			
	Fabricating	Machining	Assembly	Total plant
Direct labour	€200,000	€100,000	€300,000	€600,000
Manufacturing overhead	350,000	400,000	90,000	840,000

Jobs require varying amounts of work in the three departments. The Koopers job, for example, would have required manufacturing costs in the three departments as follows:

	Department			
	Fabricating	Machining	Assembly	Total plant
Direct materials	€3,000	€200	€1,400	€4,600
Direct labour	2,800	500	6,200	9,500
Manufacturing overhead	?	?	?	?

The company uses a plantwide overhead rate to apply manufacturing overhead cost to jobs.

Required

1 Assuming use of a plantwide overhead rate:
  (a) Compute the rate for the current year.
  (b) Determine the amount of manufacturing overhead cost that would have been applied to the Koopers job.

2 Suppose that instead of using a plantwide overhead rate, the company had used a separate predetermined overhead rate in each department. Under these conditions:
   (a) Compute the rate for each department for the current year.
   (b) Determine the amount of manufacturing overhead cost that would have been applied to the Koopers job.
3 Explain the difference between the manufacturing overhead that would have been applied using the plantwide rate in question 1 (b) above and using the departmental rates in question 2 (b).
4 Assume that it is customary in the industry to bid jobs at 150% of total manufacturing cost (direct materials, direct labour, and applied overhead). What was the company's bid price on the Koopers job? What would the bid price have been if departmental overhead rates had been used to apply overhead cost?

Chapter 6
Activity-based costing

LO Learning objectives

After studying Chapter 6, you should be able to:

1. Explain the major differences between activity-based costing and a traditional costing system
2. Distinguish between unit-level, batch-level, product-level, customer-level, and organization-sustaining activities
3. Assign costs to cost pools using a first-stage allocation
4. Compute activity rates for cost pools and explain how they can be used to target process improvements
5. Assign costs to a cost object using a second-stage allocation.

Concepts in Context

© Vonkara1

As well as costing products more accurately, activity-based costing offers a way of assessing customer profitability by analysing the huge chunk of overhead and non-manufacturing costs that traditional cost systems can struggle to measure. Take, for example, a large consumer goods manufacturer that has two distinct customer segments – major multiple/superstores and corner shop independents. The gross margins are good in the independent sector but the costs of service make the true profitability much lower than in the multiples. Why? With multiples there are a small number of large orders, a small number of drop points at the multiples' own distribution centres, and transactions are expedited electronically through EDI links. In contrast, the independents are served 'by an army of direct sales forces, each generating thousands of small paper-based orders ... [D]elivery goes to thousands of drop-off points ... payment is often by cheque (inefficient and expensive to handle) and payment is frequently late'.[1]

Activity-based costing (ABC) is a costing method that is designed to provide managers with cost information for strategic and other decisions that potentially affect capacity and therefore 'fixed' costs. Activity-based costing is also used as an element of activity-based management, an approach to management that focuses on activities.

In practice, there are many 'flavours' of activity-based costing. Consultants emphasize different aspects of activity-based costing, and companies interpret activity-based costing differently. Since so much variation occurs in practice, we focus our attention in this chapter on what we consider to be 'the best practice' – those techniques that provide managers with the most useful information for making strategic decisions. We will assume that the ABC system is used as a supplement to, rather than as a replacement for, the company's formal cost accounting system. The cost accounting methods described in Chapter 5 would continue to be used to determine product costs for external financial reports. Activity-based costing would be used to determine product and other costs for special management reports. To keep the discussion simple, we gloss over some of the relatively unimportant details that can add enormously to the complexity of activity-based costing.

LO 1

In the traditional cost accounting systems, the objective is to properly value stocks and cost of goods sold for external financial reports. In activity-based costing, the objective is to understand overhead and the profitability of products and customers. As a consequence of these differences in objectives, 'best practice' activity-based costing differs in a number of ways from traditional cost accounting.

In activity-based costing:

1. Non-manufacturing as well as manufacturing costs may be assigned to products
2. Some manufacturing costs may be excluded from product costs
3. There are a number of overhead cost pools, each of which is allocated to products and other costing objects using its own unique measure of activity
4. The allocation bases often differ from those used in traditional costing systems
5. The overhead rates, or *activity rates*, may be based on the level of activity at capacity rather than on the budgeted level of activity.

As we will see later in the chapter, these differences from traditional cost accounting systems can have dramatic impacts on the apparent costs of products and the profitability of products and customers. But first, we will briefly discuss the reasons for these departures from traditional cost accounting practices.

How costs are treated under activity-based costing

Non-manufacturing costs and activity-based costing

In traditional cost accounting, only manufacturing costs are assigned to products. Selling, general and administrative expenses are treated as period expenses and are not assigned to products. However, many of these non-manufacturing costs are also part of the costs of producing, selling, distributing and servicing products. For example, commissions paid to salespersons, shipping costs and warranty repair costs can easily be traced to individual products. To determine the profitability of products and services, such non-manufacturing costs are assigned to products in activity-based costing.

Manufacturing costs and activity-based costing

In traditional cost accounting, *all* manufacturing costs are assigned to products – even manufacturing costs that are not caused by the products. For example, a portion of the factory security guard's wages would be allocated to each product even though the guard's wages are totally unaffected by which products are made or not made during a period. In activity-based costing, a cost is assigned to a product only if there is good reason to believe that the cost would be affected by decisions concerning the product.

Plantwide overhead rate

Our discussion in Chapter 5 assumed that a single overhead rate, called a *plantwide overhead rate*, was being used throughout an entire factory and that the allocation base was direct labour-hours or machine-hours. This simple approach to overhead assignment can result in distorted unit product costs when it is used for decision-making purposes.

When cost systems were developed in the 1800s, direct labour was a larger component of product costs than it is today. Data relating to direct labour were readily available and convenient to use, and managers believed there was a high positive correlation between direct labour and overhead costs. (A positive correlation between two things means that they tend to move in tandem.) Consequently, direct labour was a useful allocation base for overhead.

However, a plantwide overhead rate based on direct labour may no longer be satisfactory. First, in many companies, direct labour may no longer be highly correlated with (i.e., move in tandem with) overhead costs. Second, because of the large variety of activities encompassed in overhead, no single allocation base may be able to reflect adequately the demands that products place on overhead resources.

On an economy-wide basis, direct labour and overhead costs have been moving in opposite directions for a long time. As a percentage of total cost, direct labour has been declining, whereas overhead has been increasing.[2] Many tasks that used to be done by hand are now done with largely automated equipment – a component of overhead. Furthermore, product diversity has increased. Companies are creating new products and services at an ever-accelerating rate that differ in volume, batch size and complexity. Managing and sustaining this product diversity requires many more overhead resources such as production schedulers and product design engineers, and many of these overhead resources have no obvious connection with direct labour.

Nevertheless, direct labour remains a viable base for applying overhead to products in many companies – particularly for external reports. In some companies there is still a high positive correlation between overhead costs and direct labour. And most companies throughout the world continue to base overhead allocations on direct labour or machine-hours. However, in those instances in which overhead costs do not move in tandem with direct labour, some other means of assigning costs must be found or product costs will be distorted. Furthermore, in service industries activity-based costing offers the chance to understand those product and customer costs which were not measured under traditional costing systems.[3]

Departmental overhead rates

Rather than use a plantwide overhead rate, many companies use departmental overhead rates. The allocation bases used in these departmental overhead rates depend on the nature of the work performed in each department. For example, overhead costs in a machining department may be allocated on the basis of the machine-hours in that department. In contrast, the overhead costs in an assembly department may be allocated on the basis of direct labour-hours in that department.

Unfortunately, even departmental overhead rates will not correctly assign overhead costs in situations where a company has a range of products that differ in volume, batch size or complexity of production.[4] This is because the departmental approach usually relies on volume as the factor in allocating overhead cost to products. For example, if the machining department's overhead is applied to products on the basis of machine-hours, it is assumed that the department's overhead costs are caused by, and are directly proportional to, machine-hours. However, the department's overhead costs are probably more complex than this and are caused by a variety of factors, including the range of products processed in the department, the number of batch set-ups that are required, the complexity of the products, and so on. Activity-based costing is a technique that is designed to reflect these diverse factors more accurately when costing products. It attempts to accomplish this goal by identifying the major *activities* such as batch set-ups, purchase order processing and so on, that consume overhead resources. An **activity** is any event that causes the consumption of overhead resources. The costs of carrying out these activities are assigned to the products that cause the activities.

The costs of idle capacity in activity-based costing

In traditional cost accounting, predetermined overhead rates are computed by dividing budgeted overhead costs by a measure of budgeted activity such as budgeted direct labour-hours. This practice results in applying the costs of unused, or idle, capacity to products, and it results in unstable unit product costs. If budgeted activity falls, the overhead rate increases because the fixed components of overhead are spread over a smaller base, resulting in increased unit product costs.

In contrast to traditional cost accounting, activity-based costing means that products are charged for the costs of capacity they use – not for the costs of capacity they don't use. In other words, the costs of idle capacity are not charged to products. This results in more stable unit costs and is consistent with the objective of assigning only those costs to products that are actually caused by the products.

Designing an activity-based costing (ABC) system

Experts agree on several essential characteristics of any successful implementation of activity-based costing. First, the initiative to implement activity-based costing must be strongly supported by top management. Second, the design and implementation of an ABC system should be the responsibility of a cross-functional team rather than of the accounting department. The team should include representatives from each area that will use the data provided by the ABC system. Ordinarily, this would include representatives from marketing, production, engineering and top management as well as technically trained accounting staff. Sometimes an outside consultant who specializes in activity-based costing acts as an adviser to the team.

The reason for insisting on strong top-management support and a multifunction team approach is rooted in the fact that it is difficult to implement changes in organizations unless those changes have the full support of those who are affected. Activity-based costing changes 'the rules of the game' since it changes some of the key measures that managers use for their decision making and for evaluating individuals' performance. Unless the managers who are directly affected by the changes in the rules have a say, there will inevitably be resistance. In addition, designing a good ABC system requires intimate knowledge of many parts of the organization's overall operations. This knowledge can only come from the people who are familiar with those operations.

Top managers must support the initiative for two reasons. First, without leadership from top management, some managers may not see any reason to change. Second, if top managers do not support the ABC system and continue to play the game by the old rules, their subordinates will quickly get the message and abandon the ABC system. Time after time, when accountants have attempted to implement an ABC system on their own without top-management support and active co-operation from other managers, the results have been ignored.

An example: introducing ABC at Classic Brass

After studying the existing cost accounting system at Classic Brass and reviewing articles in professional and trade journals, the ABC team decided to implement an activity-based costing (ABC) system. Like most other ABC implementations, the new ABC system would supplement, rather than replace, the existing cost accounting system, which would continue to be used for external financial reports.

The new ABC system would be used to prepare special reports for management decisions such as bidding for new business. The accounting manager drew the chart appearing in Exhibit 6.1 to explain the general structure of the ABC model. In activity-based costing it is assumed that cost objects such as product generate activities. For example, a customer order for a brass spittoon generates a production order, which is an activity. It is further assumed that activities consume resources. For example, a production order uses a sheet of paper and takes time for a manager to fill out. And it is assumed that consumption of resources lead to costs. The greater the number of sheets used to fill out production orders and the greater the amount o

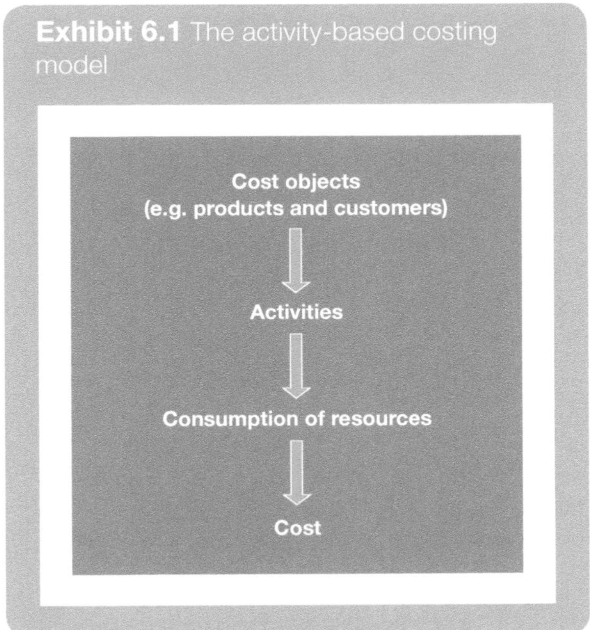

Exhibit 6.1 The activity-based costing model

time devoted to filling out such orders, the greater the cost. Activity-based costing attempts to trace through these relationships to identify how products and customers affect costs.

As in most other companies, the ABC team at Classic Brass felt that the company's traditional cost accounting system adequately measures the *direct material* and *direct labour* costs of products. Therefore, the ABC study would be concerned solely with the other costs of the company – *manufacturing overhead* and *selling, general* and *administrative costs*.

The team felt it was important to plan carefully how it would go about implementing the new ABC system at Classic Brass. Accordingly, the implementation process was broken down into the following five basic steps:

1 Identify and define activities and activity pools
2 Wherever possible, directly trace costs to activities and cost objects
3 Assign costs to activity cost pools
4 Calculate activity rates
5 Assign costs to cost objects using the activity rates and activity measures

Identifying activities to include in the ABC system

LO 2

The first major step in implementing an ABC system is to identify the activities that will form the foundation for the system. This can be difficult, time-consuming and involves a great deal of judgement. A common procedure is for the individuals on the ABC implementation team to interview everyone – or at least all supervisors and managers – in overhead departments and ask them to describe their major activities. Ordinarily, this results in a very long list of activities. The length of such lists of activities poses a problem. On the one hand, the greater the number of activities tracked in the ABC system, the more accurate the costs are likely to be. On the other hand, it is costly to design, implement, maintain and use a complex system involving large numbers of activities. Consequently, the original lengthy list of activities is usually reduced to a handful

by combining similar activities. For example, several actions may be involved in handling and moving raw materials – from receiving raw materials on the loading dock to sorting them into the appropriate bins in the storeroom. All of these activities might be combined into a single activity called material handling.

A useful way to think about activities and how to combine them is to organize them into five general levels: **unit-level, batch-level, product-level, customer-level, and organization-sustaining activities**. These levels are described as follows:[4]

1. **Unit-level activities** are performed each time a unit is produced. The costs of unit-level activities should be proportional to the number of units produced. For example, providing power to run processing equipment would be a unit-level activity since power tends to be consumed in proportion to the number of units produced.
2. **Batch-level activities** are performed each time a batch is handled or processed, regardless of how many units are in the batch. For example, tasks such as placing purchase orders, setting up equipment and arranging for shipments to customers are batch-level activities. They are incurred each time there is a batch (or a customer order). Costs at the batch level depend on the number of batches processed rather than on the number of units produced, the number of units sold or other measures of volume. For example, the cost of setting up a machine for batch processing is the same regardless of whether the batch contains one or 5,000 items.
3. **Product-level activities** relate to specific products and typically must be carried out regardless of how many batches are run or units of product are produced or sold. For example, activities such as designing a product, advertising a product and maintaining a product manager and staff are all product-level activities.
4. **Customer-level activities** relate to specific customers and include activities such as sales calls, catalogue mailings and general technical support that are not tied to any specific product.
5. **Organization-sustaining activities** are carried out regardless of which customers are served, which products are produced, how many batches are run, or how many units are made. This category includes activities such as cleaning executive offices, providing a computer network, arranging for loans, preparing annual reports to shareholders, and so on.

When combining activities in an ABC system, activities should be grouped together at the appropriate level. Batch-level activities should not be combined with unit-level activities or product-level activities with batch-level activities and so on. In general, it is best to combine only those activities that are highly correlated with each other within a level. Activities are correlated with each other if they tend to move in tandem. For example, the number of customer orders received is likely to be highly correlated with the number of completed customer orders shipped, so these two batch-level activities (receiving and shipping orders) can usually be combined with little loss of accuracy.

At Classic Brass, the ABC team, in consultation with top managers, selected the following *activity cost pools* and *activity measures*.

Activity cost pools at Classic Brass

Activity cost pool	Activity measure
Customer orders	Number of customer orders
Product design	Number of product designs
Order size	Machine-hours
Customer relations	Number of active customers
Other	Not applicable

An **activity cost pool** is a 'bucket' in which costs are accumulated that relate to a single activity in the ABC system. For example, the Customer Orders cost pool will be assigned all costs of resources that are consumed by taking and processing customer orders, including costs of processing paperwork and any costs involved in setting up machines. The measure of activity for this cost pool is simply the number of customer orders received. This is a batch-level activity, since each order generates work that occurs regardless of whether the order is for one unit or 1,000 units. The number of customer orders received is an example of an *activity measure*. An **activity measure** is an allocation base in an activity-based costing system.

The Product Design cost pool will be assigned all costs of resources consumed by designing products. The activity measure for this cost pool is the number of products designed. This is a product-level activity, since the amount of design work on a new product does not depend on the number of units ultimately ordered or batches ultimately run.

The Order Size cost pool will be assigned all costs of resources consumed as a consequence of the number of units produced, including the costs of miscellaneous factory supplies, power to run machines, and some equipment depreciation. This is a unit-level activity since each unit requires some of these resources. The activity measure for this cost pool is machine-hours.

The Customer Relations cost pool will be assigned all costs associated with maintaining relations with customers, including the costs of sales calls and the costs of entertaining customers. The activity measure for this cost pool is the number of customers the company has on its active customer list.

The Other cost pool will be assigned all overhead costs that are not associated with customer orders, product design, the size of the orders, or customer relations. These costs mainly consist of organization-sustaining costs and the costs of unused, idle capacity. These costs *will not* be assigned to products since they represent resources that are *not* consumed by products.

It is unlikely that any other company would use exactly the same activity cost pools and activities as those selected by Classic Brass. Because of the amount of judgement involved, there is considerable variation in the number and definitions of the activity cost pools and activity measures used by companies.

The mechanics of activity-based costing

After the ABC system had been designed, the team was ready to begin the process of actually computing the costs of products, customers and other objects of interest.

Tracing overhead costs to activities and cost objects

The second step in implementing an ABC system is to directly trace as many overhead costs as possible to the ultimate cost objects. At Classic Brass, the ultimate cost objects are products, customer orders, and customers. The company's manufacturing overhead and selling, general and administrative costs are listed in Exhibit 6.2. In the ABC system at Classic Brass all of these costs are considered to be 'overhead' and will be assigned to cost objects as appropriate.

One of these overhead costs – shipping – can be traced directly to customer orders. Classic Brass is directly billed for each customer order it ships, so it is a simple matter to trace these costs to the customer orders. Customers do not pay these actual shipping costs; instead they pay a standard shipping charge that can differ substantially from the actual bill that Classic Brass receives from the freight company.

No other overhead costs could be directly traced to products, customer orders, or customers. Consequently, the remainder of the overhead costs would be assigned to cost objects using the ABC system.

Assigning costs to activity cost pools

LO 3

Most overhead costs are originally classified in the company's basic accounting system according to the departments in which they are incurred. For example, salaries, supplies, rent, and so forth, incurred by the marketing department are charged to that department. In some cases, some or all of these costs can be directly traced to one of the activity cost pools in the ABC system, which is the third step in implementing activity-based costing. For example, if the ABC system has an activity called *purchase order processing*, then all of the costs of the purchasing department could probably be traced to that activity. To the extent possible, costs should be traced directly to the activity cost pools. However, it is quite common for an overhead department to be involved in several of the activities that are tracked in the ABC system. In such situations, the costs of the department are divided among the activity cost pools via an allocation process called *first-stage allocation*. The **first-stage allocation** in an ABC system is the process by which overhead costs are assigned to activity cost pools.

The immediate problem is to figure out how to divide, for example, the £500,000 of indirect factory wages at Classic Brass shown in Exhibit 6.2 among the various activity cost pools in the ABC system. The point of activity-based costing is to determine the resources consumed by cost objects. Since indirect factory worker time is a resource, we need some way of estimating the amount of indirect factory worker time that is consumed by each activity in the ABC system. Often, the best way to get this kind of information is to ask the people who are directly involved. Members of the ABC team interview indirect factory workers (e.g., supervisors, engineers, quality inspectors, etc.) and ask them what percentage of time they spend dealing with customer orders, with product design, with processing units of product (i.e., order size), and with customer relations. These interviews are conducted with considerable care. Those who are interviewed must thoroughly understand what the activities encompass and what is expected of them in the interview. In addition, departmental managers are interviewed to determine how the non-personnel costs should be distributed across the activity cost pools. In each case the key question is 'What percentage of the available resource is consumed by this activity?' For example, the production manager would be asked, 'What percentage of the available machine capacity is consumed as a consequence of the number of units processed (i.e., size of orders)?'

The results of the interviews at Classic Brass are displayed in Exhibit 6.3. For example, factory equipment depreciation is distributed 20% to Customer Orders, 60% to Order Size, and 20% to the Other cost pool. The resource in this instance is machine time. According to the estimate made by the production manager, 60% of the total available time was actually used to process units to fill orders. Each customer order requires setting up, which also requires machine time. This activity consumes 20% of the total available machine time and is entered under the Customer Orders column. The remaining 20% of available machine time represents idle time and is entered under the Other column.

Exhibit 6.2 Overhead costs (both manufacturing and non-manufacturing) at Classic Brass

Production Department:		
Indirect factory wages	£500,000	
Factory equipment depreciation	300,000	
Factory utilities	120,000	
Factory building lease	80,000	£1,000,000
Shipping costs*		40,000
General Administrative Department:		
Administrative wages and salaries	400,000	
Office equipment depreciation	50,000	
Administrative building lease	60,000	510,000
Marketing Department:		
Marketing wages and salaries	250,000	
Selling expenses	50,000	300,000
Total overhead costs		£1,850,000

*Shipping costs can be traced directly to customer orders.

Exhibit 6.3 Results of interviews: distribution of activities

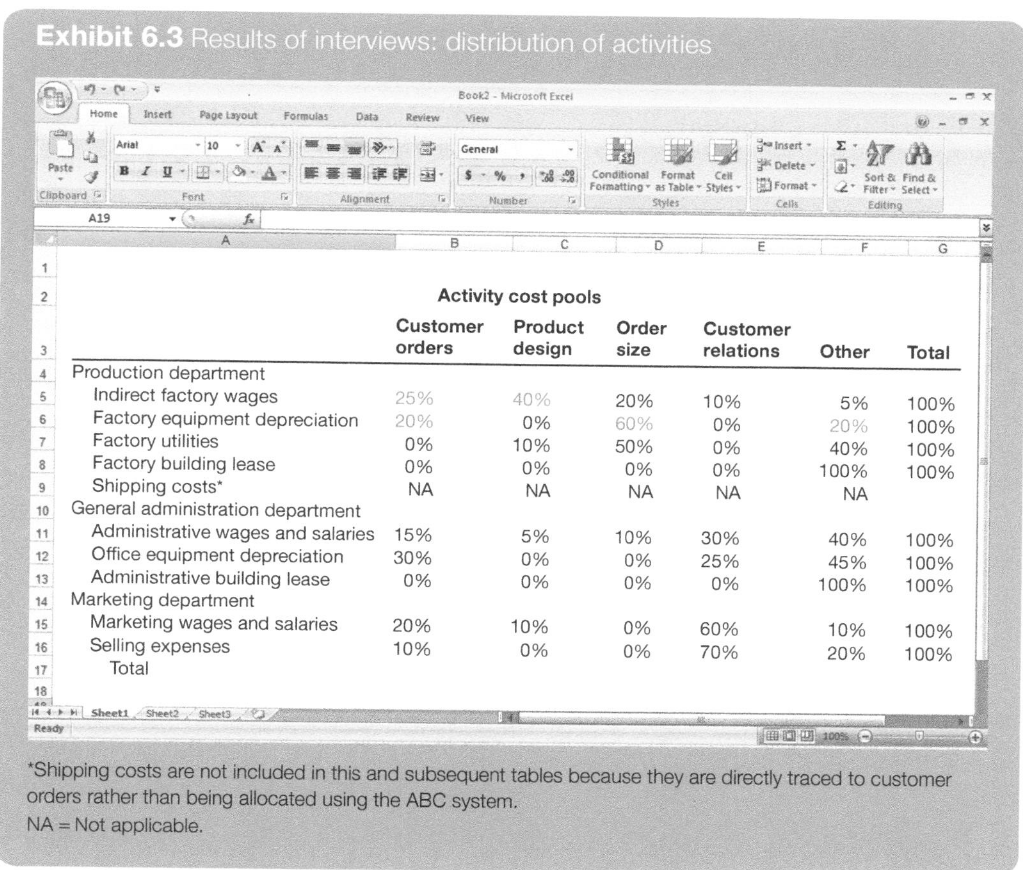

	Activity cost pools					
	Customer orders	Product design	Order size	Customer relations	Other	Total
Production department						
Indirect factory wages	25%	40%	20%	10%	5%	100%
Factory equipment depreciation	20%	0%	60%	0%	20%	100%
Factory utilities	0%	10%	50%	0%	40%	100%
Factory building lease	0%	0%	0%	0%	100%	100%
Shipping costs*	NA	NA	NA	NA	NA	
General administration department						
Administrative wages and salaries	15%	5%	10%	30%	40%	100%
Office equipment depreciation	30%	0%	0%	25%	45%	100%
Administrative building lease	0%	0%	0%	0%	100%	100%
Marketing department						
Marketing wages and salaries	20%	10%	0%	60%	10%	100%
Selling expenses	10%	0%	0%	70%	20%	100%
Total						

*Shipping costs are not included in this and subsequent tables because they are directly traced to customer orders rather than being allocated using the ABC system.
NA = Not applicable.

Exhibit 6.3 and many of the other exhibits in this chapter are presented in the form of Excel spreadsheets. It is often a good idea to use spreadsheet software in activity-based costing because of the large number of calculations involved. You *can* do all the calculations by hand, by setting up an activity-based costing system on a spreadsheet or you can use special ABC software which can save a lot of work in the long run – particularly in companies that intend periodically to update their ABC systems.

We will not go into the details of how all of the percentages in Exhibit 6.3 were determined. However, note that 100% of the factory building lease has been assigned to the Other cost pool. Classic Brass has a single production facility. It has no plans to expand or to sublease any excess space. The cost of this production facility is treated as an organization-sustaining cost since there is no way to avoid even a portion of this cost if a product or customer were dropped. (Remember that organization sustaining costs are assigned to the Other cost pool and are not allocated to products.) In contrast, some companies have separate facilities for manufacturing specific products. The costs of these separate facilities could be directly traced to the specific products.

Once the percentage distributions in Exhibit 6.3 have been established, it is a simple matter to allocate costs to the activity cost pools. The results of this first-stage allocation are displayed in Exhibit 6.4. Each cost is allocated across the activity cost pools by multiplying it by the percentages in Exhibit 6.3. For example, the indirect factory wages of £500,000 are multiplied by the 25% entry under Customer Orders in Exhibit 6.3 to arrive at the £125,000 entry under Customer Orders in Exhibit 6.4. Similarly, the indirect factory wages of £500,000 are multiplied by the 40% entry under Product Design in Exhibit 6.3 to arrive at the £200,000 entry under Product Design in Exhibit 6.4. All of the entries in Exhibit 6.4 are computed in this way.

Now that the first-stage allocations to the activity cost pools have been completed, the fourth step is to compute the activity rates.

Exhibit 6.4 First-stage allocations to activity cost pools

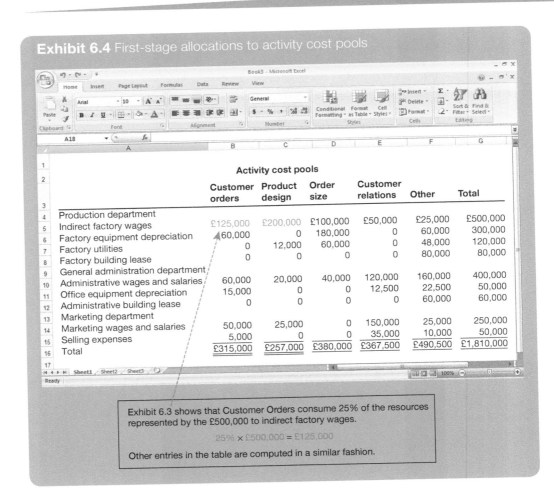

	Activity cost pools					
	Customer orders	Product design	Order size	Customer relations	Other	Total
Production department						
Indirect factory wages	£125,000	£200,000	£100,000	£50,000	£25,000	£500,000
Factory equipment depreciation	60,000	0	180,000	0	60,000	300,000
Factory utilities	0	12,000	60,000	0	48,000	120,000
Factory building lease	0	0	0	0	80,000	80,000
General administration department						
Administrative wages and salaries	60,000	20,000	40,000	120,000	160,000	400,000
Office equipment depreciation	15,000	0	0	12,500	22,500	50,000
Administrative building lease	0	0	0	0	60,000	60,000
Marketing department						
Marketing wages and salaries	50,000	25,000	0	150,000	25,000	250,000
Selling expenses	5,000	0	0	35,000	10,000	50,000
Total	£315,000	£257,000	£380,000	£367,500	£490,500	£1,810,000

Exhibit 6.3 shows that Customer Orders consume 25% of the resources represented by the £500,000 to indirect factory wages.

25% × £500,000 = £125,000

Other entries in the table are computed in a similar fashion.

Focus on Business Practice

Time-driven activity-based costing (ABC)

One of the recent innovations in ABC is a variation called 'time-driven activity-based costing' (TDABC). Rather than gathering data on the *percentage* of time spent on different areas of work such as in Exhibit 6.3, TDABC measures the *absolute* time per transactional activity. In short, it is a simpler model of ABC in which time is the only cost driver. As well as being simpler to implement, it is argued that TDABC avoids the tendency of staff to allocate 100% of their time to work activities rather than admit to having any idle time.[5]

Exercise: Consider the difficulties that there may be in trying to categorise and allocate the tasks in the many 'white collar' service activities that ABC tries to cost. How routine are the tasks and how easy would it be to make them 'countable'?

Computation of activity rates

LO 4

The activity rates that will be used for assigning overhead costs to products and customers are computed by dividing the costs listed in Exhibit 6.4 by the total activity for each activity cost pool. The results of these computations are shown in Exhibit 6.5. The total activity numbers listed across the top of the table in Exhibit 6.5 were estimated by the ABC team and represent the amount of activity actually required to produce the company's present product mix and to serve its present customers. The activity at the top of each column was divided into each of the costs in the corresponding column in Exhibit 6.4 to arrive at the activity rates in Exhibit 6.5. For example, the £125,000 entry in Exhibit 6.4 for indirect factory wages under the Customer Orders column is divided by the total of 1,000 customer orders listed at the top of Exhibit 6.5 to arrive at the activity rate of £125 for indirect factory wages under the Customer Orders column in Exhibit 6.5. Similarly, the £200,000 entry in Exhibit 6.4 for indirect factory wages under the Product Design column is divided by the total number of designs (i.e., 200 product designs) to arrive at the activity rate of £1,000 per design for indirect factory wages. Note that activity rates are not computed for the Other category of costs. This is because these organization-sustaining costs and costs of idle capacity are not allocated to products and customers.

Exhibit 6.5 Computation of activity rates

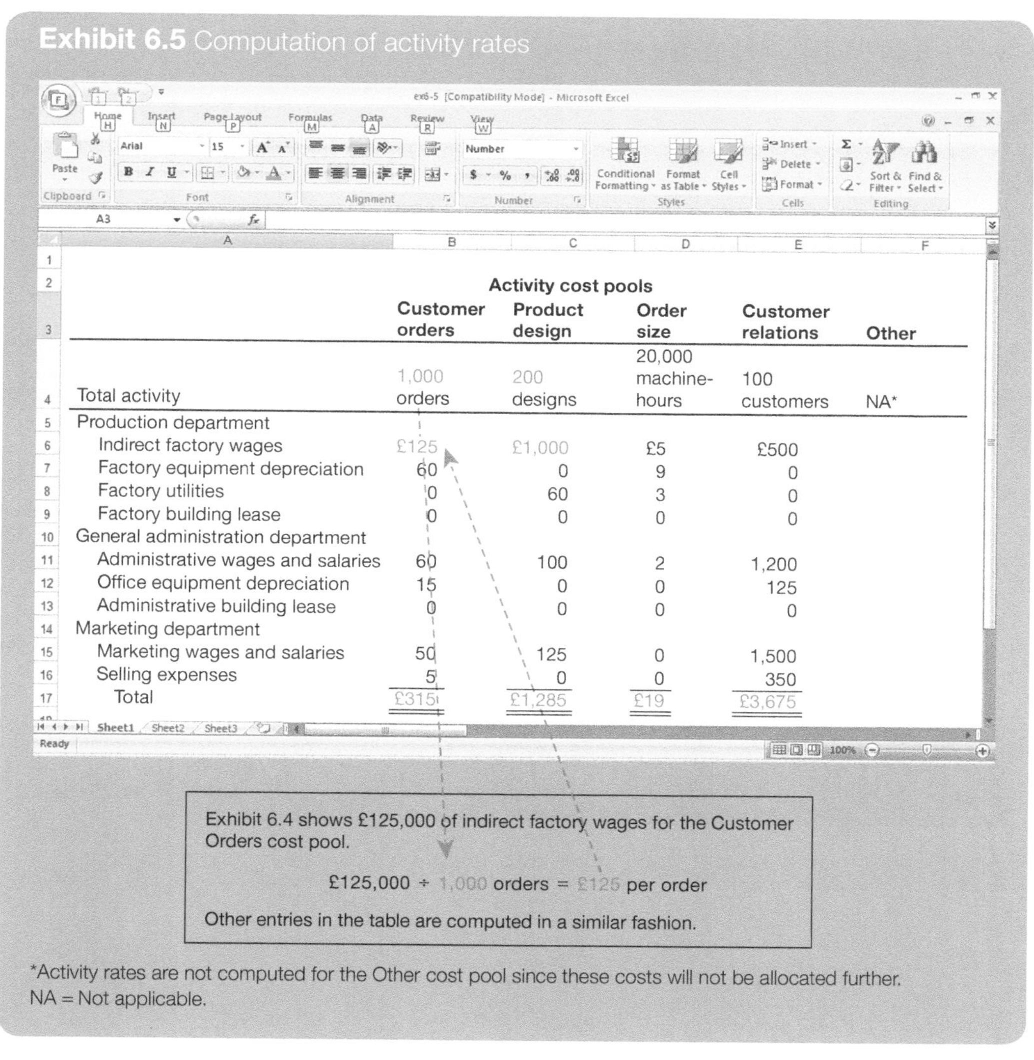

	Activity cost pools				
	Customer orders	Product design	Order size	Customer relations	Other
Total activity	1,000 orders	200 designs	20,000 machine-hours	100 customers	NA*
Production department					
Indirect factory wages	£125	£1,000	£5	£500	
Factory equipment depreciation	60	0	9	0	
Factory utilities	0	60	3	0	
Factory building lease	0	0	0	0	
General administration department					
Administrative wages and salaries	60	100	2	1,200	
Office equipment depreciation	15	0	0	125	
Administrative building lease	0	0	0	0	
Marketing department					
Marketing wages and salaries	50	125	0	1,500	
Selling expenses	5	0	0	350	
Total	£315	£1,285	£19	£3,675	

Exhibit 6.4 shows £125,000 of indirect factory wages for the Customer Orders cost pool.

£125,000 ÷ 1,000 orders = £125 per order

Other entries in the table are computed in a similar fashion.

*Activity rates are not computed for the Other cost pool since these costs will not be allocated further.
NA = Not applicable.

We urge you to study Exhibit 6.5 with care so that you are sure you know how each entry in the table was computed. Take each column in turn and divide each of the cost entries in Exhibit 6.4 under that column by the total activity at the top of the column in Exhibit 6.5. Once you see how the numbers were computed, it is really easy, although there are a lot of computations.

The entries at the bottom of Exhibit 6.5 indicate that on average a customer order consumes resources that cost £315; a product design consumes resources that cost £1,285; a unit of product consumes resources that cost £19 per machine-hour; and maintaining relations with a customer consumes resources that cost £3,675. Note that these are *average* figures. Some members of the ABC design team at Classic Brass argued that it would be unfair to charge all new products the same £1,285 product design cost regardless of how much design time they actually require. After discussing the pros and cons, the team concluded that it would not be worth the effort at the present time to keep track of actual design time spent on each new product. Similarly, some team members were uncomfortable assigning the same £3,675 cost to each customer. Some customers are undemanding – ordering standard products well in advance of their needs. Others are very demanding and consume large amounts of marketing and administrative staff time. These are generally customers who order customized products, who tend to order at the last minute, and who change their minds. While everyone agreed with this observation, the data that would be required to measure individual customers' demands on resources was not currently available. Rather than delay implementation of the ABC system, the team decided to defer such refinements to a later date.

Before proceeding further, it would be helpful to get a better idea of the overall process of assigning costs to products and other cost objects in an ABC system. Exhibit 6.6 provides a visual perspective of the ABC system at Classic Brass. We recommend that you carefully go over this exhibit. In particular, note that the Other category, which contains organization-sustaining costs and costs of idle capacity, is not allocated to products or customers.

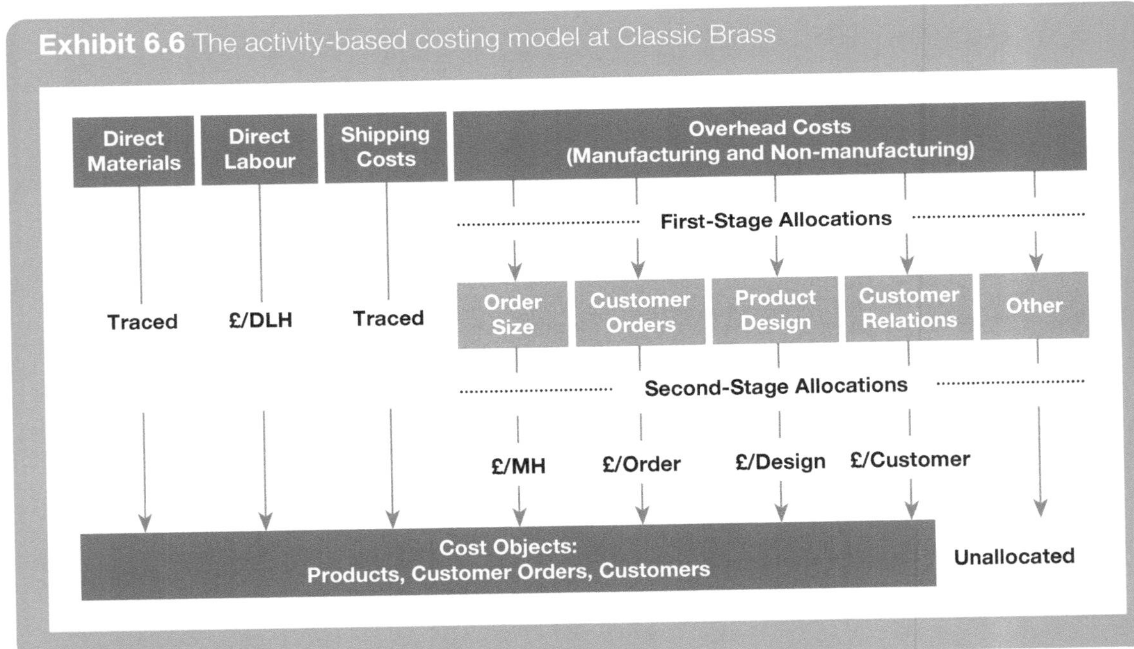
Exhibit 6.6 The activity-based costing model at Classic Brass

Computing margins using ABC

LO 5

The fifth step in the implementation of activity-based costing is called *second-stage allocation*. In **second-stage allocation**, activity rates are used to apply costs to products and customers. At Classic Brass, the ABC system might be used to apply activity costs to all of the company's products, customer orders and customers. For purposes of illustration, we will consider only one customer – Windward Yacht. This customer ordered two different products – stanchions and a compass housing. The stanchions are a standard product that does not require any design work. In contrast, the compass housing is a custom product that required extensive designing. Data concerning these two products appear in Exhibit 6.7.

We can now compute costs and margins for these orders. Note how the customer relations overhead is used for customer profitability analysis but *not* for product costing (Exhibit 6.8).

Comparison of traditional and ABC product costs

Now that the product margins have been computed using activity-based costing, it would be interesting to compare them to the product margins computed using the company's traditional cost system.

Product margins computed using the traditional cost system[6]

The costs of the two products ordered by Windward Yachts are computed under the company's traditional cost accounting system in Exhibit 6.9. The company's traditional system uses a plantwide predetermined overhead rate based on machine-hours. Since the total manufacturing overhead cost is £1,000,000

Exhibit 6.7 Data concerning the products ordered by Windward Yachts

Standard stanchions

1 This is a standard design that does not require any new design resources.
2 Four hundred units were ordered during the year, comprising two separate orders.
3 Each stanchion required 0.5 machine-hours, for a total of 200 machine-hours.
4 The selling price per unit was £34, for a total of £13,600.
5 Direct materials for 400 units totalled £2,110.
6 Direct labour for 400 units totalled £1,850.
7 Shipping costs for the two orders totalled £180.

Custom compass housing

1 This is a custom product that requires new design resources.
2 There was only one order for a single unit during the year.
3 The compass housing required 4 machine-hours.
4 The selling price was £650.
5 Direct materials were £13.
6 Direct labour was £50.
7 Shipping costs were £25.

Exhibit 6.8 Product margins – activity-based costing system (activity view)

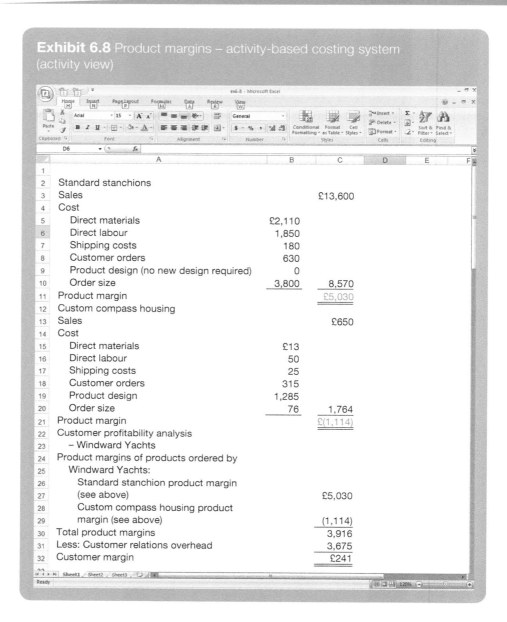

Standard stanchions		
Sales		£13,600
Cost		
Direct materials	£2,110	
Direct labour	1,850	
Shipping costs	180	
Customer orders	630	
Product design (no new design required)	0	
Order size	3,800	8,570
Product margin		£5,030
Custom compass housing		
Sales		£650
Cost		
Direct materials	£13	
Direct labour	50	
Shipping costs	25	
Customer orders	315	
Product design	1,285	
Order size	76	1,764
Product margin		£(1,114)
Customer profitability analysis – Windward Yachts		
Product margins of products ordered by Windward Yachts:		
Standard stanchion product margin (see above)		£5,030
Custom compass housing product margin (see above)		(1,114)
Total product margins		3,916
Less: Customer relations overhead		3,675
Customer margin		£241

(see Exhibit 6.2) and the total machine time is 20,000 machine-hours (see Exhibit 6.5), the predetermined manufacturing overhead rate for the company is £50 per machine-hour (£1,000,000/20,000 machine-hours = £50 per machine-hour). We see that when this predetermined manufacturing overhead rate is used to determine product costs, the stanchions show a loss of £360, whereas the compass housing shows a profit of £387.

The differences between ABC and traditional product costs

The costs of the products under the new ABC system are dramatically different from the costs computed using the old traditional costing system. The stanchions, which looked unprofitable under the traditional cost system, appear to be very profitable under the ABC system in Exhibit 6.9. And the compass housing, which looked profitable under the old cost system, appears to be unprofitable under the new costing system.

Exhibit 6.9 Product margins – traditional cost accounting system

Standard stanchions		
Margin computed using the company's old cost accounting system:		
Sales (400 units × £34)		£13,600
Cost:		
Direct materials	£2,110	
Direct labour	1,850	
Manufacturing overhead (400 units × 0.5 machine-hours per unit × £50 per machine-hour*)	10,000	13,960
Product margin		£(360)
Custom compass housing		
Margin computed using the company's old cost accounting system:		
Sales (1 unit × £650)		£650
Cost:		
Direct materials	13	
Direct labour	50	
Manufacturing overhead (1 unit × 4.0 machine-hours per unit × £50 per machine-hour)	200	263
Product margin		£387

*Predetermined manufacturing overhead rate:

$$\frac{\text{Total manufacturing overhead, £1,000,000}}{\text{Total machine-hours, 20,000}} = \text{£50 per machine-hour}$$

There are two major reasons for these changes in apparent profitability. First, under the old cost system the costs of designing products were spread across all products without regard to whether they actually required design work. Under the new ABC system, these costs are assigned only to products that actually require design work. Consequently, under the ABC system, design costs have been shifted from standard products like stanchions, which do not require any design work, to custom products like the compass housing.

Second, the Customer Orders costs, which are batch-level costs, were applied on the basis of machine-hours, a unit-level base, under the old cost system. Therefore, under the old cost system, high-volume products absorbed the bulk of these batch-level costs even though they caused no more of these costs than low-volume products that are ordered as frequently. Under the new cost system, these batch-level costs are assigned as a lump-sum to each customer order. Consequently, the new cost system shifts these costs from high-volume orders like the stanchions to low-volume orders like the compass housing.

When there are batch-level or product-level costs, activity-based costing will ordinarily shift costs from high-volume products produced in large batches to low-volume products produced in small batches. This cost shifting will usually have a greater impact on the *per unit* costs of low-volume products than on the per unit costs of high-volume products. For example, suppose that a total of £100 in batch-level cost is shifted from a high-volume, 100-unit product to a low-volume, 1-unit product. This shifting of cost will decrease the cost of the high-volume product by £1 per unit, on average, but will increase the cost of the low-volume product by £100 for the single unit. In sum, implementing activity-based costing will typically shift costs from high-volume to low-volume products, but the effects will be much more dramatic on the per unit costs of the low-volume products. The per unit costs of the low-volume products will increase far more than the per unit costs of the high-volume products will decrease.

It is important to remember another major difference between the costs of products as computed under the new ABC system at Classic Brass and product costs as computed under the old traditional cost system. Under a traditional system, only manufacturing costs are assigned to products. Under the new ABC system at Classic Brass, non-manufacturing costs are assigned to products as well as the manufacturing costs. In addition, the organization-sustaining manufacturing costs and the costs of idle capacity are *not* assigned to products under the ABC system, whereas they are assigned to products under the old traditional costing system. For these reasons, the term 'product cost' in this chapter has a different meaning than it had in Chapter 5. In the context of an ABC system like the one implemented at Classic Brass, product costs include the costs of *all* resources consumed by the product, whether they are manufacturing costs or not. Finally, as the examples below point out, ABC has been implemented in service industries as well as manufacturing.

Focus on Business Practice

Activity-based costing in healthcare

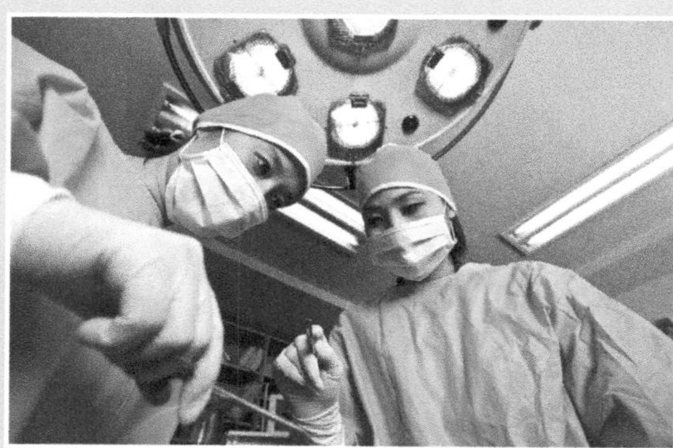
© btrenkel

A study by Yen-Ju Lin et al. (2007) reports on the use of activity-based costing (ABC) at the colorectal department at a not-for-profit teaching hospital in Taiwan. The first step in the study (which examined 183 patients) was to identify relevant activities, which was achieved by using existing clinical guidelines and care paths for the surgical procedures undertaken in the department. Activities were classified broadly in five groups, as follows: pre-surgical procedures in wards, surgical procedures in operational rooms, recovery in post-operational rooms, nursing and care in wards, and discharge planning. These five activities were further subdivided into primary activities (face-to-face care), secondary activities (such as records, charting and medication preparation related to patients) and support activities. The costs calculated on the basis of these activities were compared to the funds granted to the department from a national health insurance body. The results showed that some procedures were running at a loss (i.e. funds recouped were less than the procedure cost). The authors proposed these more accurate costs, based on ABC, could be used in two ways, (1) to negotiate better funds from the health insurance providers or governments, and (2) to seek ways to streamline activities/processes to deliver the required care within funding limits.[7]

Exercise: Why do you think ABC may be more suited to costing surgical procedures than traditional approaches?

Focus on Business Practice

Activity-based costing in a clearing bank

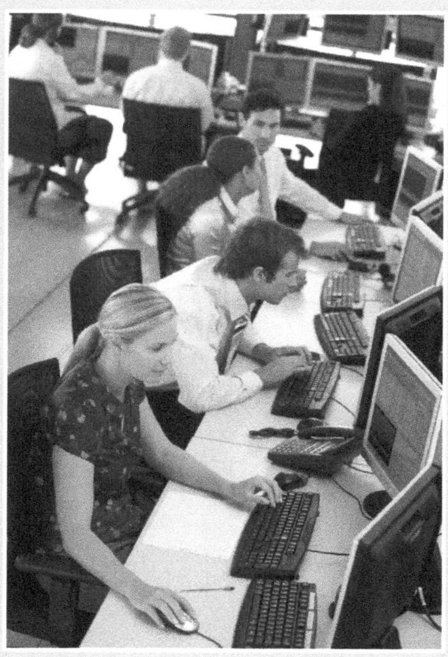
© Catherine Yeulet

Before ABC, Trafalgar Bank, a large UK-based multinational., had *some* basic cost controls based on cost centre budgets with the full allocation of overheads, and measures of performance that included sales volumes and maintaining costs at budgeted levels. ABC is well suited to the financial service sector as many service costs are process rather than volume-related. ABC can be used to analyse the profitability of customers and the new financial products. ABC may also have further applications in areas like budgeting, forecasting and performance measurement in overhead departments. The ABC system used data gathered by detailed observation and interviews that, in the first year at least, were carried out by the ABC team themselves in each of the cost centres. Flow charts were constructed to illustrate visually the processes of each area of the clearing process. Headcount driver analyses were carried out and an activity analysis schedule was created for each section describing activities, details of the cost driver(s) and the allocation base. Although some of the simpler cost-cutting exercises could have been achieved other process improvement technologies, the ABC information provided a new costing sophistication and opportunities for cost management.[8]

Exercise: Why, before ABC, did many banks not develop product costing systems similar to those widely found in manufacturing?

Summary

- Traditional cost accounting methods suffer from several defects that can result in distorted costs for decision-making purposes. All manufacturing costs – even those that are not caused by any specific product – are allocated to products. And non-manufacturing costs that are caused by products are not assigned to products. Traditional methods also allocate the costs of idle capacity to products. In effect, products are charged for resources that they do not use. And finally, traditional methods tend to place too much reliance on unit-level allocation bases such as direct labour and machine-hours. This results in over-costing high-volume products and under-costing low-volume products and can lead to mistakes when making decisions.

- Activity-based costing estimates the costs of the resources consumed by cost objects such as products and customers. The approach taken in activity-based costing assumes that cost objects generate activities that in turn consume costly resources. Activities form the link between costs and cost objects. Activity-based costing is concerned with overhead – both manufacturing overhead and selling, general and administrative overhead. The accounting for direct labour and direct material is usually unaffected.
- To build an ABC system, companies typically choose a small set of activities that summarize much of the work performed in overhead departments. Associated with each activity is an activity cost pool. To the extent possible, overhead costs are directly traced to these activity cost pools. The remaining overhead costs are assigned to the activity cost pools in the first-stage allocation. Interviews with managers often form the basis for these allocations.

Key terms

Activity An event that causes the consumption of overhead resources in an organization (p. 123).

Activity-based costing (ABC) A costing method based on activities that is designed to provide managers with cost information for strategic and other decisions that potentially affect capacity and therefore fixed costs (p. 122).

Activity cost pool A 'bucket' in which costs are accumulated that relate to a single activity in the activity-based costing system (p. 126).

Activity measure An allocation base in an activity-based costing system; ideally, a measure of the amount of activity that drives the costs in an activity cost pool (p. 127).

Batch-level activities Activities that are performed each time a batch of goods is handled or processed, regardless of how many units are in a batch. The amount of resource consumed depends on the number of batches run rather than on the number of units in the batch (p. 126).

Customer-level activities Activities that are carried out to support customers but that are not related to any specific product (p. 126).

First-stage allocation The process by which overhead costs are assigned to activity cost pools in an activity-based costing system (p. 128).

Organization-sustaining activities Activities that are carried out regardless of which customers are served, which products are produced, how many batches are run, or how many units are made (p. 126).

Product-level activities Activities that relate to specific products that must be carried out regardless of how many units are produced and sold or batches run (p. 126).

Second-stage allocation The process by which activity rates are used to apply costs to products and customers in activity-based costing (p. 133).

Unit-level activities Activities that arise as a result of the total volume of goods and services that are produced, and that are performed each time a unit is produced (p. 126).

Endnotes

1 Greco (1996).

2 Böer (1994) provides some data concerning these trends. Data maintained by the US Department of Commerce shows that since 1849, on average, material cost as a percentage of manufacturing cost has been fairly constant at 55 per cent of sales. Labour cost has always been relatively less important and has declined steadily from 23 per cent in 1849 to about 10 per cent in 1987. Overhead has grown from about 18 per cent of sales in 1947 to about 33 per cent of sales 50 years later.

3 Brignall, Fitzgerald, Johnston and Silvestro (1991).

4 See Cooper and Kaplan (1988).

5 Kaplan and Anderson (2004).

6 Note this is the same example as in Chapter 5.

7 Yen-Ju Lin et al. (2007).

8 Soin, Seal and Cullen (2002).

connect™

When you have read this chapter, log on to the Online Learning Centre for *Management Accounting for Business Decisions* at **www.mheducation.co.uk/textbooks/sealmabd1**, where you'll find multiple choice questions, practice exams and extra study tools for management accounting.

Assessment

Questions

connect™

6–1 In what fundamental ways does activity-based costing differ from traditional costing methods such as those described in Chapters 2 and 5?

6–2 Why is direct labour a poor base for allocating overhead in many companies?

6-3 Why are overhead rates in activity-based costing based on the level of activity at capacity rather than on the budgeted level of activity?

6–4 Why is top management support crucial when attempting to implement an activity-based costing system?

6–5 What are unit-level, batch-level, product-level, customer-level and organization-sustaining activities?

6–6 What types of costs should not be assigned to products in an activity-based costing system?

6–7 Why are there two stages of allocation in activity-based costing?

6–8 Why is the first stage of the allocation process in activity-based costing often based on interviews?

6–9 How can the activity rates (i.e., cost per activity) for the various activities be used to target process improvements?

6–10 When activity-based costing is used, why are manufacturing overhead costs often shifted from high-volume products to low-volume products?

Exercises

connect™

E6–1 Time allowed: 10 minutes

CD Express Ltd provides CD duplicating services to software companies. The customer provides a master CD from which CD Express makes copies. An order from a customer can be for a single copy or for thousands of copies. Most jobs are broken down into batches to allow smaller jobs, with higher priorities, to have access to the machines.

Below are listed a number of activities carried out at CD Express.

(a) Sales representatives' periodic visits to customers to keep them informed about the services provided by CD Express
(b) Ordering labels from the printer for a particular CD
(c) Setting up the CD duplicating machine to make copies from a particular master CD
(d) Loading the automatic labelling machine with labels for a particular CD
(e) Visually inspecting CDs and placing them by hand into protective plastic cases prior to shipping
(f) Preparation of the shipping documents for the order
(g) Periodic maintenance of equipment
(h) Lighting and heating the company's production facility
(i) Preparation of quarterly financial reports.

Required

Classify each of the activities above as either a unit-level, batch-level, product-level, customer-level, or organization-sustaining activity. (An order to duplicate a particular CD is a product-level activity.) Assume the order is large enough that it must be broken down into batches.

E6–2 Time allowed: 10 minutes

Listed below are a number of activities that you have observed at Ming Company, a manufacturing company. Each activity has been classified as a unit-level, batch-level, product-level, or customer-level activity.

Activity	Level of activity	Examples of activity measures
(a) Direct labour workers assemble a product	Unit	
(b) Products are designed by engineers	Product	
(c) Equipment is set up	Batch	
(d) Machines are used to shape and cut materials	Unit	
(e) Monthly bills are sent out to regular customers	Customer	
(f) Materials are moved from the receiving dock to production lines	Batch	
(g) All completed units are inspected for defects	Unit	

Required

Complete the table by providing examples of activity measures for each activity that could be used to allocate its costs to products or customers.

E6–3 Time allowed: 15 minutes

Listed below are a number of activities that you have observed at Vapo Ingman Oy, a Finnish manufacturing company. The company makes a variety of products at its plant outside Helsinki.

(a) Machine settings are changed between batches of different products
(b) Parts inventories are maintained in the storeroom (each product requires unique parts)
(c) Products are milled on a milling machine
(d) New employees are hired by the personnel office
(e) New products are designed
(f) Periodic maintenance is performed on general-purpose production equipment
(g) A bill is sent to a customer who is late in making payments
(h) Yearly taxes are paid on the company's facilities
(i) Purchase orders are issued for materials to be used in production.

Required

1 Classify each of the activities above as either a unit-level, batch-level, product-level, customer-level, or organization-sustaining activity.
2 Where possible, for each activity name one or more activity measures that might be used to assign costs generated by the activity to products or customers.

E6–4 Time allowed: 10 minutes

The operations manager of Security Home Bank has been interested in investigating the efficiency of the bank's operations. She has been particularly concerned about the costs of handling routine transactions at the bank and would like to compare these costs at the bank's various branches. If the branches with the most efficient operations can be identified, their methods can be studied and then replicated elsewhere. While the bank maintains meticulous records of wages and other costs, there has been no attempt thus far to show how those costs are related to the various services provided by the bank. The operations manager has asked for your help in conducting an activity-based costing study of bank operations. In particular, she would like to know the cost of opening an account, the cost of processing deposits and withdrawals, and the cost of processing other customer transactions.

The Westfield branch of Security Home Bank has submitted the following cost data for last year:

Teller wages	£160,000
Assistant branch manager salary	75,000
Branch manager salary	80,000
Total	£315,000

Virtually all of the other costs of the branch – rent, depreciation, utilities and so on – are organization-sustaining costs that cannot be meaningfully assigned to individual customer transactions such as depositing cheques.

In addition to the cost data above, the employees of the Westfield branch have been interviewed concerning how their time was distributed last year across the activities included in the activity-based costing study. The results of those interviews appear below:

Distribution of resource consumption across activities (percentages)

	Opening accounts	**Processing deposits and withdrawals**	**Processing other customer transactions**	**Other activities**	**Total**
Teller wages	5	65	20	10	100
Assistant branch manager salary	15	5	30	50	100
Branch manager salary	5	0	10	85	100

Required

Prepare the first-stage allocation for the activity-based costing study. (See Exhibit 6.4 for an example of a first-stage allocation.)

E6–5 Time allowed: 20 minutes

(This exercise is a continuation of E6–4; it should be assigned only if E6–4 is also assigned.) The manager of the Westfield branch of Security Home Bank has provided the following data concerning the transactions of the branch during the past year:

Activity	**Total activity at the Westfield Branch**
Opening accounts	500 new accounts opened
Processing deposits and withdrawals	100,000 deposits and withdrawals processed
Processing other customer transactions	5,000 other customer transactions processed

The lowest costs reported by other branches for these activities are displayed below:

Activity	**Lowest cost among all Security Home Bank Branches**
Opening accounts	£26.75 per new account
Processing deposits and withdrawals	£1.24 per deposit or withdrawal
Processing other customer transactions	£11.86 per other customer transaction

Required

1 Using the first-stage allocation from E6–4 and the above data, compute the activity rates for the activity-based costing system. (Use Exhibit 6.5 as a guide.) Round all computations to the nearest whole pence.

2 What do these results suggest to you concerning operations at the Westfield branch?

P6–6 Activity rates and pricing jobs

Problems

Time allowed: 45 minutes

Mercer Asbestos Removal Company is in the business of removing potentially toxic asbestos insulation and related products from buildings. There has been a long-simmering dispute between the company's estimator and the work supervisors. The onsite supervisors claim that the estimators do not take enough care in distinguishing between routine work such as removal of asbestos insulation around heating pipes in older homes and non-routine work such as removing asbestos-contaminated ceiling plaster in industrial buildings. The on-site supervisors believe that non-routine work is far more expensive than routine work and should bear higher customer charges. The estimator sums up his position in this way: 'My job is to measure the area to be cleared of asbestos. As directed by top management, I simply multiply the square meterage by £2.50 to determine the bid price. Since our average cost is only £2.175 per square metre, that leaves enough cushion to take care of the additional costs of non-routine work that shows up. Besides, it is difficult to know what is routine or not routine until you actually start tearing things apart.'

Partly to shed light on this controversy, the company initiated an activity-based costing study of all of its costs. Data from the activity-based costing system follow:

Activity cost pool	Activity measure
Job size	Thousands of square metres
Estimating and job set-up	Number of jobs
Dealing with non-routine jobs	Number of non-routine jobs
Other (costs of idle capacity and organization-sustaining costs)	Not applicable; these costs are not allocated to jobs

	Costs for the year
Wages and salaries	£300,000
Disposal fees	700,000
Equipment depreciation	90,000
On-site supplies	50,000
Office expenses	200,000
Licensing and insurance	400,000
Total cost	£1,740,000

Distribution of resource consumption across activities (percentages)

	Job size	Estimating and job set-up	Dealing with non-routine jobs	Other	Total
Wages and salaries	50	10	30	10	100
Disposal fees	60	0	40	0	100
Equipment depreciation	40	5	20	35	100
On-site supplies	60	30	10	0	100
Office expenses	10	35	25	30	100
Licensing and insurance	30	0	50	20	100

Activity cost pool	Activity for the year
Job size	800 thousand square metres
Estimating and job set-up	500 jobs
Dealing with non-routine jobs	100 non-routine jobs

Note: The 100 non-routine jobs are included in the total of 500 jobs. Both non-routine jobs and routine jobs require estimating and set-up.

Required

1. Perform the first-stage allocation of costs to the activity cost pools. (Use Exhibit 6.4 as a guide.)
2. Compute the activity rates for the activity cost pools. (Use Exhibit 6.5 as a guide.)
3. Using the activity rates you have computed, determine the total cost and the average cost per thousand square metres of each of the following jobs according to the activity-based costing system.
   (a) A routine 1,000 square metre asbestos removal job.
   (b) A routine 2,000 square metre asbestos removal job.
   (c) A non-routine 2,000 square metre asbestos removal job.

4 Given the results you obtained in Question 3 above, do you agree with the estimator that the company's present policy for bidding on jobs is adequate?

P6–7 Activity rates and activity-based management

Time allowed: 30 minutes

Aerotraiteur SA is a French company that provides passenger and crew meals to airlines operating out of the two international airports of Paris – Orly and Charles de Gaulle (CDG). The operations at Orly and CDG are managed separately, and top management believes that there may be benefits in greater sharing of information between the two operations.

To better compare the two operations, an activity-based costing system has been designed with the active participation of the managers at both Orly and CDG. The activity-based costing system is based on the following activity cost pools and activity measures:

Activity cost pool	Activity measure
Meal preparation	Number of meals
Flight-related activities	Number of flights
Customer service	Number of customers
Other (costs of idle capacity and organization-sustaining costs)	Not applicable

The operation at CDG airport serves 1.5 million meals annually on 7,500 flights for ten different airlines. (Each airline is considered one customer.) The annual cost of running the CDG airport operation, excluding only the costs of raw materials for meals, totals €29,400,000.

Annual cost of the CDG operation	
Cooks and delivery personnel wages	€24,000,000
Kitchen supplies	300,000
Chef salaries	1,800,000
Equipment depreciation	600,000
Administrative wages and salaries	1,500,000
Building costs	1,200,000
Total cost	€29,400,000

The results of employee interviews at CDG are displayed below:

Distribution of resource consumption across activities at the CDG operation (percentages)

	Meal preparation	Flight related	Customer service	Other	Total
Cooks and delivery personnel wages	75	20	0	5	100
Kitchen supplies	100	0	0	0	100
Chef salaries	30	20	40	10	100
Equipment depreciation	60	0	0	40	100
Administrative wages and salaries	0	20	60	20	100
Building costs	0	0	0	100	100

Required

1 Perform the first-stage allocation of costs to the activity cost pools. (Use Exhibit 6.4 as a guide.)
2 Compute the activity rates for the activity cost pools. (Use Exhibit 6.5 as a guide.)
3 The Orly operation has already concluded its activity-based costing study and has reported the following costs of carrying out activities at Orly:

	Meal preparation	Flight related	Customer service
Cooks and delivery personnel wages	€12.20	€780	
Kitchen supplies	0.25		
Chef salaries	0.18	32	€54,000
Equipment depreciation	0.23		
Administrative wages and salaries		45	67,000
Building costs	0.00	0	0
Total cost	€12.86	€857	€121,000

Comparing the activity rates for the CDG operation you computed in (2) above to the activity rates for Orly, do you have any suggestions for the top management of Aerotraiteur SA?

P6–8 Job and service costing

Time allowed: 35 minutes

A company has been carrying out work on a number of building contracts (including Contract ABC) over the six month period ended 31 May 2010. The following information is available:

	All contracts (including ABC)	Contract ABC
Number of contracts worked on in the six months to 31.5.10	10	–
Value	£76.2m	£6.4m
Duration (average 13 months)	8–22 months	11 months
Contract months	53*	6
Direct labour costs in the period	£9.762m	£1.017m
Raw material costs in the period	£10.817m	£1.456m
Distance from base (average)	16 kilometres	23 kilometres
Value of work certified at 31.5.10	–	£5.180m

*Contract months for 'All Contracts' are the sum contract during the six month period.

Contract ABC commenced on 1 September 2009. As at 30 November 2009 cumulative costs on the contract, held in work-in-progress, totalled £1.063m (including overheads).

The company confidently predicts that further costs after 31 May 2010 to complete Contract ABC on time (including overheads) will not exceed £0.937m.

Overheads incurred over the six month period to 31 May 2010, which are to be apportioned to individual contracts, are:

	£m
Stores operations	1.56
Contract general management	1.22
Transport	1.37
General administration	4.25
The bases of apportionment are:	
Stores operations	– contract value × contract months
Contract general management	– direct labour costs
Transport	– distance from base × contract months
General administration	– contract months

Required

1 (a) Apportion overheads to Contract ABC for the six month period to 31 May 2010 (to the nearest £000 for each overhead item).

(6 marks)

(b) Determine the expected profit/loss on Contract ABC, and the amount of profit/loss on the contract that you recommend be included in the accounts of the company for the six month period to 31 May 2010.

(7 marks)

2 The company is introducing a service costing system into its stores operations department.

3 Outline the key factors to consider when introducing the service costing system.

(7 marks)

(Total = 20 marks)

ACCA (adapted)

Chapter 7
Pricing, target costing and transfer pricing

LO Learning **objectives**

After studying Chapter 7, you should be able to:

1 Compute the profit-maximizing price using the price elasticity of demand and variable cost
2 Understand the basics of revenue management in capacity constrained businesses
3 Compute the selling price of a product using the absorption costing approach
4 Compute the mark-up percentage under the absorption costing approach
5 Compute the target cost for a new product or service
6 Understand the basics of transfer pricing

Concepts **in Context**

Airlines and hotels are industries with very high fixed costs and 'perishable products'. Since an unfilled seat or empty bedroom is a lost contribution, these industries make use of revenue-maximizing models whereby the price of an airline ticket or a room is altered according to the time of booking relative to departure time or hotel stay. These sectors have learnt the importance of altering prices in order to operate at much higher capacities than they would if prices remained fixed.[1]

© Sieto Verver

Some businesses have no pricing calculation problems. They make a product that is in competition with other, identical products for which a market price already exists. Customers will not pay more than this price, and there is no reason for any company to charge less. Under these circumstances, the company simply charges the prevailing market price. Markets for basic raw materials such as farm products and minerals follow this pattern.

In this chapter, we are concerned with the more common situation in which a company is faced with the problem of setting its own prices. Clearly, the pricing decision can be critical. If the price is set too high, customers will avoid purchasing the company's products. If the price is set too low, the company's costs may not be covered.

The usual approach in pricing is to *mark up* cost. A product's **mark-up** is the difference between its selling price and its cost. The mark-up is usually expressed as a percentage of cost. This approach is called **cost-plus pricing** because the predetermined mark-up percentage is applied to the cost base to determine a target selling price.

$$\text{Selling price} = \text{Cost} + (\text{Mark-up percentage} \times \text{Cost})$$

For example, if a company uses a mark-up of 50%, it adds 50% to the costs of its products to determine the selling price. If a product costs £10, then it would charge £15 for the product.

There are two key issues when the cost-plus approach to pricing is used. First, what cost should be used? Second, how should the mark-up be determined? Several alternative approaches are considered in this chapter, starting with the approach generally favoured by economists.

LO 1 The economists' approach to pricing

If a company raises the price of a product, unit sales ordinarily fall. Because of this, pricing is a delicate balancing act in which the benefits of higher revenues per unit are traded off against the lower volume that results from charging higher prices. The sensitivity of unit sales to changes in price is called the *price elasticity of demand.*

Elasticity of demand

A product's price elasticity should be a key element in setting its price. The **price elasticity of demand** measures the degree to which the volume of unit sales for a product or service is affected by a change in price. Demand for a product is said to be *inelastic* if a change in price has little effect on the number of units sold. The demand for designer perfumes sold by trained personnel at cosmetic counters in department stores is relatively inelastic. Lowering prices on these luxury goods has little effect on sales volume; factors other than price are more important in generating sales. On the other hand, demand for a product is said to be *elastic* if a change in price has a substantial effect on the volume of units sold. An example of a product whose demand is elastic is petrol. If a petrol station raises its price for petrol, there will usually be a substantial drop in volume as customers seek lower prices elsewhere.

Price elasticity is very important in determining prices. Managers should set higher mark-ups over cost when customers are relatively insensitive to price (i.e., demand is inelastic) and lower mark-ups when customers are relatively sensitive to price (i.e., demand is elastic). This principle is followed in department stores. Merchandise sold in the bargain basement has a much lower mark-up than merchandise sold elsewhere in the store because customers who shop in the bargain basement are much more sensitive to price (i.e. demand is elastic).

The price elasticity of demand for a product or service, ε_d, can be estimated using the following formula.[2]

$$\varepsilon_d = \frac{\ln(1 + \%\text{ change in quantity sold})}{\ln(1 + \%\text{ change in price})}$$

For example, suppose that the managers of Nature's Garden believe that every 10% increase in the selling price of their apple-almond shampoo would result in a 15% decrease in the number of bottles of shampoo sold.[3] The price elasticity of demand for this product would be computed as follows:

$$\varepsilon_d = \frac{\ln\,(1 + (-0.15))}{\ln\,(1 + (0.10))} = \frac{\ln\,(0.85)}{\ln\,(1.10)} = -1.71$$

For comparison purposes, the managers of Nature's Garden believe that another product, strawberry glycerine soap, would experience a 20% drop in unit sales if its price were increased by 10%. (Purchasers of this product are more sensitive to price than the purchasers of the apple-almond shampoo.) The price elasticity of demand for the strawberry glycerine soap is:

$$\varepsilon_d = \frac{\ln\,(1 + (-0.20))}{\ln\,(1 + (0.10))} = \frac{\ln\,(0.80)}{\ln\,(1.10)} = -2.34$$

Both of these products, like other products, have a price elasticity that is less than −1. Note also that the price elasticity of demand for the strawberry glycerine soap is larger (in absolute value) than the price elasticity of demand for the apple-almond shampoo. The more sensitive customers are to price, the larger (in absolute value) is the price elasticity of demand. In other words, a larger (in absolute value) price elasticity of demand indicates a product whose demand is more elastic.

In the next subsection, the price elasticity of demand will be used to compute the selling price that maximizes the profits of the company.

The profit-maximizing price

Under certain conditions, it can be shown that the *profit-maximizing price* can be determined by marking up *variable cost* using the following formula:[4]

$$\text{Profit-maximizing mark-up on variable cost} = \left(\frac{\varepsilon_d}{1 + \varepsilon_d}\right) - 1 \text{ Variable cost per unit}$$

Using the above mark-up is equivalent to setting the selling price using this formula:

$$\text{Profit-maximizing mark-up on variable cost} = \left(\frac{\varepsilon_d}{1 + \varepsilon_d}\right) \text{ Variable cost per unit}$$

The profit-maximizing prices for the two Nature's Garden products are computed below using these formulas:

	Apple-almond Shampoo	Strawberry glycerine soap
Price elasticity of demand (ε_d)	−1.71	−2.34
Profit-maximizing mark-up on variable cost (a)	$\left(\frac{-1.71}{-1.71+1}\right)-1$	$\left(\frac{-2.34}{-2.34+1}\right)-1$
	= 2.41 − 1 = 1.41	= 1.75 − 1 = 0.75
	or 141%	or 75%
Variable cost per unit – given (b)	£2.00	£0.40
Mark-up, (a) × (b)	2.82	0.30
Profit-maximizing price	£4.82	£0.70

Note that the 75% mark-up for the strawberry glycerine soap is lower than the 141% mark-up for the apple-almond shampoo. The reason for this is that purchasers of strawberry glycerine soap are more sensitive to price than the purchasers of apple-almond shampoo. This could be because strawberry glycerine soap is a relatively common product with close substitutes available in nearly every grocery store.

Exhibit 7.1 shows how the profit-maximizing mark-up is affected by how sensitive unit sales are to price. For example, if a 10% increase in price leads to a 20% decrease in unit sales, then the optimal mark-up on variable cost according to the exhibit is 75% – the figure computed above for the strawberry glycerine soap. Note that the optimal mark-up drops as unit sales become more sensitive to price.

Exhibit 7.1 The optimal mark-up on variable cost as a function of the sensitivity of unit sales to price

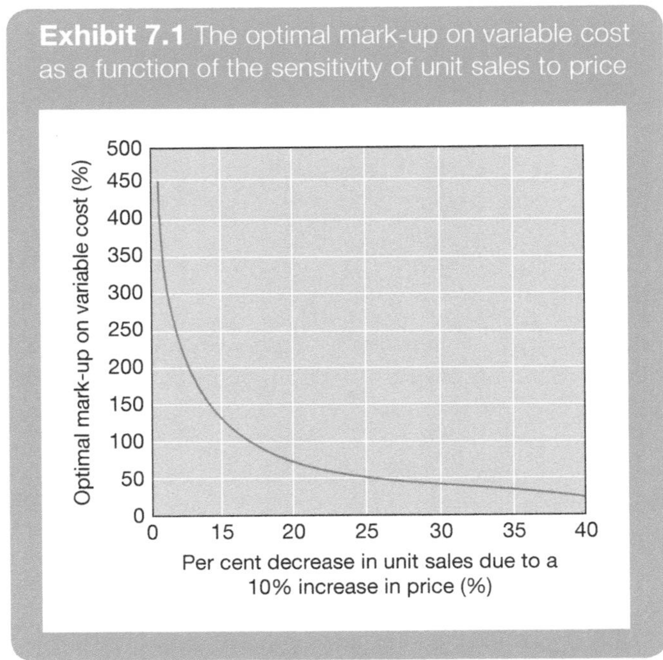

Caution is advised when using these formulas to establish a selling price. The assumptions underlying the formulas are probably not completely true, and the estimate of the percentage change in unit sales that would result from a given percentage change in price is likely to be inexact. Nevertheless, the formulas can provide valuable clues regarding whether prices should be increased or decreased. Suppose, for example, that the strawberry glycerine soap is currently being sold for £0.60 per bar. The formula indicates that the profit-maximizing price is £0.70 per bar. Rather than increasing the price by £0.10, it would be prudent to increase the price by a more modest amount to observe what happens to unit sales and to profits.

The formula for the profit-maximizing price also conveys a very important lesson. The optimal selling price should depend on two factors – the variable cost per unit and how sensitive unit sales are to changes in price. In particular, fixed costs play no role in setting the optimal price. If the total fixed costs are the same whether the company charges £0.60 or £0.70, they cannot be relevant in the decision of which price to charge for the soap. Fixed costs are relevant when deciding whether to offer a product but are not relevant when deciding how much to charge for the product.

Incidentally, we can directly verify that an increase in selling price for the strawberry glycerine soap from the current price of £0.60 per bar is warranted, based just on the forecast that a 10% increase in selling price would lead to a 20% decrease in unit sales. Suppose, for example, that Nature's Garden is currently selling 200,000 bars of the soap per year at the price of £0.60 a bar. If the change in price has no effect on the company's fixed costs or on other products, the effect on profits of increasing the price by 10% can be computed as follows:

	Present price	Higher price
Selling price	£0.60	£0.60 + (0.10 × £0.60) = £0.66
Unit sales	200,000	200,000 – (0.20 × 200,000) = 160,000
Sales	£120,000	£105,600
Variable cost	80,000	64,000
Contribution margin	£40,000	£41,600

Despite the apparent optimality of prices based on marking up variable costs according to the price elasticity of demand, surveys consistently reveal that most managers approach the pricing problem from a completely different perspective. They prefer to mark up some version of full, not variable, costs, and the mark-up is based on desired profits rather than on factors related to demand.

Revenue and yield management

LO 2

Some industries such as hotels and airlines are characterized by high fixed costs and perishability. The capacity of a plane or a hotel is fixed in the short run. Furthermore, an empty bedroom at night or an empty seat in a plane that has taken off represent a sale that is lost forever. Ideally, hotel managers would like to sell all rooms at the highest (rack) rate but they know that a trade-off develops between high occupancy and high room rates. The problem becomes one of determining how much to sell, at what price and to which market segment, so as to maximize revenue. The resolution lies in control over rates (being price restrictive if demand is high and more flexible if it is low) and restrictions to occupancy (blocking of rooms in advance) in order to maximize overall Gross revenue per period of time. These are the principles behind the technique of *yield management*. **Yield management (YM)** is the practice of achieving high capacity utilization through varying prices according to market segments and time of booking.[5]

To use YM, a hotel must know its market segments and why guests need to stay and develop appropriate marketing strategies for each market segment. To ensure the optimization of the total revenues from the room stock of a group of hotels, for example, and to allow access to its demand history, a centralized reservations system is needed. There should be some return from linking YM systems to marketing expenditure plans. For example, predicted periods of low demand from YM team meetings can trigger the need to advertise short-break packages. The overall effectiveness of a YM system is dependent upon the implementation of the following market-focused principles: identification of a customer base using a detailed segmentation strategy; developing an awareness of customers' changing needs and expectations; estimating the price elasticity of demand per market segment; responsiveness of management to cope with changing market conditions; accurate historical demand analysis, combined with a reliable forecasting method. The key performance metric in this model is the *yield percentage*:

$$\text{Yield percentage} = \frac{\text{Actual revenue}}{\text{Maximum potential revenue}}$$

The **yield percentage** will depend on the average price multiplied by the number of units sold (hotel rooms, airline seats). The maximum potential revenue is a full hotel or plane charging the maximum price.[6] With a dynamic pricing strategy, the nearer to the time that the customer who books a flight or a room actually wants to fly or stay, the higher the price. Although it may seem that the price is rising, in actuality, it is rather that the number of lower rates are restricted in advance and later bookers have only the higher priced seats or rooms left.

The absorption costing approach to cost-plus pricing

LO 3

The absorption costing approach to cost-plus pricing differs from the economists' approach both in what costs are marked up and in how the mark-up is determined. Under the absorption approach to cost-plus pricing, the cost base is the absorption costing unit product cost as defined in Chapter 5 rather than variable cost.

Setting a target selling price using the absorption costing approach

To illustrate, let us assume that the management of Ritter Company wants to set the selling price on a product that has just undergone some design modifications. The Accounting Department has provided cost estimates for the redesigned product as shown below:

	Per unit	Total
Direct materials	£6	
Direct labour	4	
Variable manufacturing overhead	3	
Fixed manufacturing overhead	–	£70,000
Variable selling, general and administrative expenses	2	
Fixed selling, general and administrative expenses	–	60,000

The first step in the absorption costing approach to cost-plus pricing is to compute the unit product cost. For Ritter Company, this amounts to £20 per unit at a volume of 10,000 units, as computed below:

Direct materials	£6
Direct labour	4
Variable manufacturing overhead	3
Fixed manufacturing overhead (£70,000 ÷10,000 units)	7
Unit product cost	£20

Ritter Company has a general policy of marking up unit product costs by 50%. A price quotation sheet for the company prepared using the absorption approach is presented in Exhibit 7.2. Note that selling, general and administrative (SG&A) costs are not included in the cost base. Instead, the mark-up is supposed to cover these expenses. Let us see how some companies compute these mark-up percentages.

LO 4

Determining the mark-up percentage

How did Ritter Company arrive at its mark-up percentage of 50%? This figure could be a widely used rule of thumb in the industry or just a company tradition that seems to work. The mark-up percentage may also be the result of an explicit computation.

As we have discussed, the mark-up over cost ideally should be largely determined by market conditions. However, a popular approach is to at least start with a mark-up based on cost and desired profit. The reasoning goes like this. The mark-up must be large enough to cover SG&A expenses and provide an adequate return on investment (ROI). Given the forecasted unit sales, the mark-up can be computed as follows:

$$\text{Mark-up percentage on absorption cost} = \frac{(\text{Required ROI} \times \text{Investment}) + \text{SG\&A expenses}}{\text{Unit sales} \times \text{Unit product cost}}$$

Exhibit 7.2 Price quotation sheet – absorption basis (10,000 units)

Direct materials	£6
Direct labour	4
Variable manufacturing overhead	3
Fixed manufacturing overhead (£70,000 ÷ 10,000 units)	7
Unit product cost	20
Mark-up to cover selling, general and administrative expenses and desired profit – 50% of unit manufacturing costs	10
Target selling price	£30

To show how the formula above is applied, assume Ritter Company must invest £100,000 to produce and market 10,000 units of the product each year. The £100,000 investment covers purchase of equipment and funds needed to carry stocks and debtors. If Ritter Company requires a 20% ROI, then the mark-up for the product would be determined as follows:

$$\text{Mark-up percentage on absorption cost} = \frac{(20\% \times 100{,}000) + (£2 \times 10{,}000 + £60{,}000)}{10{,}000 \times £20}$$

$$\text{Mark-up percentage on absorption cost} = \frac{(£20{,}000) + (£80{,}000)}{£200{,}000} = 50\%$$

As shown earlier, this mark-up of 50% leads to a target selling price of £30 for Ritter Company. As shown in Exhibit 7.3, *if the company actually sells 10,000 units* of the product at this price, the company's ROI on this product will indeed be 20%. If it turns out that more than 10,000 units are sold at this price, the ROI will be greater than 20%. If less than 10,000 units are sold, the ROI will be less than 20%. *The required ROI will be attained only if the forecasted unit sales volume is attained.*

Problems with the absorption costing approach

Using the absorption costing approach, the pricing problem looks deceptively simple. All you have to do is compute your unit product cost, decide how much profit you want, and then set your price. It appears that you can ignore demand and arrive at a price that will safely yield whatever profit you want. However, as noted above, the absorption costing approach relies on a forecast of unit sales. Neither the mark-up nor the unit product cost can be computed without such a forecast.

The absorption costing approach essentially assumes that customers *need* the forecasted unit sales and will pay whatever price the company decides to charge. However, customers have a choice. If the price is too high, they can buy from a competitor or they may choose not to buy at all. Suppose, for example, that when Ritter Company sets its price at £30, it sells only 7,000 units rather than the 10,000 units forecasted. As shown in Exhibit 7.4, the company would then have a loss of £25,000 on the product instead of a profit of £20,000. Some managers believe that the absorption costing approach to pricing is safe. This is an illusion. The absorption costing approach is safe only as long as customers choose to buy at least as many units as managers forecasted they would buy.

Exhibit 7.3 Profit statement and ROI analysis – Ritter Company actual unit sales = 10,000 units; selling price = £30

Direct materials	£6
Direct labour	4
Variable manufacturing overhead	3
Fixed manufacturing overhead (£70,000 ÷ 10,000 units)	7
Unit product cost	£20
Ritter Company Absorption costing profit statement	
Sales (£30 × 10,000 units)	£300,000
Less cost of goods sold (£20 × 10,000 units)	200,000
Gross margin	100,000
Less selling, general and administration expenses (£2 × 10,000 units £60,000)	80,000
Net operating profit	£20,000

ROI

$$\text{ROI} = \frac{\text{Net operating profit}}{\text{Average operating assets}}$$

$$= \frac{£20{,}000}{£100{,}000}$$

$$= 20\%$$

Exhibit 7.4 Profit statement and ROI analysis – Ritter Company actual unit sales = 7,000 units; selling price = £30

Direct materials	£6
Direct labour	4
Variable manufacturing overhead	3
Fixed manufacturing overhead (£70,000 ÷ 10,000 units)	10
Unit product cost	£23
Ritter Company Absorption costing profit statement	
Sales (£30 × 7,000 units)	£210,000
Less cost of goods sold (£23 × 7,000 units)	161,000
Gross margin	49,000
Less selling, general and administration expenses (£2 × 7,000 units + £60,000)	74,000
Net operating profit	£(25,000)

ROI

$$\text{ROI} = \frac{\text{Net operating profit}}{\text{Average operating assets}}$$

$$= \frac{(£25,000)}{£100,000}$$

$$= -25\%$$

Focus on Business Practice

Pricing methods for hotel services

© Manuela Weschke

Fáilte Ireland (Irish Tourist Board) provides useful business tools and guides on its website which can be used by Irish hotelier and guest house owners. One of the guides provided is on pricing. Two basic pricing methods are proposed as useful: (1) cost-plus pricing and (2) margin pricing. *Cost-plus pricing* is frequently used for food and beverages in restaurants. A typical mark-up on food costs used by chefs is cited as 200%, with 150% mark-up on beverage cost. The second approach, *margin pricing*, starts with a desired selling price of food (e.g. a menu) and deducts a required gross margin to derive the maximum costs of food ingredients. Two other pricing methods are also mentioned. *Value pricing* focuses on setting a price according to the value perceived by customers (e.g. location, premium brand). In other words, value pricing can be used when a service (e.g. WiFi, Spa treatments) differentiates from competitors. The final method is *going rate pricing*, which means services are priced the same as competitors' offerings. The guide advises this method should not be used without reference to underlying costs.[7]

Exercise: In the UK, hotel chains like Travelodge and Premier Inn frequently offer rooms for as low as £19 per night. How do you think they can justify this price? Surely such a price is not profitable?

Target costing

LO 5

Our discussion thus far has presumed that a product has already been developed, has been costed, and is ready to be marketed as soon as a price is set. In many cases, the sequence of events is just the reverse. That is, the company will already *know* what price should be charged, and the problem will be to *develop* a product that can be marketed profitably at the desired price. Even in this situation, where the normal sequence of events is reversed, cost is still a crucial factor. The company's approach will be to employ *target costing*. **Target costing** is the process of determining the maximum allowable cost for a new product and then developing a prototype that can be profitably made for that maximum target cost figure.

The target costing approach was developed in recognition that many companies have less control over price than they would like to think. The market (i.e., supply and demand) really determines prices, and a company that attempts to ignore this does so at its peril. Therefore, the anticipated market price is taken as a given in target costing. Second, target costing is more than just an approach to pricing – it takes a *strategic approach to cost management* by linking a whole series of organizational functions such as marketing, design, production and procurement.

The target cost for a product is computed by starting with the product's anticipated selling price and then deducting the desired profit, as follows:

Target cost = Anticipated selling price – Desired profit

The product development team is given the responsibility of designing the product so that it can be made for no more than the target cost.

An example of target costing

To provide a simple numerical example of target costing, assume the following situation: Handy Appliance Company feels that there is a market niche for a hand mixer with certain new features. Surveying the features and prices of hand mixers already on the market, the Marketing Department believes that a price of £30 would be about right for the new mixer. At that price, Marketing estimates that 40,000 of the new mixers could be sold annually. To design, develop, and produce these new mixers, an investment of £2,000,000 would be required. The company desires a 15% ROI. Given these data, the target cost to manufacture, sell, distribute, and service one mixer is £22.50 as shown below.

Projected sales (50,000 mixers × £30)	£1,200,000
Less desired profit (15% × £2,000,000)	300,000
Target cost for 40,000 mixers	£900,000
Target cost per mixer (£900,000/40,000 mixers)	£22.50

This £22.50 target cost would be broken down into target costs for the various functions: manufacturing, marketing, distribution, after-sales service, and so on. Each functional area would be responsible for keeping its actual costs within target.

Life-cycle costing

Traditional costing sometimes seems to focus too much on costs as they are *incurred* because incurred costs are more visible as they are 'booked' through routine cost accumulation systems. Life-cycle costing draws extensively on the techniques of target costing. Target costing is more than just a pricing technique as it *manages costs* rather than just passively measures them. The aim of target costing is to choose product and process technologies that give an acceptable profit at a planned level of output. Once a product has been designed and has gone into production, not much can be done to significantly reduce its cost. Most of the opportunities to reduce cost come from designing the product so that it is simple to make, uses inexpensive parts, and is robust and reliable. If the company has little control over market price and little control over cost once the product has gone into production, then it follows that the major opportunities for affecting profit come in the design stage where valuable features that customers are willing to pay for can be added and where most of

Exhibit 7.5 The product life-cycle: incurred versus locked-in/committed costs

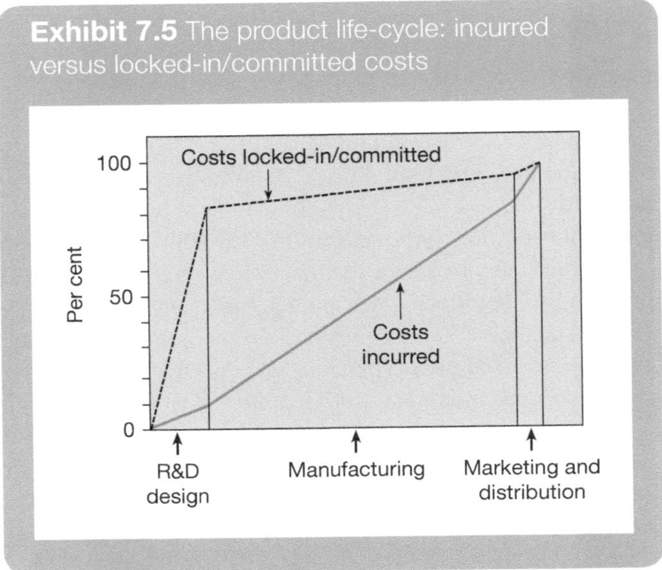

the costs are really determined. So that is where the effort is concentrated – in designing and developing the product. The difference between target costing and other approaches to product development is profound. Instead of designing the product and then finding out how much it costs, the target cost is set first and then the product is designed so that the target cost is attained.

As up to 90% of cost[8] may be committed or locked in at pre-production stages, management accountants have become more aware of the design and planning phases of the product life-cycle. The distinction between and differential timing of incurred and locked-in costs are illustrated in Exhibit 7.5. The biggest gap is at the research and development stage, where although this function may generate a relatively low proportion of a product's total cost, decisions made here lock in the costs incurred in the manufacturing and marketing phases. In recognition of the importance of the planning phase, *life-cycle* costing tries to estimate a product's costs over its lifetime.

As well as recognizing the importance of the design phase, life-cycle costing also anticipates cost improvements during the manufacturing cycle. This aspect is sometimes known as **kaizen costing** as it is part of the wider philosophy of continuous improvement. Some of the cost improvements will occur through a process of 'learning-by-doing' as workers get more adept at their tasks. Managers may routinize cost reduction through an approach known as **kaizen budgeting**. Rather than devise budgets on standard costs that are based on *past* performance, kaizen budgeting plans for *incremental* improvements in efficiency and reductions in costs.

Some problems with target and life-cycle costing

One problem with target costing is that it may reveal an unpalatable view of a company's internal operations, exposing uncompetitive practices and processes that were hidden by more traditional costing techniques. Another problem is that it may be too time-consuming. Thus, while it may be appropriate in the car industry, which is based on relatively mature technologies and lengthy product life-cycles, it is less appropriate in industries such as electronics, where the rate of innovation is extremely rapid and time-to-market must be minimized. The other feature of life-cycle costing is that it implicitly assumes a relatively orderly value chain with a dominant customer who can plan the design and delivery of the product. In an industry such as personal computers (PCs), some of the major players are the companies that supply the software (Microsoft) and the microprocessors (Intel). Leading-edge technical innovation is in the hands of these companies rather than the PC assemblers.

Focus on Business Practice

Producing the £1,300 car

© Getty Images

Target costing is widely used in the car industry. For example, at Tata Motors, engineers had to design a car that could be sold for 100,000 rupees (about £1,375)! The target cost for a new model is decomposed into target costs for each of the elements of the car – down to a target cost for each of the individual parts. The designers draft a trial blueprint, and a check is made to see if the estimated cost of the car is within reasonable distance of the target cost. If not, design changes are made, and a new trial blueprint is drawn up. This process continues until there is sufficient confidence in the design to make a prototype car according to the trial blueprint. If there is still a gap between the target cost and estimated cost, the design of the car will be further modified.

After repeating this process a number of times, the final blueprint is drawn up and turned over to the production department. In the first several months of production, the target costs will ordinarily not be achieved due to problems in getting a new model into production. However, after that initial period, target costs are compared to actual costs and discrepancies between the two are investigated with the aim of eliminating the discrepancies and achieving target costs.[9]

Exercise: Consider the possibility of target costing in other industries such as food retailing (see, e.g. Jack and Jones) (2007).

Transfer pricing

LO 6

A **transfer price** is the price charged when one segment of a company provides goods or services to another segment of the company. There are special problems in evaluating pricing goods or services transferred from one division/segment of a company to another. The problems revolve around the question of what transfer price to charge between the segments. Managers are intensely interested in how transfer prices are set, since they can have a dramatic effect on the apparent profitability of a division. Three common approaches are used to set transfer prices:

1. Allow the managers involved in the transfer to negotiate their own transfer price.
2. Set transfer prices at cost using:
   (a) Variable cost.
   (b) Full (absorption) cost.
3. Set transfer prices at the market price.

We will consider each of these transfer pricing methods in turn, beginning with negotiated transfer prices. Throughout the discussion we should keep in mind that *the fundamental objective in setting transfer prices is to motivate the managers to act in the best interests of the overall company*. In contrast, **sub-optimization** occurs when managers do not act in the best interests of the overall company or even in the best interests of their own segment.

Negotiated transfer prices

A **negotiated transfer price** is a transfer price that is agreed on between the selling and purchasing divisions. Negotiated transfer prices have several important advantages. First, this approach preserves the autonomy of the divisions and is consistent with the spirit of decentralization. Second, the managers of the divisions are likely to have much better information about the potential costs and benefits of the transfer than others in the company.

When negotiated transfer prices are used, the managers who are involved in a proposed transfer within the company meet to discuss the terms and conditions of the transfer. They may decide not to go through with the transfer, but if they do, they must agree to a transfer price. Generally speaking, we cannot predict the exact transfer price they will agree to. However, we can confidently predict two things: (1) the selling division will agree to the transfer only if the profits of the selling division increase as a result of the transfer, and (2) the purchasing division will agree to the transfer only if the profits of the purchasing division also increase as a result of the transfer. This may seem obvious, but it is an important point.

Clearly, if the transfer price is below the selling division's cost, a loss will occur on the transaction and the selling division will refuse to agree to the transfer. Likewise, if the transfer price is set too high, it will be impossible for the purchasing division to make any profit on the transferred item. For any given proposed transfer, the transfer price has both a lower limit (determined by the situation of the selling division) and an upper limit (determined by the situation of the purchasing division). The actual transfer price agreed to by the two division managers can fall anywhere between those two limits. These limits determine the **range of acceptable transfer prices** – the range of transfer prices within which the profits of both divisions participating in a transfer would increase.

An example will help us to understand negotiated transfer prices. Harris & Louder Ltd owns fast-food restaurants and snack food and beverage manufacturers in the United Kingdom. One of the restaurants, Pizza Maven, serves a variety of beverages along with pizzas. One of the beverages is ginger beer, which is served on tap. Harris & Louder has just purchased a new division, Imperial Beverages, that produces ginger beer. The managing director of Imperial Beverages has approached the managing director of Pizza Maven about purchasing Imperial Beverages' ginger beer for sale at Pizza Maven restaurants rather than its usual brand of ginger beer. Managers at Pizza Maven agree that the quality of Imperial Beverages' ginger beer is comparable to the quality of their regular brand. It is just a question of price. The basic facts are listed below:

Imperial Beverages:	
Ginger beer production capacity per month	10,000 barrels
Variable cost per barrel of ginger beer	£8 per barrel
Fixed costs per month	£70,000
Selling price of Imperial Beverages' ginger	
Pizza Maven:	
Purchase price of regular brand of ginger beer	£18 per barrel
Monthly consumption of ginger beer	2,000 barrels

The selling division's lowest acceptable transfer price

The selling division, Imperial Beverages, will be interested in a proposed transfer only if its profit increases Clearly, the transfer price must not fall below the variable cost per barrel of £8. In addition, if Imperial Beverages has insufficient capacity to fill the Pizza Maven order, then it would have to give up some of its regular sales. Imperial Beverages would expect to be compensated for the contribution margin on these lost sales. In sum, if the transfer has no effect on fixed costs, then from the selling division's standpoint, the transfer price must cover both the variable costs of producing the transferred units and any opportunity costs from lost sales.

Seller's perspective:

$$\text{Transfer price} \geq \text{Variable cost per unit} + \frac{\text{Total contribution margin on lost sales}}{\text{Number of units transferred}}$$

The purchasing division's highest acceptable transfer price

The purchasing division, Pizza Maven, will be interested in the proposal only if its profit increases. In cases like this where a purchasing division has an outside supplier, the purchasing division's decision is simple. Buy from the inside supplier if the price is less than the price offered by the outside supplier.

Purchaser's perspective:

Transfer price ≤ Cost of buying from outside supplier

We will consider several different hypothetical situations and see what the range of acceptable transfer prices would be in each situation.

Selling division with idle capacity

Suppose that Imperial Beverages has sufficient idle capacity to satisfy the demand for ginger beer from Pizza Maven without cutting into sales of ginger beer to its regular customers. To be specific, let's suppose that Imperial Beverages is selling only 7,000 barrels of ginger beer a month on the outside market. That leaves unused capacity of 3,000 barrels a month – more than enough to satisfy Pizza Maven's requirement of 2,000 barrels a month. What range of transfer prices, if any, would make both divisions better off with the transfer of 2,000 barrels a month?

1 The selling division, Imperial Beverages, will be interested in the proposal only if:

$$\text{Transfer price} \geq \text{Variable cost per unit} + \frac{\text{Total contribution margin on lost sales}}{\text{Number of units transferred}}$$

Since Imperial Beverages has ample idle capacity, there are no lost outside sales. And since the variable cost per unit is £8, the lowest acceptable transfer price as far as the selling division is concerned is also £8.

$$\text{Transfer price} \geq £8 + \frac{£0}{2{,}000} = £8$$

2 The purchasing division, Pizza Maven, can buy similar ginger beer from an outside vendor for £18. Therefore, Pizza Maven would be unwilling to pay more than £18 per barrel for Imperial Beverages' ginger beer.

Transfer price ≥ Cost of buying from outside supplier = £18

3 Combining the requirements of both the selling division and the purchasing division, the acceptable range of transfer prices in this situation is:

£8 ≤ Transfer price ≤ £18

Assuming that the managers understand their own businesses and that they are co-operative, they should be able to agree on a transfer price within this range.

Selling division with no idle capacity

Suppose that Imperial Beverages has no idle capacity; it is selling 10,000 barrels of ginger beer a month on the outside market at £20 per barrel. To fill the order from Pizza Maven, Imperial Beverages would have to divert 2,000 barrels from its regular customers. What range of transfer prices, if any, would make both divisions better off transferring the 2,000 barrels within the company?

1 The selling division, Imperial Beverage, will be interested in the proposal only if:

$$\text{Transfer price} \geq \text{Variable cost per unit} + \frac{\text{Total contribution margin on lost sales}}{\text{Number of units transferred}}$$

Since Imperial Beverage has no idle capacity, there *are* lost outside sales. The contribution margin per barrel on these outside sales is £12 (£20 – £8).

$$\text{Transfer price} \geq £8 + \frac{(20 - £8) \times 2{,}000}{2{,}000} = £8 + (£20 - £8) = £20$$

Thus, as far as the selling division is concerned, the transfer price must at least cover the revenue on the lost sales, which is £20 per barrel. This makes sense since the cost of producing the 2,000 barrels is the same whether they are sold on the inside market or on the outside. The only difference is that the selling division loses the revenue of £20 per barrel if it transfers the barrels to Pizza Maven.

2 As before, the purchasing division, Pizza Maven, would be unwilling to pay more than the £18 per barrel it is already paying for similar ginger beer from its regular supplier.

$$\text{Transfer price} \leq \text{Cost of buying from outside supplier} = £18$$

3 Therefore, the selling division would insist on a transfer price of at least £20. But the purchasing division would refuse any transfer price above £18. It is impossible to satisfy both division managers simultaneously; there can be no agreement on a transfer price and no transfer will take place. Is this good? The answer is yes. From the standpoint of the entire company, the transfer doesn't make sense. Why give up sales of £20 to save £18?

Basically, the transfer price is a mechanism for dividing between the two divisions any profit the entire company earns as a result of the transfer. If the company loses money on the transfer, there will be no profit to divide up, and it will be impossible for the two divisions to come to an agreement. On the other hand, if the company makes money on the transfer, there will be a potential profit to share, and it will always be possible for the two divisions to find a mutually agreeable transfer price that increases the profits of both divisions. If the pie is bigger, it is always possible to divide it up in such a way that everyone has a bigger piece.

Selling division has some idle capacity

Suppose now that Imperial Beverages is selling 9,000 barrels of ginger beer a month on the outside market. Pizza Maven can only sell one kind of ginger beer on tap. They cannot buy 1,000 barrels from Imperial Beverages and 1,000 barrels from their regular supplier; they must buy all their ginger beer from one source.

To fill the entire 2,000-barrel a month order from Pizza Maven, Imperial Beverages would have to divert 1,000 barrels from its regular customers who are paying £20 per barrel. The other 1,000 barrels can be made using idle capacity. What range of transfer prices, if any, would make both divisions better off transferring the 2,000 barrels within the company?

1 As before, the selling division, Imperial Beverage, will insist on a transfer price that at least covers their variable cost and opportunity cost:

$$\text{Transfer price} \geq \text{Variable cost per unit} + \frac{\text{Total contribution margin on lost sales}}{\text{Number of units transferred}}$$

Since Imperial Beverage does not have enough idle capacity to fill the entire order for 2,000 barrels, there *are* lost outside sales. The contribution margin per barrel on the 1,000 barrels of lost outside sales is £12 (£20 – £8).

$$\text{Transfer price} \geq £8 + \frac{(£20 - £8) \times 1{,}000}{2{,}000} = £8 + £6 = £14$$

Thus, as far as the selling division is concerned, the transfer price must cover the variable cost of £8 plus the average opportunity cost of lost sales of £6.

2 As before, the purchasing division, Pizza Maven, would be unwilling to pay more than the £18 per barrel it pays its regular supplier.

$$\text{Transfer price} \leq \text{Cost of buying from outside suppliers} = £18$$

3 Combining the requirements for both the selling and purchasing divisions, the range of acceptable transfer prices is:

£14 ≤ Transfer price ≤ £18

Again, assuming that the managers understand their own businesses and that they are co-operative, they should be able to agree on a transfer price within this range.

No outside supplier

If Pizza Maven has no outside supplier for the ginger beer, the highest price the purchasing division would be willing to pay depends on how much the purchasing division expects to make on the transferred units – excluding the transfer price. If, for example, Pizza Maven expects to earn £30 per barrel of ginger beer after paying its own expenses, then it should be willing to pay up to £30 per barrel to Imperial Beverages. Remember, however, that this assumes Pizza Maven cannot buy ginger beer from other sources.

Evaluation of negotiated transfer prices

As discussed earlier, if a transfer within the company would result in higher overall profits for the company, there is always a range of transfer prices within which both the selling and purchasing division would also have higher profits if they agree to the transfer. Therefore, if the managers understand their own businesses and are co-operative, then they should always be able to agree on a transfer price if it is in the best interests of the company that they do so.

The difficulty is that not all managers understand their own businesses and not all managers are co-operative. As a result, negotiations often break down even when it would be in the managers' own best interests to come to an agreement. Sometimes that is the fault of the way managers are evaluated. If managers are pitted against each other rather than against their own past performance or reasonable benchmarks, a non-cooperative atmosphere is almost guaranteed. Nevertheless, it must be admitted that even with the best performance evaluation system, some people by nature are not co-operative.

Possibly because of the fruitless and protracted bickering that often accompanies disputes over transfer prices, most companies rely on some other means of setting transfer prices. Unfortunately, as we will see below, all the alternatives to negotiated transfer prices have their own serious drawbacks.

Transfers at the cost to the selling division

Many companies set transfer prices at either the variable cost or full (absorption) cost incurred by the selling division. Although the cost approach to setting transfer prices is relatively simple to apply, it has some major defects.

First, the use of cost – particularly full cost – as a transfer price can lead to bad decisions and thus sub-optimization. Return to the example involving the ginger beer. The full cost of ginger beer can never be less than £15 per barrel (£8 per barrel variable cost + £7 per barrel fixed cost at capacity). What if the cost of buying the ginger beer from an outside supplier is less than £15 – for example, £14 per barrel? If the transfer price were bureaucratically set at full cost, then Pizza Maven would never want to buy ginger beer from Imperial Beverages, since it could buy its ginger beer from the outside supplier at less cost. However, from the standpoint of the company as a whole, ginger beer should be transferred from Imperial Beverages to Pizza Maven whenever Imperial Beverages has idle capacity. Why? Because when Imperial Beverage has idle capacity, it only costs the company £8 in variable cost to produce a barrel of ginger beer, but it costs £14 per barrel to buy from outside suppliers.

Secondly, if cost is used as the transfer price, the selling division will never show a profit on any internal transfer. The only division that shows a profit is the division that makes the final sale to an outside party.

A third problem with cost-based prices is that they do not provide incentives to control costs. If the costs of one division are simply passed on to the next, then there is little incentive for anyone to work to reduce costs. This problem can be overcome to some extent by using standard costs rather than actual costs for transfer prices.

Despite these shortcomings, cost-based transfer prices are commonly used in practice. Advocates argue that they are easily understood and convenient to use.

Transfers at market price

Some form of competitive **market price** (i.e., the price charged for an item on the open market) is often regarded as the best approach to the transfer pricing problem – particularly if transfer price negotiations routinely become bogged down.

The market price approach is designed for situations in which there is an *intermediate market* for the transferred product or service. By **intermediate market**, we mean a market in which the product or service is sold in its present form to outside customers. If the selling division has no idle capacity, the market price in the intermediate market is the perfect choice for the transfer price. The reason for this is that if the selling division can sell a transferred item on the outside market instead, then the real cost of the transfer as far as the company is concerned is the opportunity cost of the lost revenue on the outside sale. Whether the item is transferred internally or sold on the outside intermediate market, the production costs are exactly the same. If the market price is used as the transfer price, the selling division manager will not lose anything by making the transfer, and the purchasing division manager will get the correct signal about how much it really costs the company for the transfer to take place.

While the market price works beautifully when there is no idle capacity, difficulties occur when the selling division has idle capacity. Recalling once again the ginger beer example, the outside market price for the ginger beer produced by Imperial Beverages is £20 per barrel. However, Pizza Maven can purchase all of the ginger beer it wants from outside suppliers for £18 per barrel. Why would Pizza Maven ever buy from Imperial Beverages if Pizza Maven is forced to pay Imperial Beverages' market price? In some market price-based transfer pricing schemes, the transfer price would be lowered to £18, the outside vendor's market price, and Pizza Maven would be directed to buy from Imperial Beverages as long as Imperial Beverages is willing to sell. This scheme can work reasonably well, but a drawback is that managers at Pizza Maven will regard the cost of ginger beer as £18 rather than the £8, which is the real cost to the company when the selling division has idle capacity. Consequently, the managers of Pizza Maven will make pricing and other decisions based on an incorrect cost.

Unfortunately, none of the possible solutions to the transfer pricing problem are perfect – not even market-based transfer prices.

Summary

- Pricing involves a delicate balancing act. Higher prices result in more revenue per unit sold but drive down unit sales. Exactly where to set prices to maximize profit is a difficult problem, but, in general, the mark-up over cost should be highest for those products where customers are least sensitive to price. The demand for such products is said to be price inelastic.
- Managers often rely on cost-plus formulas to set target prices. In the absorption costing approach, the cost base is absorption costing unit product cost and the mark-up is computed to cover both non-manufacturing costs and to provide an adequate return on investment. However, costs will not be covered and there will not be an adequate return on investment unless the unit sales forecast used in the cost-plus formula is accurate. If applying the cost-plus formula results in a price that is too high, the unit sales forecast will not be attained.
- Some companies take a different approach to pricing. Instead of starting with costs and then determining prices, they start with prices and then determine allowable costs. Companies that use target costing estimate what a new product's market price is likely to be based on its anticipated

features and prices of products already on the market. They subtract desired profit from the estimated market price to arrive at the product's target cost. The design and development team is then given the responsibility of ensuring that the actual cost of the new product does not exceed the target cost.

- A special approach to pricing is required when goods or services are being transferred between segments or divisions of the same company. The theoretically optimal market price may not be appropriate if the company has spare capacity. Overall the aim should be to determine a price that maximizes the profit for the whole company. International transfer prices in multinational companies raise important taxation issues where the interests of the company and national taxation authorities may be in conflict.

Key terms

Cost-plus pricing A pricing method in which a predetermined mark-up is applied to a cost base to determine the target selling price (p. 150).

Intermediate market A market in which a transferred product or service is sold in its present form to outside customers (p. 164).

Kaizen budgeting Rather than base budgets on historical standards, kaizen budgeting plans for incremental improvements in efficiency and reduction in costs (p. 158).

Kaizen costing The reduction of cost during production through continuous gradual improvements that reduce waste and increase efficiency (p. 158).

Market price The price being charged for an item on the open (intermediate) market (p. 164).

Mark-up The difference between the selling price of a product or service and its cost. The mark-up is usually expressed as a percentage of cost (p. 150).

Negotiated transfer price A transfer price agreed on between buying and selling divisions (p. 159).

Price elasticity of demand A measure of the degree to which the volume of unit sales for a product or service is affected by a change in price (p. 150).

Range of acceptable transfer prices The range of transfer prices within which the profits of both the selling division and the purchasing division would increase as a result of a transfer (p. 160).

Sub-optimization An overall level of profitability that is less than a segment or a company is capable of earning (p. 159).

Target costing The process of determining the maximum allowable cost for a new product and then developing a prototype that can be profitably manufactured and distributed for that maximum target cost figure (p. 157).

Transfer price The price charged when one division or segment provides goods or services to another division or segment of an organization (p. 159).

Yield management A practice of achieving high capacity utilization through varying prices according to market segments and time of booking (p. 153).

Yield percentage A performance metric calculated by dividing actual revenue by the maximum potential revenue (p. 153).

Endnotes

1 Mattimoe and Seal (2010).

2 The term 'ln()' is the natural log function. You can compute the natural log of any number using the LN or lnx key on your calculator. For example, ln(0.85) = 20.1625.

This formula assumes that the price elasticity of demand is constant. This occurs when the relation between the selling price, p, and the unit sales, q, can be expressed in the following form: $\ln(q) = a = \varepsilon_d \ln(p)$. Even if this is not precisely true, the formula provides a useful way to estimate a product's real price elasticity.

3 The estimated change in unit sales should take into account competitors' responses to a price change.

4 The formula assumes that (a) the price elasticity of demand is constant; (b) Total cost = Total fixed cost = Variable cost per unit × q; and (c) the price of the product has no effect on the sales or costs of any other product. The formula can be derived using calculus.

5 Kimes (1989).

6 Harris (1999).

7 Pricing Methods Guide, Fáilte Ireland (Irish Tourist Board), available at http://www.businesstools.failteireland.ie/Accommodation/Hotels/Pricing-Methods.aspx#Cost-plus_pricing

8 Tanaka, Yoshikawa, Innes and Mitchell (1994).

9 Monden and Hamada (1991).

connect™

When you have read this chapter, log on to the Online Learning Centre for *Management Accounting for Business Decisions* at **www.mheducation.co.uk/textbooks/sealmabd1**, where you'll find multiple choice questions, practice exams and extra study tools for management accounting.

Assessment

Questions

connect™

7–1 What is meant by cost-plus pricing?

7–2 What does the price elasticity of demand measure? What is meant by inelastic demand? What is meant by elastic demand?

7–3 According to the economists' approach to setting prices, the profit-maximizing price should depend on which two factors?

7–4 Which product should have a larger mark-up over variable cost, a product whose demand is elastic or a product whose demand is inelastic?

7–5 When the absorption costing approach to cost-plus pricing is used, what is the mark-up supposed to cover?

7–6 What assumption does the absorption costing approach make about how consumers react to prices?

7–7 Discuss the following statement: 'Full cost can be viewed as a floor of protection. If a firm always sets its prices above full cost, it will never have to worry about operating at a loss.'

7–8 What is target costing? How do target costs enter into the pricing decision?

7–9 What are the advantages and disadvantages of cost-based transfer prices?

7–10 If a market price for a product can be determined, why isn't it always the best transfer price?

Exercises

connect™

E7–1 Time allowed: 15 minutes

Maria Lorenzi owns an ice cream stand that she operates during the summer months in West Yellowstone, Montana. Her store caters primarily to tourists passing through town on their way to Yellowstone National Park.

Maria is unsure of how she should price her ice cream cones and has experimented with two prices in successive weeks during the busy August season. The number of people who entered the store was roughly the same in the two weeks. During the first week, she priced the cones at $1.89 and 1,500 cones were sold. During the second week, she priced the cones at $1.49 and 2,340 cones were sold. The variable cost of a cone is $0.43 and consists solely of the costs of the ice cream and of the cone itself. The fixed expenses of the ice cream stand are $675 per week.

Required

1 Did Maria make more money selling the cones for $1.89 or for $1.49?

2 Estimate the price elasticity of demand for the ice cream cones.

3 Estimate the profit-maximizing price for ice cream cones.

E7–2 Time allowed: 10 minutes

Martin Company is considering the introduction of a new product. To determine a target selling price, the company has gathered the following information:

Number of units to be produced and sold each year	14,000
Unit product cost	£25
Projected annual selling, general, and administrative expenses	50,000
Estimated investment required by the company	750,000
Desired return on investment (ROI)	12%

Required

The company uses the absorption costing approach to cost-plus pricing.

1 Compute the mark-up the company will have to use to achieve the desired ROI.
2 Compute the target selling price per unit.

E7–3 Time allowed: 5 minutes

Shimada Products Corporation of Japan is anxious to enter the electronic calculator market. Management believes that in order to be competitive in world markets, the electronic calculator that the company is developing cannot be priced at more than £15. Shimada requires a minimum return of 12% on all investments. An investment of £5,000,000 would be required to acquire the equipment needed to produce the 300,000 calculators that management believes can be sold each year at the £15 price.

Required

Compute the target cost of one calculator.

E7–4 Time allowed: 15 minutes

The Reliable TV Repair Shop had budgeted the following costs for next year:

Repair technicians:	
Wages	£120,000
Fringe benefits	30,000
Repairs operation per year	90,000
Materials:	
Costs of ordering, handling, and storing parts	20% of invoice cost

In total, the company expects 10,000 hours of repair time it can bill to customers. According to competitive conditions, the company believes it should aim for a profit of £6 per hour of repair time. The competitive mark-up on materials is 40% of invoice cost. The company uses time and material pricing.

Required

1 Compute the time rate and the material loading charge that would be used to bill jobs.
2 One of the company's repair technicians has just completed a repair job that required 2.5 hours of time and £80 in parts (invoice cost). Compute the amount that would be billed for the job.

E7–5 Time allowed: 30 minutes

Sako Company's Audio Division produces a speaker that is widely used by manufacturers of various audio products. Sales and cost data on the speaker follow:

Selling price per unit on the intermediate market	£60
Variable costs per unit	42
Fixed costs per unit (based on capacity)	8
Capacity in units	25,000

Sako Company has just organized a Hi-Fi Division that could use this speaker in one of its products. The Hi-Fi Division will need 5,000 speakers per year. It has received a quote of £57 per speaker from another manufacturer. Sako Company evaluates divisional managers on the basis of divisional profits.

Required

1 Assume that the Audio Division is now selling only 20,000 speakers per year to outside customers on the intermediate market.
2 (a) From the standpoint of the Audio Division, what is the lowest acceptable transfer price for speakers sold to the Hi-Fi Division?
  (b) From the standpoint of the Hi-Fi Division, what is the highest acceptable transfer price for speakers purchased from the Audio Division?
  (c) If left free to negotiate without interference, would you expect the division managers to voluntarily agree to the transfer of 5,000 speakers from the Audio Division to the Hi-Fi Division? Why or why not?
  (d) From the standpoint of the entire company, should the transfer take place? Why or why not?
3 Assume that the Audio Division is selling all of the speakers it can produce to outside customers on the intermediate market.
4 (a) From the standpoint of the Audio Division, what is the lowest acceptable transfer price for speakers sold to the Hi-Fi Division?
  (b) From the standpoint of the Hi-Fi Division, what is the highest acceptable transfer price for speakers purchased from the Audio Division?

(c) If left free to negotiate without interference, would you expect the division managers to voluntarily agree to the transfer of 5,000 speakers from the Audio Division to the Hi-Fi Division? Why or why not?
(d) From the standpoint of the entire company, should the transfer take place? Why or why not?

E7–6 Time allowed: 20 minutes
In each of the cases below, assume that Division X has a product that can be sold either to outside customers on an intermediate market or to Division Y of the same company for use in its production process. The managers of the divisions are evaluated based on their divisional profits.

	Case	
	A	B
Division X:		
Capacity in units	200,000	200,000
Number of units being sold on the intermediate market	200,000	160,000
Selling price per unit on the intermediate market	£90	£75
Variable costs per unit	70	60
Fixed costs per unit (based on capacity)	13	8
Division Y:		
Number of units needed for production	40,000	40,000
Purchase price per unit now being paid to an outside supplier	£86	£74

Required

1 Refer to the data in case A above. Assume in this case that £3 per unit in variable costs can be avoided on intra-company sales. If the managers are free to negotiate and make decisions on their own, will a transfer take place? If so, within what range will the transfer price fall? Explain.
2 Refer to the data in case B above. In this case there will be no savings in variable costs on intra-company sales. If the managers are free to negotiate and make decisions on their own, will a transfer take place? If so, within what range will the transfer price fall? Explain.

E7–7 Time allowed: 15 minutes
Division A manufactures electronic circuit boards. The boards can be sold either to Division B of the same company or to outside customers. Last year, the following activity occurred in Division A:

Selling price per circuit board	£125
Production cost per circuit board	90
Number of circuit boards:	
Produced during the year	20,000
Sold to outside customers	16,000
Sold to Division B	4,000

Sales to Division B were at the same price as sales to outside customers. The circuit boards purchased by Division B were used in an electronic instrument manufactured by that division (one board per instrument). Division B incurred £100 in additional cost per instrument and then sold the instruments for £300 each.

Required

1 Prepare profit statements for Division A, Division B, and the company as a whole.
2 Assume that Division A's manufacturing capacity is 20,000 circuit boards. Next year, Division B wants to purchase 5,000 circuit boards from Division A rather than 4,000. (Circuit boards of this type are not available from outside sources.) From the standpoint of the company as a whole, should Division A sell the 1,000 additional circuit boards to Division B or continue to sell them to outside customers? Explain.

P7–8 Economists' approach to pricing

Problems

Time allowed: 30 minutes

The postal service of St Vincent, an island in the West Indies, obtains a significant portion of its revenues from sales of special souvenir sheets to stamp collectors. The souvenir sheets usually contain several high-value St Vincent stamps depicting a common theme, such as the life of Princess Diana. The souvenir sheets are designed and printed for the postal service by Imperial Printing, a stamp agency service company in the United Kingdom. The souvenir sheets cost the postal service $0.80 each. (The currency in St Vincent is the East Caribbean dollar.) St Vincent has been selling these souvenir sheets for $7.00 each and ordinarily sells about 100,000 units. To test the market, the postal service recently priced a new souvenir sheet at $8.00 and sales dropped to 85,000 units.

Required

1 Does the postal service of St Vincent make more money selling souvenir sheets for $7.00 each or $8.00 each?
2 Estimate the price elasticity of demand for the souvenir sheets.
3 Estimate the profit-maximizing price for souvenir sheets.
4 If Imperial Printing increases the price it charges to the St Vincent postal service for souvenir sheets to $1.00 each, how much should the St Vincent postal service charge its customers for the souvenir sheets?

P7–9 Pricing

Time allowed: 30 minutes

A small company is engaged in the production of plastic tools for the garden. Subtotals on the spreadsheet of budgeted overheads for a year reveal:

	Moulding Department	Finishing Department	General factory Overhead
Variable overhead (£000)	1,600	500	1,050
Fixed overhead (£000)	2,500	850	1,750
Budgeted activity			
Machine hours (000)	800	600	
Practical capacity			
Machine hours (000)	1,200	800	

For the purposes of reallocation of general factory overhead it is agreed that the variable overheads accrue in line with the machine hours worked in each department.

General factory fixed overhead is to be reallocated on the basis of the practical machine hour capacity of the two departments.

It has been a long-standing company practice to establish selling prices by applying a mark-up on full manufacturing cost of between 25 and 35%.

A possible price is sought for one new product which is in a final development stage. The total market for this product is estimated at 200,000 units per annum. Market research indicates that the company could expect to obtain and hold about 10% of the market. It is hoped the product will offer some improvement over competitors' products, which are currently marketed at between £90 and £100 each.

The product development department has determined that the direct material content is £9 per unit. Each unit of the product will take two labour hours (four machine hours) in the moulding department and three labour hours (three machine hours) in finishing. Hourly labour rates are £5.00 and £5.50 respectively.

Management estimate that the annual fixed costs which would be specifically incurred in relation to the product are: supervision £20,000, depreciation of a recently acquired machine £120,000 and advertising £27,000. It may be assumed that these costs are included in the budget given above. Given the state of development of this new product, management do not consider it necessary to make revisions to the budgeted activity levels given above, for any possible extra machine hours involved in its manufacture.

Required

1 Briefly explain the role of costs in pricing. *(6 marks)*

2 Prepare full cost and marginal cost information which may help with the pricing decision. *(9 marks)*

3 Comment on the cost information and suggest a price range which should be considered. *(5 marks)*

(Total = 20 marks)

ACCA *(adapted)*

P7-10 Transfer price; well-defined intermediate market

Time allowed: 45 minutes

Hrubec Products plc operates a Pulp Division that manufactures wood pulp for use in the production of various paper goods. Revenue and costs associated with a ton of pulp follow:

Selling price		£70
Less expenses:		
Variable	£42	
Fixed (based on a capacity of 50,000 tons per year)	18	60
Net profit		£10

Hrubec Products has just acquired a small company that manufactures paper cartons. This company will be treated as a division of Hrubec with full profit responsibility. The newly formed Carton Division is currently purchasing

5,000 tons of pulp per year from a supplier at a cost of £70 per ton, less a 10% quantity discount. Hrubec's managing director is anxious for the Carton Division to begin purchasing its pulp from the Pulp Division if an acceptable transfer price can be worked out.

Required

For Questions 1 and 2 below, assume that the Pulp Division can sell all its pulp to outside customers at the normal £70 price.

1 Are the managers of the Carton and Pulp Divisions likely to agree to a transfer price for 5,000 tons of pulp next year? Why or why not?

2 If the Pulp Division meets the price that the Carton Division is currently paying to its supplier and sells 5,000 tons of pulp to the Carton Division each year, what will be the effect on the profits of the Pulp Division, the Carton Division, and the company as a whole?

For Questions 3–6 below, assume that the Pulp Division is currently selling only 30,000 tons of pulp each year to outside customers at the stated £70 price.

3 Are the managers of the Carton and Pulp Divisions likely to agree to a transfer price for 5,000 tons of pulp next year? Why or why not?

4 Suppose that the Carton Division's outside supplier drops its price (net of the quantity discount) to only £59 per ton. Should the Pulp Division meet this price? Explain. If the Pulp Division does not meet the £59 price, what will be the effect on the profits of the company as a whole?

5 Refer to Question 4 above. If the Pulp Division refuses to meet the £59 price, should the Carton Division be required to purchase from the Pulp Division at a higher price for the good of the company as a whole?

6 Refer to Question 4 above. Assume that due to inflexible management policies, the Carton Division is required to purchase 5,000 tons of pulp each year from the Pulp Division at £70 per ton. What will be the effect on the profits of the company as a whole?

P7–11 Basic transfer pricing

Time allowed: 60 minutes

Alpha and Beta are divisions within the same company. The managers of both divisions are evaluated based on their own division's return on investment (ROI). Assume the following information relative to the two divisions:

	Case			
	1	2	3	4
Alpha Division:				
Capacity in units	80,000	400,000	150,000	300,000
Number of units now being sold to outside customers				
On the intermediate market	80,000	400,000	100,000	300,000
Selling price per unit on the intermediate market	£30	£90	£75	£50
Variable costs per unit	18	65	40	26
Fixed costs per unit (based on capacity)	6	15	20	9
Beta Division:				
Number of units needed annually	5,000	30,000	20,000	120,000
Purchase price now being paid to an outside supplier	£27	£89	£75*	–

*Before any quantity discount.

Managers are free to decide if they will participate in any internal transfers. All transfer prices are negotiated.

Required

1 Refer to Case 1 above. Alpha Division can avoid £2 per unit in commissions on any sales to Beta Division. Will the managers agree to a transfer and if so, within what range will the transfer price be? Explain.

2 Refer to Case 2 above. A study indicates that Alpha Division can avoid £5 per unit in shipping costs on any sales to Beta Division.

3 (a) Would you expect any disagreement between the two divisional managers over what the transfer price should be? Explain.

(b) Assume that Alpha Division offers to sell 30,000 units to Beta Division for £88 per unit and that Beta Division refuses this price. What will be the loss in potential profits for the company as a whole?

4 Refer to Case 3 above. Assume that Beta Division is now receiving an 8% quantity discount from the outside supplier.

5 (a) Will the managers agree to a transfer? If so, what is the range within which the transfer price would be?

(b) Assume that Beta Division offers to purchase 20,000 units from Alpha Division at £60 per unit. If Alpha Division accepts this price, would you expect its ROI to increase, decrease, or remain unchanged? Why?

6 Refer to Case 4 above. Assume that Beta Division wants Alpha Division to provide it with 120,000 units of a different product from the one that Alpha Division is now producing. The new product would require £21 per unit in variable costs and would require that Alpha Division cut back production of its present product by 45,000 units annually. What is the lowest acceptable transfer price from Alpha Division's perspective?

Part III

Business planning and organizational control

Chapter 8
Profit planning and controlling: budgeting

Learning objectives

After studying Chapter 8, you should be able to:

1 Understand why organizations budget and the processes they use to create budgets
2 Understand the inter-relationships and components that make up a master budget
3 Prepare a budgeted profit and loss statement and a budgeted balance sheet on static and flexible bases
4 Review some criticisms of budgeting and possible responses
5 Review the concept of zero-based budgeting

Concepts in Context

After an initial boom, many early dotcom companies have now failed. One reason seems to be that some companies thought that the old business practices such as budgeting were obsolete. The emphasis was on speed, being the first-mover and working out detailed business plans as the business developed. Frequently, many companies squandered their start-up resources before they had established a sustainable business. The collapse of dotcoms and the high tech sector around the turn of the millennium seemed to suggest that the disciplines of planning and control inherent in budgeting should not just be the concern of 'fuddy-duddy', bricks-and-mortar organizations.[1]

© Axaulya

In this chapter, we focus our attention on those steps taken by business organizations to achieve their desired levels of profits – a process that is generally called profit planning. We shall see that profit planning is accomplished through the preparation of a number of budgets, which, when brought together, form an integrated business plan known as the master budget. The master budget is an essential management tool that communicates management's plans throughout the organization, allocates resources and co-ordinates activities.

LO 1 The basic framework of budgeting

Definition of budgeting

A budget is a detailed plan for the acquisition and use of financial and other resources over a specified time period. It represents a plan for the future expressed in formal quantitative terms. The act of preparing a budget is called *budgeting*. The use of budgets to control a firm's activities is known as *budgetary control*.

The *master budget* is a summary of a company's plans that sets specific targets for sales, production, distribution and financing activities. It generally culminates in a *cash budget*, a *budgeted profit and loss account*, and a *budgeted balance sheet*. In short, it represents a comprehensive expression of management's plans for the future and how these plans are to be accomplished.

Personal budgets

Nearly everyone budgets to some extent, even though many of the people who use budgets do not recognize what they are doing as budgeting. For example, most people make estimates of their income and plan expenditures for food, clothing, housing and so on. As a result of this planning, people restrict their spending to some predetermined, allowable amount. While they may not be conscious of the fact, these people clearly go through a budgeting process. Income is estimated, expenditures are planned, and spending is restricted in accordance with the plan. Individuals also use budgets to forecast their future financial condition for purposes such as purchasing a home, financing college education, or setting aside funds for retirement. These budgets may exist only in the mind of the individual, but they are budgets nevertheless.

The budgets of a business firm serve much the same functions as the budgets prepared informally by individuals. Business budgets tend to be more detailed and to involve more work, but they are similar to the budgets prepared by individuals in most other respects. Like personal budgets, they assist in planning and controlling expenditures; they also assist in predicting operating results and financial condition in future periods.

Advantages of budgeting

Managers who have never tried budgeting are usually quick to state that budgeting is a waste of time. These managers may argue that even though budgeting may work well in some situations, it would never work well in their companies because operations are too complex or because there are too many uncertainties. In reality, however, managers who argue this way usually will be deeply involved in planning (albeit on an informal basis). These managers will have clearly defined thoughts about what they want to accomplish and when they want it accomplished. The difficulty is that unless they have some way of communicating their thoughts and plans to others, the only way their companies will ever attain the desired objectives will be through accident. In short, even though companies may attain a certain degree of success without budgets, they never attain the heights that could have been reached with a co-ordinated system of budgets.

Companies realize many benefits from a budgeting programme. Among these benefits are the following:

1. Budgets provide a means of *communicating* management's plans throughout the organization.
2. Budgets force managers to *think about* and plan for the future. In the absence of the necessity to prepare a budget, too many managers would spend all their time dealing with daily emergencies.
3. The budgeting process provides a means of *allocating resources* to those parts of the organization where they can be used most effectively.
4. The budgeting process can uncover potential *bottlenecks* before they occur.

5 Budgets *co-ordinate* the activities of the entire organization by integrating the plans of the various parts. Budgeting helps to ensure that everyone in the organization is pulling in the same direction.

6 Budgets define goals and objectives that can serve as *benchmarks* for evaluating subsequent performance.

The impact of computers on budgeting

In the past, some managers have avoided budgeting because of the time and effort involved in the budgeting process. It can be argued that budgeting is actually 'free' in that the manager's time and effort are more than offset by greater profits. Moreover, with the advent of computer spreadsheets, *any* company – large or small – can implement and maintain a budgeting programme at minimal cost. Budgeting lends itself well to readily available spreadsheet application programs.

Focus on Business Practice

Budgeting in banking firms

© Joshua Hodge Photography

Consider the following situation encountered by one of the authors at a mortgage banking firm. For years, the company operated with virtually no system of budgets whatever. Management contended that budgeting was not well suited to the firm's type of operation. Moreover, management pointed out that the firm was already profitable. Indeed, outwardly the company gave every appearance of being a well-managed, smoothly operating organization. A careful look within, however, disclosed that day-to-day operations were far from smooth, and often approached chaos. The average day was nothing more than an exercise in putting out one brush fire after another. The Cash account was always at crisis levels. At the end of a day, no one ever knew whether enough cash would be available the next day to cover required loan closings. Departments were uncoordinated, and it was not uncommon to find that one department was pursuing a course that conflicted with the course pursued by another department. Employee morale was low, and turnover was high. Employees complained bitterly that when a job was well done, nobody ever knew about it. The company was bought out by a new group who required that an integrated budgeting system be established to control operations. Within one year, significant changes were evident. Brush fires were rare. Careful planning virtually eliminated the problems that had been experienced with cash, and departmental efforts were co-ordinated and directed towards predetermined overall company goals. Although the employees were wary of the new budgeting programme initially, they became 'converted' when they saw the positive effects that it brought about. The more efficient operations caused profits to jump dramatically. Communication increased throughout the organization. When a job was well done everybody knew about it. As one employee stated, 'For the first time, we know what the company expects of us.'

Exercise: One of the key issues that emerged after the recent collapse of the Bradford & Bingley bank was the poor state of the bank's financial controls. How did that contribute to the wider banking problems that became known as the *credit crunch*?[2]

Choosing a budget period

Operating budgets are ordinarily set to cover a one-year period. The one-year period should correspond to the company's fiscal year so that the budget figures can be compared with the actual results. Many companies divide their budget year into four quarters. The first quarter is then subdivided into months, and monthly budget figures are established. These *near-term* figures can often be established with considerable accuracy. The last three quarters are carried in the budget as quarterly totals only. As the year progresses, the figures for the second quarter are broken down into monthly amounts, then the third-quarter figures are broken down, and so forth. This approach has the advantage of requiring periodic review and reappraisal of budget data throughout the year.

Continuous, perpetual or *rolling budgets* are used by a significant number of organizations. A **continuous or perpetual budget** is a 12-month budget that rolls forward one month (or quarter) as the current month (or quarter) is completed. In other words, one month (or quarter) is added to the end of the budget as each month (or quarter) comes to a close. This approach keeps managers focused on the future at least one year ahead. Advocates of continuous budgets argue that with this approach there is less danger that managers will become too focused on short-term results as the year progresses.

The self-imposed or participative budget

The success of a budget programme will be determined in large part by the way in which the budget is developed. The most successful budget programmes involve managers with cost control responsibilities in preparing their own budget estimates – rather than having a budget imposed from above. This approach to preparing budget data is particularly important if the budget is to be used to control and evaluate a manager's activities. If a budget is imposed on a manager from above, it will probably generate resentment and ill will rather than co-operation and increased productivity.

This budgeting approach, in which managers prepare their own budget estimates – called a *self-imposed budget* – is generally considered to be the most effective method of budget preparation. A **self-imposed budget** or **participative budget** is a budget that is prepared with the full co-operation and participation of managers at all levels. Exhibit 8.1 illustrates this approach to budget preparation.

A number of advantages are commonly cited for such self-imposed budgets:

1 Individuals at all levels of the organization are recognized as members of the team whose views and judgements are valued by top management.
2 The person in direct contact with an activity is in the best position to make budget estimates. Therefore, budget estimates prepared by such persons tend to be more accurate and reliable.

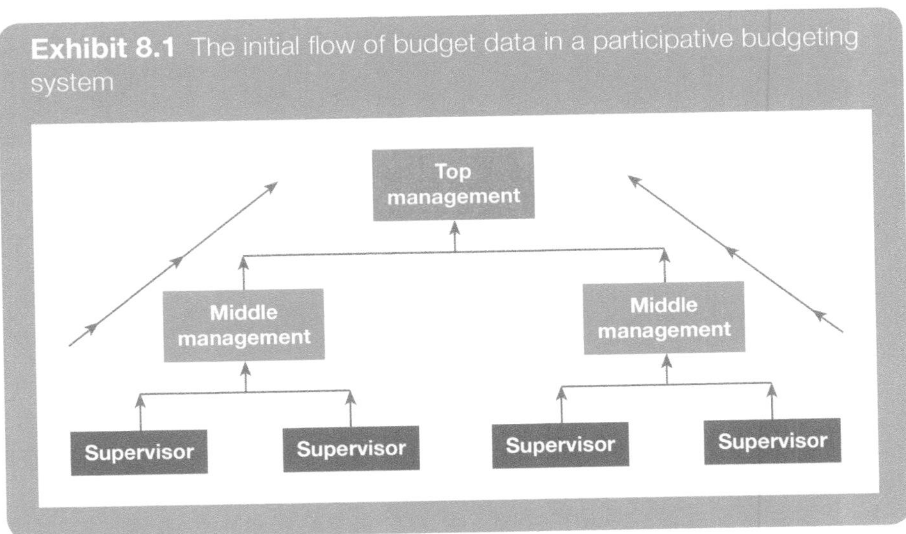

3. People are more likely to work at fulfilling a budget that they have participated in setting than they are to work at fulfilling a budget that is imposed from above.
4. A self-imposed budget contains its own unique system of control in that if people are not able to meet budget specifications, they have only themselves to blame. On the other hand, if a budget is imposed from above, they can always say that the budget was unreasonable or unrealistic to start with, and therefore was impossible to meet.

Once self-imposed budgets are prepared, are they subject to any kind of review? The answer is yes. Budget estimates prepared by lower-level managers cannot necessarily be accepted without question by higher levels of management. If no system of checks and balances is present, self-imposed budgets may be too loose and allow too much 'budgetary slack'. The result will be inefficiency and waste. Therefore, before budgets are accepted, they must be carefully reviewed by immediate superiors. If changes from the original budget seem desirable, the items in question are discussed and modified as necessary by mutual consent.

In essence, all levels of an organization should work together to produce the budget. Since top management is generally unfamiliar with detailed, day-to-day operations, it should rely on subordinates to provide detailed budget information. On the other hand, top management has a perspective on the company as a whole that is vital in making broad policy decisions in budget preparation. Each level of responsibility in an organization should contribute in the way that it best can in a *co-operative* effort to develop an integrated budget document.

We have described an ideal budgetary process that involves self-imposed budgets prepared by the managers who are directly responsible for revenues and costs. Most companies deviate from this ideal. Typically, top managers initiate the budget process by issuing broad guidelines in terms of overall target profits or sales. Lower-level managers are directed to prepare budgets that meet those targets. The difficulty is that the targets set by top managers may be unrealistically high or may allow too much slack. If the targets are too high and employees know they are unrealistic, motivation will suffer. If the targets allow too much slack, waste will occur. And, unfortunately, top managers are often not in a position to know whether the targets they have set are appropriate. Admittedly, however, in a pure self-imposed budgeting system, lower-level managers may be tempted to build into their budgets a great deal of budgetary slack and there may be a lack of direction. Nevertheless, because of the motivational advantages of self-imposed budgets, top managers should be cautious about setting inflexible targets or otherwise imposing limits on the budgeting process.

The matter of human relations

Whether or not a budget programme is accepted by lower management personnel will be reflective of (first) the degree to which top management accepts the budget programme as a vital part of the company's activities, and (second) the way in which top management uses budgeted data.

If a budget programme is to be successful, it must have the complete acceptance and support of the persons who occupy key management positions. If lower or middle management personnel sense that top management is lukewarm about budgeting, or if they sense that top management simply tolerates budgeting as a necessary evil, then their own attitudes will reflect a similar lack of enthusiasm. Budgeting is hard work, and if top management is not enthusiastic about and committed to the budget programme, then it is unlikely that anyone else in the organization will be either.

In administering the budget programme, it is particularly important that top management not use the budget as a club to pressure employees or as a way to find someone to blame for a particular problem. This type of negative emphasis will simply breed hostility, tension and mistrust rather than greater co-operation and productivity. Unfortunately, research suggests that the budget is often used as a pressure device and that great emphasis is placed on 'meeting the budget' under all circumstances.[3] Rather than being used as a pressure device, the budget should be used as a positive instrument to assist in establishing goals, in measuring operating results, and in isolating areas that are in need of extra effort or attention. Any misgivings that employees have about a budget programme can be overcome by meaningful involvement at all levels and by proper use of the programme over a period of time. Administration of a budget programme requires a great deal of insight and sensitivity on the part of management. The ultimate object must be to develop the realization that the budget is designed to be a positive aid in achieving both individual and company goals.

Management must keep clearly in mind that the human dimension in budgeting is of key importance. It is easy for the manager to become preoccupied with the technical aspects of the budget programme to the exclusion of the human aspects. Indeed, the use of budget data in a rigid and inflexible manner is the greatest single complaint of persons whose performance is being evaluated through the budget process.[4] Management should remember that the purposes of the budget are to motivate employees and to co-ordinate efforts. Preoccupation with the pounds and pence in the budget, or being rigid and inflexible in budget administration, can only lead to frustration of these purposes.

The budget committee

A standing **budget committee** will usually be responsible for overall policy matters relating to the budget programme and for co-ordinating the preparation of the budget itself. This committee generally consists of the managing director; directors in charge of various functions such as sales, production and purchasing; and the controller. Difficulties and disputes between segments of the organization in matters relating to the budget are resolved by the budget committee. In addition, the budget committee approves the final budget and receives periodic reports on the progress of the company in attaining budgeted goals.

Disputes can (and do) erupt over budget matters. Because budgets allocate resources, the budgeting process, to a large extent, determines which departments get more resources and which get relatively less. Also, the budget sets the benchmarks by which managers and their departments will be at least partially evaluated. Therefore, it should not be surprising that managers take the budgeting process very seriously and invest considerable energy and even emotion in ensuring that their interests, and those of their departments, are protected. Because of this, the budgeting process can easily degenerate into an inter-office brawl in which the ultimate goal of working together towards common goals is forgotten.

Running a successful budgeting programme that avoids inter-office battles requires considerable inter-personal skills in addition to purely technical skills. But even the best inter-personal skills will fail if, as discussed earlier, top management uses the budget process inappropriately as a club or as a way to find blame.

Focus on Business Practice

The game of budgeting

© P_Wei

Budgeting is often an intensely political process in which managers jockey for resources and relaxed goals for the upcoming year. One group of consultants describes the process in this way: Annual budgets 'have a particular urgency in that they provide the standard and most public framework against which managers are assessed and judged. It is, therefore, not surprising that budget-setting is taken seriously... Often budgets are a means for managers getting what they want. A relaxed budget will secure a relatively easy twelve months, a tight one means that their names will constantly be coming up in the monthly management review meeting. Far better to shift the burden of cost control and financial discipline to someone else. Budgeting as an intensely political exercise is conducted with all the sharper managerial skills not taught at business school, such as lobbying and flattering superiors, forced haste, regretted delay, hidden truth, half-truths, and lies.'[5]

Exercise: Why might an organization that has a high level of *trust* between managerial levels achieve a better quality of budgeting than those where mistrust is the rule?

The master budget inter-relationships

LO 2

The **master budget** consists of a number of separate but interdependent budgets. Exhibit 8.2 provides an overview of the various parts of the master budget and how they are related.

The sales budget

A **sales budget** is a detailed schedule showing the expected sales for the budget period; typically, it is expressed in both pounds and units of product. An accurate sales budget is the key to the entire budgeting process. All other parts of the master budget are dependent on the sales budget in some way, as illustrated in Exhibit 8.2. Thus, if the sales budget is sloppily done, then the rest of the budgeting process is largely a waste of time.

The sales budget will help determine how many units will have to be produced. Thus, the *production budget* is prepared after the sales budget. The production budget in turn is used to determine the budgets for manufacturing costs including the *direct materials budget*, the *direct labour budget*, and the *manufacturing overhead budget*. These budgets are then combined with data from the sales budget and the selling and administrative expense budget to determine the cash budget. In essence, the sales budget triggers a chain reaction that leads to the development of the other budgets.

As shown in Exhibit 8.2, the selling and administrative expense budget is both dependent on and a determinant of the sales budget. This reciprocal relationship arises because sales will in part be determined by the funds committed for advertising and sales promotion.

The cash budget

Once the operating budgets (sales, production, and so on) have been established, the cash budget and other financial budgets can be prepared. A **cash budget** is a detailed plan showing how cash resources will be acquired and used over some specified time period. Observe from Exhibit 8.2 that all of the operating budgets have an impact on the cash budget. In the case of the sales budget, the impact comes from the planned cash receipts to be received from sales. In the case of the other budgets, the impact comes from the planned cash expenditures within the budgets themselves.

Exhibit 8.2 The master budget inter-relationships

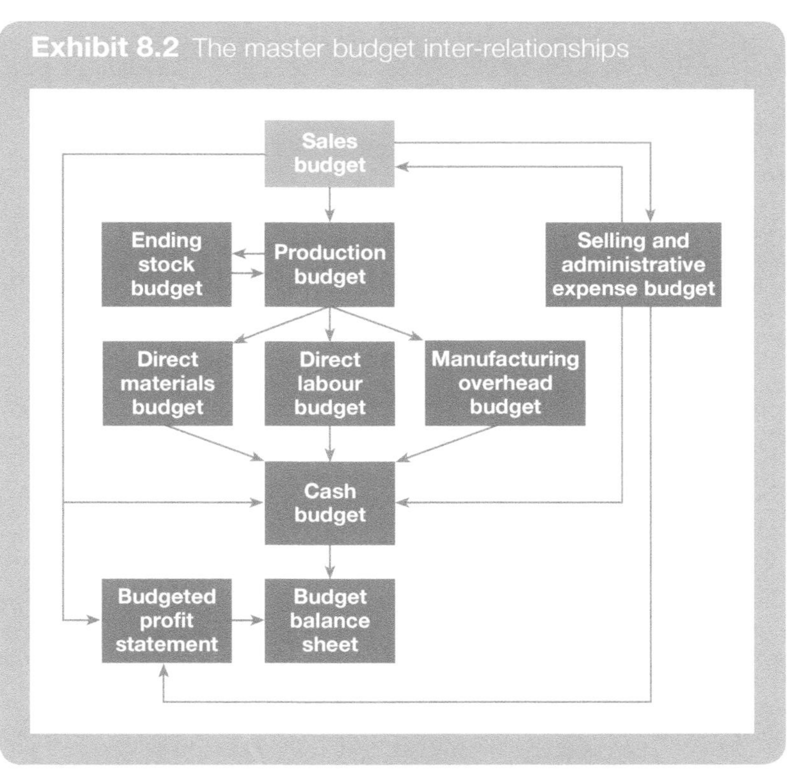

Sales forecasting – a critical step

The sales budget is usually based on the company's *sales forecast*. Sales from prior years are commonly used as a starting point in preparing the sales forecast. In addition, the manager may examine the company's unfilled back orders, the company's pricing policy and marketing plans, trends in the industry and general economic conditions. Sophisticated statistical tools may be used to analyse the data and to build models that are helpful in predicting key factors influencing the company's sales.

Preparing the master budget

The sales budget

The sales budget is the starting point in preparing the master budget. As shown earlier in Exhibit 8.2, all other items in the master budget, including production, purchases, stocks and expenses, depend on it in some way.

The sales budget is constructed by multiplying the budgeted sales in units by the selling price. Schedule 1 contains the sales budget for Hampton Freeze Ltd for the year 2011, by quarters. Notice from the schedule that the company plans to sell 100,000 cases of ice lollies during the year, with sales peaking in the third quarter.

Schedule 1

Hampton Freeze Ltd.
Sales budget
for the year ended 31 December 2011

	Quarter 1	2	3	4	Year
Budgeted sales in units (cases of lollies)	10,000	30,000	40,000	20,000	100,000
Selling price per unit	× £20	× £20	× £20	× £20	× £20
Total sales	£200,000	£600,000	£800,000	£400,000	£2,000,000

Schedule of expected cash collections

	1	2	3	4	Year
Debtors, beginning balance*	£90,000				£90,000
First-quarter sales (£200,000 × 70%, 30%)†	140,000	60,000			200,000
Second-quarter sales (£600,000 × 70%, 30%)		420,000	180,000		600,000
Third-quarter sales (£800,000 × 70%, 30%)			560,000	240,000	800,000
Fourth-quarter sales (£400,000 × 70%)‡				280,000	280,000
Total cash collections	£230,000	£480,000	£740,000	£520,000	£1,970,000

* Cash collections from last year's fourth-quarter sales. See the beginning-of-year balance sheet on page 190.

† Cash collections from sales are as follows: 70 per cent collected in the quarter of sale, and the remaining 30 per cent collected in the following year.

‡ Uncollected fourth-quarter sales appear as debtors on the company's end-of-year balance sheet (see Schedule 10 on page 194).

A schedule of expected *cash collections*, such as the one that appears in Schedule 1 for Hampton Freeze, is prepared after the sales budget. This schedule will be needed later to prepare the cash budget. Cash collections consist of collections on sales made to customers in prior periods plus collections on sales made in the current budget period. At Hampton Freeze, experience has shown that 70% of sales are collected in the quarter in which the sale is made and the remaining 30% are collected in the following quarter. So, for example, 70% of the first quarter sales of £200,000 (or £140,000) is collected during the first quarter and 30% (or £60,000) is collected during the second quarter.

The production budget

The production budget is prepared after the sales budget. The **production budget** lists the number of units that must be produced during each budget period to meet sales needs and to provide for the desired ending stock. Production needs can be determined as follows:

Budgeted sales in units	XXXX
Add desired ending stock	XXXX
Total needs	XXXX
Less beginning stock	XXXX
Required production	XXXX

Schedule 2 contains the production budget for Hampton Freeze.

Note that production requirements for a quarter are influenced by the desired level of the ending stock. Stocks should be carefully planned. Excessive stocks tie up funds and create storage problems. Insufficient stocks can lead to lost sales or crash production efforts in the following period. At Hampton Freeze, management believes that an ending stock equal to 20% of the next quarter's sales strikes the appropriate balance.

Schedule 2

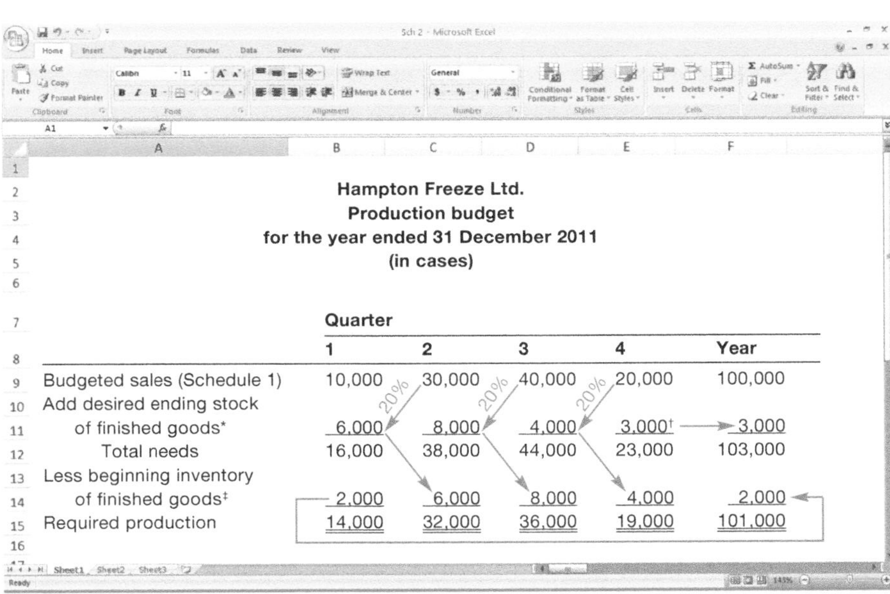

Hampton Freeze Ltd.
Production budget
for the year ended 31 December 2011
(in cases)

	Quarter 1	2	3	4	Year
Budgeted sales (Schedule 1)	10,000	30,000	40,000	20,000	100,000
Add desired ending stock of finished goods*	6,000	8,000	4,000	3,000†	3,000
Total needs	16,000	38,000	44,000	23,000	103,000
Less beginning inventory of finished goods‡	2,000	6,000	8,000	4,000	2,000
Required production	14,000	32,000	36,000	19,000	101,000

*20 per cent of next quarter's sales.
†Estimated.
‡The same as the prior quarter's *ending* stock.

The direct materials budget

Returning to Hampton Freeze's budget data, after the production requirements have been computed, a *direct materials budget* can be prepared. The **direct materials budget** details the raw materials that must be purchased to fulfil the production budget and to provide for adequate stocks. The required purchases of raw materials are computed as follows:

Raw materials needed to meet the production schedule	XXXXX
Add desired ending stock of raw materials	XXXXX
Total raw materials needs	XXXXX
Less beginning stock of raw materials	XXXXX
Raw materials to be purchased	XXXXX

Preparing a budget of this kind is one step in a company's overall **material requirements planning (MRP)**. MRP is an operations management tool that uses a computer to help manage materials and stocks. The objective of MRP is to ensure that the right materials are on hand, in the right quantities, and at the right time to support the production budget. The detailed operation of MRP is covered in most operations management books.

Schedule 3 contains the direct materials budget for Hampton Freeze. The only raw material included in that budget is high fructose sugar, which is the major ingredient in ice lollies other than water. The remaining raw materials are relatively insignificant and are included in variable manufacturing overhead. Notice that materials requirements are first determined in units (kilos, litres, and so on) and then translated into pounds by multiplying by the appropriate unit cost. Also note that the management of Hampton Freeze desires to maintain ending stocks of sugar equal to 10% of the following quarter's production needs.

The direct materials budget is usually accompanied by a schedule of expected cash disbursements for raw materials. This schedule is needed to prepare the overall cash budget. Disbursements for raw materials consist of payments for purchases on account in prior periods plus any payments for purchases in the current budget period. Schedule 3 contains such a schedule of cash disbursements.

The direct labour budget

The **direct labour budget** is also developed from the production budget. Direct labour requirements must be computed so that the company will know whether sufficient labour time is available to meet production needs. By knowing in advance just what will be needed in the way of labour time throughout the budget year, the company can develop plans to adjust the labour force as the situation may require. Firms that neglect to budget run the risk of facing labour shortages, or having to hire and lay off at awkward times. Erratic labour policies lead to insecurity and inefficiency on the part of employees.

To compute direct labour requirements, the number of units of finished product to be produced each period (month, quarter, and so on) is multiplied by the number of direct labour-hours required to produce a single unit. Many different types of labour may be involved. If so, then computations should be by type of labour needed. The direct labour requirements can then be translated into expected direct labour costs. How this is done will depend on the labour policy of the firm. In Schedule 4, the management of Hampton Freeze has assumed that the direct labour force will be adjusted as the work requirements change from quarter to quarter. In that case, the total direct labour cost is computed by simply multiplying the direct labour-hour requirements by the direct labour rate per hour as was done in Schedule 4.

However, many companies have employment policies or contracts that prevent them from laying off and rehiring workers as needed. Suppose, for example, that Hampton Freeze has fifty workers who are classified as direct labour and each of them is guaranteed at least 480 hours of pay each quarter at a rate of £7.50 per hour. In that case, the minimum direct labour cost for a quarter would be as follows:

50 workers × 480 hour × £7.50 = £180,000

Note that in Schedule 4 the direct labour costs for the first and fourth quarters would have to be increased to a £180,000 level if Hampton Freeze's labour policy did not allow it to adjust the workforce at will.

Schedule 3

Hampton Freeze Ltd.
Direct materials budget
for the year ended 31 December 2011

	Quarter 1	2	3	4	Year
Required production (units) (Schedule 2)	14,000	32,000	36,000	19,000	101,000
Raw materials needed per unit (kilos)	× 15	× 15	× 15	× 15	× 10
Production needs (kilos)	210,000	480,000	540,000	285,000	1,515,000
Add desired stock of raw materials (kilos)*	48,000	54,000	28,500	22,500	22,500
Total needs (kilos)	258,000	534,000	568,500	307,500	1,537,500
Less beginning stock of raw materials (kilos)	21,000	48,000	54,000	28,500	21,000
Raw materials to be purchased (kilos)	237,000	486,000	514,500	279,000	1,516,500
Cost of raw materials to be purchased at £0.20 per kilo	£47,400	£97,200	£102,900	£55,800	£303,300

Schedule of expected cash disbursements for materials

	1	2	3	4	Year
Creditors, beginning balance†	£25,800				£25,800
First quarter purchases (£47,000 × 50%, 50%)‡	23,700	£23,700			47,400
Second-quarter purchases (£97,200 × 50%, 50%)		48,600	£48,600		97,200
Third-quarter purchases (£102,900 × 50%, 50%)			51,450	£51,450	102,900
Fourth-quarter purchases (£55,800 × 50%)§				27,900	27,900
Total cash disbursements	£49,500	£72,300	£100,500	£79,350	£301,200

*10 per cent of the next quarter's production needs. For example, the second-quarter production needs are 480,000 kilos. Therefore, the desired ending inventory for the first quarter would be 10 per cent × 480,000 kilos – 48,000 kilos. The ending stock of 22,500 kilos for the fourth quarter is estimated.

†Cash payments for last year's fourth-quarter material purchases. See the beginning-of-year balance sheet on page 190.

‡Cash payments for purchases are as follows: 50 per cent paid for in the quarter of purchase, and the remaining 50 per cent paid for in the following quarter.

§Unpaid fourth-quarter purchases appear as creditors on the company's end-of-year balance sheet (see Schedule 10 on page 194).

The manufacturing overhead budget

The **manufacturing overhead budget** provides a schedule of all costs of production other than direct materials and direct labour. Schedule 5 shows the manufacturing overhead budget for Hampton Freeze.

Schedule 4

Hampton Freeze Ltd.
Direct labour budget
for the year ended 31 December 2011

	Quarter 1	2	3	4	Year
Units (cases) to be produced (Schedule 2)	14,000	32,000	36,000	19,000	101,000
Direct labour time per unit (hours)	× 0.8	× 0.8	× 0.8	× 0.8	× 0.8
Total hours of direct labour time needed	11,200	25,600	28,800	15,200	80,800
Direct labour cost per hour	× £7.50	× £7.50	× £7.50	× £7.50	× £7.50
Total direct labour cost*	£84,000	£192,000	£216,000	£114,000	£606,000

*This schedule assumes that the direct labour workforce will be fully adjusted to the workload (i.e., 'total hours of direct labour time needed') each quarter.

Schedule 5

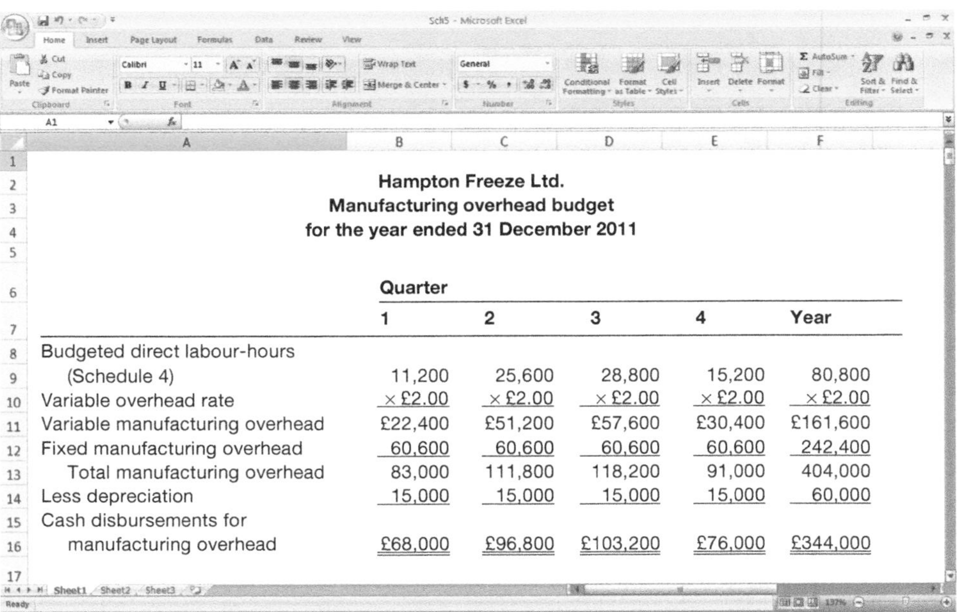

Hampton Freeze Ltd.
Manufacturing overhead budget
for the year ended 31 December 2011

	Quarter 1	2	3	4	Year
Budgeted direct labour-hours (Schedule 4)	11,200	25,600	28,800	15,200	80,800
Variable overhead rate	× £2.00	× £2.00	× £2.00	× £2.00	× £2.00
Variable manufacturing overhead	£22,400	£51,200	£57,600	£30,400	£161,600
Fixed manufacturing overhead	60,600	60,600	60,600	60,600	242,400
Total manufacturing overhead	83,000	111,800	118,200	91,000	404,000
Less depreciation	15,000	15,000	15,000	15,000	60,000
Cash disbursements for manufacturing overhead	£68,000	£96,800	£103,200	£76,000	£344,000

Note how the production costs are separated into variable and fixed components. The variable component is £2 per direct labour-hour. The fixed component is £60,600 per quarter.

The last line of Schedule 5 for Hampton Freeze shows its budgeted cash disbursements for manufacturing overhead. Since some of the overhead costs are not cash outflows, the total budgeted manufacturing overhead costs must be adjusted to determine the cash disbursements for manufacturing overhead. At Hampton Freeze, the only significant non-cash manufacturing overhead cost is depreciation, which is £15,000 per quarter. These non-cash depreciation charges are deducted from the total budgeted manufacturing overhead to determine the expected cash disbursements. Hampton Freeze pays all overhead costs involving cash disbursements in the quarter incurred.

The finished goods stock budget

Schedules 1–5 contain all of the data needed to compute unit product costs. This computation is needed for two reasons: first, to determine cost of goods sold on the budgeted profit and loss account; and second, to know what amount to put on the balance sheet stock account for unsold units. The carrying cost of the unsold units is computed on the **finished goods stock budget**.

The unit product cost computations are shown in Schedule 6. For Hampton Freeze, the absorption costing unit product cost is £13 per case of ice lollies – consisting of £3 of direct materials, £6 of direct labour and £4 of manufacturing overhead. For convenience, the manufacturing overhead is applied to units of product on the basis of direct labour-hours. The budgeted carrying cost of the expected ending stock is £39,000.

The selling and administrative expense budget

The **selling and administrative expense budget** lists the budgeted expenses for areas other than manufacturing. In large organizations, this budget would be a compilation of many smaller, individual budgets submitted by department heads and other persons responsible for selling and administrative expenses. For example, the marketing manager in a large organization would submit a budget detailing the advertising expenses for each budget period.

Schedule 6

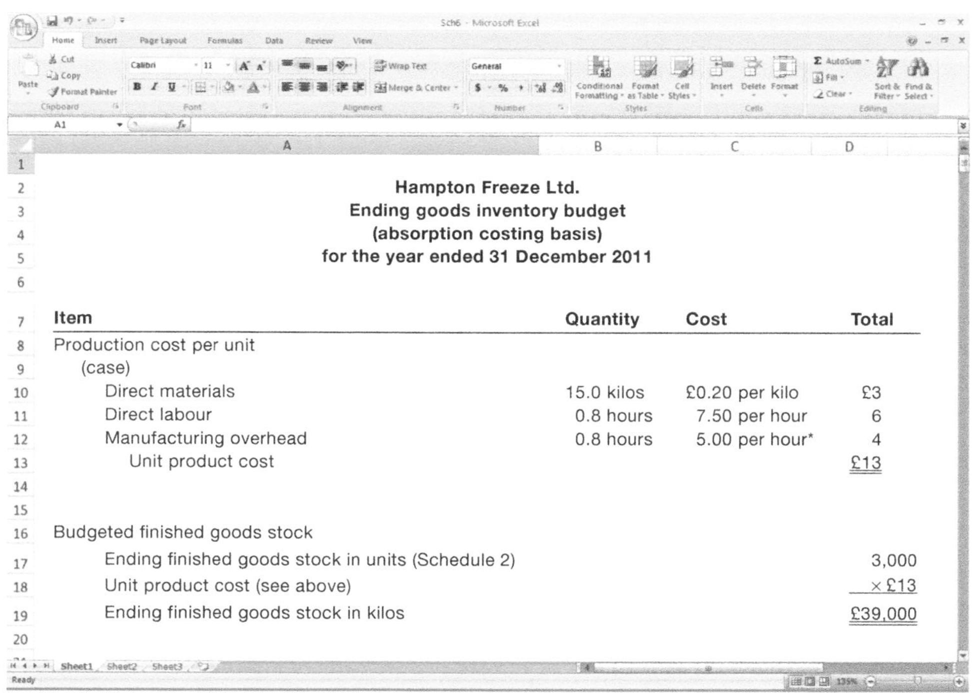

Hampton Freeze Ltd.
Ending goods inventory budget
(absorption costing basis)
for the year ended 31 December 2011

Item	Quantity	Cost	Total
Production cost per unit (case)			
Direct materials	15.0 kilos	£0.20 per kilo	£3
Direct labour	0.8 hours	7.50 per hour	6
Manufacturing overhead	0.8 hours	5.00 per hour*	4
Unit product cost			£13
Budgeted finished goods stock			
Ending finished goods stock in units (Schedule 2)			3,000
Unit product cost (see above)			× £13
Ending finished goods stock in kilos			£39,000

*£404,000 ÷ 80,800 hours = £5.

Schedule 7 contains the selling and administrative expense budget for Hampton Freeze.

Schedule 7

Hampton Freeze Ltd.
Selling and administrative expense budget
for the year ended 31 December 2011

	Quarter				
	1	**2**	**3**	**4**	**Year**
Budgeted sales in units (cases)	10,000	30,000	40,000	20,000	100,000
Variable selling and administrative expense per unit*	× £1.80	× £1.80	× £1.80	× £1.80	× £1.80
Variable expense	£18,000	£54,000	£72,000	£36,000	£180,000
Fixed selling and administrative expenses:					
Advertising	20,000	20,000	20,000	20,000	80,000
Executive salaries	55,000	55,000	55,000	55,000	220,000
Insurance		1,900	37,750		39,650
Property taxes				18,150	18,150
Depreciation	10,000	10,000	10,000	10,000	40,000
Total	85,000	86,900	122,750	103,150	397,800
Total selling and administrative expenses	103,000	140,900	194,750	139,150	577,800
Less depreciation	10,000	10,000	10,000	10,000	40,000
Cash disbursements for selling and administrative expenses	£93,000	£130,900	£184,750	£129,150	£537,800

*Commissions, clerical and shipping.

The cash budget

As illustrated in Exhibit 8.2, the cash budget pulls together much of the data developed in the preceding steps. It is a good idea to restudy Exhibit 8.2 to get the big picture firmly in mind before moving on.

The cash budget is composed of four major sections:

1 The receipts section.
2 The disbursements section.
3 The cash excess or deficiency section.
4 The financing section.

The receipts section consists of a listing of all of the cash inflows, except for financing, expected during the budget period. Generally, the major source of receipts will be from sales.

The disbursements section consists of all cash payments that are planned for the budget period. These payments will include raw materials purchases, direct labour payments, manufacturing overhead costs, and so on, as contained in their respective budgets. In addition, other cash disbursements such as equipment purchases, dividends and other cash withdrawals by owners are listed. For instance, we see in Schedule 8 that management plans to spend £130,000 during the budget period on equipment purchases and £32,000 on dividends to the owners. This is additional information that does not appear on any of the earlier schedules.

The cash excess or deficiency section is computed as follows:

Cash balance, beginning	XXXX
Add receipts	XXXX
Total cash available before financing	XXXX
Less disbursements	XXXX
Excess (deficiency) of cash available over disbursements	XXXX

Schedule 8

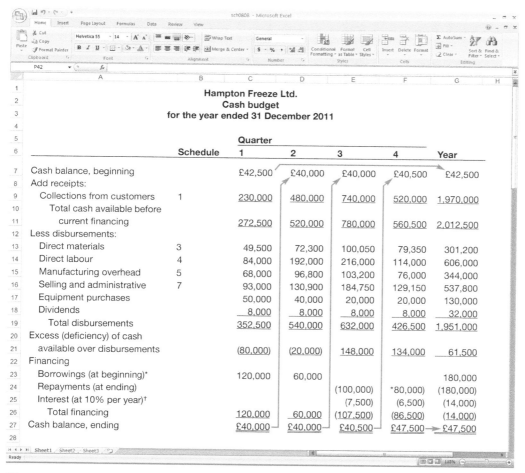

Hampton Freeze Ltd.
Cash budget
for the year ended 31 December 2011

	Schedule	Quarter 1	2	3	4	Year
Cash balance, beginning		£42,500	£40,000	£40,000	£40,500	£42,500
Add receipts:						
Collections from customers	1	230,000	480,000	740,000	520,000	1,970,000
Total cash available before current financing		272,500	520,000	780,000	560,500	2,012,500
Less disbursements:						
Direct materials	3	49,500	72,300	100,050	79,350	301,200
Direct labour	4	84,000	192,000	216,000	114,000	606,000
Manufacturing overhead	5	68,000	96,800	103,200	76,000	344,000
Selling and administrative	7	93,000	130,900	184,750	129,150	537,800
Equipment purchases		50,000	40,000	20,000	20,000	130,000
Dividends		8,000	8,000	8,000	8,000	32,000
Total disbursements		352,500	540,000	632,000	426,500	1,951,000
Excess (deficiency) of cash available over disbursements		(80,000)	(20,000)	148,000	134,000	61,500
Financing						
Borrowings (at beginning)*		120,000	60,000			180,000
Repayments (at ending)				(100,000)	*80,000)	(180,000)
Interest (at 10% per year)†				(7,500)	(6,500)	(14,000)
Total financing		120,000	60,000	(107,500)	(86,500)	(14,000)
Cash balance, ending		£40,000	£40,000	£40,500	£47,500	£47,500

*The company requires a minimum cash balance of £40,000. Therefore, borrowing must be sufficient to cover the cash deficiency of £80,000 in quarter 1 and to provide for the minimum cash balance of £40,000. All borrowings and all repayments of principal are in round £1,000 amounts.

†The interest payments relate only to the principal being repaid at the time it is repaid. For example, the interest in quarter 3 relates only to the interest due on the £100,000 principal being repaid from quarter 1 borrowing: £100,00 × ¾ × 10 per cent = £7,500. The interest paid in quarter 4 is computed as follows:

£20,000 × 10 per cent × 1 year	£2,000
£60,000 × 10 per cent × ¾	4,500
Total interest paid	£6,500

If there is a cash deficiency during any budget period, the company will need to borrow funds. If there is a cash excess during any budget period, funds borrowed in previous periods can be repaid or the idle funds can be placed in short-term or other investments.

The financing section provides a detailed account of the borrowings and repayments projected to take place during the budget period. It also includes a detail of interest payments that will be due on money borrowed. Generally speaking, the cash budget should be broken down into time periods that are as short as feasible. There can be considerable fluctuations in cash balances that would be hidden by looking at a longer time period. While a monthly cash budget is most common, many firms budget cash on a weekly or even daily basis. The quarterly cash budget for Hampton Freeze can be further refined as necessary. This budget appears in Schedule 8; it is assumed that an open line of credit can be arranged with the bank that can be used as needed to bolster the company's cash position. It is also assumed that the interest on any loans taken out with this line of credit would carry an interest rate of 10% per year. For simplicity, it is assumed that all borrowings and repayments are in round £1,000 amounts and that all borrowing occurs at the beginning of a quarter and all repayments are made at the end of a quarter.

In the case of Hampton Freeze, all loans have been repaid by year-end. If all loans are not repaid and a budgeted profit and loss account or balance sheet is being prepared, then interest must be accrued on the unpaid loans. This interest will *not* appear on the cash budget (since it has not yet been paid), but it will appear as part of interest expense on the budgeted profit and loss account and as a liability on the budgeted balance sheet.

LO 3

A budgeted profit and loss account can be prepared from the data developed in Schedules 1–8. The budgeted profit and loss account is one of the key schedules in the budget process. It shows the company's planned profit for the upcoming budget period, and it stands as a benchmark against which subsequent company performance can be measured. Schedule 9 contains the budgeted profit and loss account for Hampton Freeze.

Schedule 9

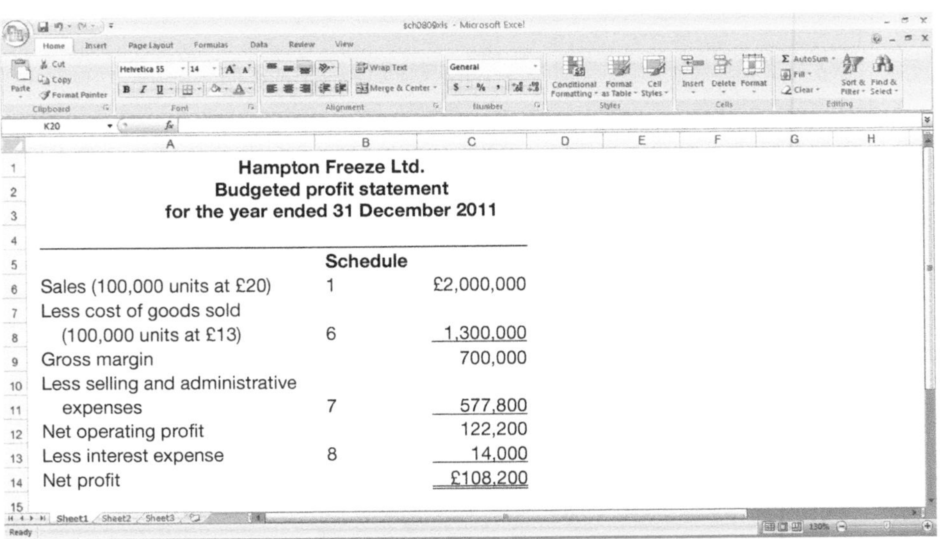

Hampton Freeze Ltd.
Budgeted profit statement
for the year ended 31 December 2011

	Schedule	
Sales (100,000 units at £20)	1	£2,000,000
Less cost of goods sold		
(100,000 units at £13)	6	1,300,000
Gross margin		700,000
Less selling and administrative		
expenses	7	577,800
Net operating profit		122,200
Less interest expense	8	14,000
Net profit		£108,200

The budgeted balance sheet

The budgeted balance sheet is developed by beginning with the current balance sheet and adjusting it for the data contained in the other budgets. Hampton Freeze's budgeted balance sheet is presented in Schedule 10. Some of the data on the budgeted balance sheet has been taken from the company's end of-year balance sheet for 2010 which appears below:

Hampton Freeze Ltd
Balance sheet
31 December 2010

Assets		
Current assets:		
Cash	£42,500	
Debtors	90,000	
Raw materials stock (21,000 kilos)	4,200	
Finished goods stock (2,000 cases)	26,000	
Total current assets		£162,700
Plant and equipment:		
Land	80,000	
Buildings and equipment	700,000	
Accumulated depreciation	(292,000)	
Plant and equipment, net		488,000
Total assets		£650,700
Liabilities and shareholders' equity		
Current liabilities:		
Creditors (raw materials)		£25,800
Shareholders' equity:		
Common stock, no par	£175,000	
Retained earnings	449,900	
Total shareholders' equity		624,900
Total liabilities and shareholders' equity		£650,700

Flexible budgeting: expanding the budgeted profit and loss account

The master budget profit and loss account in Schedule 9 focuses on a single level of activity and has been prepared using absorption costing. Some managers prefer an alternative format that focuses on a *range of* activity and that is prepared using the contribution approach. An example of a master budget profit and loss account using this alternative format is presented in Exhibit 8.3.

A statement such as that in Exhibit 8.3 is flexible, since it is geared to more than one level of activity. If, for example, the company planned to sell 2,000 units during a period but actually sold only 1,900 units, then the budget figures at the 1,900-unit level would be used to compare against actual costs and revenues. Other columns could be added to the budget as needed by simply applying the budget formulas provided. In short, a master budget profit and loss account in this expanded format can be very useful in planning and controlling operations.

Schedule 10

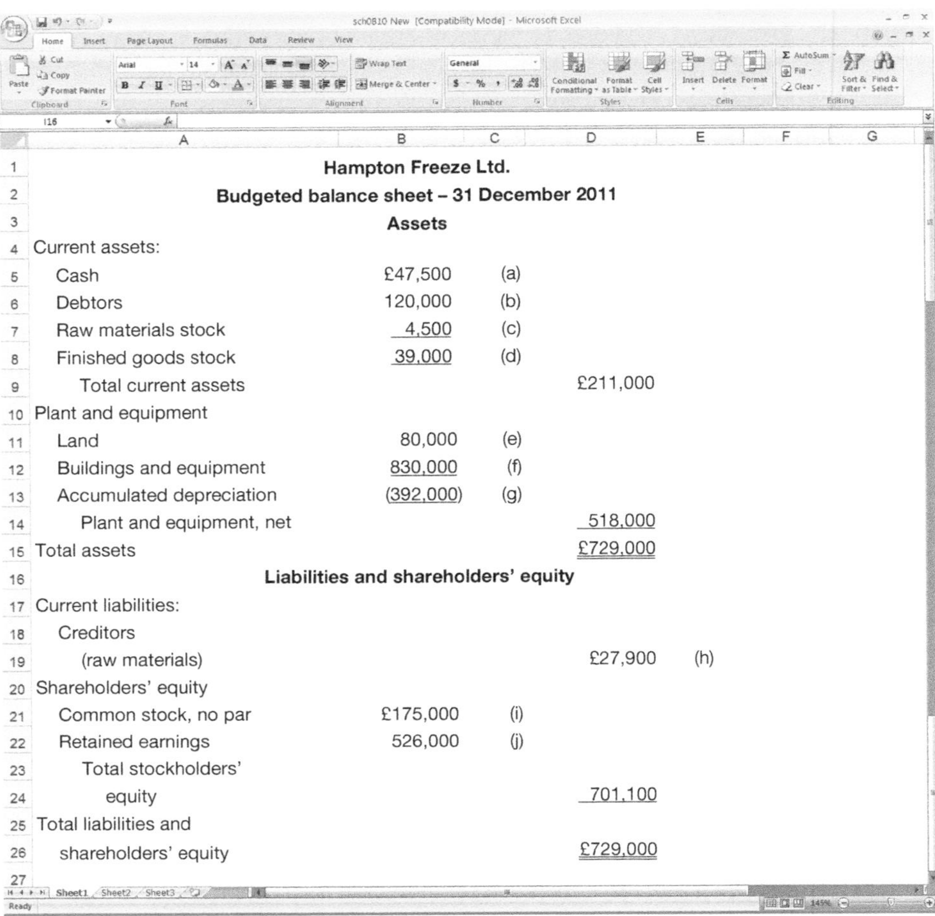

	A	B	C	D	E
1	**Hampton Freeze Ltd.**				
2	**Budgeted balance sheet – 31 December 2011**				
3	**Assets**				
4	Current assets:				
5	Cash	£47,500	(a)		
6	Debtors	120,000	(b)		
7	Raw materials stock	4,500	(c)		
8	Finished goods stock	39,000	(d)		
9	Total current assets			£211,000	
10	Plant and equipment				
11	Land	80,000	(e)		
12	Buildings and equipment	830,000	(f)		
13	Accumulated depreciation	(392,000)	(g)		
14	Plant and equipment, net			518,000	
15	Total assets			£729,000	
16	**Liabilities and shareholders' equity**				
17	Current liabilities:				
18	Creditors				
19	(raw materials)			£27,900	(h)
20	Shareholders' equity				
21	Common stock, no par	£175,000	(i)		
22	Retained earnings	526,000	(j)		
23	Total stockholders'				
24	equity			701,100	
25	Total liabilities and				
26	shareholders' equity			£729,000	

Explanation of 31 December 2011 balance sheet figures:

a The ending cash balance, as projected by the cash budget in Schedule 8.

b 30% of fourth-quarter sales, from Schedule 1 (£400,000 × 30 per cent = £120,000).

c From Schedule 3, the ending raw materials stock will be 22,500 kilos. This material costs £0.20 per kilo. Therefore, the ending stock in kilos will be 22,500 kilos × £0.20 = £4,500.

d From Schedule 6.

e From the 31 December 2010 balance sheet (no change).

f The 31 December 2010 balance sheet indicated a balance of £700,000. During 2011, £130,000 additional equipment will be purchased (see Schedule 8), bringing the 31 December 2011 balance to £830,000.

g The 31 December 2010 balance sheet indicated a balance sheet of £292,000. During 2011, £100,000 of depreciation will be taken (£60,000 on Schedule 5 and £40,000 on Schedule 7), bringing the 31 December 2011 balance to £392,000.

h One-half of the fourth-quarter raw materials purchases, from Schedule 3.

i From the 31 December 2010 balance sheet (no change).

j 31 December 2010 balance	£449,000
Add net profit, from Schedule 9	108,200
	558,100
Deduct dividends paid, from Schedule 8	32,000
31 December 2011 balance	£526,100

Exhibit 8.3 Flexible budget profit statement

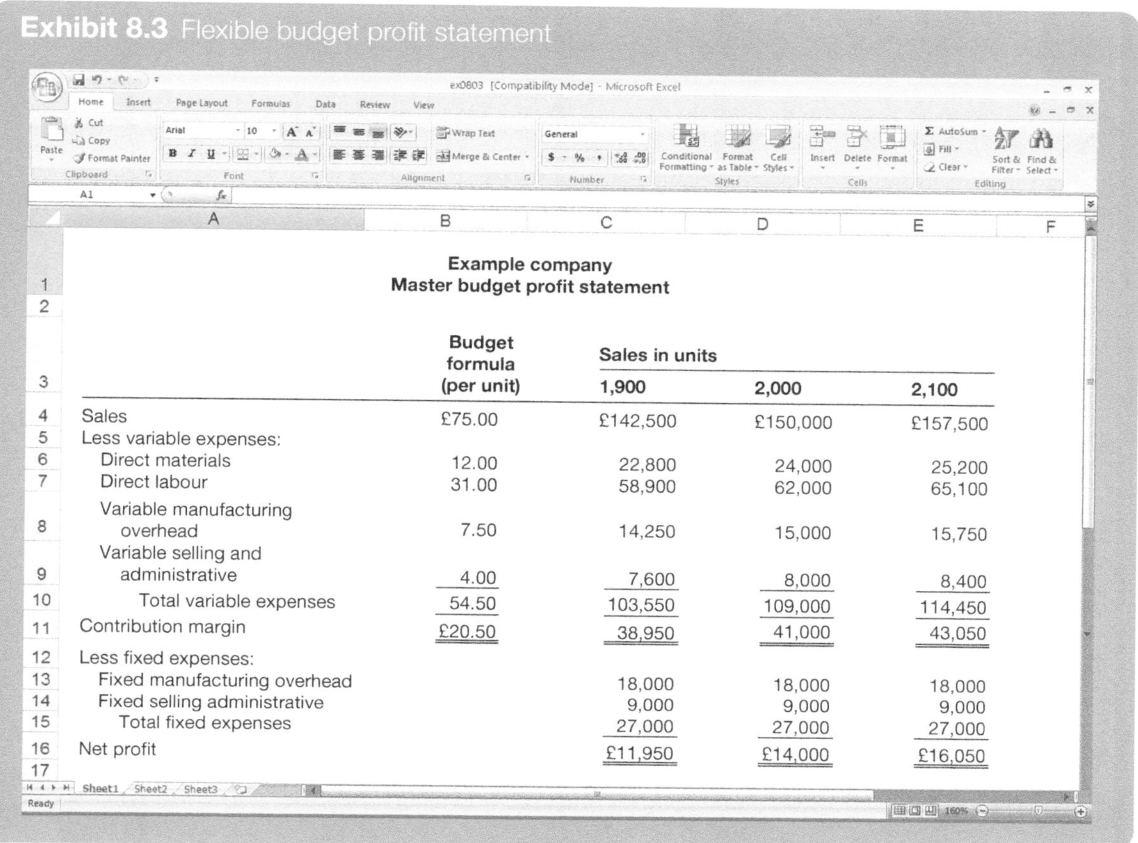

	A	B	C	D	E
1		**Example company**			
2		**Master budget profit statement**			
3		**Budget formula (per unit)**	**Sales in units** 1,900	2,000	2,100
4	Sales	£75.00	£142,500	£150,000	£157,500
5	Less variable expenses:				
6	Direct materials	12.00	22,800	24,000	25,200
7	Direct labour	31.00	58,900	62,000	65,100
8	Variable manufacturing overhead	7.50	14,250	15,000	15,750
9	Variable selling and administrative	4.00	7,600	8,000	8,400
10	Total variable expenses	54.50	103,550	109,000	114,450
11	Contribution margin	£20.50	38,950	41,000	43,050
12	Less fixed expenses:				
13	Fixed manufacturing overhead		18,000	18,000	18,000
14	Fixed selling administrative		9,000	9,000	9,000
15	Total fixed expenses		27,000	27,000	27,000
16	Net profit		£11,950	£14,000	£16,050
17					

Some criticisms of budgeting as a performance management system

LO 4

For many, if not most businesses, the budget is a key planning and control mechanism with many desirable characteristics. Yet budgeting has come in for much criticism in recent years. It has been described by Jan Wallander as 'an unnecessary evil' and Jack Welch as the 'bane of corporate America'.[6] Such criticisms of budgeting are easier to appreciate when looked at in the wider context of performance management systems. Furthermore, not only may we consider some organizational problems caused by budgeting but we can see that there are alternative, or at least supplementary, control models suggested by the performance management perspective.

One common criticism is that budgets produce a particular type of **constrained management style**, they concentrate on easy to measure events and they are *too historically based*. The last point is often linked to the view that budgets tend to be *incrementalist*. Particularly in not-for-profit organizations in the public sector, discussions about changes to budgets concentrate on marginal or incremental increases or decreases in particular departmental budgets. The problem with incrementalism is that activities become institutionalized through the budget and there is a reluctance to ask questions about fundamental purposes.

Another criticism is that budgeting makes organizations *inflexible* and *unable to respond to uncertainty*. Budgeting is seen as being *mechanistic* with *rigid, formalized* and *tightly coupled* systems. Budgeting-led organizations may be slow to recognize changes in the market and also slow to react to changes even when they have been noticed. Other criticisms of budgeting are that it is *too time consuming*, it tends to *focus on cost control* rather than value creation, it tends to be *top down*, it encourages *gaming* and *opportunism*, it reinforces departmental *barriers* and it *hinders knowledge sharing*. Overall it makes *people feel undervalued*.[7]

Much of the criticism of budgeting is driven by a changing business environment, especially the belief that competition in modern markets has increased the importance of *intellectual capital* relative to physical or tangible capital.[8] In order to respond to this new competitive challenge, it is argued that companies need to adopt a *network* rather than a hierarchical, departmental structure. A network model may still use budgets for cash forecasting but not for cost control. The aim is to avoid 'actual versus budget' reports and concentrate on relative performance. These alternative approaches draw on other forms of management control such as benchmarking and the mix of financial and non-financial measures found in approaches such as the balanced scorecard.

Reform or abandon budgeting?

Given the criticisms of budgeting, what is the appropriate response? Currently, there seems to be two main practice-led approaches. One approach is to improving budgeting and the other is to abandon it.[9] If we review the criticisms of budgeting there seems to be two main issues. One issue concerns the question of *predictability*. It could be argued that budgets work well if managers' predictions are reliable because the budget can then represent a viable plan. Conversely, budgets tend to work badly in conditions of great uncertainty and turbulent environments.[10] The other issue concerns *organizational* and *time-frame problems*. It is argued that budgeting fosters a centralizing and stifling atmosphere as well as a possible mismatch between operational strategies and annual reporting cycles. These organizational problems tend to reduce the ability of units and employees to use their initiative as they lack empowerment.

When it is advocated that organizations abandon budgeting, it may mean that budgets are still used for financial purposes but, crucially, not for *performance evaluation*. The aim is to avoid the annual performance trap associated with budgeting by working with what have been called 'relative performance contracts with hindsight'.[11] The significance of the term 'relative' is that performance is benchmarked against *internal* or *external comparators* rather than against historical standards such as last year's results. The term 'with hindsight' means that rather than referring to fixed targets set at the *beginning* of the period, 'targets are adjusted by looking back and incorporating the actual operating and economic circumstances during the period'.[12] Managerial and employee rewards tend to be based on subjective and group criteria with an 'objective to engender a philosophy doing what is best for the firm in the light of current circumstance and to promote teamwork'.[13]

LO 5

Zero-based budgeting

One way to reform budgeting is known as **zero-based budgeting**. Under a zero-based budget, managers are required to justify all budgeted expenditures, not just changes in the budget from the previous year. The baseline is zero rather than last year's budget. A zero-based budget requires considerable documentation. In addition to all the schedules in the usual master budget, the manager must prepare a series of 'decision packages' in which all the activities of the department are ranked according to their relative importance and the cost of each activity is identified. Higher-level managers can then review the decision packages and cut back in those areas that appear to be less critical or whose costs do not appear to be justified.

Under zero-based budgeting, the review is performed every year. Critics of zero-based budgeting charge that properly executed zero-based budgeting is too time consuming and too costly to justify on an annual basis. In addition, it is argued that annual reviews soon become mechanical and that the whole purpose of

Focus on Business Practice

Base budget review

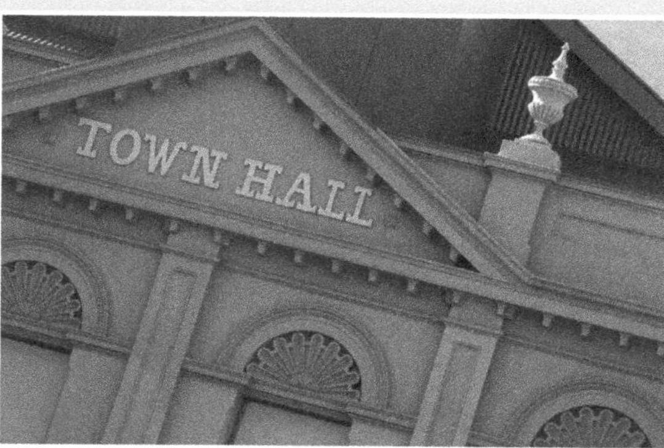

© Mark Evans

Public sector managers have tried to move away from the more traditional incremental approach by introducing priority-led budgeting and base budget review. With priority-led budgeting, budget holders are encouraged to take an investment view, (e.g. spend more now to save later) based on a three year rather than annual perspective. With base budget review, managers do not start with a blank sheet of paper (an extreme view of zero-based budgeting) but are required to take a line-by-line approach and ask 'Do we need that line and do we need that much money?'[14]

Exercise: Consider the impact of employment contracts which seem to make labour costs in the public sector more 'fixed' than in the private sector.

zero-based budgeting is then lost. Whether or not an organization should use an annual review is a matter of judgement. In some situations annual zero-based reviews may be justified; in other situations they may not because of the time and cost involved. However, most managers would at least agree that, on occasion, zero-based reviews can be very helpful.

Summary

- Our purpose has been to present an overview of the budgeting process and to show how the various operating budgets relate to each other.
- We have seen how the sales budget forms the foundation for profit planning. Once the sales budget has been set, the production budget and the selling and administrative budget can be prepared since they depend on how many units are to be sold.
- The production budget determines how many units are to be produced, so after it is prepared, the various manufacturing cost budgets can be prepared. All of these various budgets feed into the cash budget and the budgeted profit and loss account and balance sheet.
- There are many connections between these various parts of the master budget. For example, the schedule of expected cash collections, which is completed in connection with the sales budget, provides data for both the cash budget and the budgeted balance sheet.
- Although budgeting is a very widespread practice, it has come in for some criticism and some suggestions for reform and even calls the abandonment of budgeting as a performance control system.

Key terms

Budget committee A group of key management persons who are responsible for overall policy matters relating to the budget programme and for co-ordinating the preparation of the budget (p. 182).

Cash budget A detailed plan showing how cash resources will be acquired and used over some specific time period (p. 183).

Constrained management style A management approach that concentrates on easy to measure events and lacks flexibility (p. 195).

Continuous or perpetual budget A 12-month budget that rolls forward one month as the current month is completed (p. 180).

Direct labour budget A detailed plan showing labour requirements over some specific time period (p. 186).

Direct materials budget A detailed plan showing the amount of raw materials that must be purchased during a period to meet both production and stock needs (p. 186).

Finished goods stock budget A budget showing the cost expected to appear on the balance sheet for unsold units at the end of a period (p. 189).

Manufacturing overhead budget A detailed plan showing the production costs, other than direct materials and direct labour, that will be incurred over a specified time period (p. 187).

Master budget A summary of a company's plans in which specific targets are set for sales, production, distribution, and financing activities and that generally culminates in a cash budget, budgeted profit and loss account, and budgeted balance sheet (p. 183).

Material requirements planning (MRP) An operations management tool that uses a computer to help manage materials and stocks (p. 186).

Participative budget *See* Self-imposed budget (p. 180).

Production budget A detailed plan showing the number of units that must be produced during a period in order to meet both sales and stock needs (p. 185).

Sales budget A detailed schedule showing the expected sales for coming periods; these sales are typically expressed in both pounds and units (p. 183).

Self-imposed budget A method of preparing budgets in which managers prepare their own budgets. These budgets are then reviewed by the manager's supervisor, and any issues are resolved by mutual agreement (p. 180).

Selling and administrative expense budget A detailed schedule of planned expenses that will be incurred in areas other than manufacturing during a budget period (p. 189).

Zero-based budgeting A method of budgeting in which managers are required to justify all costs as if the programmes involved were being proposed for the first time (p. 196)

Endnotes

1. Bates, Rizvi, Tewari and Vardan (2001).
2. See, e.g., Aldrick (2008).
3. Carruth, McClendon and Ballard (1983).
4. Hope and Hope (1997).
5. Wildavsky (1975).
6. Wildavsky (1975).
7. Neely, Sutcliff and Heyns (2001).
8. Hope and Hope (1997).
9. Hansen, Otley and Van der Stede (2003).
10. Wallander (1999).
11. Hansen *et al.* (2003), p. 101.
12. Hansen *et al.* (2003), p. 101.
13. Hansen *et al.* (2003), p. 102.
14. Seal and Ball (2008).

connect™

When you have read this chapter, log on to the Online Learning Centre for *Management Accounting for Business Decisions* at **www.mheducation.co.uk/textbooks/sealmabd1**, where you'll find multiple choice questions, practice exams and extra study tools for management accounting.

Assessment

Questions

connect™

8–1 What is a budget? What is budgetary control?
8–2 Discuss some of the major benefits to be gained from budgeting.
8–3 What is a master budget? Briefly describe its contents.
8–4 Why is the sales forecast the starting point in budgeting?
8–5 Describe the flow of budget data in an organization. Who are the participants in the budgeting process, and how do they participate?
8–6 What is a self-imposed/participatory budget? What are the major advantages of self-imposed budgets? What caution must be exercised in their use?
8–7 How can budgeting assist a firm in its employment policies?
8–8 'The principal purpose of the cash budget is to see how much cash the company will have in the bank at the end of the year.' Do you agree? Explain.
8–9 How does zero-based budgeting differ from traditional budgeting?

Exercises

connect™

E8–1 Time allowed: 20 minutes

Silver Company makes a product that has peak sales in May of each year. These peak sales are shown in the company's sales budget for the second quarter given below:

	April	May	June	Total
Budgeted sales	£300,000	£500,000	£200,000	£1,000,000

From past experience, the company has learned that 20% of a month's sales are collected in the month of sale, that another 70% is collected in the month following sale, and that the remaining 10% is collected in the second month following sale. Bad debts are negligible and can be ignored. February sales totalled £230,000 and March sales totalled £260,000.

Required

1 Prepare a schedule of expected cash collections from sales, by month and in total, for the second quarter.
2 Assume that the company will prepare a budgeted balance sheet as of 30 June. Compute the debtors as of that date.

E8–2 Time allowed: 10 minutes

Down Under Products Ltd of Australia has budgeted sales of its popular boomerang for the next four months as follows:

	Sales in units
April	50,000
May	75,000
June	90,000
July	80,000

The company is now in the process of preparing a production budget for the second quarter. Past experience has shown that end-of-month stock levels must equal 10% of the following month's sales. The stock at the end of March was 5,000 units.

Required

Prepare a production budget for the second quarter. In your budget, show the number of units to be produced each month and for the quarter in total.

E8–3 Time allowed: 15 minutes

Three grams of musk oil are required for each bottle of Mink Caress, a very popular perfume made by a small company in western Siberia. The cost of the musk oil is 150 roubles per gram. (Siberia is located in Russia, whose currency is the rouble.) Budgeted production of Mink Caress is given below by quarters for Year 2 and for the first quarter of Year 3.

	Year 2 quarter				Year 3 quarter
	First	**Second**	**Third**	**Fourth**	**First**
Budgeted production, in bottles	60,000	90,000	150,000	100,000	70,000

Musk oil has become so popular as a perfume base that it has become necessary to carry large inventories as a precaution against stock-outs. For this reason, the stock of musk oil at the end of a quarter must be equal to 20% of the following quarter's production needs. Some 36,000 grams of musk oil will be on hand to start the first quarter of Year 2.

Required

Prepare a materials purchases budget for musk oil, by quarter and in total, for Year 2. At the bottom of your budget, show the amount of purchases in roubles for each quarter and for the year in total.

E8–4 Time allowed: 25 minutes

You have been asked to prepare a December cash budget for Ashton Company, a distributor of exercise equipment. The following information is available about the company's operations:

1 The cash balance on 1 December will be £40,000.
2 Actual sales for October and November and expected sales for December are as follows:

	October	November	December
Cash sales	£65,000	£70,000	£83,000
Sales on account	400,000	525,000	600,000

Sales on account are collected over a three-month period in the following ratio: 20% collected in the month of sale, 60% collected in the month following sale, and 18% collected in the second month following sale. The remaining 2% is uncollectable.

3 Purchases of stock will total £280,000 for December and 30% of a month's stock purchases are paid during the month of purchase. The accounts payable remaining from November's stock purchases total £161,000, all of which will be paid in December.
4 Selling and administrative expenses are budgeted at £420,000 for December. Of this amount, £50,000 is for depreciation.
5 A new web server for the Marketing Department costing £76,000 will be purchased for cash during December, and dividends totalling £9,000 will be paid during the month.
6 The company must maintain a minimum cash balance of £20,000. An open line of credit is available from the company's bank to bolster the cash position as needed.

Required

1 Prepare a schedule of expected cash collections for December.
2 Prepare a schedule of expected cash disbursements during December to suppliers for materials for stock purchases.
3 Prepare a cash budget for December. Indicate in the financing section any borrowing that will be needed during the month.

Problems

connect™

P8–5 Production and purchases budgets

Time allowed: 40 minutes

Pearl Products Limited of Shenzhen, China, manufactures and distributes toys throughout South East Asia. Three cubic centimetres (cc) of solvent H300 are required to manufacture each unit of Supermix, one of the company's products. The company is now planning raw materials needs for the third quarter, the quarter in which peak sales of Supermix occur. To keep production and sales moving smoothly, the company has the following stock requirements:

1 The finished goods stock on hand at the end of each month must be equal to 3,000 units of Supermix plus 20% of the next month's sales. The finished goods stock on 30 June is budgeted to be 10,000 units.
2 The raw materials stock on hand at the end of each month must be equal to one-half of the following month's production needs for raw materials. The raw materials stock on 30 June is budgeted to be 54,000 cc of solvent H300.
3 The company maintains no work in progress stocks.

A sales budget for Supermix for the last six months of the year follows.

	Budgeted sales in units
July	35,000
August	40,000
September	50,000
October	30,000
November	20,000
December	10,000

Required

1 Prepare a production budget for Supermix for the months July–October.
2 Examine the production budget that you prepared in Question 1 above. Why will the company produce more units than it sells in July and August, and fewer units than it sells in September and October?
3 Prepare a budget showing the quantity of solvent H300 to be purchased for July, August and September, and for the quarter in total.

P8–6 Evaluating a company's budget procedures

Time allowed: 30 minutes

Springfield Corporation operates on a calendar-year basis. It begins the annual budgeting process in late August, when the managing director establishes targets for the total pound sales and net income before taxes for the next year.

The sales target is given to the Marketing Department, where the marketing manager formulates a sales budget by product line in both units and pounds. From this budget, sales quotas by product line in units and pounds are established for each of the corporation's sales districts.

The marketing manager also estimates the cost of the marketing activities required to support the target sales volume and prepares a tentative marketing expense budget.

The operations manager uses the sales and profit targets, the sales budget by product line, and the tentative marketing expense budget to determine the pound amounts that can be devoted to manufacturing and corporate office expense. The operations manager prepares the budget for corporate expenses, and then forwards to the Production Department the product-line sales budget in units and the total pound amount that can be devoted to manufacturing.

The production manager meets with the factory managers to develop a manufacturing plan that will produce the required units when needed within the cost constraints set by the operations manager. The budgeting process usually comes to a halt at this point because the Production Department does not consider the financial resources allocated to be adequate.

When this standstill occurs, the director of finance, the operations manager, the marketing manager and the production manager meet to determine the final budgets for each of the areas. This normally results in a modest increase in the total amount available for manufacturing costs, while the marketing expense and corporate office expense budgets are cut. The total sales and profit figures proposed by the managing director are seldom changed. Although the participants are seldom pleased with the compromise, these budgets are final. Each executive then develops a new detailed budget for the operations in his or her area.

None of the areas has achieved its budget in recent years. Sales often run below the target. When budgeted sales are not achieved, each area is expected to cut costs so that the managing director's profit target can still be met. However, the profit target is seldom met because costs are not cut enough. In fact, costs often run above the original budget in all functional areas. The managing director is disturbed that Springfield has not been able to meet the sales and profit targets. He hired a consultant with considerable experience with companies in Springfield's industry. The consultant reviewed the budgets

for the past four years. He concluded that the product-line sales budgets were reasonable and that the cost and expense budgets were adequate for the budgeted sales and production levels.

Required

1. Discuss how the budgeting process as employed by Springfield Corporation contributes to the failure to achieve the managing director's sales and profit targets.
2. Suggest how Springfield Corporation's budgeting process could be revised to correct the problem.
3. Should the functional areas be expected to cut their costs when sales volume falls below budget? Explain your answer.

(*CMA, adapted*)

Chapter 9
Standard costing and variance analysis

LO Learning **objectives**

After studying Chapter 9, you should be able to:

1. Explain how direct materials standards and direct labour standards are set
2. Compute the direct materials price and quantity variances and explain their significance
3. Compute the direct labour rate and efficiency variances and explain their significance
4. Compute the variable manufacturing overhead spending and efficiency variances
5. Understand the advantages of and the potential problems with using standard costs

Concepts **in Context**

Reproduced with permission from Natuzzi SpA

Natuzzi SpA, founded and run by Pasquale Natuzzi, produces handmade leather furniture for the world market in Santeramo in Colle in southern Italy. Natuzzi is export-oriented and has, for example, about 7% of the US leather furniture market. The company's furniture is handmade by craftsmen, each of whom has a computer terminal that is linked to a sophisticated computer network. The computer terminal provides precise instructions on how to accomplish a particular task in making a piece of furniture. And the computer keeps track of how quickly the craftsman completes the task. If the craftsman beats the standard time to complete the task, the computer adds a bonus to the craftsman's pay.

The company's computers know exactly how much thread, screws, foam, leather, labour, and so on, is required for every model. 'Should the price of Argentinian hides or German dyes rise one day, employees in Santeramo enter the new prices into the computer, and the costs for all sofas with that leather and those colours are immediately recalculated. "Everything has to be clear for me," says Natuzzi. "Why this penny? Where is it going?" '[1]

How do managers control the prices that are paid for inputs and the quantities that are used? They could examine every transaction in detail, but this obviously would be an inefficient use of management time. For many companies, the answer to this control problem lies at least partially in standard costs[2] which are part of an approach to management known as management by exception.

A *standard* is a *benchmark* or '*norm*' for measuring performance. Standards are found everywhere. Your doctor evaluates your weight using standards that have been set for individuals of your age, height and gender. The food we eat in restaurants must be prepared under specified standards of cleanliness. The buildings we live in must conform to standards set in building codes. Standards are also used widely in management accounting where they relate to the *quantity* and *cost* of inputs used in manufacturing goods or providing services.

Standard costs – management by exception

Managers – often assisted by engineers and accountants – set quantity and cost standards for each major input such as raw materials and labour time. *Quantity standards* indicate how much of an input should be used in manufacturing a unit of product or in providing a unit of service. *Cost (price) standards* indicate what the cost, or purchase price, of the input should be. Actual quantities and actual costs of inputs are compared to these standards. If either the quantity or the cost of inputs departs significantly from the standards, managers investigate the discrepancy. The purpose is to find the cause of the problem and then eliminate it so that it does not recur. This process is called **management by exception**.

In our daily lives, we operate in a management by exception mode most of the time. Consider what happens when you sit down in the driver's seat of your car. You put the key in the ignition, you turn the key, and your car starts. Your expectation (standard) that the car will start is met; you do not have to open the car bonnet and check the battery, the connecting cables, the fuel lines and so on. If you turn the key and the car does not start, then you have a discrepancy (variance). Your expectations are not met, and you need to investigate why. Note that even if the car starts after a second try, it would be wise to investigate anyway. The fact that the expectation was not met should be viewed as an opportunity to uncover the cause of the problem rather than as simply an annoyance. If the underlying cause is not discovered and corrected, the problem may recur and become much worse.

Who uses standard costs?

Manufacturing, service, food, and not-for-profit organizations all make use of standards to some extent; car service centres, for example, often set specific labour time standards for the completion of certain work tasks, such as installing a carburettor or doing a valve job, and then measure actual performance against these standards. Fastfood outlets such as McDonald's have exacting standards as to the quantity of meat going into a sandwich, as well as standards for the cost of the meat. In short, you are likely to run into standard costs in virtually any line of business that you enter.

Manufacturing companies often have highly developed standard costing systems in which standards relating to materials, labour and overhead are developed in detail for each separate product. These standards are listed on a **standard cost card** that provides the manager with a great deal of information concerning the inputs that are required to produce a unit and their costs. In the following section, we provide a detailed example of the setting of standard costs and the preparation of a standard cost card.

Setting standard costs

Setting price and quantity standards is more an art than a science. It requires the combined expertise of all persons who have responsibility over input prices and over the effective use of inputs. In a manufacturing setting, this might include accountants, purchasing managers, engineers, production supervisors, line managers and production workers. Past records of purchase prices and of input usage can be helpful in setting standards. However, the standards should be designed to encourage efficient *future* operations, not a repetition of past inefficient operations.

Focus on Business Practice

Setting standards for machine running speeds

© James Grimes

Corrugated containers, more commonly known as cardboard boxes, are a relatively standardized product in terms of material content and manufacturing process. The appearance (or print) on boxes varies considerably according to customers' requirements however. The raw materials consist of heavy papers, one or two of which is corrugated (wavy) providing strength. This material, termed corrugated board, is produced in a highly automated process resulting in large flat sheets. These sheets, in turn, are cut to shape and size, and printed on according to customer orders.

A typical corrugated manufacturing plant will have one machine called a corrugator which makes the sheets of corrugated board, and four to six conversion machines which cut and print the board. For costing and production scheduling purposes, each machine is assigned a standard running speed(s). The standard running speeds are input into costing and scheduling software and updated regularly. How are these standards set and updated? When a new machine is installed at a corrugated plant, the manufacturers provide a maximum running speed (the ideal standard) and also an achievable speed (the practical standard) based on their prior installation experience. As the machine operates, data on running speed can be recorded – automatically usually – as most machines provide interfaces to production scheduling software. This actual data can be used to check against the initial standard speeds and updated if required. Some costing and scheduling software gets even smarter (e.g. Kiwiplan, www.kiwiplan.com), by using a rolling-average running speed based on a products manufacturing history. It may also be possible to have multiple standard running speeds on a machine, for example where a particularly complex customer graphic slows down the printing on a box.

Exercise: Having read the piece above, what role do you think machine operators can play in setting standard running speeds and keeping them updated?

Ideal versus practical standards

Should standards be attainable all of the time, should they be attainable only part of the time, or should they be so tight that they become, in effect, 'the impossible dream'? Opinions among managers vary, but standards tend to fall into one of two categories – either ideal or practical.

Ideal standards are those that can be attained only under the best circumstances. They allow for no machine breakdowns or other work interruptions, and they call for a level of effort that can be attained only by the most skilled and efficient employees working at peak effort 100% of the time. Some managers feel that such standards have a motivational value. These managers argue that even though employees know they will

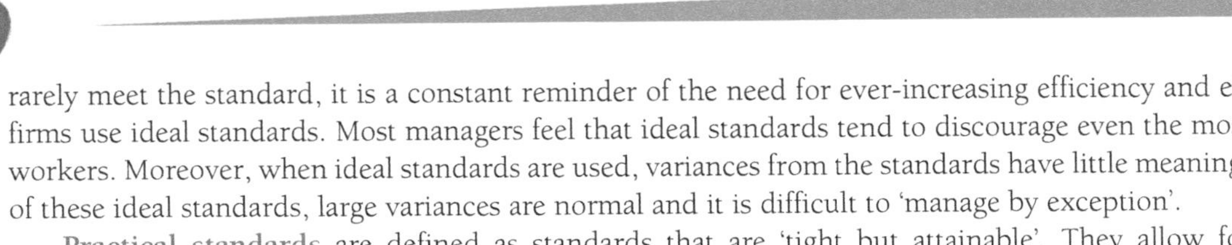

rarely meet the standard, it is a constant reminder of the need for ever-increasing efficiency and effort. Few firms use ideal standards. Most managers feel that ideal standards tend to discourage even the most diligent workers. Moreover, when ideal standards are used, variances from the standards have little meaning. Because of these ideal standards, large variances are normal and it is difficult to 'manage by exception'.

Practical standards are defined as standards that are 'tight but attainable'. They allow for normal machine downtime and employee rest periods, and they can be attained through reasonable, though highly efficient, efforts by the average worker. Variances from such a standard are very useful to management in that they represent deviations that fall outside of normal operating conditions and signal a need for management attention. Furthermore, practical standards can serve multiple purposes. In addition to signalling abnormal conditions, they can also be used in forecasting cash flows and in planning stocks. By contrast, ideal standards cannot be used in forecasting and planning; they do not allow for normal inefficiencies, and therefore they result in unrealistic planning and forecasting figures.

Throughout the remainder of this chapter, we will assume the use of practical rather than ideal standards.

LO 1

Setting direct materials standards

To illustrate the development of a standard costing system, consider the example of the Colonial Pewter Company that was organized a year ago. The company's only product at present is a reproduction of an eighteenth-century pewter bookend. The bookend is largely made by hand, using traditional metal-working tools. Consequently, the manufacturing process is labour intensive and requires a high level of skill.

The first task was to prepare price and quantity standards for the company's only significant raw material, pewter ingots. The **standard price per unit** for direct materials should reflect the final, delivered cost of the materials, net of any discounts taken. The company prepared the following documentation for the standard price of a kilo of pewter in ingot form:

Purchase price, top-grade pewter ingots, in 40-kilo ingots	£3.60
Freight, by truck, from the suppliers	0.44
Receiving and handling	0.05
Less purchase discount	(0.09)
Standard price per kilo	£4.00

Notice that the *standard price* reflects a particular grade of material (top grade), purchased in particular lot sizes (40-kilo ingots), and delivered by a particular type of carrier (truck). Allowances have also been made for handling and discounts. If everything proceeds according to these expectations, the net standard price of a kilo of pewter should therefore be £4.00.

The **standard quantity per unit** for direct materials should reflect the amount of material going into each unit of finished product, as well as an allowance for unavoidable waste, spoilage and other normal inefficiencies. The company prepared the following documentation for the standard quantity of pewter going into a pair of bookends:

Material requirements as specified in the bill of materials for a pair of bookends, in kilos	2.7
Allowance for waste and spoilage, in kilos	0.2
Allowance for rejects, in kilos	0.1
Standard quantity per pair of bookends, in kilos	3.0

A **bill of materials** is a list that shows the type and quantity of each item of material going into a unit of finished product. It is a handy source for determining the basic material input per unit, but it should be adjusted for waste and other factors, as shown above, when determining the standard quantity per unit of product. 'Waste and spoilage' in the table above refers to materials that are wasted as a normal part of the production process or that spoil before they are used. 'Rejects' refers to the direct material contained in units that are defective and must be scrapped.

Once the price and quantity standards have been set, the standard cost of material per unit of finished product can be computed as follows:

3.0 kilos per unit × £4.00 per kilo = £12 per unit

This £12 cost figure will appear as one item on the standard cost card of the product.

Setting direct labour standards

Direct labour price and quantity standards are usually expressed in terms of a labour rate and labour-hours. The **standard rate per hour** for direct labour would include not only wages earned but also fringe benefits and other labour costs. Using last month's wage records, the company determined the standard rate per hour at the Colonial Pewter Company as follows:

Basic wage rate per hour	£10
Employment taxes at 10% of the basic rate	1
Fringe benefits at 30% of the basic rate	3
Standard rate per direct labour-hour	£14

Many companies prepare a single standard rate for all employees in a department. This standard rate reflects the expected 'mix' of workers, even though the actual wage rates may vary somewhat from individual to individual due to differing skills or seniority. A single standard rate simplifies the use of standard costs and also permits the manager to monitor the use of employees within departments. According to the standard computed above, the direct labour rate for Colonial Pewter should average £14 per hour.

The standard direct labour time required to complete a unit of product (generally called the **standard hours per unit**) is perhaps the single most difficult standard to determine. One approach is to divide each operation performed on the product into elemental body movements (such as reaching, pushing, and turning over). Published tables of standard times for such movements are available. These times can be applied to the movements and then added together to determine the total standard time allowed per operation. Another approach is for an industrial engineer to do a time and motion study, actually clocking the time required for certain tasks. As stated earlier, the standard time should include allowances for coffee breaks, personal needs of employees, cleanup, and machine downtime. After consulting with the production managers, the company prepared the following documentation for the standard hours per unit:

Basic labour time per unit, in hours	1.9
Allowance for breaks and personal needs	0.1
Allowance for cleanup and machine downtime	0.3
Allowance for rejects	0.2
Standard labour-hours per unit of product	2.5

Once the rate and time standards have been set, the standard labour cost per unit of product can be computed as follows:

2.5 hours per unit × £14 per hour = £35 per unit

This £35 cost figure appears along with direct materials as one item on the standard cost card of the product.

Setting variable manufacturing overhead standards

As with direct labour, the price and quantity standards for variable manufacturing overhead are generally expressed in terms of rate and hours. The rate represents *the variable portion of the predetermined overhead rate* discussed in Chapter 5; the hours represent whatever hours base is used to apply overhead to units of product (usually machine-hours or direct labour-hours). At Colonial Pewter, the variable portion of the

Exhibit 9.1 Standard cost card – variable production cost

Input	(1) Standard quantity or hours	(2) Standard price or rate	(3) Standard cost (1) × (2)
Direct materials	3.0 kilos	£4.00	£12.00
Direct labour	2.5 hours	14.00	35.00
Variable manufacturing overhead	2.5 hours	3.00	7.50
Total standard cost per unit			£54.50

predetermined overhead rate is £3 per direct labour-hour. Therefore, the standard variable manufacturing overhead cost per unit is computed as follows:

2.5 hours per unit × £3 per hour = £7.50 per unit

This £7.50 cost figure appears along with direct materials and direct labour as one item on the standard cost card in Exhibit 9.1. Observe that the **standard cost per unit** is computed by multiplying the standard quantity or hours by the standard price or rate.

Are standards the same as budgets?

Standards and *budgets* are very similar. The major distinction between the two terms is that a standard is a *unit* amount, whereas a budget is a *total* amount. The standard cost for materials at Colonial Pewter is £12 per pair of bookends. If 1,000 pairs of bookends are to be manufactured during a budgeting period, then the budgeted cost of materials would be £12,000. In effect, *a standard can be viewed as the budgeted cost for one unit of product.*

Focus on Business Practice

Cost controlling in restaurants

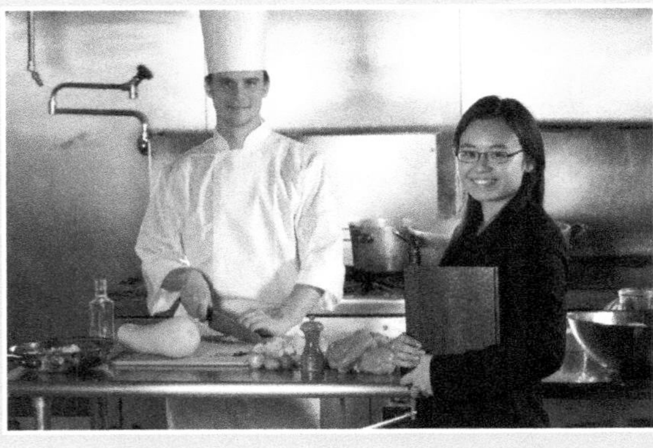

© stockstudioX

VIRBUS is a European Union funded initiative which offers an online learning, help and business management platform to the hospitality sector. One of the items to be found on their website is some useful advice to restaurateurs on controlling costs. One basic piece of advice offered is to use standard recipes as the basis of a menu, which in turn can be used to control costs and set prices. By using standard quantities/recipes for each item on a menu, kitchen staff can monitor usage of ingredients and record wastage. Apart from ingredients, labour is another major cost in restaurants. Here, VIRBUS recommends a median or average (i.e. standard) labour cost can be calculated and used for costing and pricing purposes. This labour cost can be increased to reflect additional payroll items such as overtime or social insurance. The labour cost can be combined with the hours worked by kitchen and waiting staff to determine a total labour cost per week or month if required.[3]

Exercise: Do you think a restaurant owner can ensure that standard recipes and ingredients are *always* used? Try to think of examples when this would not occur and the effects on cost.

A general model for variance analysis

An important reason for separating standards into two categories – price and quantity – is that different managers are usually responsible for buying and for using inputs and these two activities occur at different points in time. In the case of raw materials, for example, the purchasing manager is responsible for the price, and this responsibility is exercised at the time of purchase. In contrast, the production manager is responsible for the amount of the raw material used, and this responsibility is exercised when the materials are used in production, which may be many weeks or months after the purchase date. It is important, therefore, that we cleanly separate discrepancies due to deviations from price standards from those due to deviations from quantity standards. Differences between *standard* prices and *actual* prices and *standard* quantities and *actual* quantities are called **variances**. The act of computing and interpreting variances is called *variance analysis*.

Price and quantity variances

A general model for computing standard cost variances for variable costs is presented in Exhibit 9.2. This model isolates price variances from quantity variances and shows how each of these is computed. We will be using this model throughout the chapter to compute variances in direct materials, direct labour and variable manufacturing overhead.

Three things should be noted from Exhibit 9.2. First, note that a price variance and a quantity variance can be computed for all three variable cost elements – direct materials, direct labour and variable manufacturing overhead – even though the variance is not called by the same name in all cases. For example, a price variance is called a *materials price variance* in the case of direct materials but a *labour rate variance* in the case of direct labour and an *overhead spending variance* in the case of variable manufacturing overhead.

Second, note that even though a price variance may be called by different names, it is computed in exactly the same way regardless of whether one is dealing with direct materials, direct labour or variable manufacturing overhead. The same is true with the quantity variance.

Third, note that *variance analysis* is actually a type of input–output analysis. The inputs represent the actual quantity of direct materials, direct labour and variable manufacturing overhead used; the output represents the good production of the period, expressed in terms of the *standard quantity (or the standard hours) allowed for the actual output* (see column 3 in Exhibit 9.2). By **standard quantity allowed** or

Exhibit 9.2 A general model for variance analysis – variable production costs

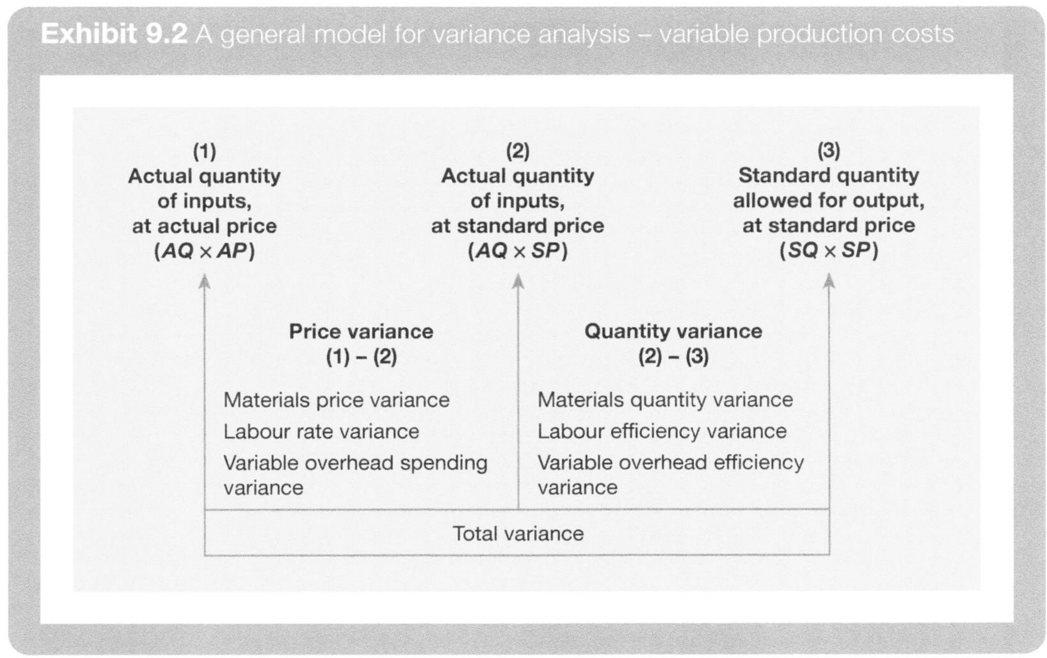

standard hours allowed, we mean the amount of direct materials, direct labour or variable manufacturing overhead *that should have been used to* produce the actual output of the period. This could be more or could be less materials, labour or overhead than was *actually* used, depending on the efficiency or inefficiency of operations. The standard quantity allowed is computed by multiplying the actual output in units by the standard input allowed per unit.

With this general model as a foundation, we will now examine the price and quantity variances in more detail.

LO 2 Using standard costs – direct materials variances

After determining standard costs for direct materials, direct labour, and variable manufacturing overhead, Colonial Pewter Company's next step was to compute the company's variances for June, the most recent month. As discussed in the preceding section, variances are computed by comparing standard costs to actual costs. To facilitate this comparison, the company referred to the standard cost data contained in Exhibit 9.1. This exhibit shows that the standard cost of direct materials per unit of product is as follows:

3.0 kilos per unit × £4.00 per kilo = £12 per unit

Colonial Pewter's purchasing records for June showed that 6,500 kilos of pewter were purchased at a cost of £3.80 per kilo. This cost figure included freight and handling and was net of the quantity discount. All of the material purchased was used during June to manufacture 2,000 pairs of pewter bookends. Using these data and the standard costs from Exhibit 9.1, the company computed the price and quantity variances shown in Exhibit 9.3.

Exhibit 9.3 Variance analysis – direct materials

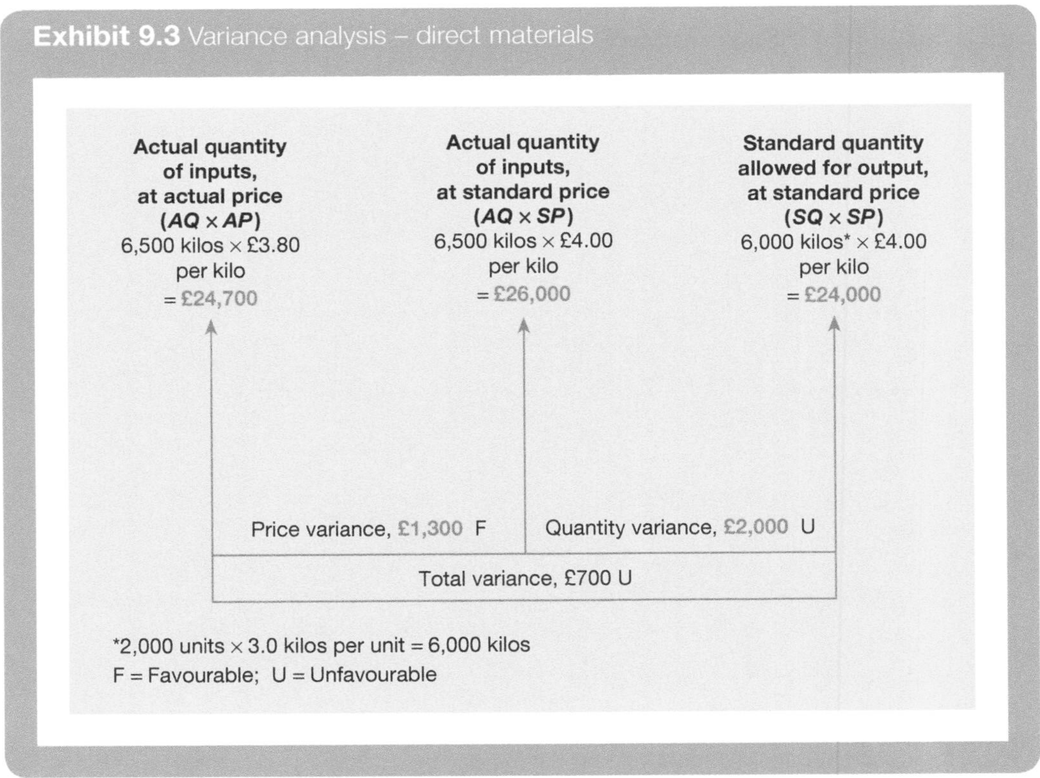

The three arrows in Exhibit 9.3 point to three different total cost figures. The first, £24,700, refers to the actual total cost of the pewter that was purchased during June. The second, £26,000, refers to what the pewter would have cost if it had been purchased at the standard price of £4.00 a kilo rather than the actual price of £3.80 a kilo. The difference between these two figures, £1,300 (£26,000 – £24,700), is the price variance. It exists because the actual purchase price was £0.20 per kilo less than the standard purchase price. Since 6,500 kilos were purchased, the total amount of the variance is £1,300 (£0.20 per kilo × 6,500 kilos). This variance is labelled favourable (denoted by F), since the actual purchase price was less than the standard purchase price. A price variance is labelled unfavourable (denoted by U) if the actual price exceeds the standard price.

The third arrow in Exhibit 9.3 points to £24,000 – the cost that the pewter would have been had it been purchased at the standard price and only the amount allowed by the standard quantity had been used. The standards call for 3 kilos of pewter per unit. Since 2,000 units were produced, 6,000 kilos of pewter should have been used. This is referred to as the standard quantity allowed for the output. If this 6,000 kilos of pewter had been purchased at the standard price of £4.00 per kilo, the company would have spent £24,000. The difference between this figure, £24,000, and the figure at the end of the middle arrow in Exhibit 9.3, £26,000, is the quantity variance of £2,000.

To understand this quantity variance, note that the actual amount of pewter used in production was 6,500 kilos. However, the standard amount of pewter allowed for the actual output is only 6,000 kilos. Therefore, a total of 500 kilos too much pewter was used to produce the actual output. To express this in monetary terms, the 500 kilos is multiplied by the standard price of £4.00 per kilo to yield the quantity variance of £2,000. Why is the standard price, rather than the actual price, of the pewter used in this calculation? The production manager is ordinarily responsible for the quantity variance. If the actual price were used in the calculation of the quantity variance, the production manager would be held responsible for the efficiency or inefficiency of the purchasing manager. Apart from being unfair, fruitless arguments between the production manager and purchasing manager would occur every time the actual price of an input is above its standard price. To avoid these arguments, the standard price is used when computing the quantity variance.

The quantity variance in Exhibit 9.3 is labelled unfavourable (denoted by U). This is because more pewter was used to produce the actual output than is called for by the standard. A quantity variance is labelled unfavourable if the actual quantity exceeds the standard quantity and is labelled favourable if the actual quantity is less than the standard quantity.

The computations in Exhibit 9.3 reflect the fact that all of the material purchased during June was also used during June. How are the variances computed if a different amount of material is purchased than is used? To illustrate, assume that during June the company purchased 6,500 kilos of materials, as before, but that it used only 5,000 kilos of material during the month and produced only 1,600 units. In this case, the price variance and quantity variance would be as shown in Exhibit 9.4.

Most firms compute the materials price variance, for example, when materials *are purchased* rather than when the materials are placed into production. This permits earlier isolation of the variance, since materials may remain in storage for many months before being used in production. Isolating the price variance when materials are purchased also permits the company to carry its raw materials in the stock accounts at standard cost. This greatly simplifies assigning raw materials costs to work in progress when raw materials are later placed into production.

Note from the exhibit that the price variance is computed on the entire amount of material purchased (6,500 kilos), as before, whereas the quantity variance is computed only on the portion of this material used in production during the month (5,000 kilos). A quantity variance on the 1,500 kilos of material that was purchased during the month but not used in production (6,500 kilos purchased – 5,000 kilos used = 1,500 kilos unused) will be computed in a future period when these materials are drawn out of stocks and used in production. The situation illustrated in Exhibit 9.4 is common for companies that purchase materials well in advance of use and store the materials in warehouses while awaiting the production process.

Exhibit 9.4 Variance analysis – direct materials, when the amount purchased differs from the amount used

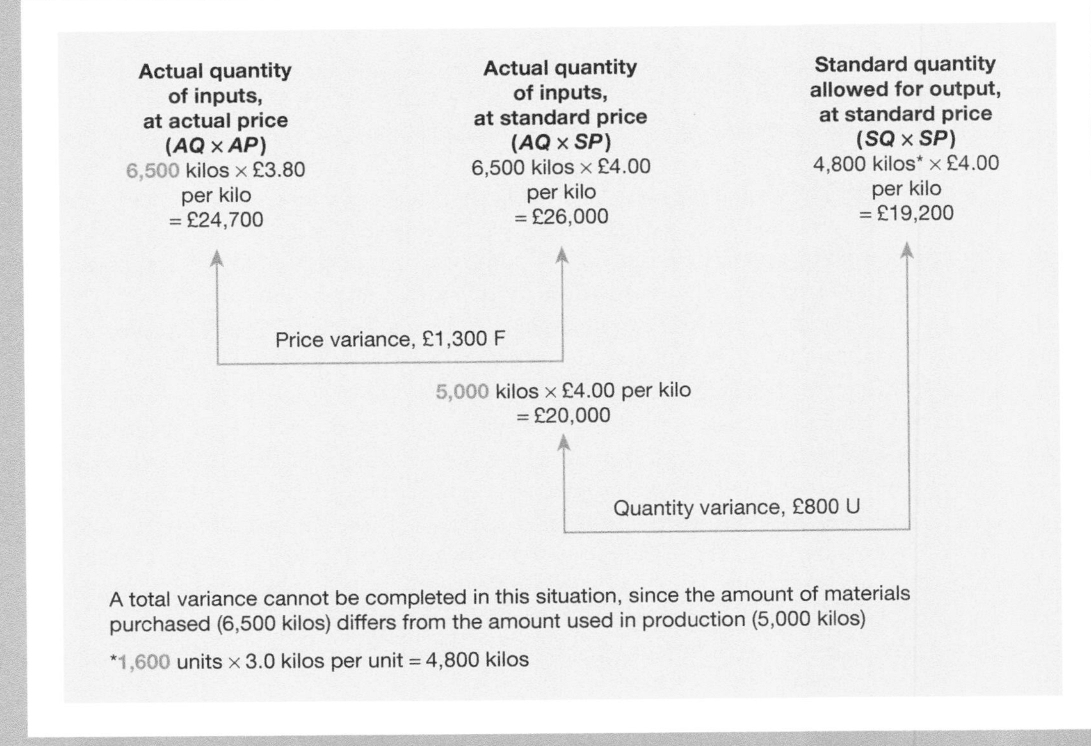

Materials price variance – a closer look

A **materials price variance** measures the difference between what is paid for a given quantity of materials and what should have been paid according to the standard that has been set. From Exhibit 9.3, this difference can be expressed by the following formula:

Materials price variance = $(AQ \times AP) - (AQ \times SP)$

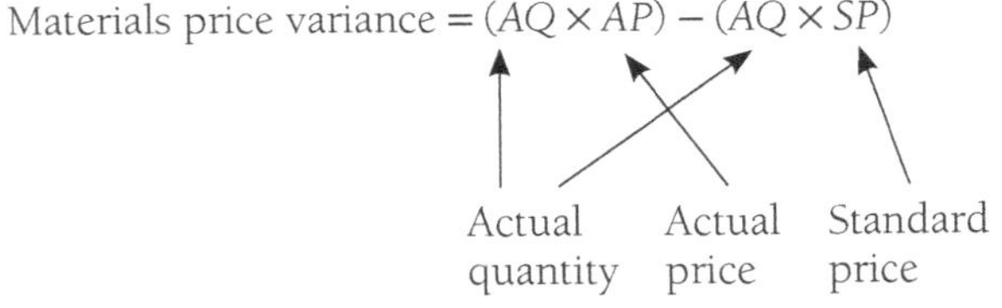

The formula can be factored into simpler form as follows:

Materials price variance = $AQ(AP - SP)$

Some managers prefer this simpler formula, since it permits variance computations to be made very quickly. Using the data from Exhibit 9.3 in this formula, we have the following:

6,500 kilos (£3.80 per kilo – £4.00 per kilo) = £1,300 F

Notice that the answer is the same as that yielded in Exhibit 9.3. If the company wanted to put these data into a performance report, the data might appear as follows:

Colonial Pewter Company Performance report – purchasing department						
Item purchased	**(1) Quantity purchased**	**(2) Actual price**	**(3) Standard price**	**(4) Difference in price (2) – (3)**	**(5) Total price variance (1) × (4)**	**Explanation**
Pewter	6,500 kilos	£3.80	£4.00	£0.20	£1,300 F	Bargained for an especially favourable price

F = Favourable; U = Unfavourable.

Isolation of variances

At what point should variances be isolated and brought to the attention of management? The answer is, the earlier the better. The sooner deviations from standard are brought to the attention of management, the sooner problems can be evaluated and corrected.

Once a performance report has been prepared, what does management do with the price variance data? The most significant variances should be viewed as 'red flags', calling attention to the fact that an exception has occurred that will require some explanation and perhaps follow-up effort. Normally, the performance report itself will contain some explanation of the reason for the variance, as shown above. In the case of Colonial Pewter Company, the purchasing manager said that the favourable price variance resulted from bargaining for an especially favourable price.

Responsibility for the variance

Who is responsible for the materials price variance? Generally speaking, the purchasing manager has control over the price paid for goods and is therefore responsible for any price variances. Many factors influence the prices paid for goods, including how many units are ordered in a lot, how the order is delivered, whether the order is a rush order, and the quality of materials purchased. A deviation in any of these factors from what was assumed when the standards were set can result in a price variance. For example, purchase of second-grade materials rather than top-grade materials may result in a favourable price variance, since the lower-grade materials would generally be less costly (but perhaps less suitable for production).

There may be times, however, when someone other than the purchasing manager is responsible for a materials price variance. Production may be scheduled in such a way, for example, that the purchasing manager must request delivery by airfreight, rather than by truck. In these cases, the production manager would bear responsibility for the resulting price variances.

A word of caution is in order. Variance analysis should not be used as an excuse to conduct witch hunts or as a means of beating line managers and workers over the head. The emphasis must be on the control function in the sense of *supporting* the line managers and *assisting* them in meeting the goals that they have participated in setting for the company. In short, the emphasis should be positive rather than negative. Excessive dwelling on what has already happened, particularly in terms of trying to find someone to blame, can be destructive to the functioning of an organization.

Materials quantity variance – a closer look

The **materials quantity variance** measures the difference between the quantity of materials used in production and the quantity that should have been used according to the standard that has been set. Although the variance is concerned with the physical usage of materials, it is generally stated in monetary terms, as shown in Exhibit 9.3. The formula for the materials quantity variance is as follows:

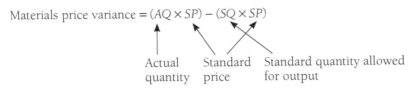

$$\text{Materials price variance} = (AQ \times SP) - (SQ \times SP)$$

Actual quantity — Standard price — Standard quantity allowed for output

Again, the formula can be factored into simpler terms:

$$\text{Materials price variance} = SP(AQ - SQ)$$

Using the data from Exhibit 9.3 in the formula, we have the following:

£4.00 per kilo (6,500 kilos – 6,000 kilos*) = £2,000 U
*2,000 units × 3.0 kilos per unit = 6,000 kilos.

The answer, of course, is the same as that yielded in Exhibit 9.3. The data might appear as follows if a formal performance report were prepared:

Colonial Pewter Company
Performance report – production department

Type of materials	(1) Standard price	(2) Actual quantity	(3) Standard quantity allowed	(4) Difference in quantity (2) – (3)	(5) Total price variance (1) × (4)	Explanation
Pewter	£4.00	6,500 kilos	6,000 kilos	500 kilos	£2,000 U	Second-grade materials unsuitable for production

F = Favourable; U = Unfavourable.

The materials quantity variance is best isolated at the time that materials are placed into production. Materials are drawn for the number of units to be produced, according to the standard bill of materials for each unit. Any additional materials are usually drawn with an excess materials requisition slip, which is different in colour from the normal requisition slips. This procedure calls attention to the excessive usage of materials *while production is still in process* and provides an opportunity for early control of any developing problem.

Excessive usage of materials can result from many factors, including faulty machines, inferior quality of materials, untrained workers and poor supervision. Generally speaking, it is the responsibility of the production department to see that material usage is kept in line with standards. There may be times, however, when the purchasing department may be responsible for an unfavourable materials quantity variance. If the purchasing department obtains inferior quality materials in an effort to economize on price, the materials may be unsuitable for use and may result in excessive waste. Thus, purchasing rather than production would be responsible for the quantity variance. At Colonial Pewter, the production manager said that second-grade materials were the cause of the unfavourable materials quantity variance for June.

LO 3 Using standard costs – direct labour variances

The next step in determining Colonial Pewter's variances for June was to compute the direct labour variances for the month. Recall from Exhibit 9.1 that the standard direct labour cost per unit of product is £35, computed as follows:

2.5 hours per unit × £14.00 per hour = £35 per unit

Exhibit 9.5 Variance analysis – direct labour

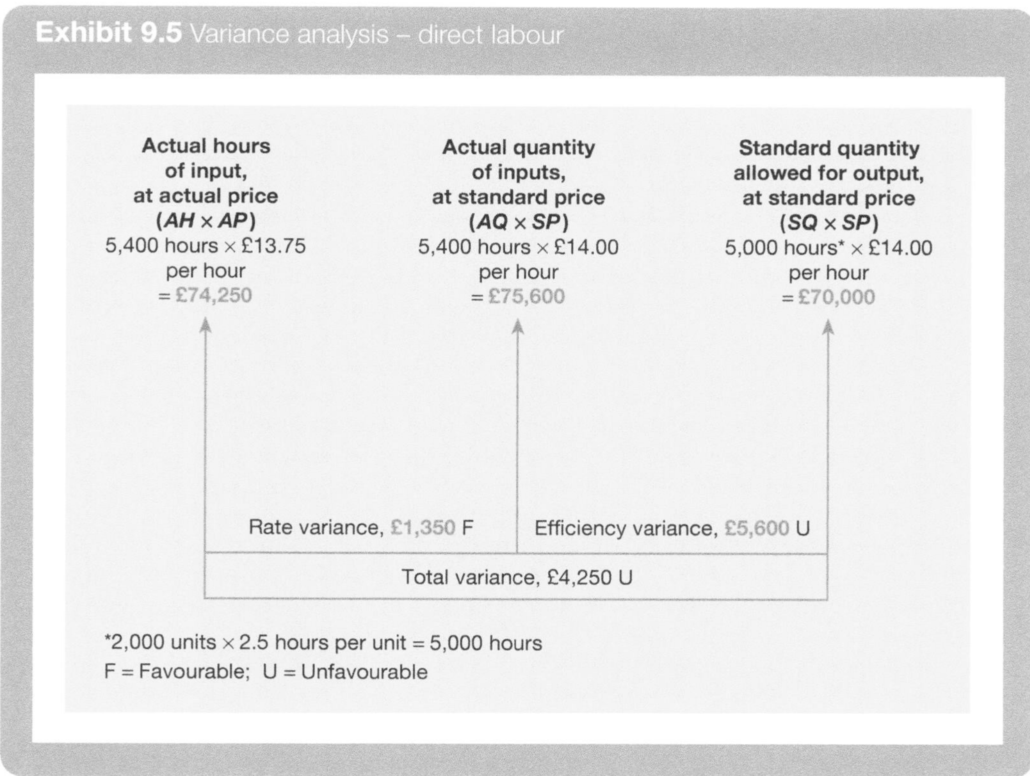

During June, the company paid its direct labour workers £74,250, including employment taxes and fringe benefits, for 5,400 hours of work. This was an average of £13.75 per hour. Using these data and the standard costs from Exhibit 9.1, the direct labour rate and efficiency variances are shown in Exhibit 9.5.

Notice that the column headings in Exhibit 9.5 are the same as those used in the prior two exhibits, except that in Exhibit 9.5 the terms *hours* and *rate* are used in place of the terms *quantity* and *price*.

Labour rate variance – a closer look

As explained earlier, the price variance for direct labour is commonly termed a **labour rate variance**. This variance measures any deviation from standard in the average hourly rate paid to direct labour workers. The formula for the labour rate variance is expressed as follows:

Labour rate variance = $(AH \times AR) - (AH \times SR)$

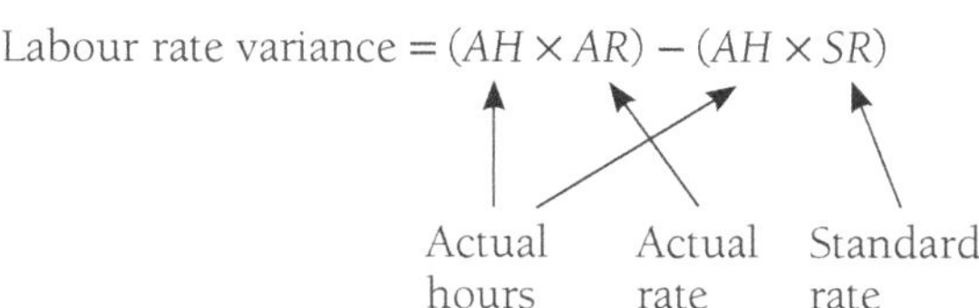

The formula can be factored into simpler form as follows:

Labour rate variance = $AH\ (AR - SR)$

Using the data from Exhibit 9.5 in the formula, we have the following:

5,400 hours (£13.75 per hour − £14.00 per hour) = £1,350 F

In most firms, the rates paid to workers are quite predictable. Nevertheless, rate variances can arise through the way labour is used. Skilled workers with high hourly rates of pay may be given duties that require little skill and call for low hourly rates of pay. This will result in unfavourable labour rate variances, since the actual hourly rate of pay will exceed the standard rate specified for the particular task being performed. A reverse situation exists when unskilled or untrained workers are assigned to jobs that require some skill or training. The lower pay scale for these workers will result in favourable rate variances, although the workers may be inefficient. Finally, unfavourable rate variances can arise from overtime work at premium rates if any portion of the overtime premium is added to the direct labour account.

Who is responsible for controlling the labour rate variance? Since rate variances generally arise as a result of how labour is used, supervisors bear responsibility for seeing that labour rate variances are kept under control.

Labour efficiency variance – a closer look

The quantity variance for direct labour, more commonly called the **labour efficiency variance**, measures the productivity of labour time. No variance is more closely watched by management, since it is widely believed that increasing the productivity of direct labour time is vital to reducing costs. The formula for the labour efficiency variance is expressed as follows

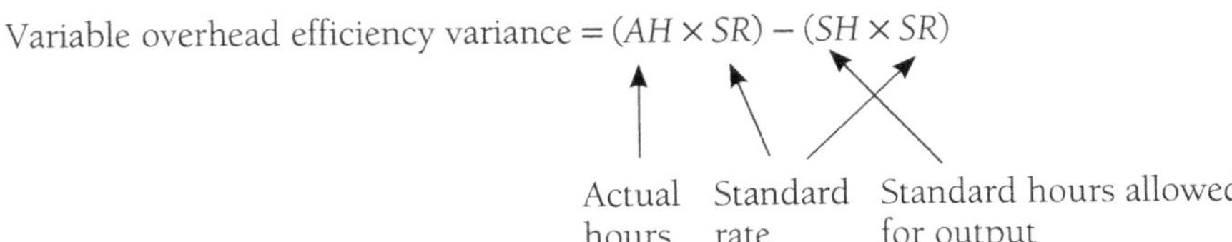

Variable overhead efficiency variance = (AH × SR) – (SH × SR)
Actual hours
Standard rate
Standard hours allowed for output

Factored into simpler terms, the formula is:

Variable overhead efficiency variance = $SR(AH - SH)$

Using the data from Exhibit 9.5 in the formula, we have the following:

£14.00 per hour (5,400 hours – 5,000 hours*) = £5,600 U
*2,000 units × hours per unit = 5,000 hours.

Possible causes of an unfavourable labour efficiency variance include poorly trained or motivated workers; poor quality materials, requiring more labour time in processing; faulty equipment, causing breakdowns and work interruptions; poor supervision of workers; and inaccurate standards. The managers in charge of production would generally be responsible for control of the labour efficiency variance. However, the variance might be chargeable to purchasing if the acquisition of poor materials resulted in excessive labour processing time.

When the labour force is essentially fixed in the short term, another important cause of an unfavourable labour efficiency variance is insufficient demand for the output of the factory. In some firms, the actual labour-hours worked is basically fixed – particularly in the short term. Managers in these firms argue that it is difficult, and perhaps even unwise, constantly to adjust the workforce in response to changes in the workload. Therefore, the only way a work centre manager can avoid an unfavourable labour efficiency variance in such firms is by keeping everyone busy all the time. The option of reducing the number of workers on hand is not available.

Thus, if there are insufficient orders from customers to keep the workers busy, the work centre manager has two options – either accept an unfavourable labour efficiency variance or build stocks. A central lesson of just-in-time production is that building stocks with no immediate prospect of sale is a bad idea. Stocks – particularly work in progress stocks – lead to high defect rates, obsolete goods, and generally inefficient operations. As a consequence, when the workforce is basically fixed in the short term, managers must be cautious about how labour efficiency variances are used. Some managers advocate dispensing with labour efficiency variances entirely in such situations – at least for the purposes of motivating and controlling workers on the shop floor.

Using standard costs – variable manufacturing overhead variances

LO 4

The final step in the analysis of Colonial Pewter's variances for June is to compute the variable manufacturing overhead variances. The variable portion of manufacturing overhead can be analysed using the same basic formulas that are used to analyse direct materials and direct labour. Recall from Exhibit 9.1 that the standard variable manufacturing overhead is £7.50 per unit of product, computed as follows:

2.5 hours per unit × £3.00 per hour = £7.50 per unit

Colonial Pewter's cost records showed that the total actual variable manufacturing overhead cost for June was £15,390. Recall from the earlier discussion of the direct labour variances that 5,400 hours of direct labour time were recorded during the month and that the company produced 2,000 pairs of bookends. The analysis of this overhead data appears in Exhibit 9.6.

Notice the similarities between Exhibits 9.5 and 9.6. These similarities arise from the fact that direct labour-hours are being used as a base for allocating overhead cost to units of product; thus, the same hourly figures appear in Exhibit 9.6 for variable manufacturing overhead as in Exhibit 9.5 for direct labour. The main difference between the two exhibits is in the standard hourly rate being used, which in this company is much lower for variable manufacturing overhead.

Manufacturing overhead variances – a closer look

The formula for **variable overhead spending variance** is expressed as follows:

Variable overhead spending variance = $(AH \times AR) - (AH \times SR)$

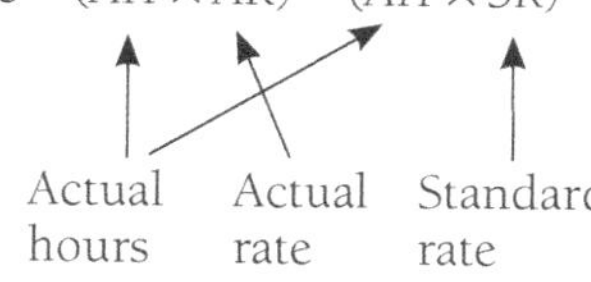

Exhibit 9.6 Variance analysis – variable manufacturing overhead

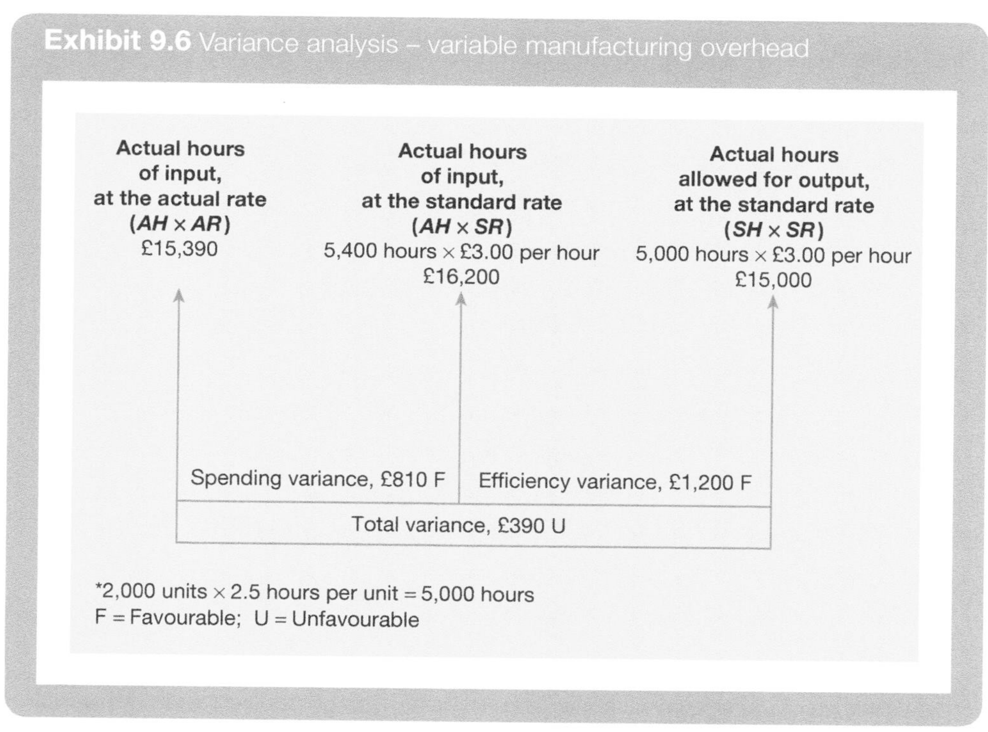

Or, factored into simpler terms:

$$\text{Variable overhead spending variance} = AH(AR - SR)$$

Using the data from Exhibit 9.6 in the formula, we have the following:

5,400 hours (£2.85 per hour* – £3.00 per hour) = £810 F
*£15,390 ÷ 5,400 hours = £2.85 per hour.

The formula for the **variable overhead efficiency variance** is expressed as follows:

$$\text{Variable overhead efficiency variance} = (AH \times SR) - (SH \times SR)$$

Or, factored into simpler terms:

$$\text{Variable overhead efficiency variance} = SR(AH - SH)$$

Again using the data from Exhibit 9.6, the computation of the variance would be as follows:

£3.00 per hour (5,400 hours – 5,000 hours*) = £1,200 U
*2,000 units × 2.5 hours per unit = 5,000 hours.

Before proceeding further, we suggest that you pause at this point and go back to review the data contained in Exhibits 9.1 to 9.6. These exhibits and the accompanying text discussion provide a comprehensive, integrated illustration of standard setting and variance analysis.

Structure of performance reports

On preceding pages we have learned that performance reports are used in a standard cost system to communicate variance data to management. Exhibit 9.7 provides an example of how these reports can be integrated in a responsibility reporting system.

Note from the exhibit that the performance reports *start at the bottom and build upwards*, with managers at each level receiving information on their own performance as well as information on the performance of each manager under them in the chain of responsibility. This variance information flows upward from level to level in a pyramid fashion, with the managing director finally receiving a summary of all activities in the organization. If the manager at a particular level (such as the production superintendent) wants to know the reasons behind a variance, he or she can ask for the detailed performance reports prepared by the various operations or departments.

In the following section, we turn our attention to the question of how a manager can determine which variances on these reports are significant enough to warrant further attention.

Variance analysis and management by exception

Variance analysis and performance reports are important elements of *management by exception*. Simply put, management by exception means that the manager's attention should be directed towards those parts of the organization where plans are not working out for one reason or another. Time and effort should not be wasted attending to those parts of the organization where things are going smoothly.

Exhibit 9.7 Upward flow of performance reports

Managing director's report

The managing director's performance report summarizes all company data. The managing director can trace the variances downwards through the company as needed to determine where top management time should be spent.

	Budget	Actual	Variance
Responsibility centre:			
Sales manager	X	X	X
Production superintendent	£26,000	£29,000	£3,000 U
Engineering head	X	X	X
Personnel supervisor	X	X	X
Controller	X	X	X
	£54,000	£61,000	£7,000 U

Production superintendent

The performance of each department head is summarized for the production superintendent. The totals on the superintendent's performance report are then passed upwards to the next level of responsibility.

	Budget	Actual	Variance
Responsibility centre:			
Cutting department	X	X	X
Machining department	X	X	X
Finishing department	£11,000	£12,500	£1,500 U
Packing department	X	X	X
	£26,000	£29,000	£3,000 U

Finishing department head

The performance report of each supervisor is summarized on the performance report of the department head. The department totals are then passed upwards to the production superintendent

	Budget	Actual	Variance
Responsibility centre:			
Sanding operation	X	X	X
Wiring operation	£5,000	£5,800	£800 U
Assembly operation	X	X	X
	£11,000	£12,500	£1,500 U

Wiring operation supervisor

The supervisor of each operation receives a performance report. The totals on these reports are then communicated upwards to the next higher level of responsibility.

	Budget	Actual	Variance
Variable costs:			
Direct materials	X	X	X
Direct labour	X	X	X
Manufacturing overhead	X	X	X
	£5,000	£5,890	£800 U

The budgets and standards discussed in this chapter and in the preceding chapter reflect management's plans. If all goes according to plan, there will be little difference between actual results and the results that would be expected according to the budgets and standards. If this happens, managers can concentrate on other issues. However, if actual results do not conform to the budget and to standards, the performance reporting system sends a signal to the manager that an 'exception' has occurred. This signal is in the form of a variance from the budget or standards.

However, are all variances worth investigating? The answer is no. Differences between actual results and what was expected will almost always occur. If every variance were investigated, management would waste a great deal of time tracking down trivial differences. Variances may occur for any of a variety of reasons – only some of which are significant and warrant management attention. For example, hotter than normal weather in the summer may result in higher than expected electrical bills for air conditioning. Or, workers may work slightly faster or slower on a particular day. Because of unpredictable random factors, one can expect that virtually every cost category will produce a variance of some kind.

How should managers decide which variances are worth investigating? One clue is the size of the variance. A variance of £5 is probably not big enough to warrant attention, whereas a variance of £5,000 might well be worth tracking down. Another clue is the size of the variance relative to the amount of spending involved. A variance that is only 0.1% of spending on an item is likely to be well within the bounds one would normally expect due to random factors. On the other hand, a variance of 10% of spending is much more likely to be a signal that something is basically wrong.

What value of *X* should be chosen? The bigger the value of *X*, the wider the band of acceptable variances that would not be investigated. Thus, the bigger the value of *X*, the less time will be spent tracking down variances, but the more likely it is that a real out-of-control situation would be overlooked. Ordinarily, if *X* is selected to be 1.0, roughly 30% of all variances will trigger an investigation even when there is no real problem. If *X* is set at 1.5, the figure drops to about 13%. If *X* is set at 2.0, the figure drops all the way to about 5%. Don't forget, however, that selecting a big value of *X* will result not only in fewer investigations but also a higher probability that a real problem will be overlooked.

LO 5

Evaluation of controls based on standard costs

Advantages of standard costs

Standard cost systems have a number of advantages.

1. As stated earlier, the use of standard costs is a key element in a management by exception approach. So long as costs remain within the standards, managers can focus on other issues. When costs fall significantly outside the standards, managers are alerted that there may be problems requiring attention. This approach helps managers focus on important issues.
2. So long as standards are viewed as reasonable by employees, they can promote economy and efficiency. They provide benchmarks that individuals can use to judge their own performance.
3. Standard costs can greatly simplify bookkeeping. Instead of recording actual costs for each job, the standard costs for materials, labour and overhead can be charged to jobs.
4. Standard costs fit naturally in an integrated system of 'responsibility accounting'. The standards establish what costs should be, who should be responsible for them, and whether actual costs are under control.

Potential problems with the use of standard costs

The use of standard costs can present a number of potential problems. Most of these problems result from improper use of standard costs and the management by exception principle or from using standard costs in situations in which they are not appropriate.[4]

1. Standard cost variance reports are usually prepared on a monthly basis and often are released days or even weeks after the end of the month. As a consequence, the information in the reports may be so stale that it is almost useless. Timely, frequent reports that are approximately correct are better than infrequent reports that are very precise but out of date by the time they are released. As mentioned earlier, some companies are now reporting variances and other key operating data daily or even more frequently.
2. If managers are insensitive and use variance reports as a club, morale may suffer. Employees should receive positive reinforcement for work well done. Management by exception, by its nature, tends to focus on the negative. If variances are used as a club, subordinates may be tempted to cover up unfavourable variances or take actions that are not in the best interests of the company to make sure the variances are favourable. For example, workers may put on a crash effort to increase output at the end of the month to avoid an unfavourable labour efficiency variance. In the rush to produce output, quality may suffer.
3. Labour quantity standards and efficiency variances make two important assumptions. First, they assume that the production process is labour-paced; if labour works faster, output will go up. However, output in many companies is no longer determined by how fast labour works; rather, it is determined by the processing speed of machines. Second, the computations assume that labour is a variable cost. However, as discussed in earlier chapters, in many companies, direct labour may

be essentially fixed. If labour is fixed, then an undue emphasis on labour efficiency variances creates pressure to build excess work in progress and finished goods inventories.

4 In some cases, a 'favourable' variance can be as bad or worse than an 'unfavourable' variance. For example, McDonald's has a standard for the amount of hamburger meat that should be in a Big Mac. If there is a 'favourable' variance, it means that less meat was used than the standard specifies. The result is a substandard Big Mac and possibly a dissatisfied customer.

5 There may be a tendency with standard cost reporting systems to emphasize meeting the standards to the exclusion of other important objectives such as maintaining and improving quality, on-time delivery, and customer satisfaction. This tendency can be reduced by using supplemental performance measures that focus on these other objectives.

6 Just meeting standards may not be sufficient; continual improvement may be necessary to survive in the current competitive environment. For this reason, some companies focus on the trends in the standard cost variances – aiming for continual improvement rather than just meeting the standards. In other companies, engineered standards are being replaced either by a rolling average of actual costs, which is expected to decline, or by very challenging target costs. This approach is sometimes known as kaizen costing which involves the reduction of cost during production through continuous gradual improvements that reduce waste and increase efficiency. While continuous improvement can be built into the costing system by setting small percentage reductions in cost, kaizen involves more than just technical changes because the philosophy relies on the development of a motivated and empowered workforce.[5]

In sum, managers should exercise considerable care in their use of a standard cost system. It is particularly important that managers go out of their way to focus on the positive, rather than just on the negative, and to be aware of possible unintended consequences.

Nevertheless, standard costs are still found in the vast majority of manufacturing companies and in many service companies, although their use is changing. For evaluating performance, standard cost variances may be supplanted by the *balanced scorecard* which we will look at in Chapter 11.

Focus on Business Practice

Survey of standard costing in global firms

© Jacob Wackerhausen

In a recent survey of major global companies,[6] it was argued that the limitations of standard costing are not always fully understood 'with users often treating it as a science rather than an art'. Among its recommendations, the report suggested that a selective use of standard costs such as direct costs may lead to better production decisions; that rapid changes in input and output prices should lead to more frequent updates of standards; that care should be taken that performance targets do not 'bake in inefficiency'; and that effective performance management should focus on the controllable elements of performance. One of the most surprising findings was continued and widespread use of spreadsheets rather than more sophisticated computer models such as enterprise resource planning systems.

Exercise: Review the advantages and disadvantages of a globalized company having a single, centralized standard costing system.

Summary

- A standard is a benchmark or 'norm' for measuring performance. In business organizations, standards are set for both the cost and the quantity of inputs needed to manufacture goods or to provide services. Quantity standards indicate how much of a cost element, such as labour time or raw materials, should be used in manufacturing a unit of product or in providing a unit of service. Cost standards indicate what the cost of the time or the materials should be.
- Standards are normally practical in nature, meaning that they can be attained by reasonable, though highly efficient, efforts. Such standards are generally felt to have a favourable motivational impact on employees.
- When standards are compared to actual performance, the difference is referred to as a variance. Variances are computed and reported to management on a regular basis for both the price and the quantity elements of materials, labour and overhead. Price and rate variances for inputs are computed by taking the difference between the actual and standard prices of the inputs and multiplying the result by the amount of input purchased. Quantity and efficiency variances are computed by taking the difference between the actual amount of the input used and the amount of input that is allowed for the actual output, and then multiplying the result by the standard price of the input.
- Not all variances require management time or attention. Only unusual or particularly significant variances should be investigated – otherwise a great deal of time would be spent investigating unimportant matters. Additionally, it should be emphasized that the point of the investigation should not be to find someone to blame. The point of the investigation is to pinpoint the problem so that it can be fixed and operations improved.
- Traditional standard cost variance reports should often be supplemented with other performance measures. Overemphasis on standard cost variances may lead to problems in other critical areas such as product quality, stocks levels, and on-time delivery.

Key terms

Bill of materials A listing of the quantity of each type of material required to manufacture a unit of product (p. 208).

Ideal standards Standards that allow for no machine breakdowns or other work interruptions and that require peak efficiency at all times (p. 207).

Labour efficiency variance A measure of the difference between the actual hours taken to complete a task and the standard hours allowed, multiplied by the standard hourly labour rate (p. 218).

Labour rate variance A measure of the difference between the actual hourly labour rate and the standard rate, multiplied by the number of hours worked during the period (p. 217).

Management by exception A system of management in which standards are set for various operating activities, with actual results then compared to these standards. Any differences that are deemed significant are brought to the attention of management as 'exceptions' (p. 206).

Materials price variance A measure of the difference between the actual unit price paid for an item and the standard price, multiplied by the quantity purchased (p. 214).

Materials quantity variance A measure of the difference between the actual quantity of materials used in production and the standard quantity allowed, multiplied by the standard price per unit of materials (p. 215).

Practical standards Standards that allow for normal machine downtime and other work interruptions and that can be attained through reasonable, though highly efficient, efforts by the average worker (p. 208).

Standard cost card A detailed listing of the standard amounts of materials, labour and overhead that should go into a unit of product, multiplied by the standard price or rate that has been set for each cost element (p. 206).

Standard cost per unit The standard cost of a unit of product as shown on the standard cost card; it is computed by multiplying the standard quantity or hours by the standard price or rate for each cost element (p. 210).

Standard hours allowed The time that should have been taken to complete the period's output as computed by multiplying the actual number of units produced by the standard hours per unit (p. 212).

Standard hours per unit The amount of labour time that should be required to complete a single unit of product, including allowances for breaks, machine downtime, cleanup, rejects, and other normal inefficiencies (p. 209).

Standard price per unit The price that should be paid for a single unit of materials, including allowances for quality, quantity purchased, shipping, receiving, and other such costs, net of any discounts allowed (p. 208).

Standard quantity allowed The amount of materials that should have been used to complete the period's output as computed by multiplying the actual number of units produced by the standard quantity per unit (p. 211).

Standard quantity per unit The amount of materials that should be required to complete a single unit of product, including allowances for normal waste spoilage, rejects and similar inefficiencies (p. 208).

Standard rate per hour The labour rate that should be incurred per hour of labour time, including employment taxes, fringe benefits and other such labour costs (p. 209).

Variable overhead efficiency variance The difference between the actual activity (direct labour-hours, machine-hours, or some other base) of a period and the standard activity allowed, multiplied by the variable part of the predetermined overhead rate (p. 220).

Variable overhead spending variance The difference between the actual variable overhead cost incurred during a period and the standard cost that should have been incurred based on the actual activity of the period (p. 219).

Variance The difference between standard prices and quantities on the one hand and actual prices and quantities on the other hand (p. 211).

Endnotes

1 Morais (1997).

2 Standard costing has been around for such a long time that recent articles are not that common. See, however, Fleischmann and Tyson (1996).

3 http://www.virbusgame.eu/virbus/mediawiki/index.php/Cost_Controlling_in_Restaurants

4 While the evils of standard cost systems are recounted in many articles and books, two particularly thorough accounts of their drawbacks can be found in Johnson (1990) and Kaplan (1986b).

5 Monden and Hamada (1991).

6 KPMG/CIMA, Standard costing: Insights from leading companies, February 2010.

connect™

When you have read this chapter, log on to the Online Learning Centre for *Management Accounting for Business Decisions* at **www.mheducation.co.uk/textbooks/sealmabd1**, where you'll find multiple choice questions, practice exams and extra study tools for management accounting.

Assessment

Questions

connect™

9–1 What is a quantity standard? What is a price standard?

9–2 Distinguish between ideal and practical standards.

9–3 If employees are chronically unable to meet a standard, what effect would you expect this to have on their productivity?

9–4 What is the difference between a standard and a budget?

9–5 What is meant by the term *variance*?

9–6 What is meant by the term *management by exception*?

9–7 Why are variances generally segregated in terms of a price variance and a quantity variance?

9–8 Who is generally responsible for the materials price variance? The materials quantity variance? The labour efficiency variance?

9–9 The materials price variance can be computed at what two different points in time? Which point is better? Why?

9–10 An examination of the cost records of the Chittenden Furniture Company reveals that the materials price variance is favourable but that the materials quantity variance is unfavourable by a substantial amount. What might this indicate?

9–11 What dangers lie in using standards as punitive tools?

9–12 'Our workers are all under labour contracts; therefore, our labour rate variance is bound to be zero.' Discuss.

9–13 What effect, if any, would you expect poor quality materials to have on direct labour variances?

9–14 If variable manufacturing overhead is applied to production on the basis of direct labour-hours and the direct labour efficiency variance is unfavourable, will the variable overhead efficiency variance be favourable or unfavourable, or could it be either? Explain.

Exercises

connect™

E9–1 Time allowed: 15 minutes

Bandar Industries Berhad of Malaysia manufactures sporting equipment. One of the company's products, a football helmet for the North American market, requires a special plastic. During the quarter ending 30 June, the company manufactured 35,000 helmets, using 22,500 kilograms of plastic in the process. The plastic cost the company RM 171,000. (The currency in Malaysia is the ringgit, which is denoted here by RM.)

According to the standard cost card, each helmet should require 0.6 kilograms of plastic, at a cost of RM 8 per kilogram.

Required

1 What cost for plastic should have been incurred in the manufacture of the 35,000 helmets? How much greater or less is this than the cost that was incurred?

2 Break down the difference computed in Question 1 above in terms of a materials price variance and a materials quantity variance.

E9–2 Time allowed: 15 minutes
Huron Company produces a commercial cleaning compound known as Zoom. The direct materials and direct labour standards for one unit of Zoom are given below:

	Standard quantity or hours	Standard price or rate	Standard cost
Direct materials	4.6 kilos	£2.50 per kilo	£11.50
Direct labour	0.2 hours	12.00 per hour	2.40

During the most recent month, the following activity was recorded:

1 Twenty thousand kilos of material were purchased at a cost of £2.35 per kilo.
2 All of the material purchased was used to produce 4,000 units of Zoom.
3 A total of 750 hours of direct labour time was recorded at a total labour cost of £10,425.

Required

1 Compute the direct materials price and quantity variances for the month.
2 Compute the direct labour rate and efficiency variances for the month.

E9–3 Time allowed: 10 minutes
Refer to the data in E9–2. Assume that instead of producing 4,000 units during the month, the company produced only 3,000 units, using 14,750 kilos of material in the production process. (The rest of the material purchased remained in stocks.)

Required

Compute the direct materials price and quantity variances for the month.

E9–4 Time allowed: 20 minutes
Erie Company manufactures a small cassette player called the Jogging Mate. The company uses standards to control its costs. The labour standards that have been set for one Jogging Mate cassette player are as follows:

Standard hours	Standard rate per hour	Standard cost
18 minutes	£12.00	£3.60

During August, 5,750 hours of direct labour time were recorded in the manufacture of 20,000 units of the Jogging Mate. The direct labour cost totalled £73,600 for the month.

Required

1 What direct labour cost should have been incurred in the manufacture of the 20,000 units of the Jogging Mate? By how much does this differ from the cost that was incurred?
2 Break down the difference in cost from Question 1 above into a labour rate variance and a labour efficiency variance.
3 The budgeted variable manufacturing overhead rate is £4 per direct labour-hour. During August, the company incurred £21,850 in variable

manufacturing overhead cost. Compute the variable overhead spending and efficiency variances for the month.

E9–5 Time allowed: 30 minutes

Dawson Toys Ltd produces a toy called the Maze. The company has recently established a standard cost system to help control costs and has established the following standards for the Maze toy:

Direct materials: 6 microns per toy at £0.50 per micron
Direct labour: 1.3 hours per toy at £8 per hour

During July, the company produced 3,000 Maze toys. Production data for the month on the toy follow:

Direct materials: 25,000 microns were purchased for use in production at a cost of £0.48 per micron. Some 5,000 of these microns were still in stock at the end of the month
Direct labour: 4,000 direct labour-hours were worked at a cost of £36,000

Required

1 Compute the following variances for July:
   (a) Direct materials price and quantity variances.
   (b) Direct labour rate and efficiency variances.

2 Prepare a brief explanation of the significance and possible causes of each variance.

Problems

connect™

P9–6 Standard costing

Time allowed: 45 minutes

As a recently appointed assistant management accountant you are attending a monthly performance meeting. You have with you a statement of monthly actual costs, a summary of cost variances and other pieces of information you have managed to collect, as shown below:

	£
Actual cost of direct material purchased and used	62,700
Actual direct wages paid	97,350
Variable overheads incurred	19,500
Fixed overheads incurred	106,500

The variances from standard cost were:

Direct material price variance	5,700 Adv.
Direct material usage variance	3,000 Fav.
Direct labour rate variance	1,650 Fav.
Direct labour efficiency variance	9,000 Fav.
Variable overhead variance	1,500 Adv.
Fixed overhead expenditure variance	1,500 Adv.
Fixed overhead volume variance	15,000 Adv.

The actual wage rate paid for the period was £8.85 per hour. It takes three standard hours to produce one unit of the finished product.

The single direct material used in the period cost 30p per kilogram above the standard price. Five kilograms of raw material input is allowed for as standard for one unit of output.

All figures relate to the single product which is manufactured at the plant. There were no stocks at the beginning or end of the accounting period. Variable and fixed overhead absorption rates are based on standard hours produced.

Managers from various functions have brought to the meeting measures which they have collected for their own areas of responsibility. In order to demonstrate the link between the accounting values and their measures you decide to work from the variances to confirm some of them.

Required

1 The formula for the calculation of the labour cost variance is:

$$(SH \times SR) - (AH \times AR)$$

Provide formulae for the calculation of the labour rate variance and labour efficiency variance using similar notation to that above. Demonstrate how they will sum to the labour cost variance given above. *(2 marks)*

2 Using variance formulae, such as those above, or otherwise, determine:
   (a) the actual number of direct labour hours worked
   (b) the standard rate of pay per direct labour-hour
   (c) the standard hours of production
   (d) the actual production in units
   (e) the actual quantity of direct material consumed
   (f) the actual price paid for the direct material (per kilogram)
   (g) the standard direct material usage in kilograms for the actual number of units produced. *(10 marks)*

3 From Question 2 above and any other calculations which may be appropriate, compute the standard cost per unit of finished product. Show separately standard prices and standard quantities for each element of cost. *(4 marks)*

4 Briefly interpret the overhead variances given in the question. *(4 marks)*

(Total 20 marks)

ACCA (adapted)

P9–7 Hospital; basic variance analysis

Time allowed: 45 minutes

John Fleming, chief administrator for Valley View Hospital, is concerned about costs for tests in the hospital's lab. Charges for lab tests are consistently higher at Valley View than at other hospitals and have resulted in many complaints. Also, because of strict regulations on amounts reimbursed for lab tests, payments received from insurance companies and governmental units have not been high enough to provide an acceptable level of profit for the lab.

Mr Fleming has asked you to evaluate costs in the hospital's lab for the past month. The following information is available:

1. Basically, two types of tests are performed in the lab – blood tests and smears. During the past month, 1,800 blood tests and 2,400 smears were performed in the lab.
2. Small glass plates are used in both types of tests. During the past month, the hospital purchased 12,000 plates at a cost of £28,200. This cost is net of a 6% quantity discount. Some 1,500 of these plates were still on hand unused at the end of the month; there were no plates on hand at the beginning of the month.
3. During the past month, 1,150 hours of labour time were recorded in the lab. The cost of this labour time was £13,800.
4. Variable overhead cost last month in the lab for utilities and supplies totalled £7,820.

Valley View Hospital has never used standard costs. By searching industry literature, however, you have determined the following nationwide averages for hospital labs:

Plates:	Two plates are required per lab test. These plates cost £2.50 each and are disposed of after the test is completed.
Labour:	Each blood test should require 0.3 hours to complete, and each smear should require 0.15 hours to complete. The average cost of this lab time is £14 per hour.
Overhead:	Overhead cost is based on direct labour-hours. The average rate for variable overhead is £6 per hour.

Mr Fleming would like a complete analysis of the cost of plates, labour and overhead in the lab for the last month so that he can get to the root of the lab's cost problem.

Required

1. Compute a materials price variance for the plates purchased last month and a materials quantity variance for the plates used last month.
2. For labour cost in the lab:
   (a) Compute a labour rate variance and a labour efficiency variance.
   (b) In most hospitals, one-half of the workers in the lab are senior technicians and one-half are assistants. In an effort to reduce costs, Valley View Hospital employs only one-quarter senior technicians and three-quarters assistants. Would you recommend that this policy be continued? Explain.
3. Compute the variable overhead spending and efficiency variances. Is there any relationship between the variable overhead efficiency variance and the labour efficiency variance? Explain.

P9–8 Straightforward variance analysis

Time allowed: 45 minutes

Becton Labs Ltd produces various chemical compounds for industrial use. One compound, called Fludex, is prepared by means of an elaborate distilling

process. The company has developed standard costs for one unit of Fludex, as follows:

	Standard quantity	Standard price or rate	Standard cost
Direct materials	2.5 grams	£20.00 per gram	£50.00
Direct labour	1.4 hours	12.50 per hour	17.50
Variable manufacturing overhead	1.4 hours	3.50 per hour	4.90
			£72.40

During November, the following activity was recorded by the company relative to production of Fludex:

1 Materials purchased, 12,000 grams at a cost of £225,000.
2 There was no beginning stocks of materials on hand to start the month; at the end of the month, 2,500 grams of material remained in the warehouse unused.
3 The company employs 35 lab technicians to work on the production of Fludex. During November, each worked an average of 160 hours at an average rate of £12 per hour.
4 Variable manufacturing overhead is assigned to Fludex on the basis of direct labour-hours. Variable manufacturing overhead costs during November totalled £18,200.
5 During November, 3,750 good units of Fludex were produced. The company's management is anxious to determine the efficiency of the activities surrounding the production of Fludex.

Required

1 For materials used in the production of Fludex:
   (a) Compute the price and quantity variances.
   (b) The materials were purchased from a new supplier who is anxious to enter into a long-term purchase contract. Would you recommend that the company sign the contract? Explain.
2 For direct labour employed in the production of Fludex:
   (a) Compute the rate and efficiency variances.
   (b) In the past, the 35 technicians employed in the production of Fludex consisted of 20 senior technicians and 15 assistants. During November, the company experimented with only 15 senior technicians and 20 assistants in order to save costs. Would you recommend that the new labour mix be continued? Explain.
3 Compute the variable overhead spending and efficiency variances. What relationship can you see between this efficiency variance and the labour efficiency variance?

Chapter 10
Long-term decision making: capital investment appraisal

LO Learning objectives

After studying Chapter 10, you should be able to:

1 Determine the acceptability of an investment project using the net present value method
2 Determine the acceptability of an investment project using the internal rate of return method
3 Compare the net present value and internal rate of return methods
4 Determine the payback period for an investment
5 Compute the simple rate of return for an investment

Concepts in Context

Neil is a commercial manager working in a large hotel chain. His job is to appraise possible sites for new hotels. He has data for each town and city on transport, businesses, and tourism as well as on competitor hotels in the area. His team uses these data to estimate future guest volumes and revenues. The projected net cash flows are then analysed using investment appraisal techniques in order to evaluate the financial viability of a new hotel.

© Jay Spooner

The term 'investment decision making' or, alternatively, 'capital budgeting', is used to describe how managers plan significant outlays on projects that have long-term implications such as the purchase of new equipment and the introduction of new products. Most companies have many more potential projects than can actually be funded. Hence, managers must carefully select those projects that promise the greatest future return. How well managers make these capital budgeting decisions is a critical factor in the long-run profitability of the company.

Capital budgeting involves *investment* – a company must commit funds now in order to receive a return in the future. Investments are not limited to shares and bonds. Purchase of inventory or equipment is also an investment. For example, Wetherspoons makes an investment when it opens a new pub/restaurant. Eon makes an investment when it installs a new computer to handle customer billing. Jaguar makes an investment when it redesigns a model and must retool its production lines. All of these investments are characterized by a commitment of funds today in the expectation of receiving a return in the future in the form of additional cash inflows or reduced cash outflows.

Focus on Business Practice

Investing in renewable energy

© TebNad

Renewable energy projects are in vogue with investors and energy firms. Wind farms are increasingly common, particularly in remote upland areas and offshore. Energy and utility companies who invest in wind energy projects do incur high development costs – in the region of £1 million per megawatt of electricity. Debt finance is typically available for such projects, helped by guaranteed cash flows over 15–20 years from energy sales to utility companies. The return on investment is thus dependent on the price agreed in the longer term, as ongoing running costs are low compared to initial investment costs. Take for example the London Array, a proposed project to construct the world's largest offshore wind farm in the Thames estuary. The estimated investment cost of the project in early 2009 was £3 billion. However, the global economic recession and falling electricity prices has seen one backer (Royal Dutch Shell) withdraw from the project. In May 2009, two other firms behind the project, German energy concern Eon and Danish firm Dong Energy, joined forces with Abu Dhabi firm Masdar to sign contracts for a £2 billion investment. Work on the project will be in two phases, starting in 2011.[1]

Exercise: Using the internet or other sources, find the costs and savings from installing a domestic wind turbine in your own home.

Capital budgeting – planning investments

Typical capital budgeting decisions

What types of business decisions require capital budgeting analysis? Virtually any decision that involves an outlay now in order to obtain some return (increase in revenue or reduction in costs) in the future. Typical capital budgeting decisions include:

1 Cost reduction decisions. Should new equipment be purchased to reduce costs?

2 Expansion decisions. Should a new plant, warehouse, or other facility be acquired to increase capacity and sales?
3 Equipment selection decisions. Which of several available machines would be the most cost effective to purchase?
4 Equipment replacement decisions. Should old equipment be replaced now or later?

The time value of money

As stated earlier, business investments commonly promise returns that extend over fairly long periods of time. Therefore, in approaching capital budgeting decisions, it is necessary to employ techniques that recognize *the time value of money*. A pound today is worth more than a pound a year from now. The same concept applies in choosing between investment projects. Those projects that promise returns earlier in time are preferable to those that promise returns later in time.

The capital budgeting techniques that recognize the two above characteristics of business investments most fully are those that involve discounted cash flows. We will spend most of this chapter illustrating the use of discounted cash flow methods in making *capital budgeting decisions*.

Discounted cash flows – the net present value method

There are two approaches to making capital budgeting decisions by means of discounted cash flows. One is the *net present value* method, and the other is the *internal rate of return method* (sometimes called the *time-adjusted rate of return method*). The net present value method is discussed in this section; the internal rate of return method is discussed in the next section.

The net present value method illustrated

LO 1

Under the net present value method, the present value of all cash inflows is compared to the present value of all cash outflows that are associated with an investment project. The difference between the present value of these cash flows, called the **net present value**, determines whether or not the project is an acceptable investment. To illustrate, let us assume the following data:

- Harper Company is contemplating the purchase of a machine capable of performing certain operations that are now performed manually. The machine will cost £5,000, and it will last for five years. At the end of the five-year period, the machine will have a zero scrap value. Use of the machine will reduce labour costs by £1,800 per year. Harper Company requires a minimum return of 20% before taxes on all investment projects.

Should the machine be purchased? Harper Company must determine whether a cash investment now of £5,000 can be justified if it will result in a £1,800 reduction in cost each year over the next five years. It may appear that the answer is obvious since the total cost savings is £9,000 (5 × £1,800). However, the company can earn a 20% return by investing its money elsewhere. It is not enough that the cost reductions cover just the original cost of the machine; they must also yield at least a 20% return or the company would be better off investing the money elsewhere.

To determine whether the investment is desirable, it is necessary to discount the stream of annual £1,800 cost savings to its present value and then to compare this discounted present value with the cost of the new machine. Since Harper Company requires a minimum return of 20% on all investment projects, this rate is used in the discounting process. Exhibit 10.1 shows how this analysis is done.

According to the analysis, Harper Company should purchase the new machine. The present value of the cost savings is £5,384, as compared to a present value of only £5,000 for the investment required (cost of the machine). Deducting the present value of the investment required from the present value of the cost savings gives a net present value of £384. Whenever the net present value is zero or greater, as in

Exhibit 10.1 Net present value analysis of a proposed project

Initial cost	£5,000		
Life of the project (years)	5		
Annual cost savings	£1,800		
Salvage value	0		
Required rate of return	20%		

Item Year	Year(s)	Amount of cash flow	20% factor	Present value of cash flows
Annual cost savings	1–5	£1,800	2.991*	£5,384
Initial investment	Now	(5,000)	1.000	(5,000)
Net present value				£384

*From Exhibit 10A.4 in Appendix 10A at the end of the chapter.

our example, an investment project is acceptable. Whenever the net present value is negative (the present value of the cash outflows exceeds the present value of the cash inflows), an investment project is not acceptable. In sum:

If the net present value is ...	Then the project is ...
Positive	Acceptable, since it promises a return greater than a required rate of return
Zero	Acceptable, since it promises a return equal to the required rate of return
Negative	Not acceptable, since it promises a return less than the required rate of return

A full interpretation of the solution would be as follows: The new machine promises more than the required 20% rate of return. This is evident from the positive net present value of £384. Harper Company could spend up to £5,384 for the new machine and still obtain the minimum required 20% rate of return. The net present value of £384, therefore, shows the amount of 'cushion' or 'margin of error'. One way to look at this is that the company could underestimate the cost of the new machine by up to £384, or overestimate the net present value of the future cash savings by up to £384, and the project would still be financially attractive.

Emphasis on cash flows

In capital budgeting decisions, the focus is on cash flows and not on accounting profit. The reason is that accounting profit is based on accrual concepts that ignore the timing of cash flows into and out of an organization. From a capital budgeting standpoint the timing of cash flows is important, since a pound received today is more valuable than a pound received in the future. Therefore, even though the accounting profit figure is useful for many things, it is not used in discounted cash flow analysis. Instead of determining accounting profit, the manager must concentrate on identifying the specific cash flows associated with an investment project.

What kinds of cash flows should the manager look for? Although the specific cash flows will vary from project to project, certain types of cash flows tend to recur, as explained in the following paragraphs.

Typical cash outflows

Most projects will have an immediate cash outflow in the form of an initial investment in equipment or other assets. Any salvage value realized from the sale of old equipment can be recognized as a cash inflow or as a reduction in the required investment. In addition, some projects require that a company expand its working capital. **Working capital** is current assets (cash, debtors and stock) less current liabilities. When a company takes on a new project, the balances in the current asset accounts will often increase. For example, opening a new Tesco store would require additional cash in sales registers, increased debtors for new customers, and more stock to fill the shelves. These additional working capital needs should be treated as part of the initial investment in a project. Also, many projects require periodic outlays for repairs and maintenance and for additional operating costs. These should all be treated as cash outflows for capital budgeting purposes.

Typical cash inflows

On the cash inflow side, a project will normally either increase revenues or reduce costs. Either way, the amount involved should be treated as a cash inflow for capital budgeting purposes. (In regard to this point, notice that so far as cash flows are concerned, *a reduction in costs is equivalent to an increase in revenues.*) Cash inflows are also frequently realized from salvage of equipment when a project is terminated. In addition, upon termination of a project, any working capital that was tied up in the project can be released for use elsewhere and should be treated as a cash inflow. Working capital is released, for example, when a company sells off its stock or collects its receivables. (If the released working capital is not shown as a cash inflow at the termination of a project, then the project will go on being charged for the use of the funds forever!)

In summary, the following types of cash flows are common in business investment projects:

Cash outflows:
- Initial investment (including installation costs)
- Increased working capital needs
- Repairs and maintenance
- Incremental operating costs.

Cash inflows:
- Incremental revenues
- Reduction in costs
- Salvage value
- Release of working capital

Recovery of the original investment

When computing the present value of a project, depreciation is not deducted for two reasons.

First, depreciation is not a current cash outflow. Second, as discussed above, discounted cash flow methods of making capital budgeting decisions focus on *cash flows.* Although depreciation is a vital concept in computing profit for financial statements, it is not relevant in an analytical framework that focuses on cash flows. A second reason for not deducting depreciation is that discounted cash flow methods *automatically* provide for return of the original investment, thereby making a deduction for depreciation unnecessary.

Simplifying assumptions

In working with discounted cash flows, at least two simplifying assumptions are usually made.

The first assumption is that all cash flows other than the initial investment occur at the end of a period. This is somewhat unrealistic in that cash flows typically occur somewhat uniformly throughout a period. The purpose of this assumption is just to simplify computations.

The second assumption is that all cash flows generated by an investment project are immediately reinvested. It is further assumed that the reinvested funds will yield a rate of return equal to the discount rate. Unless these conditions are met, the return computed for the project will not be accurate.

Choosing a discount rate

To use the net present value method, we must choose some rate of return for discounting cash flows to their present value. The firm's cost of capital is usually regarded as the most appropriate choice for the discount rate. The **cost of capital** is the average rate of return the company must pay to its long-term creditors and shareholders for the use of their funds. The mechanics involved in cost of capital computations are covered in finance texts and will not be considered here.

LO 2 Discounted cash flows – the internal rate of return method

The **internal rate of return** (or **time-adjusted rate of return**) can be defined as the interest yield promised by an investment project over its useful life. It is sometimes referred to simply as the **yield** on a project. The internal rate of return is computed by finding the discount rate that equates the present value of a project's cash outflows with the present value of its cash inflows. In other words, the internal rate of return is that discount rate which will cause the net present value of a project to be equal to zero.

The internal rate of return method illustrated

To illustrate the internal rate of return method, let us assume the following data:

- Glendale School is considering the purchase of a large tractor-pulled lawn mower. At present, the lawn is mowed using a small hand-pushed petrol mower. The large, tractor-pulled mower will cost £16,950 and will have a useful life of ten years. It will have only a negligible scrap value, which can be ignored. The tractor-pulled mower would do the job much more quickly than the old mower and would result in a labour saving of £3,000 per year.

To compute the internal rate of return promised by the new mower, we must find the discount rate that will cause the net present value of the project to be zero. How do we do this? The simplest and most direct approach *when the net cash inflow is the same every year* is to divide the investment in the project by the expected net annual cash inflow. This computation will yield a factor from which the internal rate of return can be determined. The formula is as follows:

$$\text{Factor of the internal rate of return} = \frac{\text{Investment required}}{\text{Net annual cash flow}} \qquad (1)$$

The factor derived from formula (1) is then located in the present value tables to see what rate of return it represents. Using formula (1) and the data for Glendale School's proposed project, we get:

$$\frac{\text{Investment required}}{\text{Net annual cash flow}} = \frac{£16{,}950}{£3{,}000} = 5.650$$

Thus, the discount factor that will equate a series of £3,000 cash inflows with a present investment of £16,950 is 5.650. Now we need to find this factor in Exhibit 10A.4 in Appendix 10A to see what rate of return it represents. We should use the 10-period line in Exhibit 10A.4 since the cash flows for the project continue for 10 years. If we scan along the 10-period line, we find that a factor of 5.650 represents a 12% rate of return. Therefore, the internal rate of return promised by the mower project is 12%. We can verify this by computing the project's net present value using a 12% discount rate. This computation is made in Exhibit 10.2.

Notice from Exhibit 10.2 that using a 12% discount rate equates the present value of the annual cash inflows with the present value of the investment required in the project, leaving a zero net present value. The 12% rate therefore represents the internal rate of return promised by the project.

Exhibit 10.2 Evaluation of the mower purchase using a 12% discount rate

		Initial cost		£16,950
		Life of the project (years)		10
		Annual cost savings		£3,000
		Salvage value		0
Item	**Year(s)**	**Amount of cash flow**	**20% factor**	**Present value of cash flows**
Annual cost savings	1–10	£3,000	5.650*	£16,950
Initial investment	Now	(16,950)	1.000	(16,950)
Net present value				£0

*From Exhibit 10A.4 in Appendix 10A.

Salvage value and other cash flows

The technique just demonstrated works very well if a project's cash flows are identical every year. But what if they are not? For example, what if a project will have some salvage value at the end of its life in addition to the annual cash inflows? Under these circumstances, a trial-and-error process is necessary to find the rate of return that will equate the cash inflows with the cash outflows. This trial-and-error process can be carried out by hand, or it can be carried out by means of computer software programs such as spreadsheets that perform the necessary computations in seconds. In short, erratic or uneven cash flows should not prevent a manager from determining a project's internal rate of return.

Using the internal rate of return

Once the internal rate of return has been computed, what does the manager do with the information? The internal rate of return is compared to the company's *required rate of return*. The **required rate of return** is the minimum rate of return that an investment project must yield to be acceptable. If the internal rate of return is *equal* to or *greater than* the required rate of return, then the project is acceptable. If it is less than the required rate of return, then the project is rejected. Quite often, the company's cost of capital is used as the required rate of return. The reasoning is that if a project cannot provide a rate of return at least as great as the cost of the funds invested in it, then it is not profitable.

In the case of the Glendale School example used earlier, let us assume that the district has set a minimum required rate of return of 15% on all projects. Since the large mower promises a rate of return of only 12%, it does not clear this hurdle and would therefore be rejected as a project.

The cost of capital as a screening tool

As we have seen in preceding examples, the cost of capital often operates as a screening device, helping the manager screen out undesirable investment projects. This screening is accomplished in different ways, depending on whether the company is using the internal rate of return method or the net present value method in its capital budgeting analysis.

When the internal rate of return method is used, the cost of capital is used as the hurdle rate that a project must clear for acceptance. If the internal rate of return of a project is not great enough to clear the cost of capital hurdle, then the project is ordinarily rejected. We saw the application of this idea in the Glendale School example, where the hurdle rate was set at 15%.

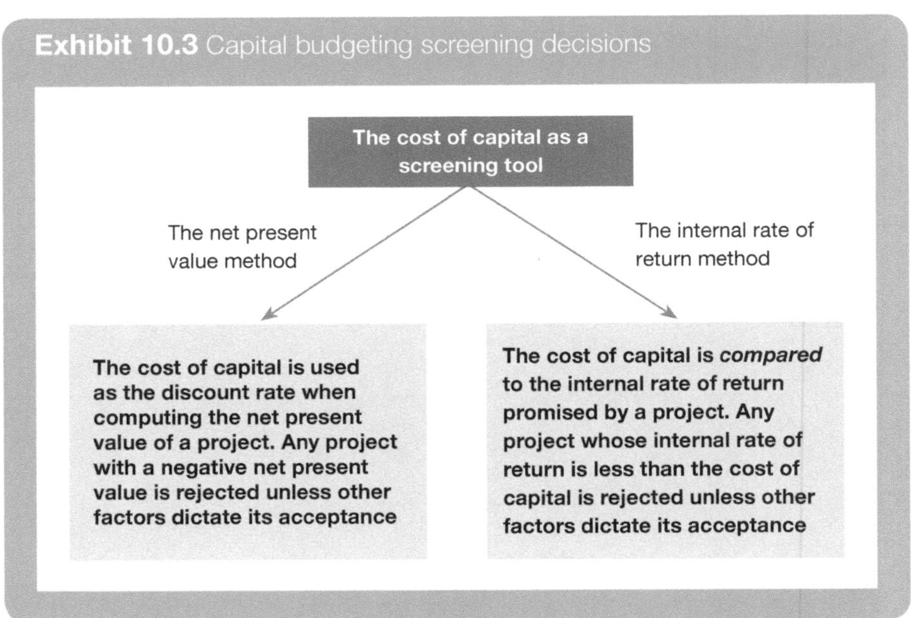
The cost of capital as a screening tool
The net present value method
The internal rate of return method
The cost of capital is used as the discount rate when computing the net present value of a project. Any project with a negative net present value is rejected unless other factors dictate its acceptance
The cost of capital is *compared* to the internal rate of return promised by a project. Any project whose internal rate of return is less than the cost of capital is rejected unless other factors dictate its acceptance
Exhibit 10.3 Capital budgeting screening decisions

When the net present value method is used, the cost of capital is the discount rate used to compute the net present value of a proposed project. Any project yielding a negative net present value is rejected unless other factors are significant enough to require its acceptance. The use of the cost of capital as a screening tool is summarized in Exhibit 10.3.

LO 3 Comparison of the net present value and the internal rate of return methods

The net present value method has several important advantages over the internal rate of return method.

First, the net present value method is often simpler to use. As mentioned earlier, the internal rate of return method may require hunting for the discount rate that results in a net present value of zero. This can be a very laborious trial-and-error process, although it can be automated to some degree using a computer spreadsheet.

Second, a key assumption made by the internal rate of return method is questionable. Both methods assume that cash flows generated by a project during its useful life are immediately reinvested elsewhere. However, the two methods make different assumptions concerning the rate of return that is earned on those cash flows. The net present value method assumes the rate of return is the discount rate, whereas the internal rate of return method assumes the rate of return is the internal rate of return on the project. Specifically, if the internal rate of return of the project is high, this assumption may not be realistic. It is generally more realistic to assume that cash inflows can be reinvested at a rate of return equal to the discount rate – particularly if the discount rate is the company's cost of capital or an opportunity rate of return. For example, if the discount rate is the company's cost of capital, this rate of return can actually be realized by paying off the company's creditors and buying back the company's stock with cash flows from the project. In short, when the net present value method and the internal rate of return method do not agree concerning the attractiveness of a project, it is best to go with the net present value method. Of the two methods, it makes the more realistic assumption about the rate of return that can be earned on cash flows from the project.

Focus on Business Practice

Investment appraisal in software engineering

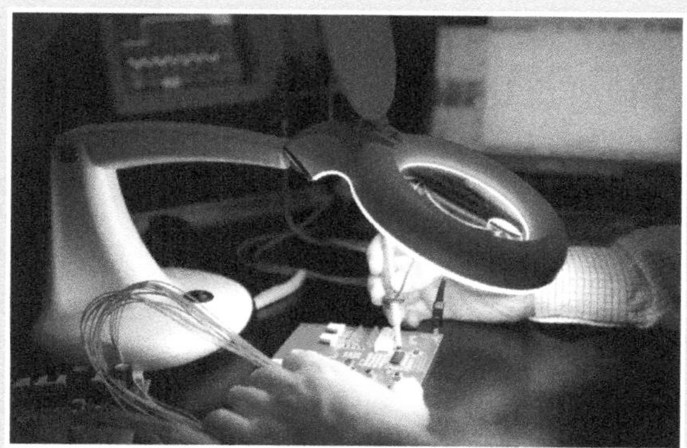

© Matthew Barnett

According to an editorial in *IEEE Software* in 2004, software engineers view the term 'return on investment' (ROI) with suspicion, due mainly to its (mis-)use by many software vendors trying to increase sales of their product. One of the issues faced in evaluating investments in software (bought or in-house developed) is that accurate cash flows representing the costs and revenues/cost savings of any proposed software project as a 'must have'. Identifying all cash flow associated with software is not an easy task. However, the authors propose that software engineers should acquaint themselves with the investment evaluation techniques like net present value, as in many businesses software is strategically important and must undergo rigorous investment appraisal. This knowledge can help software engineers in two ways. First, it may help them to understand the strategic nature of the software they are working on. Second, it may help them do their own investment analysis on whether software should be upgraded/modified versus completely rewritten.[2]

Exercise: Do you think it is necessary to evaluate investment in software which is viewed as a 'must have' for an organization? For example, no bank could trade nowadays without ATMs and internet banking.

Other approaches to capital budgeting decisions

Discounted cash flow methods have gained widespread acceptance as decision-making tools. Other methods of making capital budgeting decisions are also used, however, and are preferred by some managers. In this section, we discuss two such methods known as *payback* and *simple rate of return*.

The payback method

LO 4

The payback method centres on a span of time known as the payback period. The **payback period** can be defined as the length of time that it takes for a project to recoup its initial cost out of the cash receipts that it generates. This period is sometimes referred to as 'the time that it takes for an investment to pay for itself'. The basic premise of the payback method is that the more quickly the cost of an investment can be recovered, the more desirable is the investment.

The payback period is expressed in years. *When the net annual cash inflow is the same every year*, the following formula can be used to compute the payback period:

$$\text{Payback period} = \frac{\text{Investment required}}{\text{Net annual cash flow}^{*}} \qquad (2)$$

*If new equipment is replacing old equipment, this becomes incremental net annual cash inflow.

To illustrate the payback method, assume the following data:

- York Company needs a new milling machine. The company is considering two machines: machine A and machine B. Machine A costs £15,000 and will reduce operating costs by £5,000 per year. Machine B costs only £12,000 but will also reduce operating costs by £5,000 per year.

Which machine should be purchased according to the payback method?

$$\text{Machine A payback period} = \frac{£15{,}000}{£5{,}000} = 3.0 \text{ years}$$

$$\text{Machine B payback period} = \frac{£12{,}000}{£5{,}000} = 2.4 \text{ years}$$

According to the payback calculations, York Company should purchase machine B, since it has a shorter payback period than machine A.

Evaluation of the payback method

The payback method is not a true measure of the profitability of an investment. Rather, it simply tells the manager how many years will be required to recover the original investment. Unfortunately, a shorter payback period does not always mean that one investment is more desirable than another.

To illustrate, consider again the two machines used in the example above. Since machine B has a shorter payback period than machine A, it *appears* that machine B is more desirable than machine A. But, if we add one more piece of data, this illusion quickly disappears. Machine A has a projected 10-year life, and machine B has a projected 5-year life. It would take two purchases of machine B to provide the same length of service as a single purchase of machine A. Under these circumstances, machine A would be a much better investment than machine B, even though machine B has a shorter payback period. Unfortunately, the payback method has no inherent mechanism for highlighting differences in useful life between investments. Such differences can be very important, and relying on payback alone may result in incorrect decisions.

A further criticism of the payback method is that it does not consider the time value of money. A cash inflow to be received several years in the future is weighed equally with a cash inflow to be received right now. To illustrate, assume that for an investment of £8,000 you can purchase either of the two following streams of cash inflows:

Year	0	1	2	3	4	5	6	7	8
Stream 1		0	0	0	£8,000	£2,000	£2,000	£2,000	£2,000
Stream 2		£2,000	£2,000	£2,000	£2,000	£8,000	0	0	0

Which stream of cash inflows would you prefer to receive in return for your £8,000 investment? Each stream has a payback period of 4.0 years. Therefore, if payback alone were relied on in making the decision, you would be forced to say that the streams are equally desirable. However, from the point of view of the time value of money, stream 2 is much more desirable than stream 1.

On the other hand, under certain conditions the payback method can be very useful. For one thing, it can help identify which investment proposals are in the 'ballpark'. That is, it can be used as a screening tool to help answer the question, 'Should I consider this proposal further?' If a proposal does not provide a payback within some specified period, then there may be no need to consider it further. In addition, the payback period is often of great importance to new firms that are 'cash poor'. When a firm is cash poor, a project with a short payback period but a low rate of return might be preferred over another project with a high rate of return but a long payback period. The reason is that the company may simply need a faster return of its cash investment. And finally, the payback method is sometimes used in industries where products become obsolete very rapidly – such as consumer electronics. Since products may last only a year or two, the payback period on investments must be very short.

Payback and uneven cash flows

When the cash flows associated with an investment project change from year to year, the simple payback formula that we outlined earlier is no longer usable, and the computations involved in deriving the payback period can be fairly complex. Consider the following data:

Year	Investment	Cash inflow
1	£4,000	£1,000
2		0
3		2,000
4	2,000	1,000
5		500
6		3,000
7		2,000
8		2,000

What is the payback period on this investment? The answer is 5.5 years, but to obtain this figure it is necessary to track the unrecovered investment year by year. The steps involved in this process are shown in Exhibit 10.4. By the middle of the sixth year, sufficient cash inflows will have been realized to recover the entire investment of £6,000 (£4,000 + £2,000).

The simple/accounting rate of return method

LO 5

The **simple rate of return** method is another capital budgeting technique that does not involve discounted cash flows. The method is also known as the accounting rate of return, the unadjusted rate of return, and the financial statement method.

Unlike the other capital budgeting methods that we have discussed, the simple rate of return method does not focus on cash flows. Rather, it focuses on accounting profit. The approach is to estimate the revenues that will be generated by a proposed investment and then to deduct from these revenues all of the

Exhibit 10.4 Payback and uneven cash flows

Year	(1) Beginning unrecovered investment	(2) Additional Investment	(3) Total Unrecovered Investment (1) + (2)	(4) Cash inflow	(5) Ending unrecovered Investment (3) – (4)
1	£4,000		£4,000	£1,000	£3,000
2	3,000		3,000	0	3,000
3	3,000		3,000	2,000	1,000
4	1,000	£2,000	3,000	1,000	2,000
5	2,000		2,000	500	1,500
6	1,500		1,500	3,000	0
7	0		0	2,000	0
8	0		0	2,000	0

projected operating expenses associated with the project. This profit figure is then related to the initial investment in the project, as shown in the following formula:

$$\text{Simple rate of return} = \frac{\begin{array}{c}\text{Incremental revenues} - \text{Incremental expenses} \\ \text{including depreciation} = \text{Incremental net profit}\end{array}}{\text{Initial investment}^{*}} \qquad (3)$$

*The investment should be reduced by any salvage from the sale of old equipment. Or, if a cost reduction project is involved, formula (3) becomes:

$$\text{Simple rate of return} = \frac{\text{Cost savings} - \text{Depreciation on new equipment}}{\text{Initial investment}^{*}} \qquad (4)$$

*The investment should be reduced by any salvage from the sale of old equipment.

- Brigham Tea Ltd is a processor of a non-tannic acid tea. The company is contemplating purchasing equipment for an additional processing line. The additional processing line would increase revenues by £90,000 per year. Incremental cash operating expenses would be £40,000 per year. The equipment would cost £180,000 and have a nine-year life. No salvage value is projected.

Required

1 Compute the simple rate of return.
2 Compute the internal rate of return and compare it to the simple rate of return.

Solution

1 By applying the formula for the simple rate of return found in equation (3), we can compute the simple rate of return:

$$\text{Simple rate of return} = \frac{\left[\begin{array}{c}\text{£90,000} \\ \text{incremental} \\ \text{revenues}\end{array}\right] - \left[\begin{array}{c}\text{£40,000 cash operating} \\ \text{expenses + £20,000} \\ \text{depreciation}\end{array}\right]}{\text{£180,000 initial investment}}$$

$$= \frac{\text{£30,000}}{\text{£180,000}}$$

$$= 16.7\%$$

2 The rate computed in (1) above, however, is far below the internal rate of return of approximately 24%:

$$\text{Factor of the internal rate of return} = \frac{\text{£180,000}}{\text{£50,000}} = 3.600$$

*£30,000 profit + £20,000 depreciation = £50,000; or the annual cash inflow can be computed as £90,000 increased revenues – £40,000 cash expenses = £50,000.

By scanning across the nine-year line in Exhibit 10A.4 in Appendix 10A, we can see that the internal rate of return is approximately 24%.

- Midshires Farms Ltd hires people on a part-time basis to sort eggs. The cost of this hand-sorting process is £30,000 per year. The company is investigating the purchase of an egg-sorting machine that would cost £90,000 and have a 15-year useful life. The machine would have negligible salvage value, and it would cost £10,000 per year to operate and maintain. The egg-sorting equipment currently being used could be sold now for a scrap value of £2,500.

Required

Compute the simple rate of return on the new egg-sorting machine.

A cost reduction project is involved in this situation. By applying the formula for the simple rate of return found in equation (4), we can compute the simple rate of return as follows:

Solution

$$\text{Simple rate of return} = \frac{\text{£}20{,}000^{*} \text{ cost savings} - \text{£}6{,}000^{\dagger} \text{ depreciation on new equipment}}{\text{£}90{,}000 - \text{£}2{,}500}$$

$$= 16.0\%$$

* £30,000 – £10,000 = £20,000 cost savings.

† £90,000 ÷ 15 years = £6,000 depreciation.

Criticisms of the simple rate of return

The most damaging criticism of the simple rate of return method is that it does not consider the time value of money. A pound received ten years from now is viewed as being just as valuable as a pound received today. Thus, the manager can be misled if the alternatives being considered have different cash flow patterns. For example, assume that project A has a high simple rate of return but yields the bulk of its cash flows many years from now. Another project, B, has a somewhat lower simple rate of return but yields the bulk of its cash flows over the next few years. Project A has a higher simple rate of return than project B; however, project B might in fact be a much better investment if the time value of money were considered.

Summary

- Investment decisions should take into account the time value of money since a pound today is more valuable than a pound received in the future. The net present value and internal rate of return methods both reflect this fact. In the net present value method, future cash flows are discounted to their present value so that they can be compared on a valid basis with current cash outlays.
- The difference between the present value of the cash inflows and the present value of the cash outflows is called the project's net present value. If the net present value of the project is negative, the project is rejected.
- The discount rate in the net present value method is usually a minimum required rate of return such as the company's cost of capital.
- The internal rate of return is the rate of return that equates the present value of the cash inflows and the present value of the cash outflows, resulting in a zero net present value. If the internal rate of return is less than the company's minimum required rate of return, the project is rejected.
- Some companies prefer to use either payback or the simple rate of return to evaluate investment proposals. The payback period is the number of periods that are required to recover the initial investment in the project. The simple rate of return is determined by dividing a project's accounting profit by the initial investment in the project.

Key terms

Capital budgeting The process of planning significant outlays on projects that have long-term implications, such as the purchase of new equipment or the introduction of a new product (p. 234).

Cost of capital The overall cost to an organization of obtaining investment funds, including the cost of both debt sources and equity sources (p. 238).

Internal rate of return The discount rate at which the net present value of an investment project is zero; thus, the internal rate of return represents the interest yield promised by a project over its useful life. This term is synonymous with time-adjusted rate of return (p. 238).

Net present value The difference between the present value of the cash inflows and the present value of the cash outflows associated with an investment project (p. 235).

Payback period The length of time that it takes for a project to recover its initial cost out of the cash receipts that it generates (p. 241).

Required rate of return The minimum rate of return that an investment project must yield to be acceptable (p. 239).

Simple rate of return The rate of return computed by dividing a project's annual accounting profit by the initial investment required (p. 243).

Time-adjusted rate of return This term is synonymous with internal rate of return (p. 238).

Working capital The excess of current assets over current liabilities (p. 237).

Yield A term synonymous with internal rate of return and time-adjusted rate of return (p. 238).

Endnotes

1 http://www.guardian.co.uk/business/2009/may/12/wind-farm-electricity-london-array; http://www.guardian.co.uk/business/2009/apr/08/london-array-seeks-bailout; http://www.seai.ie/Renewables/Wind_Energy/Wind_Farm_Development/Financing_wind_farms/

2 Erdogmus, Favaro and Strigel (2004).

connect

When you have read this chapter, log on to the Online Learning Centre for *Management Accounting for Business Decisions* at **www.mheducation.co.uk/textbooks/sealmabd1**, where you'll find multiple choice questions, practice exams and extra study tools for management accounting.

Future value and present value tables

Appendix 10A

Exhibit 10A.1 Future value of £1; $F_n = P(1+r)^n$

Periods	4%	6%	8%	10%	12%	14%	20%
1	1.040	1.060	1.080	1.100	1.120	1.140	1.200
2	1.082	1.124	1.166	1.210	1.254	1.300	1.440
3	1.125	1.191	1.260	1.331	1.405	1.482	1.728
4	1.170	1.263	1.361	1.464	1.574	1.689	2.074
5	1.217	1.338	1.469	1.611	1.762	1.925	2.488
6	1.265	1.419	1.587	1.772	1.973	2.195	2.986
7	1.316	1.504	1.714	1.949	2.211	2.502	3.583
8	1.369	1.594	1.851	2.144	2.476	2.853	4.300
9	1.423	1.690	1.999	2.359	2.773	3.252	5.160
10	1.480	1.791	2.159	2.594	3.106	3.707	6.192
11	1.540	1.898	2.332	2.853	3.479	4.226	7.430
12	1.601	2.012	2.518	3.139	3.896	4.818	8.916
13	1.665	2.133	2.720	3.452	4.364	5.492	10.699
14	1.732	2.261	2.937	3.798	4.887	6.261	12.839
15	1.801	2.397	3.172	4.177	5.474	7.138	15.407
20	2.191	3.207	4.661	6.728	9.646	13.473	38.338
30	3.243	5.744	10.063	17.450	29.960	50.950	237.380
40	4.801	10.286	21.275	45.260	93.051	199.880	1469.800

Exhibit 10A.2 Future value of an annuity of £1 in arrears; $F_n = \frac{(1+r)_n - 1}{r}$

Periods	4%	6%	8%	10%	12%	14%	20%
1	1.000	1.000	1.000	1.000	1.000	1.000	1.000
2	2.040	2.060	2.080	2.100	2.120	2.140	2.220
3	3.122	3.184	3.246	3.310	3.374	3.440	3.640
4	4.247	4.375	4.506	4.641	4.779	4.921	5.368
5	5.416	5.637	5.867	6.105	6.353	6.610	7.442
6	6.633	6.975	7.336	7.716	8.115	8.536	9.930
7	7.898	8.394	8.923	9.487	10.089	10.730	12.916
8	9.214	9.898	10.637	11.436	12.300	13.233	16.499
9	10.583	11.492	12.488	13.580	14.776	16.085	20.799
10	12.006	13.181	14.487	15.938	17.549	19.337	25.959
11	13.486	14.972	16.646	18.531	20.655	23.045	32.150
12	15.026	16.870	18.977	21.385	24.133	27.271	39.580
13	16.627	18.882	21.495	24.523	28.029	32.089	48.497
14	18.282	21.015	24.215	27.796	32.393	37.581	59.196
15	20.024	23.276	27.152	31.773	37.280	43.842	72.035
20	29.778	36.778	45.762	57.276	75.052	91.025	186.690
30	56.085	79.058	113.283	164.496	241.330	356.790	1181.900
40	95.026	154.762	259.057	442.597	767.090	1342.000	7343.900

Exhibit 10A.3 Present value of £1; $F_n = \frac{F_n}{(1+r)^n}$

Period	4%	5%	6%	8%	10%	12%	14%	16%	18%	20%	22%	24%	26%	28%	30%	40%
1	0.962	0.952	0.926	0.943	0.909	0.893	0.877	0.862	0.847	0.833	0.820	0.806	0.794	0.781	0.769	0.714
2	0.925	0.907	0.857	0.890	0.826	0.797	0.769	0.743	0.718	0.684	0.672	0.650	0.630	0.610	0.592	0.510
3	0.889	0.864	0.794	0.840	0.751	0.712	0.675	0.641	0.609	0.579	0.551	0.524	0.500	0.477	0.455	0.364
4	0.855	0.823	0.735	0.792	0.683	0.636	0.592	0.552	0.516	0.482	0.451	0.423	0.397	0.373	0.350	0.260
5	0.822	0.784	0.681	0.747	0.621	0.567	0.519	0.476	0.437	0.402	0.370	0.341	0.315	0.291	0.269	0.186
6	0.790	0.746	0.630	0.705	0.564	0.507	0.456	0.410	0.370	0.335	0.303	0.275	0.250	0.227	0.207	0.133
7	0.760	0.711	0.583	0.665	0.513	0.452	0.400	0.352	0.314	0.279	0.249	0.222	0.198	0.178	0.159	0.095
8	0.731	0.677	0.540	0.627	0.467	0.404	0.351	0.305	0.266	0.233	0.204	0.179	0.157	0.139	0.123	0.068
9	0.703	0.645	0.500	0.592	0.424	0.361	0.308	0.263	0.225	0.194	0.167	0.144	0.125	0.108	0.094	0.048
10	0.676	0.614	0.463	0.558	0.386	0.322	0.270	0.227	0.191	0.162	0.137	0.116	0.099	0.085	0.073	0.035
11	0.650	0.585	0.429	0.527	0.350	0.287	0.237	0.195	0.162	0.135	0.112	0.094	0.079	0.066	0.056	0.025
12	0.625	0.557	0.397	0.497	0.319	0.257	0.208	0.168	0.137	0.112	0.092	0.076	0.062	0.052	0.043	0.018
13	0.601	0.530	0.368	0.469	0.290	0.229	0.182	0.145	0.116	0.093	0.075	0.061	0.050	0.040	0.033	0.013
14	0.577	0.505	0.340	0.442	0.263	0.205	0.160	0.125	0.099	0.078	0.062	0.049	0.039	0.032	0.025	0.009
15	0.555	0.481	0.315	0.417	0.239	0.183	0.140	0.108	0.084	0.065	0.051	0.040	0.031	0.025	0.020	0.006
16	0.534	0.458	0.292	0.394	0.218	0.163	0.123	0.093	0.071	0.054	0.042	0.032	0.025	0.019	0.015	0.005
17	0.513	0.436	0.270	0.371	0.198	0.146	0.108	0.080	0.060	0.045	0.034	0.026	0.020	0.015	0.012	0.003
18	0.494	0.416	0.250	0.350	0.180	0.130	0.095	0.069	0.051	0.038	0.027	0.021	0.016	0.012	0.009	0.002
19	0.476	0.396	0.232	0.331	0.164	0.116	0.083	0.060	0.043	0.031	0.023	0.017	0.012	0.009	0.007	0.002
20	0.456	0.377	0.215	0.312	0.149	0.104	0.073	0.051	0.037	0.026	0.019	0.014	0.010	0.007	0.005	0.001
21	0.439	0.359	0.199	0.294	0.135	0.093	0.064	0.044	0.031	0.022	0.015	0.011	0.008	0.006	0.004	0.001
22	0.422	0.342	0.184	0.278	0.123	0.083	0.056	0.038	0.026	0.018	0.013	0.009	0.006	0.004	0.003	0.001
23	0.406	0.326	0.170	0.262	0.112	0.074	0.049	0.033	0.022	0.015	0.010	0.007	0.005	0.003	0.002	
24	0.390	0.310	0.158	0.247	0.102	0.066	0.043	0.028	0.019	0.013	0.008	0.006	0.004	0.003	0.002	
25	0.375	0.295	0.146	0.233	0.092	0.059	0.038	0.024	0.016	0.010	0.007	0.005	0.003	0.002	0.001	
26	0.361	0.281	0.135	0.220	0.084	0.053	0.033	0.021	0.014	0.009	0.006	0.004	0.002	0.002	0.001	
27	0.347	0.268	0.125	0.207	0.076	0.047	0.029	0.018	0.011	0.007	0.005	0.003	0.002	0.001	0.001	
28	0.333	0.255	0.116	0.196	0.069	0.042	0.026	0.016	0.010	0.006	0.004	0.002	0.002	0.001	0.001	
29	0.321	0.243	0.107	0.185	0.063	0.037	0.022	0.014	0.008	0.005	0.003	0.002	0.001	0.001	0.001	
30	0.308	0.231	0.099	0.174	0.057	0.033	0.020	0.012	0.007	0.004	0.003	0.002	0.001	0.001		
40	0.208	0.142	0.046	0.097	0.022	0.011	0.005	0.003	0.001	0.001						

Exhibit 10A.4 Present value of an annuity of £1 in arrears; $P_n = \frac{1}{r}\left[1 - \frac{1}{(1+r)^n}\right]$

Period	4%	5%	6%	8%	10%	12%	14%	16%	18%	20%	22%	24%	26%	28%	30%	40%
1	0.962	0.952	0.943	0.926	0.909	0.893	0.877	0.862	0.847	0.833	0.820	0.806	0.781	0.794	0.769	0.714
2	1.886	1.859	1.833	1.783	1.736	1.690	1.647	1.605	1.566	1.528	1.492	1.457	1.424	1.392	1.361	1.224
3	2.775	2.723	2.673	2.577	2.487	2.402	2.322	2.246	2.174	2.106	2.042	1.981	1.923	1.868	1.816	1.589
4	3.630	3.546	3.465	3.312	3.170	3.037	2.914	2.798	2.690	2.589	2.494	2.404	2.320	2.241	2.166	1.879
5	4.452	4.330	4.212	3.993	3.791	3.605	3.433	3.274	3.127	2.991	2.864	2.745	2.635	2.532	2.436	2.035
6	5.242	5.076	4.917	4.623	4.355	4.111	3.889	3.685	3.498	3.326	3.167	3.030	2.885	2.759	2.643	2.168
7	6.002	5.786	5.582	5.206	4.868	4.564	4.288	4.039	3.812	3.605	3.416	3.242	3.083	2.937	2.802	2.263
8	6.733	6.463	6.210	5.747	5.335	4.968	4.639	4.344	4.078	3.837	3.619	3.421	3.421	3.076	2.925	2.331
9	7.435	7.108	6.802	6.247	7.759	5.328	4.946	4.607	4.303	4.031	3.786	3.566	3.366	3.184	3.019	2.379
10	8.111	7.722	7.360	6.710	6.145	5.650	5.216	4.833	4.494	4.192	3.923	3.682	3.465	3.629	3.092	2.414
11	8.760	8.306	7.887	7.139	6.495	5.988	5.453	5.029	4.656	4.327	4.035	3.776	3.544	3.335	3.147	2.438
12	9.385	8.863	8.384	7.536	6.814	6.194	5.660	5.197	4.793	4.430	4.127	3.851	3.606	3.387	3.190	2.456
13	9.986	9.394	8.853	7.904	7.103	6.424	5.842	5.342	4.910	4.533	4.203	3.912	3.656	3.427	3.223	2.468
14	10.563	9.899	9.295	8.244	7.367	6.628	6.002	5.468	5.008	4.611	4.265	3.962	3.695	3.459	3.249	2.477
15	11.118	10.380	9.712	8.559	7.606	6.811	6.142	5.575	5.092	4.675	4.315	4.001	3.726	3.483	3.268	2.484
16	11.652	10.838	10.106	8.851	7.824	6.974	6.265	5.669	5.162	4.730	4.357	4.033	3.751	3.503	3.283	2.489
17	12.166	11.274	10.477	9.122	8.022	7.120	6.373	5.749	5.222	4.775	4.391	4.059	3.771	3.518	3.295	2.492
18	12.659	11.690	10.828	9.372	8.201	7.250	6.467	5.818	5.273	4.812	4.419	4.080	3.786	3.529	3.304	2.494
19	13.134	12.085	11.158	9.604	8.365	7.366	6.550	5.877	5.316	4.844	4.442	4.097	3.799	3.539	3.311	2.496
20	13.590	12.462	11.470	9.818	8.514	7.469	6.623	5.929	5.353	4.870	4.460	4.110	3.808	3.546	3.316	2.497
21	14.029	12.821	11.764	10.017	8.649	7.562	6.687	5.973	5.384	4.891	4.476	4.121	3.186	3.551	3.320	2.498
22	14.451	13.163	12.042	10.201	8.772	7.645	6.743	6.011	5.410	4.909	4.499	4.130	3.822	3.556	3.323	2.498
23	14.857	13.489	12.303	10.371	8.883	7.718	6.792	6.044	5.432	4.295	4.499	4.137	3.827	3.559	3.325	2.499
24	15.247	13.799	12.550	10.529	8.985	7.784	6.835	6.073	5.451	4.937	4.507	4.143	3.831	3.562	3.327	2.499
25	15,622	14.094	12.783	10.675	9.077	7.843	6.873	6.097	5.467	4.948	4.514	4.147	3.834	3.564	3.329	2.499
26	15.983	14.375	13.003	10.810	9.161	7.896	6.906	6.118	5.480	4.956	4.520	4.151	3.837	3.566	3.330	2.500
27	16.330	14.643	13.211	10.935	9.237	7.943	6.935	6.136	5.492	4.964	4.525	4.154	3.839	3.567	3.331	2.500
28	16.663	14.898	13.406	11.051	9.307	7.984	6.961	6.152	5.502	4.970	4.528	4.157	3.840	3.568	3.331	2.500
29	16.984	15.141	13.591	11.158	9.370	8.022	6.983	6.166	5.510	4.975	4.531	4.159	3.841	3.569	3.332	2.500
30	17.292	15.373	13.765	11.258	9.427	8.055	7.003	6.177	5.517	4.979	4.534	4.160	3.842	3.569	3.332	2.500
40	19.793	17.159	15.046	11.925	9.779	8.244	7.105	6.234	5.548	4.997	4.544	4.166	3.846	3.571	3.333	2.500

Assessment

Questions

connect

10–1 Why can't accounting profit figures be used in the net present value and internal rate of return methods of making capital budgeting decisions?

10–2 Why are discounted cash flow methods of making capital budgeting decisions superior to other methods?

10–3 What is net present value? Can it ever be negative? Explain.

10–4 Identify two simplifying assumptions associated with discounted cash flow methods of making capital budgeting decisions.

10–5 If a firm has to pay interest of 14% on long-term debt, then its cost of capital is 14%. Do you agree? Explain.

10–6 What is meant by an investment project's internal rate of return? How is the internal rate of return computed?

10–7 Explain how the cost of capital serves as a screening tool when dealing with (a) the net present value method and (b) the internal rate of return method.

10–8 What is meant by the term *payback period*? How is the payback period determined?

10–9 How can the payback method be useful to the manager?

10–10 What is the major criticism of the payback and simple rate of return methods of making capital budgeting decisions?

Exercises

connect

E10–1 Consider each of the following situations independently. (Ignore income taxes.)

Time allowed: 10 minutes

1 In three years, when he is discharged from the Air Force, Steve wants to buy a power boat that will cost £8,000. What lump-sum amount must he invest now to have the £8,000 at the end of three years if he can invest money at:

(a) 10%?

(b) 14%?

2 Annual cash inflows that will arise from two competing investment projects are given below:

	Investment	
Year	A	B
1	£3,000	£12,000
2	6,000	9,000
3	9,000	6,000
4	12,000	3,000
	£30,000	£30,000

Each investment project will require the same investment outlay. You can invest money at an 18% rate of return. Compute the present value of the cash inflows for each investment.

3 Julie has just retired. Her company's retirement programme has two options as to how retirement benefits can be received. Under the first option, Julie would receive a lump sum of £150,000 immediately as her full retirement benefit. Under the second option, she would receive £14,000 each year for 20 years plus a lump-sum payment of £60,000 at the end of the 20-year period. If she can invest money at 12%, which option would you recommend that she accept? Use present value analysis.

E10–2 Time allowed: 15 minutes

Each of the following parts is independent. (Ignore income/corporation taxes.)

1 The Atlantic Medical Clinic can purchase a new computer system that will save £7,000 annually in billing costs. The computer system will last for eight years and have no salvage value. What is the maximum purchase price that the Atlantic Medical Clinic should be willing to pay for the new computer system if the clinic's required rate of return is:
   (a) 16%?
   (b) 20%?

2 The Caldwell *Herald* newspaper reported the following story:
   Frank Ormsby of Caldwell is the state's newest millionaire. By choosing the six winning numbers on last week's state lottery, Mr Ormsby has won the week's grand prize totalling £1.6 million. The State Lottery Commission has indicated that Mr Ormsby will receive his prize in 20 annual instalments of £80,000 each.
   (a) If Mr Ormsby can invest money at a 12% rate of return, what is the present value of his winnings?
   (b) Is it correct to say that Mr Ormsby is the 'state's newest millionaire'? Explain your answer.

3 Fraser Company will need a new warehouse in five years. The warehouse will cost £500,000 to build. What lump-sum amount should the company invest now to have the £500,000 available at the end of the five-year period? Assume that the company can invest money at:
   (a) 10%
   (b) 14%.

E10-3 Time allowed: 15 minutes

Perot Industries has £100,000 to invest. The company is trying to decide between two alternative uses of the funds. The alternatives are:

	Project	
	A	B
Cost of equipment required	£100,000	–
Working capital investment required	–	£100,000
Annual cash inflows	21,000	16,000
Salvage value of equipment in six years	8,000	–
Life of the project	6 years	6 years

The working capital needed for project B will be released at the end of six years for investment elsewhere. Perot Industries' discount rate is 14%.

Which investment alternative (if either) would you recommend that the company accept? Show all computations using the net present value format. Prepare a separate computation for each project.

E10–4 Time allowed: 30 minutes

Complete the following cases (ignore income taxes).

1. Preston Company requires a minimum return of 14% on all investments. The company can purchase a new machine at a cost of £84,900. The new machine would generate cash inflows of £15,000 per year and have a 12-year useful life with no salvage value. Compute the machine's net present value. Is the machine an acceptable investment? Explain.
2. The Walton *Daily News* is investigating the purchase of a new auxiliary press that has a projected life of 18 years. It is estimated that the new press will save £30,000 per year in cash operating costs. If the new press costs £217,500, what is its internal rate of return? Is the press an acceptable investment if the company's required rate of return is 16%? Explain.
3. Refer to the data above for the Walton *Daily News*. How much would the annual cash inflows (cost savings) have to be for the new press to provide the required 16% rate of return? Round your answer to the nearest whole pound.

E10–5 Time allowed: 30 minutes

Solve the three following present value exercises:

1. The Cambro Foundation, a non-profit organization, is planning to invest £104,950 in a project that will last for three years. The project will provide cash inflows as follows:

Year 1	£30,000
Year 2	40,000
Year 3	?

   Assuming that the project will yield exactly a 12% rate of return, what is the expected cash inflow for Year 3?
2. Lukow Products is investigating the purchase of a piece of automated equipment that will save £400,000 each year in direct labour and stock carrying costs. This equipment costs £2,500,000 and is expected to have a 15-year useful life with no salvage value. The company requires a minimum 20% return on all equipment purchases. Management anticipates that this equipment will provide intangible benefits such as greater flexibility, higher quality of output, and experience in automation. What pound value per year would management have to attach to these intangible benefits to make the equipment an acceptable investment?
3. The Matchless Dating Service has made an investment in video and recording equipment that costs £106,700. The equipment is expected to generate cash inflows of £20,000 per year. How many years will the equipment have to be used to provide the company with a 10% rate of return on its investment?

E10–6 Time allowed: 10 minutes

A piece of labour-saving equipment has just come onto the market that Mitsui Electronics Ltd could use to reduce costs in one of its plants in Japan. Relevant data relating to the equipment follow (currency is in thousands of yen, denoted by ¥).

Purchase cost of the equipment	¥432,000
Annual cost savings that will be provided by the equipment	¥90,000
Life of the equipment	12 years

Required

1 Compute the payback period for the equipment. If the company requires a payback period of four years or less, would the equipment be purchased?

2 Compute the simple rate of return on the equipment. Use straight-line depreciation based on the equipment's useful life. Would the equipment be purchased if the company requires a rate of return of at least 14%?

E10–7 Time allowed: 10 minutes

Nick's Novelties Ltd is considering the purchase of electronic pinball machines to place in amusement houses. The machines would cost a total of £300,000, have an eight-year useful life, and have a total salvage value of £20,000. Based on experience with other equipment, the company estimates that annual revenues and expenses associated with the machines would be as follows:

Revenues from use		£200,000
Less operating expenses:		
Commissions to amusement houses	£100,000	
Insurance	7,000	
Depreciation	35,000	
Maintenance	18,000	160,000
Profit		£40,000

Required (ignore taxes)

1 Assume that Nick's Novelties Ltd will not purchase new equipment unless it provides a payback period of four years or less. Would the company purchase the pinball machines?

2 Compute the simple rate of return promised by the pinball machines. If the company requires a simple rate of return of at least 12%, will the pinball machines be purchased?

Problems

connect™

P10–8 Basic net present value analysis

Time allowed: 20 minutes

Joyce Mines of Ireland is contemplating the purchase of equipment to exploit a mineral deposit that is located on land to which the company has mineral rights. An engineering and cost analysis has been made, and it is expected that the following cash flows would be associated with opening and operating a mine in the area:

Cost of new equipment and timbers	€275,000
Working capital required	100,000
Net annual cash receipts	120,000*
Cost to construct new roads in three years	40,000
Salvage value of equipment in four years	€65,000

*Receipts from sales of ore, less out-of-pocket costs for salaries, utilities, insurance, and so forth.

It is estimated that the mineral deposit would be exhausted after four years of mining. At that point, the working capital would be released for reinvestment elsewhere. The company's discount rate is 20%.

Required (ignore taxes)

Determine the net present value of the proposed mining project. Should the project be accepted? Explain.

P10–9 Basic net present value analysis

Time allowed: 20 minutes

The Sweetwater Candy Company would like to buy a new machine that would automatically 'dip' chocolates. The dipping operation is currently done largely by hand. The machine the company is considering costs £120,000. The manufacturer estimates that the machine would be usable for 12 years but would require the replacement of several key parts at the end of the sixth year. These parts would cost £9,000, including installation. After 12 years, the machine could be sold for about £7,500.

The company estimates that the cost to operate the machine will be only £7,000 per year. The present method of dipping chocolates costs £30,000 per year. In addition to reducing costs, the new machine will increase production by 6,000 boxes of chocolates per year. The company realizes a contribution margin of £1.50 per box. A 20% rate of return is required on all investments.

Required (ignore taxes)

1. What are the net annual cash inflows that will be provided by the new dipping machine?
2. Compute the new machine's net present value. Use the incremental cost approach and round all pound amounts to the nearest whole pound.

P10–10 Simple rate of return; payback

Time allowed: 30 minutes

Paul Swanson has an opportunity to acquire a franchise from The Yogurt Place plc to dispense frozen yogurt products under The Yogurt Place name. Mr Swanson has assembled the following information relating to the franchise:

1. A suitable location in a large shopping mall can be rented for £3,500 per month.

2 Remodelling and necessary equipment would cost £270,000. The equipment would have an estimated 15-year life and an estimated £18,000 salvage value. Straight-line depreciation would be used, and the salvage value would be considered in computing depreciation deductions.
3 Based on similar outlets elsewhere, Mr Swanson estimates that sales would total £300,000 per year. Ingredients would cost 20% of sales.
4 Operating costs would include £70,000 per year for salaries, £3,500 per year for insurance, and £27,000 per year for utilities. In addition, Mr Swanson would have to pay a commission to The Yogurt Place plc of 12.5% of sales.

Rather than obtain the franchise, Mr Swanson could invest his funds in long-term corporate bonds that would yield a 12% annual return.

Required (ignore taxes)

1 Prepare a profit statement that shows the expected profit each year from the franchise outlet. Use the contribution format.
2 Compute the simple rate of return promised by the outlet. If Mr Swanson requires a simple rate of return of at least 12%, should he obtain the franchise?
3 Compute the payback period on the outlet. If Mr Swanson wants a payback of four years or less, should the outlet be opened?

P10–11 Net present value analysis of a new product

Time allowed: 50 minutes

Matheson Electronics has just developed a new electronic device which, when mounted on a car, will tell the driver how many miles the car is travelling per litre of petrol.

The company is anxious to begin production of the new device. To this end, marketing and cost studies have been made to determine probable costs and market potential. These studies have provided the following information:

1 New equipment would have to be acquired to produce the device. The equipment would cost £315,000 and have a 12-year useful life. After 12 years, it would have a salvage value of about £15,000.
2 Sales in units over the next 12 years are projected to be as follows:

Year	Sales in units
1	6,000
2	12,000
3	15,000
4–12	18,000

3 Production and sales of the device would require working capital of £60,000 to finance debtors, inventories and day-to-day cash needs. This working capital would be released at the end of the project's life.
4 The devices would sell for £35 each; variable costs for production, administration and sales would be £15 per unit.

5 Fixed costs for salaries, maintenance, property taxes, insurance and straight-line depreciation on the equipment would total £135,000 per year. (Depreciation is based on cost less salvage value.)
6 To gain rapid entry into the market, the company would have to advertise heavily. The advertising programme would be:

Year	Amount of yearly advertising
1–2	£180,000
3	150,000
4–12	120,000

7 Matheson Electronics' board of directors has specified that all new products must have a return of at least 14% to be acceptable.

Required (ignore taxes)

1 Compute the net cash inflow (cash receipts less yearly cash operating expenses) anticipated from sale of the device for each year over the next 12 years.
2 Using the data computed in Question 1 above and other data provided in the problem, determine the net present value of the proposed investment. Would you recommend that Matheson accepts the device as a new product?

P10–12 Opening a small business; net present value

Time allowed: 30 minutes

In eight years, John Duncan will retire. He has £150,000 to invest, and is exploring the possibility of opening a self-service car wash. The car wash could be managed in the free time he has available from his regular occupation, and it could be closed easily when he retires. After careful study, Mr Duncan has determined the following:

1 A building in which a car wash could be installed is available under an eight-year lease at a cost of £1,700 per month.
2 Purchase and installation costs of equipment would total £150,000. In eight years the equipment could be sold for about 10% of its original cost.
3 An investment of an additional £2,000 would be required to cover working capital needs for cleaning supplies, change funds, and so forth. After eight years, this working capital would be released for investment elsewhere.
4 Both a car wash and a vacuum service would be offered with a wash costing £1.50 and the vacuum costing 25 pence per use.
5 The only variable costs associated with the operation would be 23 pence per wash for water and 10 pence per use of the vacuum for electricity.
6 In addition to rent, monthly costs of operation would be: cleaning, £450; insurance, £75; and maintenance, £500.
7 Gross receipts from the car wash would be about £1,350 per week. According to the experience of other car washes, 70% of the customers using the wash would also use the vacuum.

Mr Duncan will not open the car wash unless it provides at least a 10% return, since this is the amount that could be earned by simply placing the £150,000 in high-grade securities.

Required (ignore taxes)

1 Assuming that the car wash will be open 52 weeks a year, compute the expected net annual cash receipts (gross cash receipts less cash disbursements) from its operation. (Do not include the cost of the equipment, the working capital, or the salvage value in these computations.)
2 Would you advise Mr Duncan to open the car wash? Show computations using the net present value method of investment analysis. Round all pound figures to the nearest whole pound.

P10-13 Simple rate of return; payback

Time allowed: 30 minutes

Sharkey's Fun Centre contains a number of electronic games as well as a miniature golf course and various rides located outside the building. Paul Sharkey, the owner, would like to construct a water slide on one portion of his property. Mr Sharkey has gathered the following information about the slide:

1 Water slide equipment could be purchased and installed at a cost of £330,000. According to the manufacturer, the slide would be usable for 12 years after which it would have no salvage value.
2 Mr Sharkey would use straight-line depreciation on the slide equipment.
3 To make room for the water slide, several rides would be dismantled and sold. These rides are fully depreciated, but they could be sold for £60,000 to an amusement park in a nearby city.
4 Mr Sharkey has concluded that about 50,000 more people would use the water slide each year than have been using the rides. The admission price would be £3.60 per person (the same price that the Fun Centre has been charging for the rides).
5 Based on experience at other water slides, Mr Sharkey estimates that incremental operating expenses each year for the slide would be: salaries, £85,000; insurance, £4,200; utilities, £13,000; and maintenance, £9,800.

Required

1 Prepare a profit statement showing the expected profit each year from the water slide.
2 Compute the simple rate of return expected from the water slide. Based on this computation, should the water slide be constructed if Mr Sharkey requires a simple rate of return of at least 14% on all investments?
3 Compute the payback period for the water slide. If Mr Sharkey requires a payback period of five years or less, would the water slide be constructed?

P10–14 Simple rate of return; payback; internal rate of return

Time allowed: 30 minutes

Honest John's Used Cars plc has always hired students from the local university to wash the cars on the lot. Honest John is considering the purchase of an automatic car wash that would be used in place of the students. The following information has been gathered by Honest John's accountant to help Honest John make a decision on the purchase:

1. Payments to students for washing cars total £15,000 per year at present.
2. The car wash would cost £21,000 installed, and it would have a 10-year useful life. Honest John uses straight-line depreciation on all assets. The car wash would have a negligible salvage value in 10 years.
3. Annual out-of-pocket costs associated with the car wash would be: wages of students to operate the wash, keep the soap bin full and so forth, £6,300; utilities, £1,800; and insurance and maintenance, £900.
4. Honest John now earns a return of 20% on the funds invested in his stock of used cars. He feels that he would have to earn an equivalent rate on the car wash for the purchase to be attractive.

Required (ignore taxes)

1. Determine the annual savings that would be realized in cash operating costs if the car wash were purchased.
2. Compute the simple rate of return promised by the car wash. (*Hint:* Note that this is a cost reduction project.) Will Honest John accept this project if he expects a 20% return?
3. Compute the payback period on the car wash. Honest John (who has a reputation for being something of a penny-pincher) will not purchase any equipment unless it has a payback of four years or less. Will he purchase the car wash equipment?
4. Compute (to the nearest whole %) the internal rate of return promised by the car wash. Based on this computation, does it appear that the simple rate of return would normally be an accurate guide in investment decisions?

Chapter 11
Strategic management accounting and the balanced scorecard

LO Learning objectives

After studying Chapter 11, you should be able to:

1 Define the concepts of strategy and strategic management accounting
2 Understand the impact of corporate strategy on management accounting
3 Understand some basic strategic models and their relationship with management accounting techniques
4 Understand how a balanced scorecard fits together and how it supports a company's strategy

Concepts in Context

The term strategic management accounting (SMA) has been used to describe the process of 'provision and analysis of management accounting data about a business and its competitors for use in developing and monitoring business strategy'.[1] We may illustrate the basic ideas of SMA by looking at one of the leading retailers in the United Kingdom, Tesco, which has tailored its key performance indicators to the economics of its business. For example, rather than maximize EVA, Tesco has realized that its main fixed assets are its stores. With this type of asset base, the company aims to reduce the cost of building good quality new stores through strategic partnering with construction companies. In order to check its market positioning, the company is constantly monitoring the prices of its merchandise relative to the prices charged by its main competitors. As well as promoting customer loyalty, it uses its store card as a database for targeting the specific needs of individual customers as revealed through their purchase patterns. It also keeps a close eye on non-financial indicators such as the length of queues at the check-outs.

© Joshua Hodge Photography

In this chapter we will review both short- and long-term financial planning but in the context of *strategic choice*. **Strategic choice** means that companies can *choose* which industries and products they want to compete in but it also means that different companies in the *same* industry may decide to adopt different strategies with quite different implications for management accounting and control. For example, a company's strategy may determine whether management will be concentrating on a tight control of costs, maintaining quality or LO 1 generating new product ideas.

As more and more reliance is placed on bought-in goods and services, a higher proportion of costs are generated by a firm's suppliers, which suggests that major improvements in cost, quality and innovation are LO 2 potentially available through the effective management of the firm's supply chain. In *strategic* as opposed to *traditional* management accounting, there is a recognition that managers may have some freedom to choose which industry they operate in, which technology is used and how the organization is structured. Thus, rather than passively adapting to given competitive, technological and organizational circumstances, **strategic management accounting (SMA)** helps managers make choices through information support. Strategic management accounting is also concerned with the *implementation* of strategies by setting up control systems that drive through the chosen strategies. For example, if a company wishes to pursue a low-cost strategy then traditional budgetary control may help implementation. However, few companies compete on price alone so additional performance measures may be non-financial, such as delivery or queuing time.

As described above, Tesco's approach in linking its goals and its management information systems demonstrates many of the principles of SMA. The company has decided how it is going to compete, reviewed its internal and external operations and chosen key performance indicators that enable it to monitor the development of its chosen business model. The search for data is driven by decision needs rather than by what is simply easily available.

Some basic techniques of strategic management accounting

SMA has an orientation towards the firm's environment. The relevant environment may be in its value chain, that is, its 'upstream' relations with suppliers and 'downstream' relations with its customers. The other relevant environment is its competitive position relative to both existing and potential competitors. Its competitive position will not just depend on price but on a **marketing mix**.

Sometimes SMA will use existing information and sometimes new information will be sought. For example, the increased emphasis on marketing may involve the use of techniques such as **attribute costing** that costs product attributes that appeal to customers, using brand value as a basis for managerial decisions and measuring the costs of quality. The competitive position is monitored through competitor cost assessment through estimates of competitors' costs based on an appraisal of facilities, technology, economies of scale, market share, volume, unit costs and return on sales. Strategic management accounting is also concerned with the long run through the use of target and **life-cycle costing** that looks at the costs incurred throughout the life of a product as it goes through various stages such as development and full production.

LO 3 SMA and the concept of strategic positioning

Both the choice of strategic options and the ongoing search for strategic information may be informed by a variety of corporate strategy models. In short, a further development of SMA integrates the more outward and forward-looking aspects of the strategic intelligence approach with some well-known models of strategic choice.

Some strategic choice models involve deciding on a company's *strategic position*. For example, following Miles and Snow,[2] should the company be a **defender** concentrating on reducing costs and/or improving quality, a **prospector** continually searching for market opportunities or an analyser which combines the defender and prospector positions? Or, following Michael Porter,[3] should the company concentrate on **cost leadership** (aiming to be the lowest-cost producer in an industry) or **product differentiation** (maintain a price premium based on superior product quality)? Porter argues that: '[T]he worst strategic error is to be *stuck in the middle* or to try simultaneously to pursue all the strategies. This is a recipe for strategic mediocrity and below-average performance, because pursuing all strategies simultaneously means that a firm is not able to achieve any of them because of their inherent contradictions.'

The implications for management accounting of these positional strategies could be that a company that seeks cost leadership may use standard costing with flexible budgets for manufacturing cost control. With product cost being the key input to pricing decisions, it may also analyse costs of competitors in order to review its positioning. If the company is a differentiator then traditional costing may be less important, and more attention is paid to new product development and marketing expenditures.

Porter's generic strategy model may be linked to another of his innovations, the concept of the **value chain**. The value chain,[4] which is illustrated in Exhibit 11.1, consists of the major business functions that add value to a company's products and services. All these functions, from research and development through product design, manufacturing, marketing, distribution and customer service, are required to bring a product or service to the customer and generate revenues.

With value-chain analysis, the aim is to find linkages between value-creating activities, which result in lower costs and/or enhanced differentiation. John Shank's *strategic cost management*[5] approach shows how Porter's ideas on strategic positioning and gaining competitive advantage can have an impact on management accounting. Shank advocates a cost-driver analysis, which suggests that costs are driven by *structural* and *executional* factors. **Structural drivers** consider factors such as scale, scope, experience, technology and complexity, while **executional drivers** include factors such as work force involvement, quality management capacity utilization, plant lay-out efficiency, product configuration effectiveness, and exploitation of linkages.

Strategic investment appraisal: investment appraisal with strategic 'bolt-ons'?

In Chapter 10, we considered the various techniques of investment appraisal such as net present value (NPV) and internal rate of return. In principle, many strategic decisions, such as acquisitions or major marketing initiatives, could be analysed using these techniques by estimating and discounting future net cash flows and choosing the option that seems to give the highest return or largest NPV. Yet some advocates of more strategic approaches have argued that the conventional investment appraisal approach may set up business problems in a misleading way with an overemphasis on financial calculation leaving strategic issues either neglected or treated in an *ad hoc*, 'bolt-on' manner. John Shank argues that the NPV model follows four steps:

Step 1	Identifying spending proposals
Step 2	Quantitative analysis of incremental cash flows
Step 3	Qualitative issues that cannot be fitted into NPV are then treated in an *ad hoc* manner
Step 4	Decision – *Yes/No*

According to Shank, in conventional capital budgeting/investment appraisals, *Step 1* is hardly analysed since the investment proposals just appear out of thin air. *Step 2*, in contrast, gets a great deal of attention with

Exhibit 11.1 Business functions making up the value chain

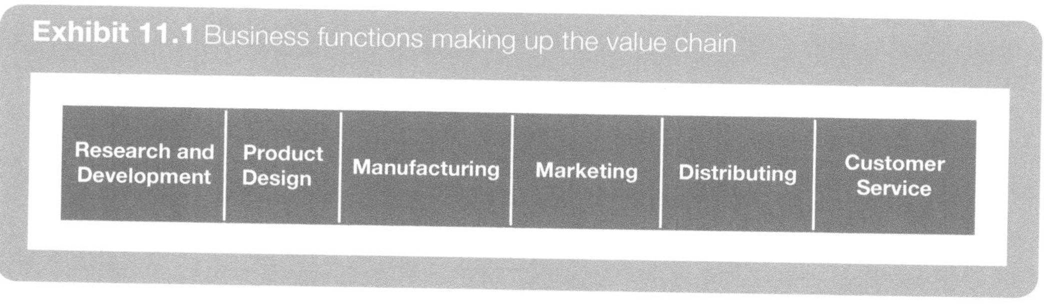

elaborate considerations of relevant cash flows and sophisticated treatments of risk. *Step 3* is a 'step-child' concerned with 'soft-issues' that cannot be handled in *Step 2*. *Step 4*, the decision, *then generally flows out of Step 2*.

Shank[6] argues that the finance framework sets up strategic problems in a misleading way and argues that pure NPV analysis misses the richness of real business problems and is often merely set up to rationalize a prior decision. He illustrates the point with a case study, *Mavis Machines*.

The Mavis Machines case

Mavis Machines is a small metal working company producing drill bits for oil exploration. At present, the shop has four large manual lathes each operated by a skilled worker. The question facing the Managing Director of Mavis Machines is whether the company should install a numerically controlled lathe to replace all manual lathes. The numerical lathe would require only one operator but with different skills in computerized automation.

The decision can be set up using an NPV model and produces a very high rate of internal rate of return, as shown in Exhibit 11.2.

Exhibit 11.2 Summary of the quantitative analysis of the automation project in Mavis Machines

Net Investment		
Purchase price		$680,000
Less:		
Trade-in value of old machines		(240,000)
Tax saving from trade-in (46%)		(108,000)
Book value	476,000	
Selling price	240,000	
Loss on resale	236,000	
Investment tax credit (10%)		(68,000)
Net		**($263,400)**
Annual cash savings		
Labour – six operators (3/shift × 2 shifts) × $20,800 each		($124,800)
Factory space savings (no difference in cash flows)		0
Other cash savings (supplies, maintenance and power)		20,000
Total, pre-tax		$144,800
Less additional taxes (46%)		(60,600)
Cash saved – pre-tax	144,800	
Additional depreciation	(13,000)*	
Additional taxable income	131,800	
Annual after tax cash savings		**$84,200**
(ignoring inflation in savings in future years)		
*Old depreciation = $590 – $20/15 = $38,000		
New depreciation = $680 – $68/12 = $51,000		
Difference = $13,000		
Summary of cash flows*		
Period 0 (263,400) 12 year IRR = 32 + %, real		
Periods 1–12 $84,200		

*Ignoring the minor impact from the lost salvage values in year 12.

The main cash savings stem from the need for fewer workers. However, other significant savings can be made in the net cost of the initial investment because of the healthy trade-in value of the relatively modern manual lathes. Indeed, 60% of the attractiveness of the project comes from the scrap value of the old machines, which suggests that the previous replacement decision might have been faulty. In an NPV approach other factors such as *flexibility, marketing* and *corporate image* are treated in rather an *ad hoc* manner.

An alternative strategic approach suggests a different perspective on the choice. Indeed when explicit strategic models are used to explore the issues the emphasis on a positive NPV in the financial analysis is eclipsed by other factors. *Competitive analysis* suggests that as a small machine shop, Mavis is best positioned as a *niche* player rather than a cost leader. The manual lathes and the skilled operators give it more product flexibility and greater security than one numerical lathe. Its strength lies in its flexibility to vary its products and sources of raw material. *Value chain analysis* suggested that it would lose both buyer and seller power because it would be more dependent only on those suppliers that could meet stringent quality requirements and would be more dependent on a single customer. There were also questions concerning the ease of maintenance of the new machine and the likely impact that firing eight workers out of a small workforce would have on morale and the firm's local reputation.

Strategic investment appraisal: an iterative model

Does the criticism of NPV by Shank and others mean that the material in Chapter 10 is of limited relevance for strategic decisions? Not according to Tomkins and Carr,[7] who suggest that strategic investment decisions may be modelled to include both financial and strategic analysis as shown in Exhibit 11.3. They suggest that a three-stage is followed:

1. The firm decides which markets to be in, by assessing both customer requirements and the relative ability of rivals to meet them. The firm will generate a number of investment possibilities based on product attributes related to volume of sales.
2. Analysis of the value chain assesses the means by which the attributes of the product can be delivered. This analysis will review possible suppliers and distributors as part of an iterative process to check on performance throughout the whole product life cycle.
3. The first two steps may then be modelled in terms of a cost and attribute driver analysis to see if the attributes can be delivered at an acceptable profit. The process is iterative in that a first assessment may suggest unacceptable low levels of profitability. The next assessment may then consider whether the profitability can be improved through piecemeal cost savings or whether existing delivery systems must be changed more radically through process re-engineering. Tomkins and Carr call this search for improvement, a process of 'probing' that uses discounted cash flow analysis but which also draws on an array of market, technological and other data.[8]

Modelling and monitoring strategy: the balanced scorecard and other non-financial measures

LO 4

So far in this chapter although we have discussed strategic choice, our focus on *financial metrics* of various sorts is arguably inappropriate for strategic decision making. We will now consider a very influential model, the *balanced scorecard*, which may be used by organizations to develop, implement and control strategy through a balanced use of financial and *non-financial* indicators. Rather than focus on an individual strategic investment, the balanced scorecard is concerned with the maintenance of an outward and forward-looking stance on a continuous and routine basis through a systematic process of monitoring and reporting on a variety of different performance dimensions.

A **balanced scorecard (BSC)** consists of an integrated set of performance measures that are derived from the company's strategy and that support the company's strategy throughout the organization.[9] A strategy is

Exhibit 11.3 A systematic formal analysis for strategic investment decisions

Reprinted from Management Accounting Research, 7/2, Tomkins, C and Carr, C., 'Reflections on the papers in this issue and a commentary on the state of strategic management accounting', 271–80, Copyright (1996), with permission from Elsevier.

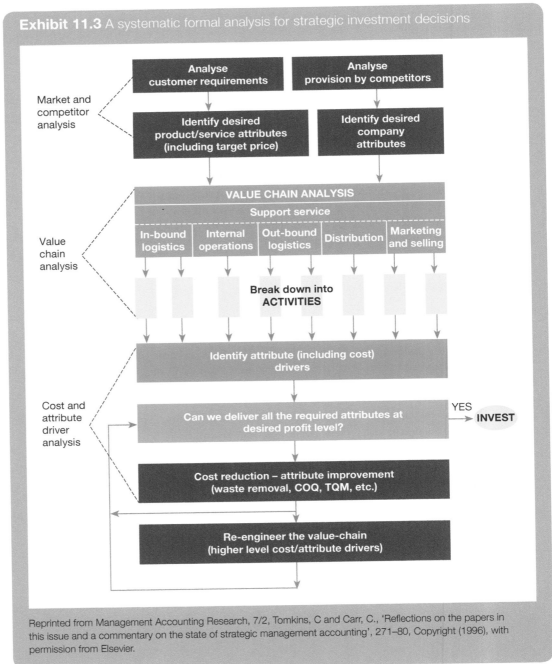

essentially a theory about how to achieve the organization's goals. For example, low-cost European carriers such as easyJet and Ryanair have copied Southwestern Airlines' strategy of offering passengers low prices and fun on short-haul jet service. The low prices result from the absence of costly frills such as meals and assigned seating. The fun is provided by flight attendants who go out of their way to entertain passengers with their antics. This is an interesting strategy. Southwestern Airlines consciously hires people who have a sense of humour and who enjoy their work. Hiring and retaining such employees probably costs no more – and may cost less – than retaining grumpy flight attendants who view their jobs as a chore. Southwestern Airlines' strategy is to build loyal customers through a combination of 'fun' – which does not cost anything to provide – and low prices that are possible because of the lack of costly frills offered by competing airlines. The theory is that low prices and fun[10] will lead to loyal customers, which, in combination with low costs, will lead to high profits. So far, this theory has worked.

Under the balanced scorecard approach, top management translates its strategy into performance measures that employees can understand and can do something about. For example, the amount of time passengers have to wait in line to have their baggage checked might be a performance measure for a supervisor in charge of the check-in counter at an airport. This performance measure is easily understood by the supervisor, and can be improved by the supervisor's actions.

Common characteristics of balanced scorecards

Performance measures used in the balanced scorecard approach tend to fall into the four groups illustrated in Exhibit 11.4: financial, customer, internal business processes, and learning and growth. Internal business processes are what the company does in an attempt to satisfy customers. For example, in a manufacturing company, assembling a product is an internal business process. In an airline, handling baggage is an internal business process. The basic idea is that learning is necessary to improve internal business processes; improving business processes is necessary to improve customer satisfaction; and improving customer satisfaction is necessary to improve financial results.

Note that the emphasis in Exhibit 11.4 is on *improvement* – not on just attaining some specific objective such as profits of £10 million. In the balanced scorecard approach, continual improvement is encouraged. In many industries, this is a matter of survival. If an organization does not continually improve, it will eventually lose out to competitors that do.

Exhibit 11.4 From strategy to performance measures: the balanced scorecard

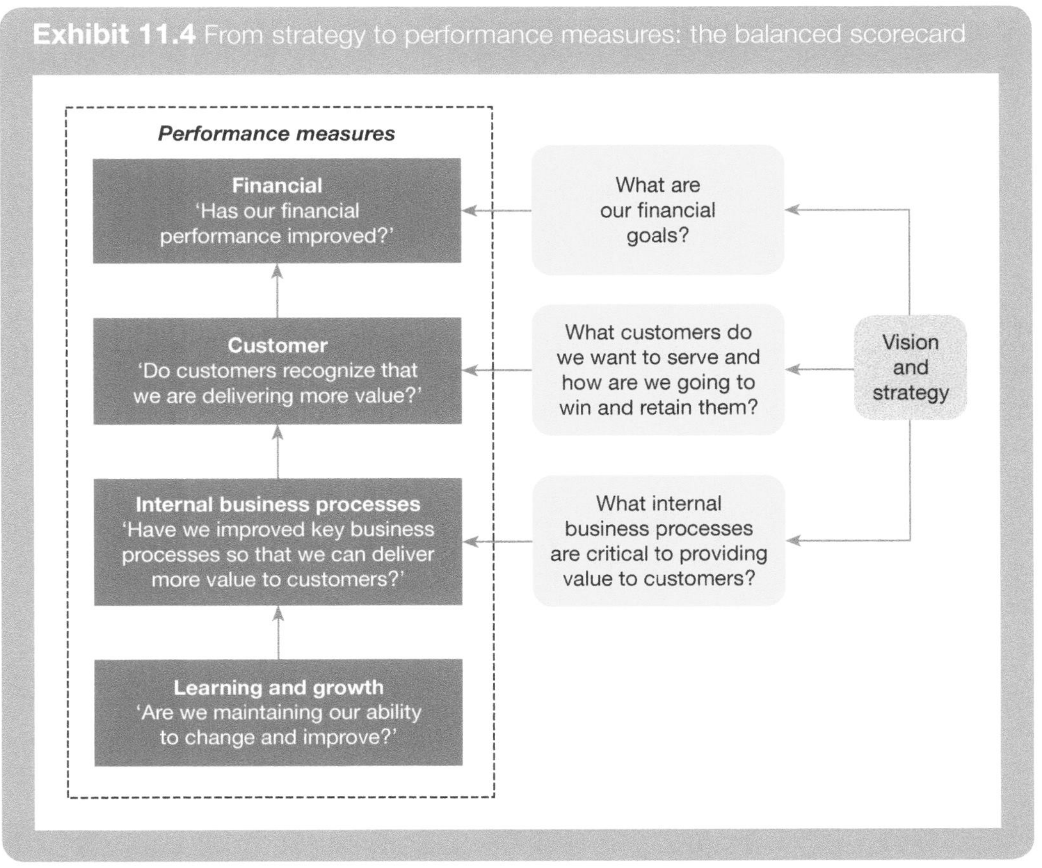

Financial performance measures appear at the top of Exhibit 11.4. Ultimately, most companies exist to provide financial rewards to owners. There are exceptions. Some companies may have loftier goals, such as providing environmentally friendly products to consumers. However, even non-profit organizations must generate enough financial resources to stay in operation.

Ordinarily, top managers are responsible for the financial performance measures – not lower level managers. The supervisor in charge of checking in passengers can be held responsible for how long passengers have to queue. However, this supervisor cannot reasonably be held responsible for the entire company's profit. That is the responsibility of the airline's top managers.

Exhibit 11.5 lists some examples of performance measures that can be found on the balanced scorecards of companies. However, few companies, if any, would use all of these performance measures, and almost all companies would add other performance measures. Managers should carefully select the performance measures for their company's balanced scorecard, keeping the following points in mind. First and foremost, the performance measures should be consistent with, and follow from, the company's strategy. If the

Exhibit 11.5 Examples of performance measures for balanced scorecards

Customer perspective performance measure	**Desired change**
Customer satisfaction as measured by survey results	+
Number of customer complaints	–
Market share	+
Product returns as a percentage of sales	–
Percentage of customers retained from last period	+
Number of new customers	+
Internal business processes perspective performance measure	**Desired change**
Percentage of sales from new products	+
Time to introduce new products to market	–
Percentage of customer calls answered within 20 seconds	+
On-time deliveries as a percentage of all deliveries	+
Work in progress inventory as a percentage of sales	–
Unfavourable standard cost variances	–
Defect-free units as a percentage of completed units	+
Delivery cycle time*	–
Throughput time*	–
Manufacturing cycle efficiency*	+
Quality costs	–
Set-up time	–
Time from call by customer to repair of product	–
Percentage of customer complaints settled on first contact	+
Time to settle a customer claim	–
Learning and growth perspective performance measure	**Desired change**
Suggestions per employee	+
Value-added employee†	+
Employee turnover	–
Hours of in-house training per employee	+

*Explained later in this chapter.

†Value-added is revenue less externally purchased materials, supplies and services.

performance measures are not consistent with the company's strategy, people will find themselves working at cross-purposes. Second, the scorecard should not have too many performance measures. This can lead to a lack of focus and confusion.

While the entire organization will have an overall balanced scorecard, each responsible individual will have his or her own personal scorecard as well. This scorecard should consist of items the individual can personally influence that relate directly to the performance measures on the overall balanced scorecard. The performance measures on this personal scorecard should not be overly influenced by actions taken by others in the company or by events that are outside of the individual's control.

With those broad principles in mind, we will now take a look at how a company's strategy affects its balanced scorecard.

A company's strategy and the balanced scorecard

Returning to the performance measures in Exhibit 11.5, each company must decide which customers to target and what internal business processes are crucial to attracting and retaining those customers. Different companies, having different strategies, will target different customers with different kinds of products and services. Take the car industry as an example. BMW stresses engineering and handling; Volvo, safety; Jaguar, luxury detailing; and Toyota,[11] reliability. Because of these differences in emphases, a one-size-fits-all approach to performance measurement will not work even within this one industry. Performance measures must be tailored to the specific strategy of each company.

Suppose, for example, that Jaguar's strategy is to offer distinctive, richly finished luxury automobiles to wealthy individuals who prize handcrafted, individualized products. Part of Jaguar's strategy might be to create such a large number of options for details, such as leather seats, interior and exterior colour combinations, and wooden dashboards, that each car becomes virtually one of a kind. For example, instead of just offering tan or blue leather seats in standard cowhide, the company may offer customers the choice of an almost infinite palate of colours in any of a number of different exotic leathers. For such a system to work effectively, Jaguar would have to be able to deliver a completely customized car within a reasonable amount of time – and without incurring more cost for this customization than the customer is willing to pay. Exhibit 11.6 suggests how Jaguar might reflect this strategy in its balanced scorecard.

If the balanced scorecard is correctly constructed, the performance measures should be linked together on a cause-and-effect basis. Each link can then be read as a hypothesis in the form 'If we improve this performance measure, then this other performance measure should also improve.' Starting from the bottom of Exhibit 11.6, we can read the links between performance measures as follows. If employees acquire the skills to install new options more effectively, then the company can offer more options and the options can be installed in less time. If more options are available and they are installed in less time, then customer surveys should show greater satisfaction with the range of options available. If customer satisfaction improves, then the number of cars sold should increase. In addition, if customer satisfaction improves, the company should be able to maintain or increase its selling prices, and if the time to install options decreases, the costs of installing the options should decrease. Together, this should result in an increase in the contribution margin per car. If the contribution margin per car increases and more cars are sold, the result should be an increase in profits.

In essence, the balanced scorecard articulates a theory of how the company can attain its desired outcomes (financial, in this case) by taking concrete actions. While the strategy laid out in Exhibit 11.6 seems plausible, it should be regarded as only a theory that should be discarded if it proves to be invalid. For example, if the company succeeds in increasing the number of options available and in decreasing the time required to install options and yet there is no increase in customer satisfaction, the number of cars sold, the contribution margin per car, or profits, the strategy would have to be reconsidered. One of the advantages of the balanced scorecard is that it continually tests the theories underlying management's strategy. If a strategy is not working, it should become evident when some of the predicted effects (i.e. more car sales) do not occur. Without this feedback, management may drift on indefinitely with an ineffective strategy based on faulty assumptions.

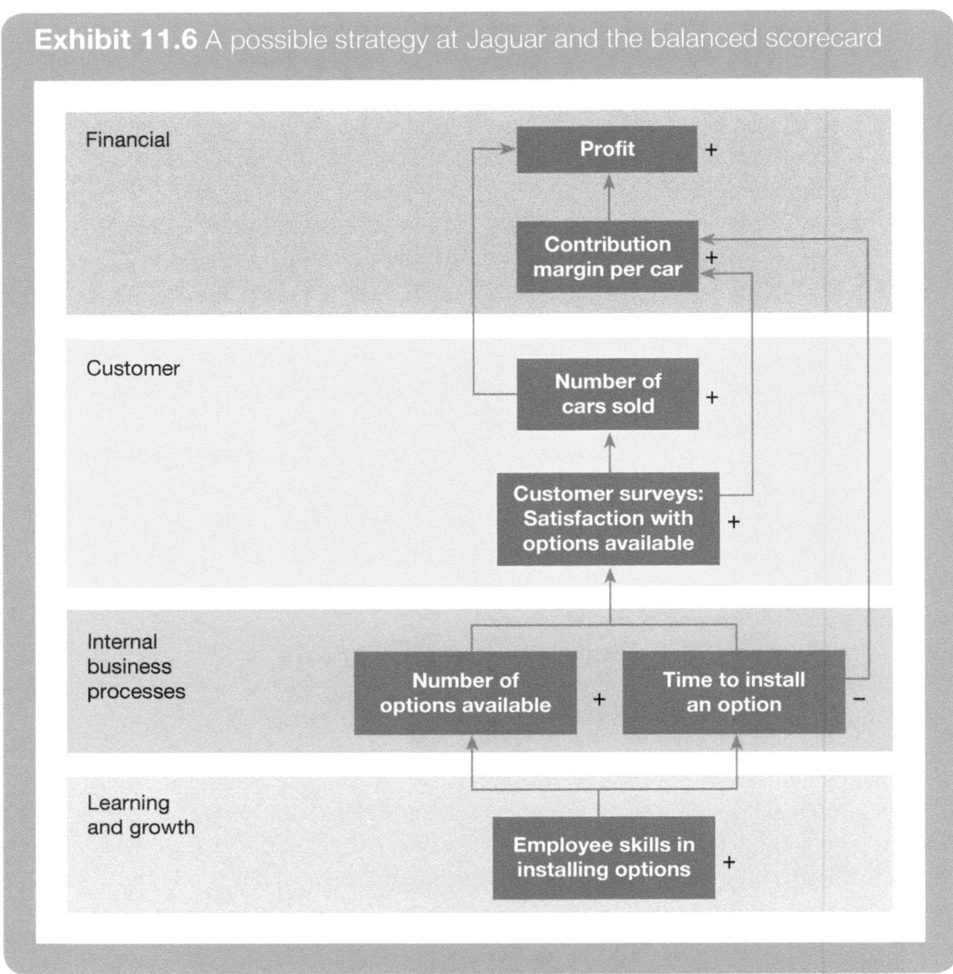

Exhibit 11.6 A possible strategy at Jaguar and the balanced scorecard

Advantages of timely feedback

Whatever performance measures are used, they should be reported on a frequent and timely basis. For example, data about defects should be reported to the responsible managers at least once a day so that action can quickly be taken if an unusual number of defects occurs. In the most advanced companies, any defect is reported *immediately*, and its cause is tracked down before any more defects can occur. Another common characteristic of the performance measures under the balanced scorecard approach is that managers focus on trends in the performance measures over time. The emphasis is on progress and *improvement* rather than on meeting any specific standard.

Some measures of internal business process performance

Most of the performance measures listed in Exhibit 11.5 are self-explanatory. However, three are not – *delivery cycle time, throughput time* and *manufacturing cycle efficiency* (MCE). These three important performance measures are discussed next.

Delivery cycle time

The amount of time between when an order is received from a customer to when the completed order is shipped is called the **delivery cycle time**. This time is clearly a key concern to many customers, who would like the delivery cycle time to be as short as possible. Cutting the delivery cycle time may give a company

Focus on Business Practice

A health service scorecard

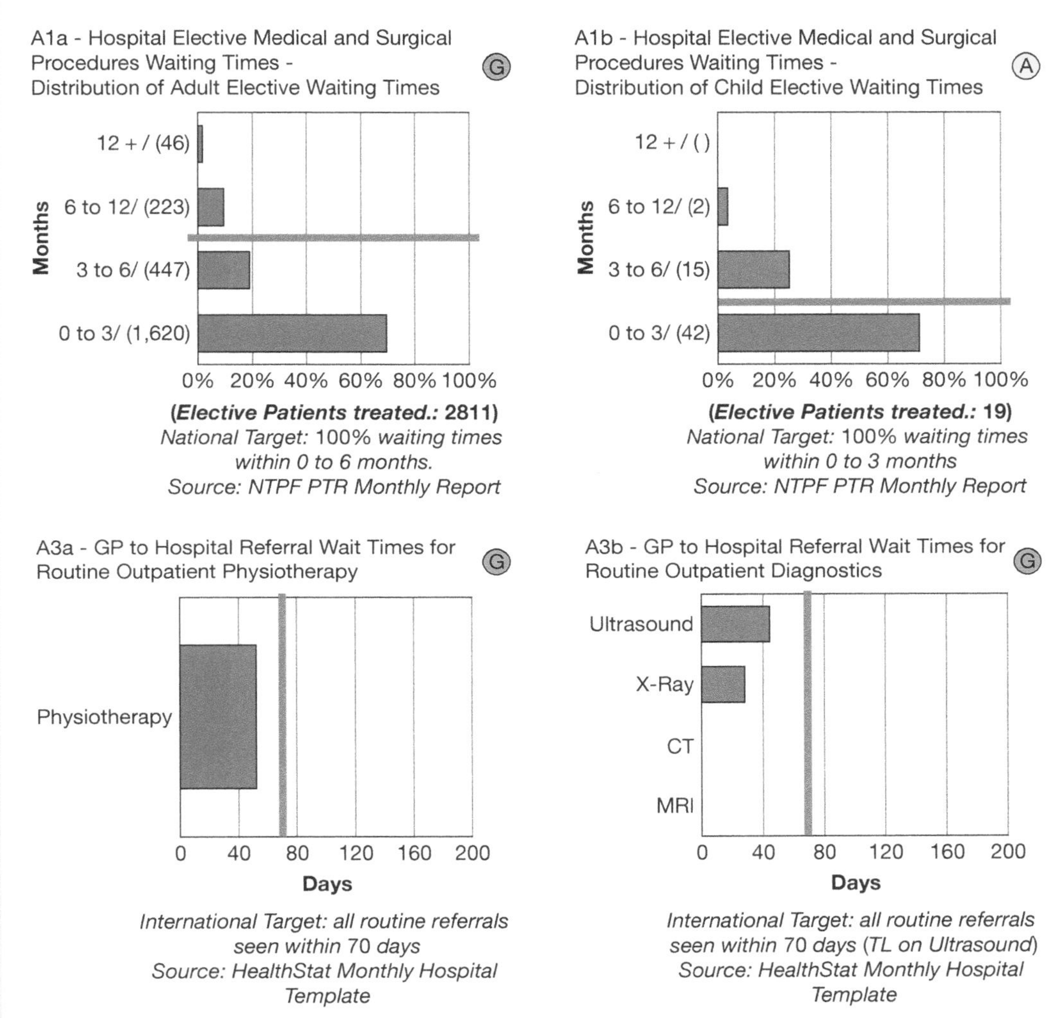

Reproduced with permission from Healthstat.

Many businesses and services use a balanced scorecard type system to report on key operating statistics and performance indicators. The Health Service Executive (HSE) is the state agency responsible for the running of the public health service in Ireland. It has over 100,000 employees and an annual budget of approximately €15 billion. The HSE uses a reporting system called HealthStat to monitor its performance in delivering health and care services.

HealthStat is described by the HSE as 'a comprehensive databank of performance information for Irish public health services'. To provide a comprehensive view of how services are delivered, HealthStat groups performance indicators under three headings: (1) Access – measuring waiting time for services; (2) Integration – checks that patients receive the correct services, in the right location and are informed about their treatment; and (3) Resources – whether a hospital or care facility is making best use of its financial and human resources. In total, 18 performance

metrics across these three headings are reported on a monthly basis. Each metric is compared to a national target – these targets have been set against best international practice and are regularly reviewed. Each month, a traffic-light type dashboard (green = better than target, amber = below target, but improving, red = well below target) is compiled and reported to clinical managers, hospitals and the HSE's board. The data are also released to the public via the HSE's website – see example above. According to the HSE, HealthStat, being the first unified reporting systems used by the HSE, provides all staff and managers with a platform to monitor and improve service delivery.[12]

Exercise: Looking at the example given, do you think these performance metrics take into account factors like quality of care received, willingness of medical professionals to communicate to patients and so on? Should such things be included in performance measurements?

a key competitive advantage – and may be necessary for survival – and therefore many companies would include this performance measure on their balanced scorecard.

Throughput (manufacturing cycle) time

The amount of time required to turn raw materials into completed products is called **throughput time**, or manufacturing cycle time. The relationship between the delivery cycle time and the throughput (manufacturing cycle) time is illustrated in Exhibit 11.7.

Note that, as shown in Exhibit 11.7, the throughput time, or manufacturing cycle time, is made up of process time, inspection time, move time and queue time. Process time is the amount of time in which work is actually done on the product. Inspection time is the amount of time spent ensuring that the product is not defective. Move time is the time required to move materials or partially completed products from workstation to workstation. Queue time is the amount of time a product spends waiting to be worked on, to be moved, to be inspected, or in storage waiting to be shipped.

As shown at the bottom of Exhibit 11.7, the only one of these four activities that adds value to the product is process time. The other three activities – inspecting, moving and queueing – add no value and should be eliminated as much as possible.

Exhibit 11.7 Delivery cycle time and throughput (manufacturing cycle) time

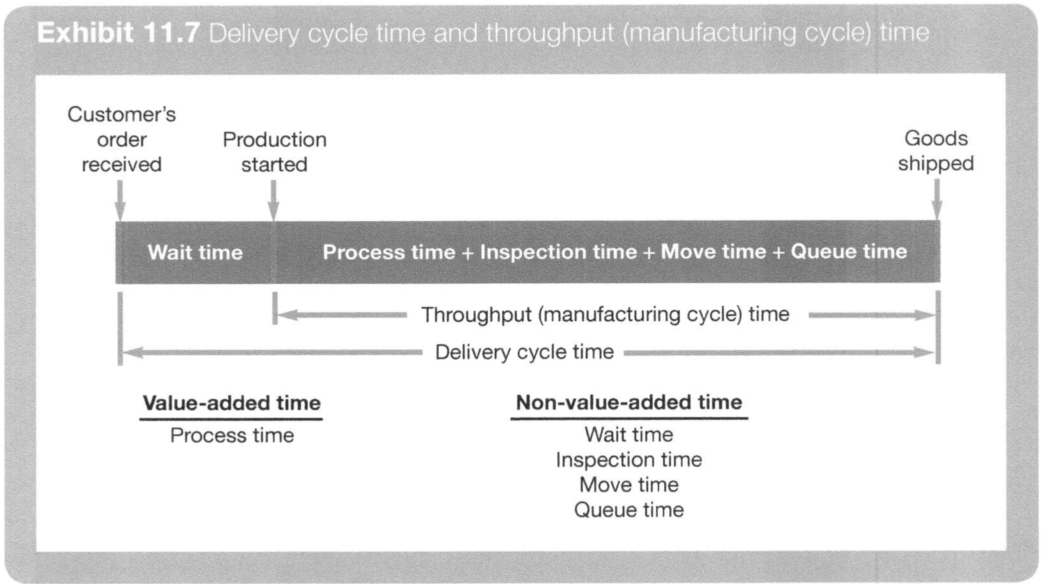

Manufacturing cycle efficiency (MCE)

Through concerted efforts to eliminate the non-value-added activities of inspecting, moving and queueing, some companies have reduced their throughput time to only a fraction of previous levels. In turn, this has helped to reduce the delivery cycle time from months to only weeks or hours. The throughput time, which is considered to be a key measure in delivery performance, can be put into better perspective by computing the **manufacturing cycle efficiency (MCE)**. The MCE is computed by relating the value-added time to the throughput time. The formula is as follows:

$$\text{MCE} = \frac{\text{Value-added time}}{\text{Throughput (manufacturing cycle) time}}$$

If the MCE is less than 1, then non-value-added time is present in the production process. An MCE of 0.5, for example, would mean that half of the total production time consisted of inspection, moving and similar non-value-added activities. In many manufacturing companies, the MCE is less than 0.1 (10%), which means that 90% of the time a unit is in process is spent on activities that do not add value to the product. By monitoring the MCE, companies are able to reduce non-value-added activities and thus get products into the hands of customers more quickly and at a lower cost.

We would like to emphasize a few points concerning the balanced scorecard. First, the balanced scorecard should be tailored to the company's strategy; each company's balanced scorecard should be unique. The examples given in this chapter are just that – examples. They should not be interpreted as general templates to be fitted to each company. Second, the balanced scorecard reflects a particular strategy, or theory, about how a company can further its objectives by taking specific actions. The theory should be viewed as tentative and subject to change if the actions do not in fact lead to attaining the company's financial and other goals. If the theory (i.e. strategy) changes, then the performance measures on the balanced scorecard should also change. The balanced scorecard should be viewed as a dynamic system that evolves as the company's strategy evolves.[13,14]

The balanced scorecard should not be seen just as 'a four bucket' model[15] with four boxes that must be filled. Organizations may choose to have five main dimensions. For example, banks may wish to have an extra box labelled risk management. As we have seen recently with the world-wide 'credit crunch', banks that have failed to manage risk have suffered financially or even gone out of business completely.

Focus on Business Practice

Risk and the balanced scorecard

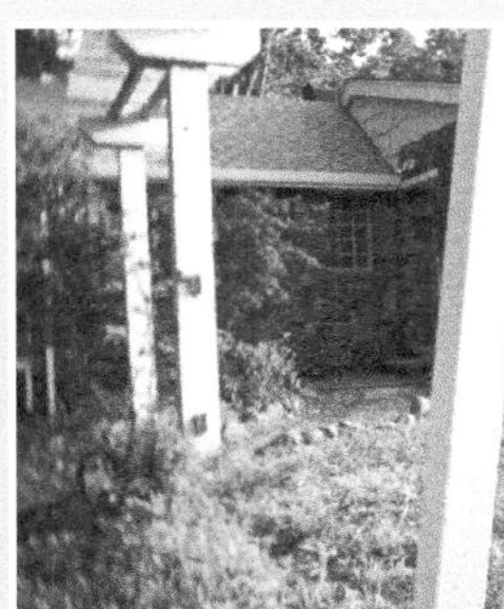

© slobo

The author was recently involved in a research project looking at the implementation of the balanced scorecard in a major European bank. The bank had 'customized' the scorecard by including 'risk' as a major objective. Relative to some of its competitors, this bank did seem to be better prepared for the credit crunch with a much less risky approach to lending. Another interesting feature of the bank was the way that each employee had a personal scorecard which was aligned to the local business unit through to corporate objectives. The scorecard implementation had a board level corporate champion and was 'owned' by both human resource and finance functions.[16]

Exercise: Not all performance indicators in the balanced scorecard are positively related. Consider in this example the potential trade-off between risk and financial return.

Summary

- Profit and shareholder value metrics may be used for business planning but they may not provide sufficient information for developing and implementing strategies.
- Strategic management accounting has evolved from the collection of competitor information to attempts to match management accounting systems with an organization's strategic position.
- A balanced scorecard consists of an integrated system of performance measures that are derived from and support the company's strategy. Different companies will have different balanced scorecards because they have different strategies. A well-constructed balanced scorecard provides a means for guiding the company and also provides feedback concerning the effectiveness of the company's strategy.

Key terms

Attribute costing Costing the product attributes that appeal to customers (p. 260).

Balanced scorecard (BSC) An integrated set of performance measures that is derived from and supports the organization's strategy (p. 263).

Cost leadership Aiming to be the lowest cost producer in an industry (p. 260).

Defender A company which concentrates on reducing costs and/or improving quality in existing markets/products (p. 260).

Delivery cycle time The amount of time required from receipt of an order from a customer to shipment of the completed goods (p. 268).

Executional drivers Cost factors such as work force involvement, quality management capacity utilization, plant lay-out efficiency, product configuration effectiveness, and exploitation of linkages (p. 261).

Life-cycle costing Analyses costs incurred throughout the life of a product from development through to full production (p. 260).

Manufacturing cycle efficiency (MCE) Process (value-added) time as a percentage of throughput time (p. 271).

Marketing mix Price is one element in product competitiveness together with product, promotion and place (p. 260).

Product differentiation Aims to maintain a price premium based on superior product quality (p. 261).

Prospector A company that is continually searching for market opportunities (p. 260).

Strategic choice Choosing not only which industries and products to compete in but also how a company plans to compete (p. 260).

Strategic management accounting The use of management accounting information to help managers choose where and how to compete (p. 260).

Structural drivers Factors such as scale, scope, experience, technology and complexity (p. 261).

Throughput time The amount of time required to turn raw materials into completed products (p. 270).

Value chain The major business functions that add value to a company's products and services (p. 261).

Endnotes

1. Simmonds (1981).
2. Miles and Snow (1978).
3. Porter (1980).
4. Porter (1985).
5. Shank (1996).
6. Shank (1996).
7. Tomkins and Carr (1996).
8. For a discussion of strategic investment appraisal see also Northcott and Alkaraan (2007).
9. The balanced scorecard concept was developed by Robert Kaplan and David Norton. For further details, see their articles Kaplan and Norton (1992) (1996a) (1996b), (1997) and (2004). In the 1960s, the French developed a concept similar to the balanced scorecard called Tableau de Bord or 'dashboard'. For details, see Lebas (1994).
10. Some low cost airlines have only copied the 'no-frills' and seem less concerned with 'fun'. There is also an emerging trend to encourage online check-in.
11. Of course, Toyota, *as a company*, is associated with the development of lean production, which, as we have seen is based on trying to achieve both low cost, reliability, and high quality specifications. It may not try to achieve all these characteristics *in a particular model*.
12. http://www.hse.ie/eng/staff/Healthstat/about/
13. Kaplan and Norton (1996b).
14. For a critical evaluation of the BSC see Norreklit (2000).
15. Ittner and Larcker (2003).
16. Ye and Seal (2009).

connect

When you have read this chapter, log on to the Online Learning Centre for *Management Accounting for Business Decisions* at **www.mheducation.co.uk/textbooks/sealmabd1**, where you'll find multiple choice questions, practice exams and extra study tools for management accounting.

Assessment

Questions

connect™

11–1 Why is market share an important indicator to monitor?
11–2 What aspects of a competitor's costs should be analysed in a strategic assessment?
11–3 What sources are useful for strategic intelligence gathering?
11–4 What is the difference between a prospector and a defender company?
11–5 What is the difference between a cost leader and a product differentiator?
11–6 What are the three steps/dimensions that combine financial and strategic analysis as proposed by Tomkins and Carr?
11–7 What are the implications of the 'strategy as collision' model?
11–8 Why does the balanced scorecard include financial performance measures as well as measures of how well internal business processes are doing?
11–9 What is the difference between the delivery cycle time and the throughput time? What four elements make up the throughput time? Into what two classes can these four elements be placed?
11–10 Why does the balanced scorecard differ from company to company?

Exercises

connect™

E11–1 Time allowed: 20 minutes

Management of Mittel Rhein AG of Köln, Germany, would like to reduce the amount of time between when a customer places an order and when the order is shipped. For the first quarter of operations during the current year the following data were reported:

	Days
Inspection time	0.3
Wait time (from order to start of production)	14.0
Process time	2.7
Move time	1.0
Queue time	5.0

Required

1 Compute the throughput time, or velocity of production.
2 Compute the manufacturing cycle efficiency (MCE) for the quarter.
3 What percentage of the throughput time was spent in non-value-added activities?
4 Compute the delivery cycle time.

Problems

connect™

P11–2 Perverse effects of some performance measures

Time allowed: 30 minutes

There is often more than one way to improve a performance measure. Unfortunately, some of the actions taken by managers to make their performance look better may actually harm the organization. For example, suppose the marketing department is held responsible only for increasing the performance measure 'total revenues'. Increases in total revenues may be achieved by working harder and smarter, but they can also usually be achieved by simply cutting prices. The increase in volume from cutting prices almost always results in greater total revenues; however, it does not always lead to greater total profits. Those who design performance measurement systems need to keep in mind that managers who are under pressure to perform may take actions to improve performance measures that have negative consequences elsewhere.

Required

For each of the following situations, describe actions that managers might take to show improvement in the performance measure but which do not actually lead to improvement in the organization's overall performance.

1. Concerned with the slow rate at which new products are brought to market, top management of a consumer electronics company introduces a new performance measure – speed-to-market. The research and development department is given responsibility for this performance measure, which measures the average amount of time a product is in development before it is released to the market for sale.
2. The Chief Executive of a telephone company has been under public pressure from city officials to fix the large number of public pay phones that do not work. The company's repair people complain that the problem is vandalism and damage caused by theft of coins from coin boxes – particularly in high crime areas in the city. The Chief Executive says she wants the problem solved and has pledged to city officials that there will be substantial improvement by the end of the year. To ensure that this is done, she makes the managers in charge of installing and maintaining pay phones responsible for increasing the percentage of public pay phones that are fully functional.
3. A manufacturing company has been plagued by the chronic failure to ship orders to customers by the promised date. To solve this problem, the production manager has been given the responsibility of increasing the percentage of orders shipped on time. When a customer calls in an order, the production manager and the customer agree to a delivery date. If the order is not completed by that date, it is counted as a late shipment.
4. Concerned with the productivity of employees, the board of directors of a large multinational corporation has dictated that the manager of each subsidiary will be held responsible for increasing the revenue per employee of his or her subsidiary.

P11–3 Strategic analysis

Time allowed: 45 minutes

M-HK provides a passenger ferry service between two large cities separated by the mouth of a major river. The ferries are frequent, well-supported by passengers and cover the distance between the cities in one hour. M-HK also transports passengers and goods by water ferry to other cities located on the

river mouth. There are other ferry operators providing services between each of these locations besides M-HK.

Required

1. Explain what strategic information is required by M-HK's management in respect of customer demand, competition, competitiveness, and finance in order to plan its future ferry services. *(10 marks)*
2. Using the information in your answer to Question 1, discuss how M-HK's Chartered Management Accountant should provide reports to M-HK's senior management for operational and strategic planning purposes. *(15 marks)*

(Total = 25 marks)

CIMA Management Accounting – Business Strategy, May 2001

P11–4 Strategic analysis

Time allowed: 45 minutes

R is a large high-class hotel situated in a thriving city. It is part of a worldwide hotel group owned by a large number of shareholders. The majority of the shares are held by individuals, each holding a small number; the rest are owned by financial institutions.

The hotel provides full amenities, including a heated swimming pool, as well as the normal facilities of bars, restaurants and good-quality accommodation. There are many other hotels in the city which all compete with R. The city in which R is situated is old and attracts many foreign visitors, particularly in its summer season.

Required

1. State the main stakeholders with whom relationships need to be established and maintained by the management of R. Explain why it is important that relationships are developed and maintained with each of these stakeholders. *(10 marks)*
2. Explain how the management of R should carry out a benchmarking exercise on its services, and recommend ways in which the outcomes should be evaluated. *(15 marks)*
   Note: Do NOT describe different methods of benchmarking in answering this question. *(Total = 25 marks)*

CIMA Management Accounting – Business Strategy, May 2001

P11-5 Balanced scorecard

Time allowed: 45 minutes

The Royal Hotel Ltd is privately owned and situated in Keswick, an inland resort in the English Lake District. It is a medium-sized hotel with 50 bedrooms. Whilst high standards of building maintenance exist, the hotel has been conservatively managed by William Wordsworth, who owns 100% of its share capital. The hotel currently offers accommodation and restaurant facilities only, and has experienced little innovation in services offered during recent years.

William Wordsworth intends to retire in five years' time, so he has invited Pam Ayres to join him in partnership, with a view to her taking a controlling interest in the hotel on his retirement. She has recently qualified with a Master's Degree from the University of Birmingham, and has some knowledge of the latest approaches to the measurement of business performance. She has conducted a preliminary investigation of the hotel's performance over the past two years, to form a basis for taking a decision on joining William in partnership. The data she has gathered, based on the balanced scorecard approach to performance measurement, is presented in Appendix 1 and Appendix 2.

Appendix 1: Financial data

	Current year	Previous year
Estimated market value of the business	£2,000,000	£2,000,000
Turnover	£1,000,000	£950,000
Net profit	£200,000	£188,000
Current assets (cash, stock and credit card debtors)	£30,000	£25,000
Current liabilities (trade creditors)	£7,000	£10,000

Appendix 2: Non-financial data

Customer perspective

	Current year	Previous year
Room occupancy (during the 300 days the hotel is open each year)	55%	65%
Market share of overnight hotel accommodation in Keswick	4.33%	3.67%
Customer satisfaction rating (score maximum 100%)	55%	65%
Customers indicating they would return to the Royal Hotel if visiting Keswick again	25%	45%

Internal business processes

	Current year	Previous year
Audited percentage of procedures done according to job specification	75%	85%
Year on year employee retention rate	30%	50%
Customer rating of staff responsiveness (score maximum 100%)	60%	85%
Customer rating of staff competence (score maximum 100%)	50%	90%
Customer rating of staff courtesy (score maximum 100%)	60%	78%

Learning and growth perspective

	Current year	Previous year
Royal Hotel percentage of revenue from accommodation and restaurant	100%	100%
Keswick hotels industry average percentage of revenue from accommodation and restaurants	65%	75%
Average percentage of staff with hotel and restaurant qualifications	55%	65%

Required

1. Assess the financial performance of the Royal Hotel based only on the information provided in Appendix 1.
2. Explain why the information in Appendix 2 is likely to give a better indication of future success than the information in Appendix 1.
3. Using all the information at your disposal, assess the future prospects of the Royal Hotel, and advise Pam Ayres on the desirability of becoming a partner in the business

(*Thanks to Alan Coad, University of Birmingham*)

Chapter 12
Performance measurement and management control in segmented organizations

LO Learning **objectives**

After studying Chapter 12, you should be able to:

1 Differentiate between performance measurement in cost centres, profit centres and investment centres
2 Compute the return on investment (ROI)
3 Show how changes in sales, expenses and assets affect an organization's ROI
4 Compute residual income and understand its strengths and weaknesses
5 Compute economic value added (EVA) and other value management metrics

Concepts **in Context**

© Andriy Petrenko

Quaker Oats provides an example of how the use of a specific performance measure can change the way a company operates. Prior to adopting EVA, 'its businesses had one overriding goal – increasing quarterly earnings. To do it, they guzzled capital. They offered sharp price discounts at the end of each quarter, so plants ran overtime turning out huge shipments of Gatorade, Rice-A-Roni, 100 per cent Natural Cereal, and other products. Managers led the late rush, since their bonuses depended on raising operating profits each quarter ... Pumping up sales requires many warehouses (capital) to hold vast temporary inventories (more capital). But who cared? Quaker's operating businesses paid no charge for capital in internal accounting, so they barely noticed. It took EVA to spotlight the problem. One plant has trimmed inventories from $15 million to $9 million, even though it is producing much more, and Quaker has closed five of 15 warehouses, saving $6 million a year in salaries and capital costs.'[1]

Once an organization grows beyond a few people, it becomes impossible for the top manager to make decisions about everything. For example, the managing director of the Novotel Hotel chain cannot be expected to decide whether a particular hotel guest at the Novotel in Sheffield should be allowed to check out later than the normal checkout time. To some degree, managers have to delegate decisions to those who are at lower levels in the organization. However, the degree to which decisions are delegated varies from organization to organization.

Decentralization in organizations

A **decentralized organization** is one in which decision making is not confined to a few top executives but rather is spread throughout the organization, with managers at various levels making *key operating decisions* relating to their sphere of responsibility. Decentralization is a matter of degree, since all organizations are decentralized to some extent out of necessity. At one extreme, a strongly decentralized organization is one in which there are few, if any, constraints on the freedom of even the lowest-level managers and employees to make decisions. At the other extreme, in a strongly centralized organization, lower-level managers have little freedom to make a decision. Although most organizations fall somewhere between these two extremes, there is a pronounced trend towards more and more decentralization.

Advantages and disadvantages of decentralization

Decentralization has many benefits, including:

1. Top management is relieved of much day-to-day problem solving and is left free to concentrate on strategy, on higher-level decision making, and on co-ordinating activities.
2. Decentralization provides lower-level managers with vital experience in making decisions. Without such experience, they would be ill-prepared to make decisions when they are promoted.
3. Added responsibility and decision-making authority often result in increased job satisfaction. It makes the job more interesting and provides greater incentives for people to put out their best efforts.
4. Lower-level managers generally have more detailed and up-to-date information about conditions in their own area of responsibility than top managers. Therefore, the decisions of lower-level managers are often based on better information.
5. It is difficult to evaluate a manager's performance if the manager is not given much latitude in what he or she can do.

Decentralization has four major disadvantages:

1. Lower-level managers may make decisions without fully understanding the 'big picture'. While top-level managers typically have less detailed information about operations than the lower-level managers, they usually have more information about the company as a whole and may have a better understanding of the company's strategy. This situation can be avoided to some extent with the use of modern management information systems that can, in principle, give every manager at every level the same information that goes to the managing director and other top-level managers.
2. In a truly decentralized organization, there may be a lack of co-ordination among autonomous managers. This problem can be reduced by clearly defining the company's strategy and communicating it effectively throughout the organization.
3. Lower-level managers may have objectives that are different from the objectives of the entire organization. For example, some managers may be more interested in increasing the sizes of their departments than in increasing the profits of the company.[2] To some degree, this problem can be overcome by designing performance evaluation systems that motivate managers to make decisions that are in the best interests of the company.
4. In a strongly decentralized organization, it may be more difficult effectively to spread innovative ideas. Someone in one part of the organization may have a terrific idea that would benefit other parts of the organization, but without strong central direction the idea may not be shared with and adopted by other parts of the organization.

Decentralization and segment reporting

Effective decentralization requires *segmental reporting*. In addition to the company-wide profit and loss account, reports are needed for individual segments of the organization. A **segment** is a part or activity of an organization about which managers would like cost, revenue or profit data. Examples of segments include divisions of a company, sales territories, individual stores, service centres, manufacturing plants, marketing departments, individual customers and product lines. As we shall see, a company's operations can be segmented in many ways. For example, a supermarket chain like Tesco or Sainsbury can segment their businesses by geographic region, by individual store, by the nature of the merchandise (i.e., green groceries, canned goods, paper goods), by brand name, and so on. In this chapter, we learn how to construct profit and loss accounts for such business segments. These segmented profit and loss accounts are useful in analysing the profitability of segments and in measuring the performance of segment managers.

Cost, profit and investment centres

LO 1

Decentralized companies typically categorize their business segments into cost centres, profit centres and investment centres – depending on the responsibilities of the managers of the segments.[3]

Cost centre

A **cost centre** is a business segment whose manager has control over costs but not over revenue or investment funds. Service departments such as accounting, finance, general administration, legal, personnel and so on, are usually considered to be cost centres. In addition, manufacturing facilities are often considered to be cost centres. The managers of cost centres are expected to minimize cost while providing the level of services or the amount of products demanded by other parts of the organization. For example, the manager of a production facility would be evaluated at least in part by comparing actual costs to how much the costs should have been for the actual number of units produced during the period.

Profit centre

In contrast to a cost centre, a **profit centre** is any business segment whose manager has control over both cost and revenue. Like a cost centre, however, a profit centre generally does not have control over investment funds. For example, the manager in charge of an amusement park would be responsible for both the revenues and costs, and hence the profits, of the amusement park but may not have control over major investments in the park. Profit centre managers are often evaluated by comparing actual profit to targeted or budgeted profit.

Investment centre

An **investment centre** is any segment of an organization whose manager has control over cost, revenue and investments in operating assets. For example, the managing director of the Truck Division at General Motors (one of the companies that pioneered decentralization in the last century)[4] would have a great deal of discretion over investments in the division. The managing director of the Truck Division would be responsible for initiating investment proposals, such as funding research into more fuel-efficient engines for sport-utility vehicles. Once the proposal has been approved by the top level of managers at General Motors and the board of directors, the managing director of the Truck Division would then be responsible for making sure that the investment pays off. Investment centre managers are usually evaluated using return on investment or residual income measures as discussed later in the chapter.

Responsibility centres

A **responsibility centre** is broadly defined as any part of an organization whose manager has control over cost, revenue or investment funds. Cost centres, profit centres and investment centres are all known as responsibility centres.

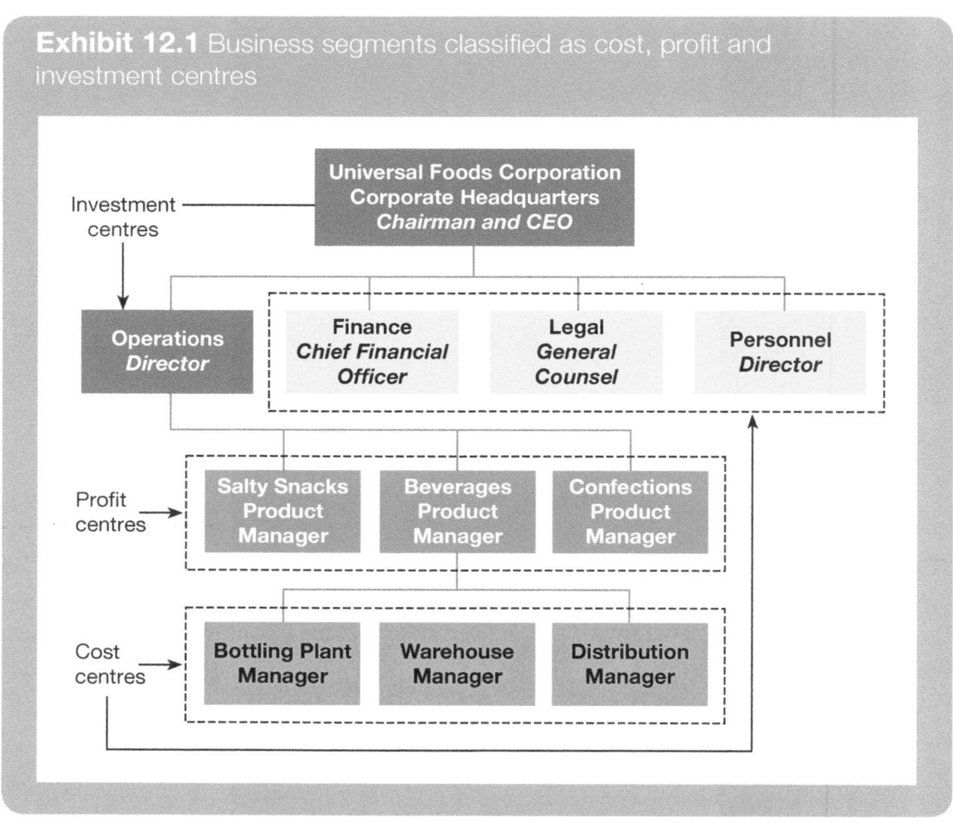

Exhibit 12.1 Business segments classified as cost, profit and investment centres

A partial organization chart for Universal Foods Corporation, a company in the snack food and beverage industry, appears in Exhibit 12.1. This partial organization chart indicates how the various business segments of the company are classified in terms of responsibility. Note that the cost centres are the departments and work centres that do not generate significant revenues by themselves. These are staff departments such as finance, legal and personnel, and operating units such as the bottling plant, warehouse and beverage distribution centre. The profit centres are business segments that generate revenues and include the beverage, salty snacks and confections product segments. The managing director of operations oversees allocation of investment funds across the product segments and is responsible for revenues and costs and so is treated as an investment centre. And finally, corporate headquarters is an investment centre, since it is responsible for all revenues, costs and investments. In this chapter we are going to focus on the management of investment centres.

LO 2 Rate of return for measuring managerial performance

When a company is truly decentralized, segment managers are given a great deal of autonomy. So great is this autonomy that the various profit and investment centres are often viewed as being virtually independent businesses, with their managers having about the same control over decisions as if they were in fact running their own independent firms. With this autonomy, fierce competition often develops among managers, with each striving to make his or her segment the 'best' in the company.

Competition between investment centres is particularly keen for investment funds. How do top managers in corporate headquarters go about deciding who gets new investment funds as they become available, and how do these managers decide which investment centres are most profitably using the funds that have already been entrusted to their care? One of the most popular ways of making these judgments is to measure the rate of return that investment centre managers are able to generate on their assets. This rate of return is called *the return on investment (ROI)*.

The return on investment (ROI) formula

The **return on investment (ROI)** is defined as net operating profit divided by average operating assets:

$$\text{ROI} = \frac{\text{Net operating profit}}{\text{Average operating assets}}$$

There are some issues about how to measure net operating profit and average operating assets, but this formula seems clear enough. The higher the return on investment of a business segment, the greater the *profit generated per pound invested* in the segment's operating assets.

Net operating profit and operating assets defined

Note that *net operating profit*, rather than net profit, is used in the ROI formula. **Net operating profit** is profit before interest and taxes and is sometimes referred to as EBIT (earnings before interest and taxes). The reason for using net operating profit in the formula is that the profit figure used should be consistent with the base to which it is applied. Notice that the base (i.e., denominator) consists of *operating assets*. Thus, to be consistent we use net operating profit in the numerator.

Operating assets include cash, debtors, inventory, plant and equipment, and all other assets held for productive use in the organization. Examples of assets that would not be included in the operating assets category (i.e., examples of non-operating assets) would include land held for future use, an investment in another company, or a factory building rented to someone else. The operating assets base used in the formula is typically computed as the average of the operating assets between the beginning and the end of the year.

Plant and equipment: net book value or gross cost?

A major issue in ROI computations is the monetary measure of plant and equipment that should be included in the operating assets base. To illustrate the problem involved, assume that a company reports the following amounts for plant and equipment on its balance sheet:

Plant and equipment	£3,000,000
Less accumulated depreciation	900,000
Net book value	£2,100,000

What amount of plant and equipment should the company include with its operating assets in computing ROI? One widely used approach is to include only the plant and equipment's *net book value* – that is, the plant's original cost less accumulated depreciation (£2,100,000 in the example above). A second approach is to ignore depreciation and include the plant's entire *gross cost* in the operating assets base (£3,000,000 in the example above). Both of these approaches are used in actual practice, even though they will obviously yield very different operating asset and ROI figures.

The following arguments can be raised for using *net book value* to measure *operating assets* and for using *gross cost* to measure operating assets in ROI computation.

Arguments for using net book value to measure operating assets in ROI computations:

1. The net book value method is consistent with how plant and equipment are reported on the balance sheet (i.e., cost less accumulated depreciation to date).
2. The net book value method is consistent with the computation of operating profit, which includes depreciation as an operating expense.

Arguments for using gross cost to measure operating assets in ROI computations:

1. The gross cost method eliminates both the age of equipment and the method of depreciation as factors in ROI computations. (Under the net book value method, ROI will tend to increase over time as net book value declines due to depreciation.)
2. The gross cost method does not discourage replacement of old, worn out equipment. (Under the net book value method, replacing fully depreciated equipment with new equipment can have a dramatic, adverse effect on ROI.)

Managers generally view consistency as the most important of the considerations above. As a result, a majority of companies use the net book value approach in ROI computations. In this text, we will also use the net book value approach unless a specific exercise or problem directs otherwise.

LO 3 Controlling the rate of return

When we first defined the return on investment, we used the following formula:

$$\text{ROI} = \frac{\text{Net operating profit}}{\text{Average operating assets}}$$

We can modify this formula slightly by introducing sales as follows:

$$\text{ROI} = \frac{\text{Net operating profit}}{\text{Sales}} \times \frac{\text{Sales}}{\text{Average operating assets}}$$

The first term on the right-hand side of the equation is the *margin*, which is defined as follows:

$$\text{Margin} = \frac{\text{Net operating profit}}{\text{Sales}}$$

The **margin** is a measure of management's ability to control operating expenses in relation to sales. The lower the operating expenses per pound of sales, the higher the margin earned.

The second term on the right-hand side of the preceding equation is *turnover* which is defined as follows:

$$\text{Turnover} = \frac{\text{Sales}}{\text{Average operating assets}}$$

Turnover is a measure of the sales that are generated for each pound invested in operating assets.

The following alternative form of the ROI formula, which we will use most frequently, combines margin and turnover:

$$\text{ROI} = \text{Margin} \times \text{Turnover}$$

Which formula for ROI should be used – the original one stated in terms of net operating profit and average operating assets or this one stated in terms of margin and turnover? Either can be used – they will always give the same answer. However, the margin and turnover formulation provides some additional insights.

Some managers tend to focus too much on margin and ignore turnover. To some degree at least, the margin can be a valuable indicator of a manager's performance. Standing alone, however, it overlooks one crucial area of a manager's responsibility – the investment in operating assets. Excessive funds tied up in operating assets, which depresses turnover, can be just as much of a drag on profitability as excessive operating expenses, which depresses margin. One of the advantages of ROI as a performance measure is that it forces the manager to control the investment in operating assets as well as to control expenses and the margin.

Exhibit 12.2 Elements of return on investment (ROI)

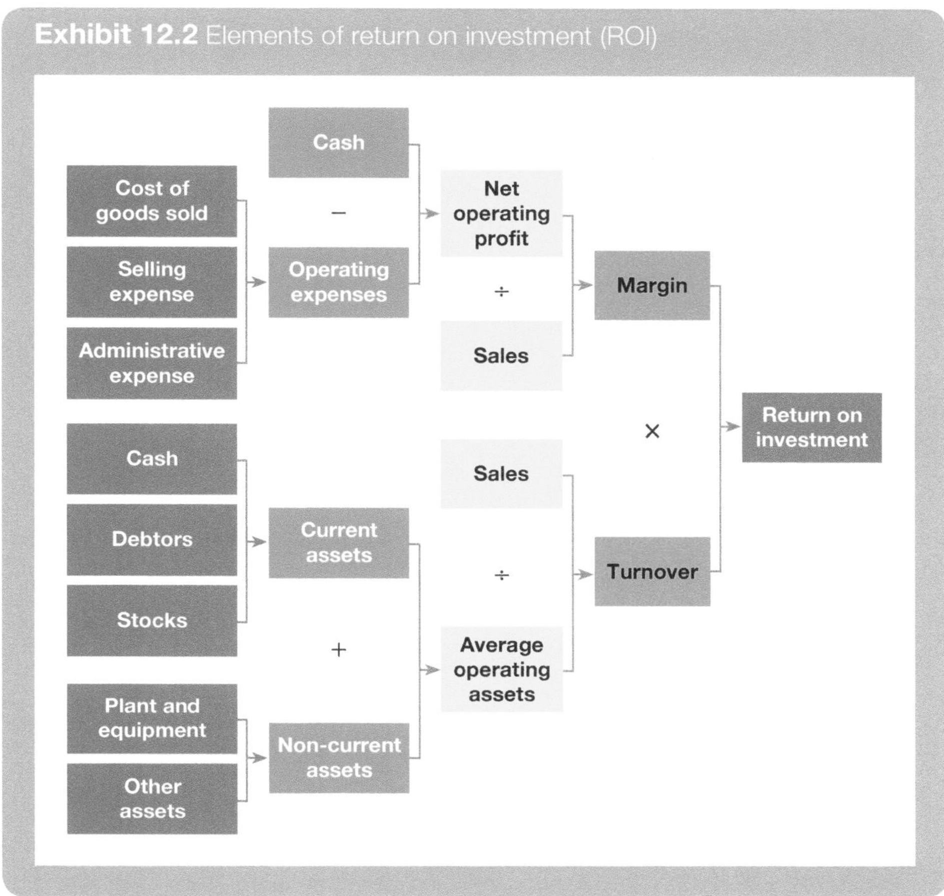

Du Pont pioneered the ROI concept and recognized the importance of looking at both margin and turnover in assessing the performance of a manager. The ROI formula is now widely used as the key measure of the performance of an investment centre. The ROI formula blends together many aspects of the manager's responsibilities into a single figure that can be compared to the returns of competing investment centres, the returns of other firms in the industry, and to the past returns of the investment centre itself.

Du Pont also developed the diagram that appears in Exhibit 12.2. This exhibit helps managers understand how they can control ROI. An investment centre manager can increase ROI in basically three ways:

1. Increase sales
2. Reduce expenses
3. Reduce assets.

To illustrate how the rate of return can be improved by each of these three actions, consider how the manager of the Raffles Burger Grill is evaluated. Burger Grill is a small chain of upmarket casual restaurants that has been rapidly adding outlets via franchising. The Raffles franchise is owned by a group of local surgeons who have little time to devote to management and little expertise in business matters. Therefore, they delegate operating decisions – including decisions concerning investment in operating assets such as inventories – to a professional manager they have hired. The manager is evaluated largely based on the ROI the franchise generates.

The following data represent the results of business activity for the most recent month:

Net operating profit	£10,000
Sales	100,000
Average operating assets	50,000

The rate of return generated by the Raffles Burger Grill investment centre is as follows:

ROI = Margin × Turnover

$$\frac{\text{Net operating profit}}{\text{Sales}} \times \frac{\text{Sales}}{\text{Average operating assets}}$$

$$\frac{£10{,}000}{£1{,}000{,}000} \times \frac{£100{,}000}{£50{,}000}$$

10% × 2 = 20%

As we stated above, to improve the ROI figure, the manager can (1) increase sales, (2) reduce expenses, or (3) reduce the operating assets.

(1) Increase sales

Assume that the manager of the Raffles Burger Grill is able to increase sales from £100,000 to £110,000. Assume further that either because of good cost control or because some costs in the company are fixed, the net operating profit increases even more rapidly, going from £10,000 to £12,000 per period. The operating assets remain constant.

$$\text{ROI} = \frac{£12{,}000}{£110{,}000} \times \frac{£110{,}000}{£50{,}000}$$

10.91% × 2.2 = 24% (as compared to 20% above)

(2) Reduce expenses

Assume that the manager of the Raffles Burger Grill is able to reduce expenses by £1,000 so that net operating profit increases from £10,000 to £11,000. Both sales and operating assets remain constant.

$$\text{ROI} = \frac{£11{,}000}{£100{,}000} \times \frac{£100{,}000}{£50{,}000}$$

11% × 2 = 22% (as compared to 20% above)

(3) Reduce assets

Assume that the manager of the Raffles Burger Grill is able to reduce operating assets from £50,000 to £40,000. Sales and net operating profit remain unchanged.

$$\text{ROI} = \frac{£10{,}000}{£100{,}000} \times \frac{£100{,}000}{£40{,}000}$$

10% × 2.5 = 25% (as compared to 20% above)

A clear understanding of these three approaches to improving the ROI figure is critical to the effective management of an investment centre. We will now look at each approach in more detail.

Increase sales

In first looking at the ROI formula, one is inclined to think that the sales figure is neutral, since it appears as the denominator in the margin computation and as the numerator in the turnover computation. We *could* cancel out the sales figure, but we do not do so for two reasons. First, this would tend to draw attention away from the fact that the rate of return is a function of *two* variables, margin and turnover. And second, it would tend to conceal the fact that a change in sales can affect both the *margin* and the turnover in an organization. To explain, a change in sales can affect the margin if expenses increase or decrease at a different rate than sales. For example, a company may be able to keep a tight control on its costs as its sales goup, with the result that net operating profit increases more rapidly than sales and increases the margin. Or a company may have fixed expenses that remain constant as sales go up, resulting in an increase in the net operating profit and in the margin. Either (or both) of these factors could have been responsible for the increase in the margin percentage from 10 to 10.91 illustrated in (1) above.

Further, a change in sales can affect the *turnover* if sales either increase or decrease without a proportionate increase or decrease in the operating assets. In the first approach above, for example, sales increased from £100,000 to £110,000, but the operating assets remained unchanged. As a result, the turnover increased from 2 to 2.2 for the period.

Reduce expenses

Often the easiest route to increased profitability and to a stronger ROI figure is simply to cut the 'fat' out of an organization through a concerted effort to control expenses. When margins begin to be squeezed, this is generally the first line of attack by a manager. Discretionary fixed costs usually come under scrutiny first, and various programmes are either curtailed or eliminated in an effort to cut costs. Managers must be careful, however, not to cut out muscle and bone along with the fat. Also, they must remember that frequent cost-cutting binges can destroy morale. Most managers now agree that it is best to stay 'lean and mean' all the time.

Reduce operating assets

Managers have always been sensitive to the need to control sales, operating expenses and operating margins. However, they have not always been equally sensitive to the need to control investment in operating assets. Firms that have adopted the ROI approach to measuring managerial performance report that one of the first reactions of investment centre managers is to trim their investment in operating assets. The reason, of course, is that these managers soon realize that an excessive investment in operating assets reduces turnover and hurts the ROI. As these managers reduce their investment in operating assets, funds are released that can be used elsewhere in the organization.

How can an investment centre manager control the investment in operating assets? One approach is to eliminate unneeded stock. Just-in-time (JIT) purchasing and JIT manufacturing have been extremely helpful in reducing stocks of all types, with the result that ROI figures have improved dramatically in some companies. Another approach is to devise various methods of speeding up the collection of debtors. For example, many firms now employ the lockbox technique by which customers in distant states send their payments directly to post office boxes in their area. The funds are received and deposited by a local bank on behalf of the payee firm. This speeds up the collection process, since the payments are not delayed in the postal system. As a result of the speedup in collection, the Debtors balance is reduced and the asset turnover is increased.

Criticisms of ROI

Although ROI is widely used in evaluating performance, it is not a perfect tool. The method is subject to the following criticisms:

1. Just telling managers to increase ROI may not be enough. Managers may not know how to increase ROI; they may increase ROI in a way that is inconsistent with the company's strategy; or they may take actions that increase ROI in the short run but harm the company in the long run (such as cutting back on research and development). This is why ROI is best used as part of a balanced scorecard. A balanced scorecard can provide concrete guidance to managers, make it more likely that actions taken are consistent with the company's strategy, and reduce the likelihood that short-run performance will be enhanced at the expense of long-term performance.

2 A manager who takes over a business segment typically inherits many committed costs over which the manager has no control. These committed costs may be relevant in assessing the performance of the business segment as an investment but make it difficult fairly to assess the performance of the manager relative to other managers.

3 As discussed in the next section, a manager who is evaluated based on ROI may reject profitable investment opportunities.

Focus on Business Practice

Performance management at Deere & Company

© BanksPhotos

Deere & Company is a world leader in providing advanced products and services for agriculture, forestry, construction, lawn and turf care, landscaping and irrigation. They also provide financial services worldwide and manufacture and market engines used in heavy equipment. In recessionary times, a firm like Deere & Company would be expected to experience declining performance as investment in new equipment declines and construction halts. And Deere & Company has lived up to these expectations with a 45% drop in construction equipment sales and a 15% drop in agricultural equipment sales in 2009. Despite this, Deere & Company still posted profit of $873 million for the year. This strong performance is due in some part to a tight focus on costs and lean manufacturing processes, and may also be in part to the needs of developing economies like China and India where increasing food output means greater agricultural equipment sales. The solid performance may also be attributed in part to a novel 'profit driver' introduced by former CEO Bob Lane. All managers at Deere & Company must 'pay' a 1% per month (12% per annum) charge before reporting any gain. Or in other words, Lane regarded a 12% annual profit as breakeven (see also the later *Focus on Business Practice* on EVA).[5]

Exercise: Assuming the above 12% charge is the minimum return on investment required by Deere & Company, would they proceed with investments which yield a lower return? Why or why not?

Residual income[6] – another measure of performance

Another approach to measuring an investment centre's performance focuses on a concept known as *residual income*. **Residual income** is the net operating profit that an investment centre earns above the minimum required return on its operating assets. **Economic value added (EVA)** is a similar concept that differs in some details from residual income.[7] For example, under the economic value added concept, funds used for research and development are treated as investments rather than as expenses.[8] However, for our purposes, we will not draw any distinction between residual income and economic value added.

When residual income or economic value added is used to measure performance, the purpose is to maximize the total amount of residual income or economic value added, not to maximize overall ROI. For purposes of illustration, consider the following data for an investment centre – the Scottish Division of Alaskan Marine Services Corporation.

Alaskan Marine Services Corporation Scottish Division Basic data for performance evaluation	
Average operating assets	£100,000
Net operating profit	£20,000
Minimum required rate of return	15%

Alaskan Marine Services Corporation has long had a policy of evaluating investment centre managers based on ROI, but it is considering a switch to residual income. The finance director of the company, who is in favour of the change to residual income, has provided the following table that shows how the performance of the division would be evaluated under each of the two methods:

Marine Services Corporation Scottish Division	**Alternative performance measures**	
	ROI	**Residual income**
Average operating assets	£100,000 (a)	£100,000
Net operating profit	£20,000 (b)	£20,000
ROI, (b) ÷ (a)	20%	
Minimum required return (15% × £100,000)		15,000
Residual income		£5,000

The reasoning underlying the residual income calculation is straightforward. The company is able to earn a rate of return of at least 15% on its investments. Since the company has invested £100,000 in the Scottish Division in the form of operating assets, the company should be able to earn at least £15,000 (15% × £100,000) on this investment. Since the Scottish Division's net operating profit is £20,000, the residual income above and beyond the minimum required return is £5,000. If *residual income* is adopted as the performance measure to replace ROI, the manager of the Scottish Division would be evaluated based on the growth from year to year in residual income.

Motivation and residual income

One of the primary reasons why the chief accountant of Marine Services Corporation would like to switch from ROI to residual income has to do with how managers view new investments under the two performance measurement schemes. The residual income approach encourages managers to make investments that are profitable for the entire company but that would be rejected by managers who are evaluated by the ROI formula.

To illustrate this problem, suppose that the manager of the Scottish Division is considering purchasing a computerized diagnostic machine to aid in servicing marine diesel engines. The machine would cost £25,000 and is expected to generate additional operating profit of £4,500 a year. From the standpoint of the company, this would be a good investment since it promises a rate of return of 18% (£4,500/£25,000), which is in excess of the company's minimum required rate of return of 15%.

If the manager of the Scottish Division is evaluated based on residual income, she would be in favour of the investment in the diagnostic machine as shown below:

Marine Services Corporation
Scottish Division
Performance evaluated using residual income

	Present	New project	Overall
Average operating assets	£100,000	£25,000	£125,000
Net operating profit	£20,000	£4,500	£24,500
Minimum required return	15,000	3,750*	18,750
Residual income	£5,000	£750	£5,750

*£25,000 × 15% = £3,750.

Since the project would increase the residual income of the Scottish Division, the manager would want to invest in the new diagnostic machine.

Now suppose that the manager of the Scottish Division is evaluated based on ROI. The effect of the diagnostic machine on the division's ROI is computed below:

Marine Services Corporation
Scottish Division
Performance evaluated using ROI

	Present	New project	Overall
Average operating assets (a)	£100,000	£25,000	£125,000
Net operating profit (b)	£20,000	£4,500†	
ROI, (b)/(a)	20%	18%	19.6%

†£25,000 × 18% = £4,500.

The new project reduces the division's ROI from 20% to 19.6%. This happens because the 18% rate of return on the new diagnostic machine, while above the company's 15% minimum rate of return, is below the division's present ROI of 20%. Therefore, the new diagnostic machine would drag the division's ROI down even though it would be a good investment from the standpoint of the company as a whole. If the manager of the division is evaluated based on ROI, she will be reluctant even to propose such an investment.

Basically, a manager who is evaluated based on ROI will reject any project whose rate of return is below the division's current ROI even if the rate of return on the project is above the minimum required rate of return for the entire company. In contrast, any project whose rate of return is above the minimum required rate of return for the company will result in an increase in residual income. Since it is in the best interests of the company as a whole to accept any project whose rate of return is above the minimum required rate of return, managers who are evaluated based on residual income will tend to make better decisions concerning investment projects than managers who are evaluated based on ROI.

Divisional comparison and residual income

The residual income approach has one major disadvantage. It cannot be used to compare the performance of divisions of different sizes. You would expect larger divisions to have more residual income than smaller divisions, not necessarily because they are better managed but simply because of the bigger numbers involved.

As an example, consider the following residual income computations for Division X and Division Y:

	Division	
	X	Y
Average operating assets (a)	£1,000,000	£250,000
Net operating profit	£120,000	£40,000
Minimum required return: 10% × (a)	100,000	25,000
Residual income	£20,000	£15,000

Observe that Division X has slightly more residual income than Division Y, but that Division X has £1,000,000 in operating assets as compared to only £250,000 in operating assets for Division Y. Thus, Division X's greater residual income is probably more a result of its size than the quality of its management. In fact, it appears that the smaller division is better managed, since it has been able to generate nearly as much residual income with only a quarter as much in operating assets to work with. This problem can be reduced to some degree by focusing on the percentage change in residual income from year to year rather than on the absolute amount of the residual income.

ROI, RI and the balanced scorecard

Simply exhorting managers to increase ROI is not sufficient. Managers who are told to increase ROI will naturally wonder how this is to be accomplished. The Du Pont scheme, which is illustrated in Exhibit 12.2, provides managers with some guidance. Generally speaking, ROI can be increased by increasing sales, decreasing costs, and/or decreasing investments in operating assets. However, it may not be obvious to managers how they are supposed to increase sales, decrease costs and decrease investments in a way that is consistent with the company's strategy. For example, a manager who is given inadequate guidance may cut back on investments that are critical to implementing the company's strategy.

For that reason, when managers are evaluated based on ROI, a *balanced scorecard* approach is advised. And indeed, ROI, or residual income, is typically included as one of the financial performance measures on a company's balanced scorecard. The balanced scorecard provides a way of communicating a company's strategy to managers throughout the organization. The scorecard indicates how the company intends to improve its financial performance. A well-constructed balanced scorecard should answer questions such as: 'What internal business processes should be improved?' and 'Which customer should be targeted and how will they be attracted and retained at a profit?' In short, a well-constructed balanced scorecard can provide managers with a road map that indicates how the company intends to increase its ROI. In the absence of such a road map of the company's strategy, managers may have difficulty understanding what they are supposed to do to increase ROI and they may work at cross-purposes rather than in harmony with the overall strategy of the company. Other critics of EVA are also concerned that a single top-down metric will not be enough to guide the generation of corporate wealth.[9]

Focus on Business Practice

GEC – right metric, wrong strategy?

© gaspr13

GEC was an example of a company that seemed to thrive while it used ROI but then collapsed as it adopted value-based management/residual income. Yet a more sophisticated analysis might suggest that it was the choice of strategy rather than the adoption of a particular metric that led to problems. The company focused on telecoms just at the height of the so-called Dotcom bubble – when many other companies also decided to focus on that industry. As a consequence, there was overcapacity in that industry and a fall in profitability.[10]

Exercise: Perhaps GEC should have paid more attention to actions of its competitors as suggested by the principles of SMA?

The problem of single period metrics: the bonus bank approach

The problem with ROI, RI and EVA is that they are all single period metrics. Thus, although it can be shown that under certain assumptions the capitalized value of residual income equals the net present value of the company,[11] a one-period measure cannot capture the economic value of a division or investment. From this point of view, investment decisions based on these techniques will not be identical to those based on the 'correct' NPV rule.

Advocates of EVA have tried to respond to this problem by basing executive remuneration on a 'bonus bank' system. The aim of this approach is that bonuses are not just based on a single year's performance but may be accumulated over a number of years. The aim is to discourage managers who may be able to boost EVA in the very short term, take a bonus and then leave the company. In fact, one of the distinguishing features of EVA over RI is the great care that is devoted to designing managerial compensation schemes that are aligned with shareholder wealth objectives.[12]

Focus on Business Practice

Value-based management at Allianz

© Dmitriy Shironosov

At *Allianz*, the company explains the principles behind its use of EVA®. They calculate EVA® as normalized profit minus capital charges, where capital charges are defined as a measure of the company's capital multiplied by the cost of capital. New investment in each division is based on their risk-return profile and their strategic position. Using this process, the divisions can only ensure that they receive growth capital if they:

- operate in a profitable market or business;
- transform their market position into sustainable creation of value and a leading market position;
- maintain an orientation and competency that fits within the long-term strategy of the *Allianz Group*; and
- are able to generate distributable earnings in an amount that is at least equal to their cost of capital.

The requirement to meet the cost of capital is just the minimum. Over the medium-term, the objective is to generate a return of 15% or more on the capital employed. Therefore, companies must determine what business activities will increase their value and concentrate their efforts and resources on these activities. Further, new value drivers must be created, for example, through new products, more cost-effective processes and optimized distribution channels. Local management must also prevent value being destroyed along the complete **value chain**. If value diminishes, countermeasures must be implemented immediately. Because EVA® is an important factor in managing the business, senior management compensation is based on this measurement to a significant extent.[13]

Exercise: Consider what issues might be neglected by a company that uses ROI rather than EVA as a key performance metric.

Summary

- Segment reports can provide information for evaluating the profitability and performance of divisions, product lines, sales territories and other segments of a company. Under the contribution approach to segment reporting, only those costs that are traceable are assigned to a segment. Fixed common costs and other non-traceable costs are not allocated to a segment. A cost is considered to be traceable to a segment only if the cost is caused by the segment and eliminating the segment would result in avoiding the cost.
- Costs that are traceable to a segment are further classified as either variable or fixed. The contribution margin is sales less variable costs. The segment margin is the contribution margin less the traceable fixed costs of the segment.
- For purposes of evaluating the performance of managers, there are at least three kinds of business segments – cost centres, profit centres and investment centres.
- Return on investment (ROI) is widely used to evaluate investment centre performance. However, there is a trend towards using residual income or economic value added instead of ROI.
- The residual income and economic value added approaches encourage profitable investments in many situations where the ROI approach would discourage investment.

Key terms

Cost centre A business segment whose manager has control over cost but has no control over revenue or the use of investment funds (p. 281).

Decentralized organization An organization in which decision making is not confined to a few top executives but rather is spread throughout the organization (p. 280).

Economic value added (EVA) A concept similar to residual profit (p. 288).

Investment centre A business segment whose manager has control over cost and over revenue and that also has control over the use of investment funds (p. 281).

Margin Net operating profit divided by sales (p. 284).

Net operating profit Profit before interest and profit taxes have been deducted (p. 283).

Operating assets Cash, debtors, inventory, plan and equipment, and all other assets held for productive use in an organization (p. 283).

Profit centre A business segment whose manager has control over cost and revenue but has no control over the use of investment funds (p. 281).

Residual income The net operating profit that an investment centre earns above the required return on its operating assets (p. 288).

Responsibility centre Any business segment whose manager has control over cost, revenue or the use of investment funds (p. 281).

Return on investment (ROI) Net operating profit divided by average operating assets. It also equals margin multiplied by turnover (p. 283).

Segment Any part or activity of an organization about which the manager seeks cost, revenue or profit data (p. 281).

Turnover The amount of sales generated in an investment centre for each pound invested in operating assets. It is computed by dividing sales by the average operating assets figure (p. 284).

Endnotes

1 Tully (1993).

2 There is a similar problem with top-level managers.

3 Some companies classify business segments that are responsible mainly for generating revenue, such as an insurance sales office, as revenue centres. Other companies would consider this to be just another type of profit centre, since costs of some kind (salaries, rent, utilities) are usually deducted from the revenues in the segment's profit statement.

4 See Johnson and Kaplan (1987).

5 Deere's Harvest, *Time*, May 24, 2010 – also at http://www.time.com/time/magazine/article/0,9171,1971431-1,00.html

6 Since residual income was developed in America, the term 'income' rather than 'profit' is used.

7 The basic idea underlying residual income and economic value added has been around for over 100 years. In recent years, economic value added has been popularized and trademarked by the consulting firm Stern, Stewart & Co.

8 Over 100 different adjustments could be made for deferred taxes, LIFO reserves, provisions for future liabilities, mergers and acquisitions, gains or losses due to changes in accounting rules, operating leases, and other accounts, but most companies make only a few. For further details, see Young and O'Byrne (2001).

9 See, for example, Mouritsen (1998).

10 Seal (2010).

11 O'Hanlon and Peasnell (1998).

12 See, for example, Young and O'Byrne (2001).

13 www.allianz.co.uk

When you have read this chapter, log on to the Online Learning Centre for *Management Accounting for Business Decisions* at **www.mheducation.co.uk/textbooks/sealmabd1**, where you'll find multiple choice questions, practice exams and extra study tools for management accounting.

Assessment

Questions

connect

12–1 What is meant by the term *decentralization*?
12–2 What benefits result from decentralization?
12–3 Distinguish between a cost centre, a profit centre and an investment centre.
12–4 Define a segment of an organization. Give several examples of segments.
12–5 What is meant by the terms *margin* and *turnover*?
12–6 What are the three basic approaches to improving return on investment (ROI)?
12–7 What is meant by residual income?
12–8 In what way can the use of ROI as a performance measure for investment centres lead to bad decisions? How does the residual income approach overcome this problem?

Exercises

E12–1 Time allowed: 15 minutes

Selected operating data for two divisions of Outback Brewing Ltd of Australia are given below:

	Division	
	Queensland	**New South Wales**
Sales	£4,000,000	£7,000,000
Average operating assets	2,000,000	2,000,000
Net operating profit	360,000	420,000
Property, plant, and equipment (net)	950,000	800,000

Required

1 Compute the rate of return for each division using the return on investment (ROI) formula stated in terms of margin and turnover.
2 As far as you can tell from the data, which divisional manager seems to be doing the better job? Why?

E12–2 Time allowed: 15 minutes

Provide the missing data in the following tabulation:

	Division		
	Alpha	**Bravo**	**Charlie**
Sales	£?	£11,500,000	£?
Net operating profit	?	920,000	210,000
Average operating assets	800,000	?	?
Margin	4%	?	7%
Turnover	5	?	?
Return on investment (ROI)	?	20%	14%

E12–3 Time allowed: 20 minutes

Meiji Isetan Corp. of Japan has two regional divisions with headquarters in Osaka and Yokohama. Selected data on the two divisions follow (in millions of yen, denoted by ¥):

	Division	
	Osaka	Yokohama
Sales	¥3,000,000	¥9,000,000
Net operating profit	210,000	720,000
Average operating assets	1,000,000	4,000,000

Required

1. For each division, compute the return on investment (ROI) in terms of margin and turnover. Where necessary, carry computations to two decimal places.
2. Assume that the company evaluates performance by use of residual profit and that the minimum required return for any division is 15%. Compute the residual profit for each division.
3. Is Yokohama's greater amount of residual profit an indication that it is better managed? Explain.

E12–4 Time allowed: 30 minutes

Selected sales and operating data for three divisions of a multinational structural engineering firm are given below:

	Division		
	Asia	Europe	North America
Sales	£12,000,000	£14,000,000	£25,000,000
Average operating assets	3,000,000	7,000,000	5,000,000
Net operating profit	600,000	560,000	800,000
Minimum required rate of return	14%	10%	16%

Required

1. Compute the return on investment (ROI) for each division using the formula stated in terms of margin and turnover.
2. Compute the residual income for each division.
3. Assume that each division is presented with an investment opportunity that would yield a 15% rate of return.
4. (a) If performance is being measured by ROI, which division or divisions will probably accept the opportunity? Reject? Why?
   (b) If performance is being measured by residual income, which division or divisions will probably accept the opportunity? Reject? Why?

Problems

connect

P12–5 Return on investment (ROI); comparison of company performance

Time allowed: 30 minutes

Comparative data on three companies in the same industry are given below:

	Company		
	A	B	C
Sales	£600,000	£500,000	£?
Net operating profit	84,000	70,000	?
Average operating assets	300,000	?	1,000,000
Margin	?	?	3.5%
Turnover	?	?	2
ROI	?	7%	?

Required

1. What advantages can you see in breaking down the ROI computation into two separate elements, margin and turnover?
2. Fill in the missing information above, and comment on the relative performance of the three companies in as much detail as the data permit. Make specific recommendations on steps to be taken to improve the return on investment, where needed. (Adapted from National Association of Accountants, Research Report No. 35, p. 34)

P12–6 Return on investment (ROI) and residual income

Time allowed: 20 minutes

Financial data for Joel de Paris plc for last year follow:

Joel de Paris plc
Balance sheet

	Ending balance	Beginning balance
Assets		
Cash	£120,000	£140,000
Debtors	530,000	450,000
Stock	380,000	320,000
Plant and equipment, net	620,000	680,000
Investment in Buisson SA	280,000	250,000
Land (undeveloped)	170,000	180,000
Total assets	£2,100,000	£2,020,000
Liabilities and shareholders' equity		
Creditors	£310,000	£360,000
Long-term debt	1,500,000	1,500,000
Shareholders' equity	290,000	160,000
Total liabilities and shareholders' equity	£2,100,000	£2,020,000

Joel de Paris plc Profit and loss account		
Sales		£4,050,000
Less operating expenses		3,645,000
Net operating profit		405,000
Less interest and taxes:		
Interest expense	£150,000	
Tax expense	110,000	260,000
Net profit		£145,000

The company paid dividends of £15,000 last year. The 'Investment in Buisson', on the balance sheet represents an investment in the shares of another company.

Required

1. Compute the company's margin, turnover and ROI for last year.
2. The board of directors of Joel de Paris Inc has set a minimum required return of 15%. What was the company's residual income last year?

P12–7 Return on investment (ROI) and residual income

Time allowed: 30 minutes

'I know headquarters wants us to add on that new product line', said Dell Havasi, manager of Billings Company's Office Products Division. 'But I want to see the numbers before I make any move. Our division has led the company for three years, and I don't want any letdown.'

Billings Company is a decentralized organization with five autonomous divisions. The divisions are evaluated on the basis of the return that they are able to generate on invested assets, with year-end bonuses given to the divisional managers who have the highest ROI figures. Operating results for the company's Office Products Division for the most recent year are given below:

Sales	£10,000,000
Less variable expenses	6,000,000
Contribution margin	4,000,000
Less fixed expenses	3,200,000
Net operating profit	£800,000
Divisional operating assets	£4,000,000

The company had an overall ROI of 15% last year (considering all divisions). The Office Products Division has an opportunity to add a new product line that would require an additional investment in operating assets of £1,000,000. The cost and revenue characteristics of the new product line per year would be:

Sales	£2,000,000
Variable expenses	60% of sales
Fixed expenses	£640,000

Required

1 Compute the Office Products Division's ROI for the most recent year; also compute the ROI as it will appear if the new product line is added.

2 If you were in Dell Havasi's position, would you be inclined to accept or reject the new product line? Explain.

3 Why do you suppose headquarters is anxious for the Office Products Division to add the new product line?

4 Suppose that the company views a return of 12% on invested assets as being the minimum that any division should earn and that performance is evaluated by the residual income approach.

5 (a) Compute the Office Products Division's residual income for the most recent year; also compute the residual income as it will appear if the new product line is added.

(b) Under these circumstances, if you were in Dell Havasi's position, would you accept or reject the new product line? Explain.

Chapter 13
Management control and business process improvement

Learning objectives

After studying Chapter 13, you should be able to:

1 Understand a business process improvement view of organization
2 Review some business process improvement innovations and how management accounting can support them
3 Understand the impact of lean thinking and six sigma on process management
4 Consider how outsourcing and shared service centres are changing the nature and location of management accounting information

Concepts in Context

© Ryan KC Wong

A Dell personal computer (PC) is basically made up of a central processing unit (CPU), an operating system and a memory. The CPU comes from Intel or Advanced Micro Devices; the operating system from Microsoft; while the memory has multiple sources. The main direct innovation comes from suppliers with only indirect innovation from the PC manufacturers. The PC has a life cycle of three months to two years with 50% of profits achieved within the first three to six months of the life cycle. The industry typically experiences deep discounting when new processors, operating systems or memory are introduced. Thus older components become obsolete very quickly. In the PC industry, supply chains are no longer linear but networked – 'information moves independently of product at internet speeds'.[1]

In earlier chapters we introduced the concepts of responsibility accounting and organizational segmentation. The focus of the analysis was the department, the functional area and the business segment such as a division. In this chapter, we take a different perspective on the management of the organization. The focus is on the management of *business processes* rather than organizational structures such as departments or divisions. A **business process** is any series of steps that is followed in order to carry out some task in a business. For example, the steps followed to make a large seafood pizza at Pizza Hut are a business process. The steps followed by your bank when you deposit a cheque are a business process.

In many organizations, one process such as order fulfilment can be fragmented across departments and controlled bureaucratically. No one is responsible for the whole process as firms are built up as 'functional silos' with vertical structures that each deal with just a piece of a process. In Exhibit 13.1, there is an illustration of the contrast between a business process perspective and a departmental or divisional perspective. The departmental perspective is sometimes visualized as tending to produce a 'silo mentality' with some flows up and down the silo but little communication between individual 'silos'. The business process perspective challenges managers to find metrics which monitor the processes *across* the organization which serve customers and thus generate value.

Over the last few years, new technology, especially *enterprise resource planning* (ERP) packages have generated improved operations management information which may enable the integration of 'end-to-end' business processes from procurement through to final delivery and payment. Even more recently, the internet has created whole new business models with cost and revenue streams that are only just beginning to be understood. We will be looking at techniques that seek to improve business processes such as *benchmarking* and practices, such as *activity-based management* (ABM) and *business process re-engineering* (BPR), that aim to identify and eliminate non-value adding activities.[2]

Exhibit 13.1 The process perspective contrasted to the departmental 'silo mentality'

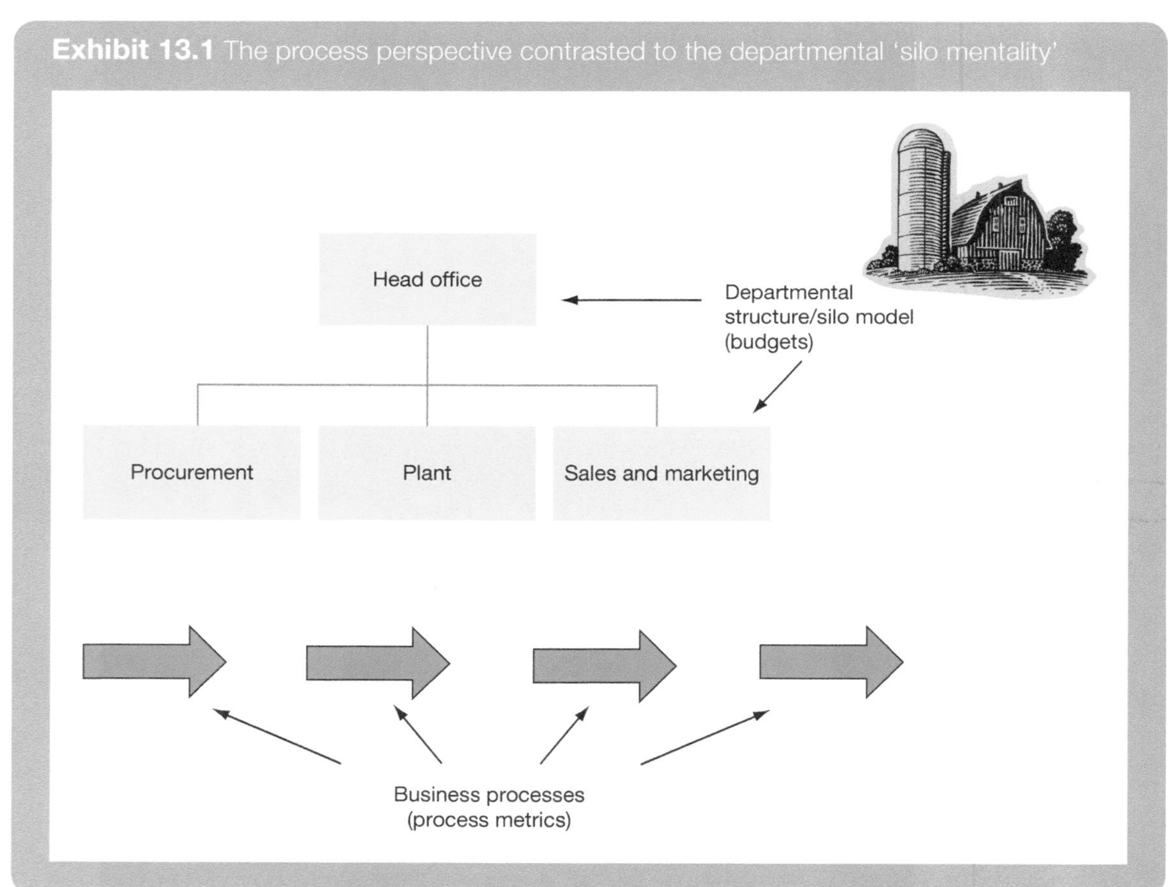

Many of these business process improvement techniques are associated with the philosophy of the *lean enterprise* or *lean production*. **Lean production** techniques were first introduced in manufacturing but are increasingly being applied in service sectors, including not-for-profit organizations in the public sector.[3] Indeed, there are some similarities between inventories in manufacturing and queues of customers in services particularly since both are the result of failing to match supply and demand. Lean principles also involve other focuses of attention such as the reduction of waste and virtual elimination of defects.

Business process improvement

LO 1

The accounting metrics and procedures that have been used in the management of departmental and divisional organizational structures have been around for a very long time and are long-standing topics in management accounting and management texts.[4] In contrast, business process management (BPM) is relatively new, especially in Western businesses. Many of the philosophies and models considered in this chapter have only become widespread in the last 20 years. Some of the approaches have been regarded as management 'fads' and have been criticized as lacking sound theoretical frameworks.[5] The lack of an organizing framework has recently been addressed with a proposal[6] that there are five key themes in BPM – process strategy, process architecture, process ownership, process measurement and process improvement. From a management accounting perspective, process ownership is an important issue because it relates to the problem of establishing responsibility for processes when traditionally management accounting systems, such as budgets, have been organized on a departmental or divisional basis rather than on a business process basis. Indeed some of the critics of budgeting argue that budgeting inevitably reinforces a 'silo mentality'.[7]

Process measurement is clearly at the heart of the management accounting project. Recognizing that financial reporting is directed towards financial stakeholders rather than customers, a process management perspective inevitably embraces measures that take a more balanced view of stakeholders with an explicit concern with customer metrics and with measures that both drive organizational improvement and link strategy with operations. The obvious candidate for this task is the balanced scorecard or some variation of that approach.

Finally, the theme of process improvement is supported by a huge array of potential improvement tools some of which have evolved out of management accounting and some of which have influenced the development of the finance function. These process improvement tools will be looked at in more detail below.

Just-in-time (JIT)

LO 2

When companies use the **just-in-time (JIT)** production and stock control system, they purchase materials and produce units only as needed to meet actual customer demand. In a JIT system, stocks are reduced to the minimum and in some cases to zero. The JIT approach can be used in both merchandising and manufacturing companies. It has the most profound effects, however, on the operations of manufacturing companies, which maintain three classes of stock – *raw materials, work in progress* and *finished goods*.

Traditionally, manufacturing companies have maintained large amounts of all three kinds of stock to act as buffers so that operations can proceed smoothly even if there are unanticipated disruptions. Raw materials stock provide insurance in case suppliers are late with deliveries. Work in progress stock are maintained in case a workstation is unable to operate due to a breakdown or other reason. Finished goods stock are maintained to accommodate unanticipated fluctuations in demand.

While these stock provide buffers against unforeseen events, they have a cost. In addition to the money tied up in the stock, experts argue that the presence of stock encourages inefficient and sloppy work, results in too many defects, and dramatically increases the amount of time required to complete a product. None of this is obvious – if it were, companies would have long ago reduced their stocks.

The JIT concept

Under ideal conditions, a company operating a JIT system would purchase *only* enough materials each day to meet that day's needs. Moreover, the company would have no goods still in progress at the end of the day, and all goods completed during the day would have been shipped immediately to customers. As this sequence suggests, 'just-in-time' means that raw materials are received just in time to go into production, manufactured parts are completed *just in time* to be assembled into products, and products are completed *just in time* to be shipped to customers.

Although few companies have been able to reach this ideal, many companies have been able to reduce stock to only a fraction of their previous levels. The result has been a substantial reduction in ordering and warehousing costs, and much more effective operations.

How does a company avoid a build-up of parts and materials at various workstations and still ensure a smooth flow of goods when JIT is in use? In a JIT environment, the flow of goods is controlled by a *pull approach*. The pull approach can be explained as follows: At the final assembly stage, a signal is sent to the preceding workstation as to the exact amount of parts and materials that will be needed *over the next few hours* to assemble products to fill customer orders, and only that amount of parts and materials is provided. The same signal is sent back through each preceding workstation so that a smooth flow of parts and materials is maintained with no appreciable stock build-up at any point. Thus, all workstations respond to the pull exerted by the final assembly stage, which in turn responds to customer orders. As one worker explained, 'Under a JIT system you don't produce anything, anywhere, for anybody unless they ask for it somewhere downstream. Stocks are an evil that we're taught to avoid.' The pull approach is illustrated in Exhibit 13.2.

The pull approach described above can be contrasted to the *push approach* used in conventional manufacturing systems. In conventional systems, when a workstation completes its work, the partially completed goods are 'pushed' forward to the next workstation regardless of whether that workstation is ready to receive them. The result is an unintentional stockpiling of partially completed goods that may not be completed for days or even weeks. This ties up funds and also results in operating inefficiencies. For one thing, it becomes very difficult to keep track of where everything is when so much is scattered all over the factory floor.

Another characteristic of conventional manufacturing systems is an emphasis on 'keeping everyone busy' as an end in itself. This inevitably leads to excess stock – particularly work in progress stock – for reasons that will be more fully explored in a later section on the theory of constraints. In JIT, the traditional emphasis on keeping everyone busy is abandoned in favour of producing only what customers actually want – even if that means some workers are idle.

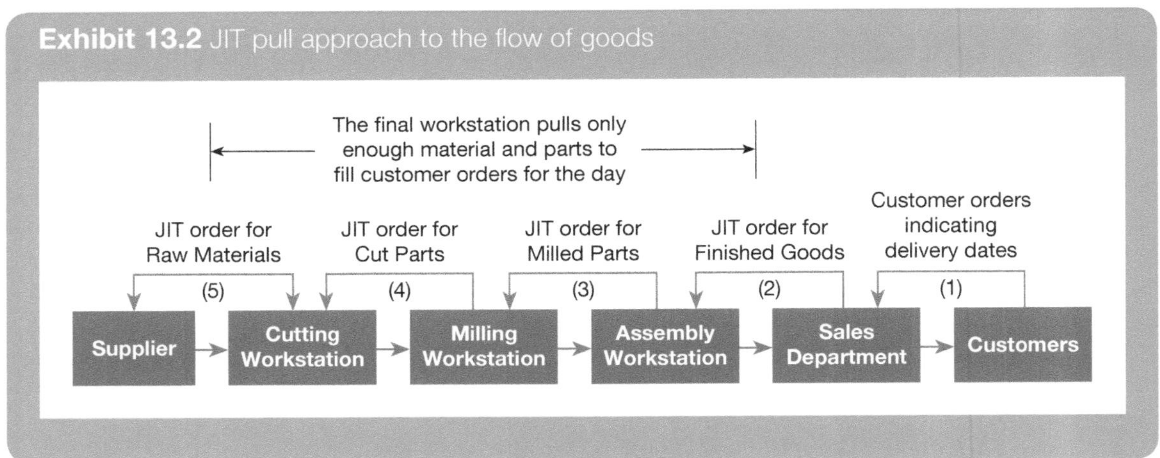

Exhibit 13.2 JIT pull approach to the flow of goods

JIT purchasing

Any organization with stock – retail, wholesale, distribution, service, or manufacturing – can use *JIT purchasing*. Under JIT purchasing:

1. *A company relies on a few ultra reliable suppliers.* Rather than soliciting bids from suppliers each year and going with the low bidder, the dependable suppliers are rewarded with long-term contracts.
2. *Suppliers make frequent deliveries in small lots just before the goods are needed.* Rather than deliver a week's (or a month's) supply of an item at one time, suppliers must be willing to make deliveries as often as several times a day, and in the exact quantities specified by the buyer. Undependable suppliers who do not meet delivery schedules are weeded out. Dependability is essential, since a JIT system is highly vulnerable to any interruption in supply. If a single part is unavailable, the entire assembly operation may have to be shut down. Or, in the case of a merchandising company, if the supplier allows stock to get down to zero, customers may be turned away unsatisfied.
3. *Suppliers must deliver defect-free goods.* Because of the vulnerability of a JIT system to disruptions, defects cannot be tolerated. Indeed, suppliers must become so reliable that incoming goods do not have to be inspected.

Companies that adopt JIT purchasing often realize substantial savings from streamlined operations. Note that a company does not have to eliminate all stock to use the JIT approach. Indeed, retail organizations must maintain some stock or they could not operate. But the amount of time a product spends on a shelf or in a warehouse can be greatly reduced.

Key elements in a JIT system

In addition to JIT purchasing, four key elements are usually required for the successful operation of a JIT manufacturing system. These elements include improving the plant layout, reducing the set-up time needed for production runs, striving for zero defects, and developing a flexible workforce.

Improving plant layout

To implement JIT properly, a company typically must improve the manufacturing *flow lines* in its plant. A flow line is the physical path taken by a product as it moves through the manufacturing process as it is transformed from raw materials to completed goods.

Traditionally, companies have designed their plant floors so that similar machines are grouped together. Such a functional layout results in all drill presses in one place, all lathes in another place, and so forth. This approach to plant layout requires that work in progress be moved from one group of machines to another – frequently across the plant or even to another building. The result is extensive material-handling costs, large work in progress stock, and unnecessary delays.

An improved plant layout can dramatically increase *throughput*, which is the total volume of production through a facility during a period, and it can dramatically reduce throughput time (also known as *cycle time*), which is the time required to make a product.

Reduced set-up time

Set-ups involve activities – such as moving materials, changing machine settings, setting up equipment, and running tests – that must be performed whenever production is switched over from making one type of item to another. For example, it may not be a simple matter to switch over from making 1.25 cm brass screws to making 2 cm brass screws on a manually controlled milling machine. Many preparatory steps must be performed, and these steps can take hours. Because of the time and expense involved in such set-ups, many managers believe set-ups should be avoided and therefore items should be produced in large batches. For example, one batch of 400 units requires only one set-up, whereas four batches of 100 units each would require four set-ups. The problem with big batches is that they create large amounts of stock that must wait for days, weeks, or even months before further processing at the next workstation or before they are sold.

Smaller batches reduce the level of stock, make it easier to respond quickly to the market, reduce cycle times, and generally make it much easier to spot manufacturing problems before they result in a large number of defective units.

Zero defects and JIT

Defective units create big problems in a JIT environment. If a completed order contains a defective unit, the company must ship the order with less than the promised quantity or it must restart the whole production process to make just one unit. At minimum, this creates a delay in shipping the order and may generate a ripple effect that delays other orders. For this and other reasons, defects cannot be tolerated in a JIT system. Companies that are deeply involved in JIT tend to become zealously committed to a goal of *zero defects*. Even though it may be next to impossible to attain the zero defect goal, companies have found that they can come very close.

Flexible workforce

Workers on a JIT line must be multiskilled and flexible. Workers are often expected to operate all of the equipment on a JIT product flow line. Moreover, workers are expected to perform minor repairs and do maintenance work when they would otherwise be idle. In contrast, on a conventional assembly line a worker performs a single task all the time every day and all maintenance work is done by a specialized maintenance crew.

Benefits of a JIT system

The main benefits of JIT are the following:

1. Working capital is bolstered by the recovery of funds that were tied up in stock
2. Areas previously used to store stock are made available for other, more productive uses
3. Throughput time is reduced, resulting in greater potential output and quicker response to customers
4. Defect rates are reduced, resulting in less waste and greater customer satisfaction.

As a result of benefits such as those cited above, more companies are embracing JIT each year. Most companies find, however, that simply reducing stock is not enough. To remain competitive in an ever changing and ever more competitive business environment, companies must strive for continuous improvement.

Focus on Business Practice

Business improvement practices at Toyota

© ricardoazoury

Many of the business improvement practices introduced in this chapter such as JIT and lean production are associated with the Japanese (and now global) car manufacturer, *Toyota*. Some well-publicised recalls of recent models do not mean that that the business process philosophies and practices are faulty. According to some, *Toyota* 'remains the benchmark...' and '... stands out for innovating in ways that are likely to shape our future'.[8] It has been argued that Toyota 'forgot' some of its principles of quality and knowledge management as it strove for rapid global growth. In particular, it forgot its 'three nevers' by building a new product, in a new factory with a new workforce.

Exercise: Review the important roles played by learning-by-doing/tacit knowledge and attitude of mind for the successful implementation of business process improvement policies.

Managing constraints

Profits can be increased by effectively managing the organization's constraints. One aspect of managing constraints is to decide how best to utilize them. If the constraint is a bottleneck in the production process, we have seen that the manager should select the product mix that maximizes the total contribution margin. In addition, the manager should take an active role in managing the constraint itself by increasing the efficiency of the bottleneck operation and by increasing its capacity. Such efforts directly increase the output of finished goods and will often pay off in an almost immediate increase in profits.

It is often possible for a manager to effectively increase the capacity of the bottleneck, which is called **relaxing (or elevating) the constraint**. In the case of Mountain Goat Cycles in Chapter 4, the stitching machine operator could be asked to work overtime. This would result in more available stitching time and hence more finished goods that can be sold. The benefits from relaxing the constraint in such a manner are often enormous and can be easily quantified. The manager should first ask, 'What would I do with additional capacity at the bottleneck if it were available?'

Managers should focus much of their attention on managing bottlenecks. As we have discussed, managers should emphasize products that most profitably utilize the constrained resource. They should also make sure that products are processed smoothly through the bottlenecks, with minimal lost time due to breakdowns and set-ups. And they should try to find ways to increase the capacity at the bottlenecks.

The capacity of a bottleneck can be effectively increased in a number of ways, including:

- *Working* overtime on the bottleneck
- Subcontracting some of the processing that would be done at the bottleneck
- *Investing in additional machines* at the bottleneck
- *Shifting* workers from processes that are not bottlenecks to the process that is a bottleneck
- *Focusing business process improvement efforts* such as TQM and BPR on the bottleneck
- Reducing *defective units*. Each defective unit that is processed through the bottleneck and subsequently scrapped takes the place of a good unit that could be sold.

The last three methods of increasing the capacity of the bottleneck are particularly attractive, since they are essentially free and may even yield additional cost savings. These somewhat ad hoc examples have been generalized in the *theory of constraints (TOC)*.

The theory of constraints

A constraint is anything that prevents you from getting more of what you want. Every individual and every organization faces at least one constraint, so it is not difficult to find examples of constraints. You may not have enough time to study thoroughly for every subject and to go out with your friends at the weekend, so time is your constraint. Since a constraint prevents you from getting more of what you want, the **theory of constraints (TOC)** maintains that effectively managing the constraint is a key to success.

TOC and continuous improvement

In TOC, an analogy is often drawn between a business process and a chain. If you want to increase the strength of a chain, what is the most effective way to do this? Should you concentrate your efforts on strengthening the strongest link, the largest link, all the links, or the weakest link? Clearly, focusing effort on the weakest link will bring the biggest benefit.

Continuing with this analogy, the procedure to follow in strengthening the chain is straightforward. First, identify the weakest link, which is the constraint. Second, do not place a greater strain on the system than the weakest link can handle. Third, concentrate improvement efforts on strengthening the weakest link. Fourth, if the improvement efforts are successful, eventually the weakest link will improve to the point where it is no longer the weakest link. At this point, the new weakest link (i.e. the new constraint) must be identified, and improvement efforts must be shifted over to that link. This simple sequential process provides a powerful strategy for continuous improvement. The TOC approach is a perfect complement to TQM and process re-engineering – it focuses improvement efforts where they are likely to be most effective.

Exhibit 13.3 Processing surgery patients at an NHS facility (simplified)

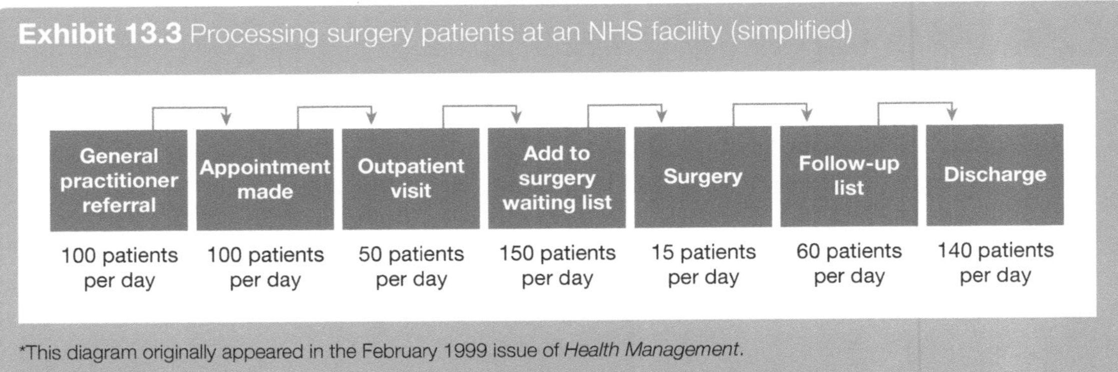

*This diagram originally appeared in the February 1999 issue of *Health Management*.

An example of TOC

A simple example will be used to illustrate the role of a constraint. In Exhibit 13.3, bottlenecks in the National Health Service contribute to the waiting lists that characterize the health care system. The key constraint or bottleneck is in surgery where the maximum number of patients that can be processed is 15 patients a day. Other parts of the systems such as general practitioners (100 patients per day) and outpatients (50 patients per day) could process higher numbers. The key to increasing the overall capacity of the system is to improve the capacity in surgery – improvements in other areas may simply lead to longer waiting lists. If efforts are focused on the first bottleneck in surgery, subsequent improvements may lead to a situation when another part of the system takes over as the weakest link and hence a focus for management attention.

The impact of TOC on management accounting

Conventional management accounting has two possible conflicts with TOC. If non-bottleneck machines have a production cut then they begin to look inefficient. Labour efficiency variances may also worsen. Furthermore, a reduction in work in progress may lead to a fall in reported profit. The TOC solution is to change the usual measures by focusing on throughput, stock and operational expense. The theory has its own special definitions:

$$\text{Throughput} = \text{Sales} - \text{Material and purchased services}$$

$$\text{Inventory} = \text{Stock} + \text{Machines and buildings}$$

$$\text{Operating expense} = \text{Non-material conversion costs especially labour costs}$$

$$\text{Net profit} = \text{Throughput} - \text{Operational expense}$$

$$\text{ROI} = \frac{\text{Throughput} - \text{Operational expense}}{\text{Inventory}}$$

Note that direct labour is treated as a fixed cost. Traditional accounting such as standard costing focuses on controlling operational expenses ('cost world'), JIT focuses on cutting stock ('JIT world'). In contrast, 'Throughput world' focuses on throughput even if it means conflicting with JIT by holding buffer stocks or with cost world by tolerating slack labour.

Throughput accounting[9]

One response to the theory of constraints is a technique that determines the optimum use of bottleneck activity called **throughput accounting (TA)**. The main idea is to rank products by calculating the throughput accounting ratio:

$$\text{TA ratio} = \frac{\text{Return per factory hour}}{\text{Cost per factory hour}}$$

where

$$\text{Return per factory hour} = \frac{\text{Sales price} - \text{Material cost}}{\text{Time on key resource}}$$

And

$$\text{Cost per factory hour} = \frac{\text{Total factory cost}}{\text{Total time available on key resource}}$$

Although it incorporates some of the terminology of the theory of constraints, it could be argued that throughput accounting does not reflect the true spirit of the TOC philosophy with its emphasis on the active management of bottlenecks.[10]

Total quality management (TQM)

One approach to process improvement is known as **total quality management (TQM)**. There are two major characteristics of TQM: (1) a focus on serving customers and (2) systematic problem solving using teams made up of frontline workers. A variety of specific tools are available to aid teams in their problem solving. One of these tools, **benchmarking**, involves studying organizations that are among the best in the world at performing a particular task.

The plan-do-check-act cycle

Perhaps the most important and pervasive TQM problem-solving tool is the *plan-do-check-act (PDCA)* cycle, which is also referred to as the Deming Wheel.[11] The **plan-do-check-act cycle** is a systematic, fact-based approach to continuous improvement. The basic elements of the PDCA cycle are illustrated in Exhibit 13.4. The PDCA cycle applies the scientific method to problem solving. In the Plan phase, the problem-solving team analyses data to identify possible causes for the problem and then proposes a solution. In the Do phase, an experiment is conducted. In the Check phase, the results of the experiment are analysed. And in the Act phase, if the results of the experiment are favourable, the plan is implemented. If the results of the experiment are not favourable, the team goes back to the original data and starts all over again.

An important element of TQM is its focus on the customer. The accounting and consulting firm KPMG Peat Marwick periodically surveys its customers' satisfaction with its services. The firm's managing director points out that it costs four times as much to gain a new customer as to keep an old customer, and the most satisfied customers are generally the most profitable customers for the firm. 'For each complaint that you hear, there are fifty you don't. If you don't monitor clients' satisfaction, you may find out about their dissatisfaction as they walk out the door.'[12]

In sum, TQM provides tools and techniques for continuous improvement based on facts and analysis; and if properly implemented, it avoids counterproductive organizational infighting.

Some criticisms of TQM

There have been a number of criticisms of TQM. They may not always be justified but managers should be aware of possible pitfalls. TQM has been accused of draining innovation from organizations by standardizing

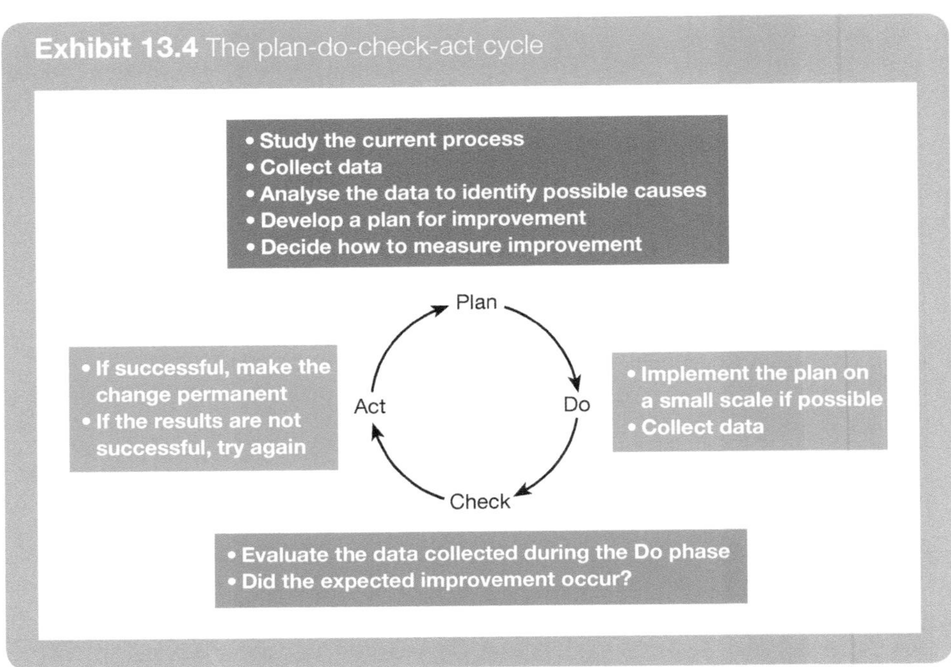
• Study the current process
• Collect data
• Analyse the data to identify possible causes
• Develop a plan for improvement
• Decide how to measure improvement
Plan
Do
Check
Act
• Implement the plan on a small scale if possible
• Collect data
• Evaluate the data collected during the Do phase
• Did the expected improvement occur?
• If successful, make the change permanent
• If the results are not successful, try again

Exhibit 13.4 The plan-do-check-act cycle

internal processes. It is also accused of making organizations more efficient at what they are doing irrespective of whether they should be doing it. The spectre is that TQM results in a finely honed organization that is a world class producer of wagon wheels or manual typewriters. Like other management change initiatives, TQM suffers from the 'Flavour of the month' syndrome. Typically, organizational members have been bombarded with so many fads that they may merely go through the motions of implementation of TQM hoping that senior managers will soon embrace a new 'three letter acronym'.

Benchmarking

Much of the data gathered through the introduction of quality management may be used as a basis for comparison with other organizations. In particular, it may be useful to identify organizations that are the best at performing specific activities or producing particular products in order to learn how they achieve their relatively high performance. This process is known as benchmarking. With *quality management*, the focus may be on *non-financial* measures as much as financial measures such as costs. Later in the chapter, we can see an example of *cost* benchmarking based on ABC data.

In order to achieve the best result from benchmarking a number of principles should be adhered to. Benchmarking may be seen as an exercise that proceeds according to a sequence of steps.

- *Step 1: Internal and competitive analysis.* At this preliminary stage the organization chooses the areas for analysis and undertakes basic comparisons between internal data and external data. External data may be found in marketing reports, consumer surveys, government statistics. It may not be confined to the firm's industry. For example, the particular part of the organization chosen for benchmarking may involve an activity where the best performers are in a completely different industry. For example, a theatre may study the ticketing procedures used in the airline industry. Although there may be a danger of not comparing like with like such as when a tyre retailer sees a formula one team as an appropriate benchmark for tyre-changing, there may still be lessons that can be learnt even from such apparently 'unfair' comparisons.

- *Step 2: Building a benchmarking team.* Changes in practice may involve both radical reorganization and long-term commitment. Thus benchmarking teams must ideally have the backing of senior management, the support of the workforce and a long-term orientation. Typically, teams will be from a number of functional areas representing different professional specialisms and change must be supported by dedicated training programmes.
- *Step 3: Choosing benchmarking partners and sharing information.* This step strikes a balance between the need to *'stretch' performance* and not comparing like with like. Furthermore, if partners are really going to learn from each other then detailed information about operational performance has to be shared, implying an atmosphere of co-operation and trust rather than competition. If trust is absent then information may be shared on the basis of quid pro quo or as part of an industry-wide initiative. Alternatively, information may be gathered on a unilateral basis through activities such as reverse engineering. As we saw in Chapter 11, the collection of data on competitors is an important part of strategic management accounting and may be based wholly on competitive rather than co-operative principles.
- *Step 4: Taking action to meet the benchmark.* It is at this stage that the internal implementation of the external analysis may run into difficulties, especially if best practice threatens job security and/or managerial empires. The issues of organizational change take us beyond the material normally found in management accounting books. However, management accountants and others such as politicians and senior managers should be aware of the technical limitations of benchmarking exercises. Organizational resistance is not always based on vested interests.

Some problems with benchmarking

Using external comparators can lead to criticism on the basis that measures are 'their numbers not ours'. It is therefore important that a consistent set of measures is used with a close match between internal and external indicators. Benchmarking has been described as being a mixed metaphor.[13] On the one hand, we have the language of collaboration with an emphasis on organizational learning. On the other hand, we have descriptions of benchmarking that often convey notions of competition, of being a one-sided attempt by the initiator of the benchmarking exercise to close a perceived performance gap. Even when benchmarking is a public policy initiative, governments often send out a mixed message that both inculcates a 'league table mentality' and tries to nurture a non-blame, learning model.

Six sigma

LO 3

Another approach to business improvement is known as **six sigma**. It is a strategic, company-wide, approach that focuses on quality and reliability. The key aims are to:

- Improve quality as perceived by the customer
- Reduce errors (defects) in the process
- Ensure processes are capable of producing repeatable outputs
- Reduce the variation in these outputs
- Identify the root causes of quality issues and errors
- Prioritize solution options to make the biggest gain
- Monitor and control processes within defined quality criteria.

The term 'six sigma' comes from statistics as the approach focuses on *variation reduction* through statistical analysis. The statistical basis of the approach may be illustrated in Exhibit 13.5, in which it is argued that business improvement can come from focusing on *variation from the mean* rather than average times.

Exhibit 13.5 A six sigma approach to problem solving[14]

The problem: a focus on 'average' isn't sufficient

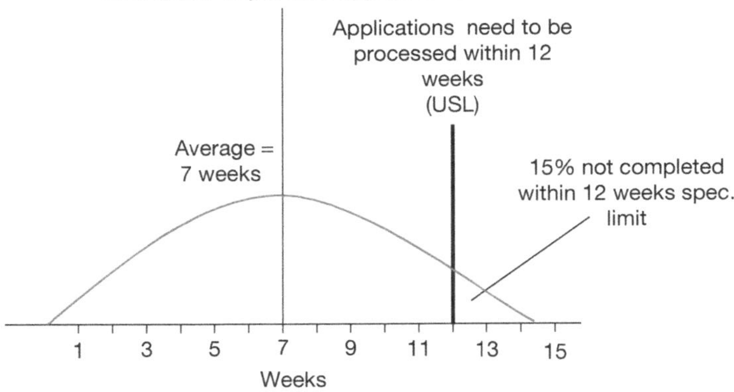

- Processing time **varies significantly** – some can take 1 or 2 weeks, some can take up to 15 weeks
- **Lack of predictability** for business and customer
- How would you ensure customer requirement are satisfied more often?

Six sigma solution: variation provides a more complete understanding of performance – process capability

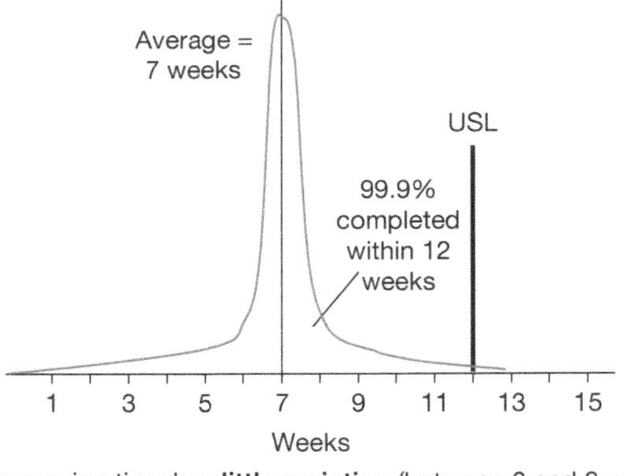

Reduced variation
Increased performance

- Processing time has **little variation** (between 6 and 8 weeks)
- Much **higher probability** of meeting **customer specification** – nearly all applications are completed within 12 weeks
- The business could spread its resource, by targeting a longer processing time such as 11 weeks and the majority of applications would still be processed on time.

Source: © Joel Cohen. Reproduced with permission.

Business process re-engineering (BPR) and lean production

Business process re-engineering is a more radical approach to improvement than either TQM, benchmarking or six sigma. Instead of tweaking the existing system in a series of incremental improvements, a business process is diagrammed in detail, questioned, and then completely redesigned in order to eliminate unnecessary steps, to reduce opportunities for errors, and to reduce costs. While process re-engineering is similar in some respects to TQM, its proponents view it as a more sweeping approach to change. One difference is that while TQM emphasizes a team approach involving people who work directly in the processes, process re-engineering is more likely to be imposed from above and more likely to use outside consultants.

Lean production

BPR is closely associated with the concept of the lean enterprise. The lean enterprise may be created from scratch or through the transformation of existing firms. Process re-engineering focuses on *simplification* and *elimination of wasted effort*. A central idea of process re-engineering is that *all activities that do not add value to a product or service should be eliminated.*[15] Activities that do not add value to a product or service that customers are willing to pay for are known as **non-value-added activities**. For example, moving large batches of work in progress from one workstation to another is a non-value-added activity that can be eliminated by redesigning the factory layout. The starting point for re-engineering is not 'How do we do something faster or cheaper or better?' but rather 'Why do we do something at all? Is it to meet demands of customers or internal organization?' In short, re-engineering is not piecemeal – it is 'all-or-nothing'.

Many of the business process improvement tools can be summarized by a very long-standing and robust philosophy known as lean production.[16] Lean enterprises try to organize work around *business processes* rather than on a departmental basis with a traditional emphasis on specialization and a division of labour.

There are five core principles to represent lean production:

1. Specify the *value desired by the customer*
2. Identify the value stream for each product providing that value and challenge all of the *wasted* steps
3. Make the product *flow continuously*
4. Introduce *pull* between all steps where continuous flow is impossible
5. *Manage towards perfection* so that the number of steps and the amount of time and information needed to serve the customer continually falls.

An emphasis on eliminating 'waste'

As can be seen, many of the principles of lean production may also be found in other approaches to process improvement such as JIT. However, lean production places a great deal of emphasis on the elimination of *waste*, where waste is defined as anything that does not add value to the final product or service, in the eyes of the customer; an activity the customer would not want to pay for if they knew it was happening. There are seven possible areas of manufacturing waste: *transport, inventory, motion, waiting, overproduction, over-processing and defects*. In services, the seven possible areas of waste are: *delay, duplication, unnecessary movement, unclear communication, incorrect inventory, opportunity lost and errors*.

Lean accounting

In order to support a lean approach to creating value, accounting measures have to be used selectively and supplemented with non-financial performance measures. The key emphasis should be on measuring flow through the whole process rather than on the more traditional approach of local machine or labour utilization. Such measures include production by the hour, cycle times and so on. The emphasis is on measuring and minimizing stock, work in progress and other forms of working capital such as accounts receivables.

Managers need to understand the capacity of the process and constantly seek ways that will increase throughput. Financial information should be timely and relevant. In practice, that means providing management information in real time or at least so that operations be supported as they take place rather than 'after the event'. The emphasis will probably be on contribution costing rather than the more complicated and time consuming standard costing. Revenues will be based on actual deliveries to customers rather than production for stock. In short, lean thinking synthesizes the key insights of JIT, TQM and TOC. Finally, the philosophy for the accounting system should be on continuous improvement with information that is both forward and outward looking.

Focus on Business Practice

Lean thinking in public services

© Catherine Yeulet

Although it began in manufacturing, lean thinking has spread to the service sector. In recent years it has also been introduced in the public services. The same principles of focusing on meeting customer needs, streamlining flows along process lines and reducing waste are very relevant. Lean offers potential not only for cost savings but for improving the service offered to citizens and even improving staff morale. All these issues are becoming increasingly important as governments seek to reduce public spending in the post-credit crunch era.[17]

Exercise: Consider an organization that you are familiar with. How does that organization generate value for its customers? Are there some areas of the organization that do not seem to be part of that value adding process?

LO 4

Organizational change and the finance function

We have already seen how business process improvement thinking has changed operations. Yet these concepts are also being applied to areas of the business usually seen as support functions, such as human resources, IT and finance. Applying concepts such as lean and six sigma, the finance function is being scrutinized as never before with a view to relocating what are seen as routine transactions in specialized **shared service centres**. Whether retained in-house or outsourced to third party providers, this organizational change has implications for the production, dissemination and application of management accounting information in ways that are only just beginning to be understood. For example, Exhibit 13.6 shows how different areas of the organization will draw on different aspects of the various management accounting practices introduced throughout this book.

Exhibit 13.6 The diverse roles of management accounting within large corporations

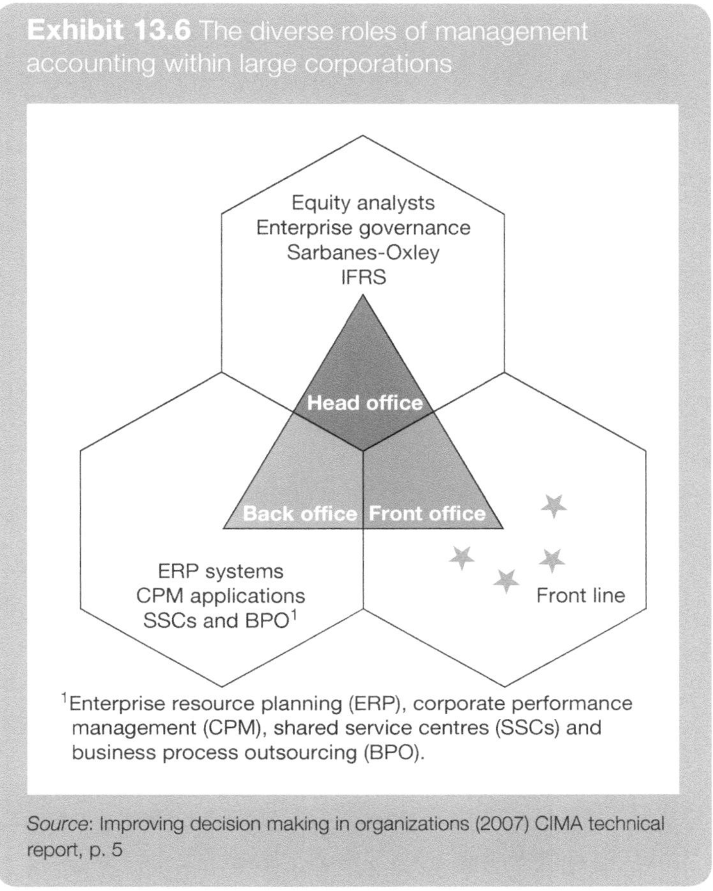

Source: Improving decision making in organizations (2007) CIMA technical report, p. 5

Focus on Business Practice

The logic of the shared service centre

© Dmitry Ersler

The Shared Services Centre (SSC) was originally conceived to reduce headcount and increase efficiency through using better IT, business process re-engineering and cutting out duplication between divisions. But shared services have a commercial logic that goes beyond cost cutting. If it was just about cost cutting then a third party outsourcing specialist could also do those tasks. Shared service centres define and preserve what a company does for all its stakeholders. The SSC provides accountability, visibility and transparency – all aspects that can lead to improved enterprise governance. By placing the common support services outside of the operating business units, the SSC creates a new visibility of those processes leaving the business units to focus on their core competencies.

Exercise: Discuss the viewpoint that shared services are concerned with what we have earlier defined as overhead costs?

Summary

- The business process perspective challenges managers to find metrics which monitor the processes *across* the organization which serve customers and thus generate value.
- There are a number of business process improvement tools such as JIT, TOC, TQM, benchmarking, six Sigma and lean production.
- The philosophies of lean production can be applied in service and public sectors as well as in manufacturing.
- New organizational forms such as shared service centres and outsourcing are having an increasing impact on the delivery of business services. These restructurings raise fundamental questions about the status of services such as the finance function.

Key terms

Benchmarking A comparison with organizations that are the best at performing specific activities or producing particular products in order to learn how they achieve their relatively high performance (p. 309).

Business process A series of steps that is followed in order to carry out some task in a business (p. 302).

Business process re-engineering involves mapping and then redesigning business processes in order to eliminate unnecessary steps, reduce opportunities for errors, and lower costs. (p. 313).

Just-in-time (JIT) A production system in which materials are purchased and produced only as needed to meet actual customer demand so that stocks are reduced to the minimum and in some cases to zero (p. 303).

Lean production The identification of a value stream and challenging all forms of waste or non-value adding activity (p. 303).

Non-value-added activities are activities in an organization that do not add value to that organization's products or services. (p. 313).

Plan-do-check-act cycle is a systematic, fact-based approach to continuous improvement (p. 309).

Relaxing (or elevating) the constraint Increasing the capacity of a bottleneck (p. 307).

Shared service centres Organizations which specialize in the delivery of the routine transactions of support services that are required by the operating units of large organizations (p. 314).

Six sigma An approach that focuses on the variation from the mean rather than average times (p. 311).

Theory of constraints (TOC) A management approach that emphasizes the importance of managing constraints (p. 307).

Throughput accounting(TA) Ranking products by calculating the throughput accounting ratio (p. 309).

Total quality management(TQM) An approach to quality that focuses on serving customers and using teams made up of frontline workers to aim for zero defects (p. 309).

Endnotes

1. Kuglin and Rosenbaum (2001).
2. See Hansen and Mouritsen (2007) for a discussion of the relationship between operations management and management accounting.
3. Radnor, Walley, Stephens, and Bucci (2006).
4. Seal (2010).
5. See e.g. the criticisms of Ittner and Larcker (2001).
6. Smart, Maddern and Maull (2009)
7. Hope and Fraser, 1997.
8. Fischer (2010).
9. Galloway and Waldron (1988).
10. See Dugdale and Jones (1998); Jones and Dugdale (1998).
11. Dr W. Edwards Deming, a pioneer in TQM, introduced many of the elements of TQM to Japanese industry after the Second World War. TQM was further refined and developed at Japanese companies such as Toyota.
12. Madonna (1992).
13. Cox, Mann, and Sampson (1997).
14. Thanks to Joel Cohen for this example.
15. Hammer and Champy (1995).
16. See Womack, Jones, and Roos (1990).
17. In the hot seat: Reducing costs in public sector organizations in an age of austerity, Deloitte Research paper, http://www.deloitte.com/view/en_GB/uk/industries/government-public-sector/, 12 April, 2010.

connect

When you have read this chapter, log on to the Online Learning Centre for *Management Accounting for Business Decisions* at **www.mheducation.co.uk/textbooks/sealmabd1**, where you'll find multiple choice questions, practice exams and extra study tools for management accounting.

Assessment

Questions

connect™

13–1 What are six ways of relaxing a constraint?

13–2 In what way does throughput accounting misrepresent the theory of constraints?

Exercises

connect™

E13–1 Time allowed: 15 minutes

Listed below are a number of terms that relate to just-in-time, total quality management, process re-engineering, and theory of constraints:

Benchmarking	Non-value-added activities
Business process	Plan-do-check-act cycle
Constraint	Process re-engineering
Frequent	Pull
Just-in-time	Set-up
Non-constraint	Total quality management

Choose the term or terms above that most appropriately complete the following statements:

1 To successfully operate a JIT system, a company must learn to rely on a few suppliers who are willing to make ______ deliveries.

2 ______ is an incremental approach to improvement, whereas ______ tends to be a much more radical approach that involves completely redesigning business processes.

3 A production system in which units are produced and materials are purchased only as needed to meet actual customer demand is called ______.

4 In just-in-time, the flow of goods is controlled by what is described as a ______ approach to manufacturing.

5 Increasing the rate of a ______ as the result of an improvement effort is unlikely to have much effect on profits.

6 ______ involves studying the business processes of companies that are considered among the best in the world at performing a particular task.

7 The activities involved in getting equipment ready to produce a different product are called a ______.

8 The theory of constraints suggests that improvement efforts should be focused on the company's ______.

9 The ______ is a systematic, fact-based approach to continuous improvement that resembles the scientific method.

10 In process re-engineering, two objectives are to simplify and to eliminate ______.

11 A ______ is any series of steps that are followed in order to carry out some task in a business.

Problems

connect™

P13–2 Pricing/ABC/throughput accounting

Time allowed: 45 minutes

LM Hospital is a private hospital whose management is considering the adoption of an activity-based costing (ABC) system for the year 2010/11. The main reason for its introduction would be to provide more accurate information for pricing purposes. With the adoption of new medical technology, the amount of time that some patients stay in hospital has decreased considerably, and the management feels that the current pricing strategy may no longer reflect the different costs incurred.

Prices are currently calculated by determining the direct costs for the particular type of operation and adding a markup of 135%. With the proposed ABC system, the management expects to use a markup for pricing purposes of 15% on cost. This percentage will be based on all costs except facility sustaining costs. It has been decided that the hospital support activities should be grouped into three categories – admissions and record keeping, caring for patients, and facility sustaining.

The hospital has four operating theatres that are used for 9 hours a day for 300 days a year. It is expected that 7,200 operations will be performed during the coming year. The hospital has 15 consultant surgeons engaged in operating theatre work and consultancy. It is estimated that each consultant surgeon will work at the hospital for 2,000 hours in 2010/11.

The expected costs for 2010/11 are:

	£
Nursing services and administration	9,936,000
Linen and laundry	920,000
Kitchen and food costs (3 meals a day)	2,256,000
Consultant surgeons' fees	5,250,000
Insurance of buildings and general equipment	60,000
Depreciation of buildings and general equipment	520,000
Operating theatre	4,050,000
Pre-operation costs	1,260,000
Medical supplies – used in the hospital wards	1,100,000
Pathology laboratory (where blood tests, etc. are carried out)	920,000
Updating patient records	590,000
Patient/bed scheduling	100,000
Invoicing and collections	160,000
Housekeeping activities, including ward maintenance, window cleaning, etc.	760,000

Other information for 2010/11:

Nursing hours	480,000
Number of pathology laboratory tests	8,000
Patient days	44,000
Number of patients	9,600

Information relating to specific operations for 2010/11:

	ENT (ear, nose and throat)	Cataract
Time of stay in hospital	4 days	1 day
Operation time	2 hours	0.5 hour
Consultant surgeon's time (which includes time in the operating theatre)	3 hours	0.85 hour

Required

1 Before making the final decision on the costing/pricing system, management has selected two types of operation for review: an ear, nose and throat (ENT) operation and a cataract operation.
   (a) Calculate the prices that would be charged under each method for the two types of operation. (Your answer should include an explanation and calculations of the cost drivers you have used.) *(10 marks)*
   (b) Comment on the results of your calculations and the implications for the proposed pricing policy. *(5 marks)*
2 Critically assess the method you have used to calculate the ABC prices by selecting two items/categories above which you feel should have been dealt with in a different way. *(5 marks)*
3 Explain whether the concept of throughput accounting could be used in a hospital. *(5 marks)*

(Total = 25 marks)

Adapted from CIMA Management Accounting – Decision Making, May 2001

P13–3 Cost management/JIT

Time allowed: 45 minutes

The WYE hotel group operates a chain of 50 hotels. The size of each hotel varies, as do the services that each hotel provides. However, all of the hotels operated by the group provide a restaurant, swimming pool, lounge bar, guest laundry service and accommodation.

Some of the hotels also provide guest entertainment, travel bureaux and shopping facilities. The Managing Director of the group is concerned about the high level of running costs being incurred by the hotels.

Required

1 Explain how cost reduction, value analysis and zero-based budgeting techniques could be used by the WYE hotel group to improve the profitability of its hotels. *(15 marks)*
2 M plc is a food manufacturer. It operates a just-in-time (JIT) system with computer-controlled, automated processing and packaging equipment. The focus of M plc's weekly management reports is on the variance analysis that is generated from a standard absorption costing system that uses labour hours as the basis of overhead absorption.

3 Explain why standard costing systems based upon absorption costing principles may be inappropriate in the modern manufacturing environment of companies such as M plc. *(10 marks)*

(Total = 25 marks)

CIMA Management Accounting – Performance Management, May 2001

P13–4 Group exercise

Time allowed: 15 minutes per person

Use your experience as an individual, as a customer and/or as an employee to identify examples of waste and bottlenecks in organizations that you deal with. Suggest ways that might make the operation less wasteful and thus more 'lean'. Discuss possible reasons for the persistence of wasteful activities.

Bibliography

Aldrick, P. 2008. 'Management failure' added to problems, admits chairman, *Daily Telegraph*, 3 June.

Arthur, A. 2000. How to build your own project budget, *Management Accounting (UK)*, April, pp. 20–22.

Bain, P. and Taylor, P. 2000. Entrapped by the 'electronic panopticon'? Worker resistance in the call centre, *New Technology, Work and Employment*, 15(1), pp. 21–28.

Bates, M., Rizvi, S., Tewari, P. and Vardan, D. 2001. How fast is too fast? *McKinsey Quarterly*, 3, pp. 52–61.

Böer, G. 1994. Five modern management accounting myths, *Management Accounting (US)*, January, pp. 22–27.

Brignall, T.J., Fitzgerald, L., Johnston, R. and Silvestro, R., 1991. Product costing in service organisation. *Management Accounting Research,* 2, pp. 249–261.

Burns, J. and Scapens, R. 2000. Conceptualising management accounting change: an institutional framework, *Management Accounting Research*, 11, pp. 3–25.

Carruth. P., McClendon, T. and Ballard, M. 1983. What supervisors don't like about budget evaluations, *Management Accounting (US)*, 64(8), February, p. 42.

CIMA, 2001a. *Activity-based Management – An Overview*. CIMA technical briefing, April, p. 2.

Cooper, R. and Kaplan, R.S. 1988. How cost accounting distorts product costs, *Management Accounting (US)*, April, pp. 20–27.

Cox, W.J., Mann, L. and Sampson, D. 1997. Benchmarking as a mixed metaphor: disentangling assumptions of competition and collaboration, *Journal of Management Studies*, 43, pp. 285–314.

Cugini, A., Caru, A. and Zerbini, F. 2007. The cost of customer satisfaction: a framework for strategic cost management in service industries, *European Accounting Review*, 16, pp. 499–530.

Dugdale, D. and Jones, T.C. 1998. Throughput accounting: transformation practices? *British Accounting Review*, 30(3), pp. 203–20.

Erdogmus, H., Favaro, J. and Strigel, W. 2004. Return on investment, *IEEE Software*, May/June, pp. 18–21.

Fischer, B. 2010 That was Kaizen; this is now, *Financial Management*, April, p.12.

Fleischmann, R.K. and Tyson, T. 1996. A guide to the historical controversies and organizational contexts of standard costs, *Journal of Accounting Education*, 14 (1), pp. 37–56.

Galloway, D. and Waldron, D. 1988. Throughput accounting – 1: the need for a new language for manufacturing, *Management Accounting*, November, pp. 34–35.

Getlin, J. 2008. Author's creation, Disney's jackpot, *Los Angeles Times*, 13 February. http://articles. Latimes.com/2008/Feb/13/entertainment/ et-cheetan 13 (accessed 10 March 2010.)

Greco, S. 1996. Are we making money yet?, *Inc*, July, pp. 52–61.

Hammer, M. and Champy, J. 1995. *Reengineering the Corporation: A Manifesto for Business Revolution*, London: Nicolas Brealey.

Hansen, A. and Mouritsen, J. 2007. Management accounting and changing operations management, in T. Hopper, D. Northcott and R. Scapens (eds.), *Issues in Management Accounting* (3rd edn). Harlow: Pearson Education, pp. 3–25.

Hansen, S., Otley, D. and Van der Stede, W. 2003. Practice developments in budgeting: an overview and research perspective, *Journal of Management Accounting Research*, 15, pp. 95–116.

Harris, P.J. 1999 *Profit Planning* (Hospitality Managers Pocket Book Series, 2nd edn) Oxford: Butterworth-Heinemann.

Harris, P.J. 1999, *Profit Planning* (Hospitality Managers Pocket Book Series, 2nd edn.), Oxford: Butterworth-Heinemann.

Hayward, C. 2002. Out of site, *Financial Management*, February, pp. 26–27.

Hood, C. 1995. The 'new public management' in the 1980s: variations on a theme, *Accounting, Organizations and Society*, 20(2/3), pp. 93–109.

Hope, J. and Fraser, R. 1997. Beyond budgeting, *Management Accounting*, December.

Hope J. and Hope, T. 1997. *Competing in the Third Wave: The Ten Key Management Issues of the Information Age*. Boston: Harvard Business School Press.

IFAC (International Federation of Accountants), 2005. *International Guidance document on Environmental Management Accounting*. New York: IFAC.

Ittner, C. and Larcker, D. 2001. Assessing empirical research in managerial accounting: a value-based management perspective, *Journal of Accounting and Economics*, 32, pp. 349–410.

Ittner, C. and Larcker, D. 2003. Coming up short on nonfinancial performance measurement, *Harvard Business Review*, November, pp. 88–95.

Jack, L. and Jones, J. 2007. Facing up to the new realities: the case for relevant costing and target cost management in agriculture, *Journal of Applied Accounting Research*, 8 (3), pp. 117–45.

Johnson, H.T. 1990. Performance measurement for competitive excellence, in R. Kaplan (ed.), *Measures for Manufacturing Excellence*, Boston, MA: Harvard Business School Press, pp. 63–90.

Johnson, H.T. and Kaplan, R.S. 1987. *Relevance Lost: The Rise and Fall of Management Accounting*, Boston, MA: Harvard University Press.

Jones, T.C. and Dugdale, D. 1998. Theory of constraints: transforming ideas? *British Accounting Review*, 30(1), pp. 73–94.

Kaplan, R. 1986b. Accounting lag: the obsolescence of cost accounting systems. *California Management Review*, Winter, pp. 174–99.

Kaplan, and Anderson, S. 2004. Time driven activity-based costing, *Harvard Business Review*, November, pp. 131–138.

Kaplan, R. and Norton, D. 1992. The balanced scorecard – measures that drive performance, *Harvard Business Review*, January/February, pp. 71–79.

Kaplan, R. and Norton, D. 1996a. Using the balanced scorecard as a strategic management system, *Harvard Business Review*, January/February, pp. 75–85.

Kaplan, R. and Norton, D. 1996b. *Translating Strategy into Action: The Balanced Scorecard*, Boston, MA: Harvard Business School Press.

Kaplan, R. and Norton, D. 1997. Why does a business need a balanced scorecard? *Journal of Cost Management*, May/June, pp. 5–10.

Kaplan, R. and Norton, D. 2004. *Strategy Maps: Converting Intangible Assets into Tangible Outcomes*, Boston, MA: Harvard Business School Press.

Kimes, S. 1989. Yield management: a tool for capacity-constrained service firms, in C.H. Lovelock (ed.) (1992) *Managing Services, Marketing, Operations and Human Resources*, Upper Saddle River, New Jersey: Prentice Hall.

Kuglin, F. and Rosenbaum, B. 2001. *The Supply Chain Network @ Internet Speed*, New York: American Management Association.

Lebas, M. 1994. Managerial accounting in France: overview of past tradition and current practice, *The European Accounting Review*, 3(3), pp. 471–87.

Lord, R. 1995. Interpreting and measuring operating leverage, *Issues in Accounting Education*, Fall, pp. 317–29.

Madonna, J. 1992. A service company measures, monitors and improves quality, *Leadership and Empowerment for Total Quality*, The Conference Board Report No. 992, New York, pp. 9–11.

Mattimoe, R. and Seal, W. (2010) Pricing in a service sector context: accounting and marketing logics in the hotel industry, *European Accounting Review* (in press).

May, M. 2002. *Transforming the Finance Function: Adding Company-wide Value in a Technology Driven Environment* (2nd edn). London: Prentice Hall.

Miles, R. and Snow, C. 1978. *Organizational Strategy, Structure, and Process*, New York: McGraw-Hill.

Monden, Y. and Hamada, K. 1991. Target costing and kaizen costing in Japanese automobile companies, *Journal of Management Accounting Research*, 3 (Fall), pp. 16–34.

Morais, R. 1997. A methodical man, *Forbes*, 11 August, pp. 70–72.

Mouritsen, J. 1998. Driving growth: economic value added versus intellectual capital, *Management Accounting Research*, 9, pp. 461–82.

Neely, A., Sutcliff, M. and Heyns, H. 2001. *Driving Value through Strategic Planning and Budgeting*, New York: Accenture.

Norreklit, H. 2000. The balance on the balanced scorecard – a critical analysis of some of its assumptions, *Management Accounting Research*, 11, pp. 65–88.

Northcott, D. and Alkaraan, F. 2007. Strategic investment appraisal, in T. Hopper, D. Northcott and R. Scapens (eds), *Issues in Management Accounting* (3rd edn). Harlow: Pearson Education, pp. 199–221.

O'Hanlon, J. and Peasnell, K. 1998. Wall Street's contribution to management accounting: the Stern Stewart EVA, financial management system, *Management Accounting Research* 9, pp. 421–44.

Olson, O., Guthrie, J. and Humphrey, C. (eds) 1998. *Global Warning! Debating International Developments in New Public Financial Management*, Oslo: Cappelen Akademisk Forlag.

Porter, M. 1980. *Competitive Strategy: Techniques for Analyzing Industries and Competitors*. New York: Free Press.

Porter, M. 1985. *Competitive Advantage: Creating and Sustaining Superior Performance*, New York: Free Press.

Radnor, Z., Walley, P., Stephens, A. and Bucci, G. 2006. *Evaluation of the lean approach to business management and its use in the public sector*. Report by Warwick Business School for Scottish Executive Social Research.

Reed, J. and Schafer, D. 2010. Carmakers join forces in green new world, *Financial Times*, 10 April, p. 15.

Scapens, R., Ezzamel, M., Burns, J. and Baldvinsdottir, G. 2003. *The Future Direction of UK Management Accounting Practice,* London: Elsevier/CIMA Publishing.

Seal, W.B. 2010. Managerial discourse and the link between theory and practice: from ROI to value-based management, *Management Accounting Research* (in press).

Seal, W.B. and Ball, A., 2008. *Re-Inventing Budgeting: the impact of third way modernization on local government budgeting*. Elsevier/CIMA.

Shank, J. 1996. Analyzing technology investments – from NPV to strategic cost management, *Management Accounting Research*, 7, pp. 185–97.

Simmonds, K. 1981. Strategic management accounting, *Management Accounting*, 59(4), pp. 26–29.

Smart, P., Maddern, H. and Maull, R. 2009. Understanding business process management: implications for theory and practice, *British Journal of Management*, 20(4), pp. 491–507.

Soin, K., Seal, W. and Cullen, J. 2002. ABC and organizational change: an institutional perspective, *Management Accounting Research*, 13, pp. 249–71.

Tanaka, M., Yoshikawa, T., Innes, J. and Mitchell, F. 1994. *Contemporary Cost Management*, London: Chapman and Hall.

Thrift, N. (2005) *Knowing Capitalism*, London: Sage.

Tomkins, C. and Carr, C. 1996. Reflections on the papers in this issue and a commentary on the state of strategic management accounting, *Management Accounting Research*, 7, pp. 271–80.

Tully, S. 1993. The real key to creating wealth, *Fortune*, 20 September, pp. 38–50.

US Environmental Protection Agency 1997. *Full Cost Accounting for Municipal Solid Waste Management*: A Handbook, Washington, DC: US EPA.

Wallander, J. 1999. Budgeting: An unnecessary evil, *Scandinavian Journal of Management*, 15, pp. 405–21.

Wildavsky, A. 1975. *Budgeting: A Comparative Theory of Budgetary Process*, Boston: Little Brown.

Wilke, J. 1994. At Digital Equipment, a resignation reveals key problem: selling, *Wall Street Journal*, 26 April, pp. A1, A11.

Womack, J.P., Jones, D.T. and Roos, D. 1990. *The Machine that Changed the World*, New York: Rawson Associates.

Ye, L. and Seal, W.B. 2009. The balanced scorecard, *Financial Management*, September, pp. 27–28.

Yen-Ju Lin, B., Chao, T., Yao, Y., Tu, S-M., Wu, C-C., Chern, J-Y., Chao, S-H. and Shaw, K-Y. 2007. How can activity-based costing methodology be performed as a powerful tool to calculate costs and secure appropriate patient care?, *Journal of Medical Systems*, 31, pp. 85–90.

Young, S.D. and O'Byrne, S.E. 2001. *EVA and Value-based Management*, New York: McGraw-Hill.

Glossary

Absorption costing A costing method that includes all manufacturing costs – direct materials, direct labour and both variable and fixed overhead – as part of the cost of a finished unit of product. This term is synonymous with full cost (p. 106).

Activity An event that causes the consumption of overhead resources in an organization (p. 123).

Activity-based costing (ABC) A costing method based on activities that is designed to provide managers with cost information for strategic and other decisions that potentially affect capacity and therefore fixed costs (p. 122).

Activity cost pool A 'bucket' in which costs are accumulated that relate to a single activity in the activity-based costing system (p. 126).

Activity measure An allocation base in an activity-based costing system; ideally, a measure of the amount of activity that drives the costs in an activity cost pool (p. 127).

Administrative costs All executive, organizational and clerical costs associated with the general management of an organization rather than with manufacturing, marketing or selling (p. 17).

Allocation base A measure of activity such as direct labour-hours or machine-hours that is used to assign costs to cost objects (p. 108).

Avoidable cost Any cost that can be eliminated (in whole or in part) by choosing one alternative over another in a decision-making situation. In managerial accounting, this term is synonymous with relevant cost and differential cost (p. 76).

Attribute costing Costing the product attributes that appeal to customers (p. 260).

Balanced scorecard (BSC) An integrated set of performance measures that is derived from and supports the organization's strategy (p. 263).

Batch-level activities Activities that are performed each time a batch of goods is handled or processed, regardless of how many units are in a batch. The amount of resource consumed depends on the number of batches run rather than on the number of units in the batch (p. 126).

Benchmarking A comparison with organizations that are the best at performing specific activities or producing particular products in order to learn how they achieve their relatively high performance (p. 309).

Bill of materials A listing of the quantity of each type of material required to manufacture a unit of product (p. 208).

Bottleneck A machine or process that limits total output because it is operating at capacity (p. 89).

Break-even point The level of sales at which profit is zero. The break-even point can also be defined as the point where total sales equals total expenses or as the point where total contribution margin equals total fixed expenses (p. 45).

Budget A detailed plan for the future, usually expressed in formal quantitative terms (p. 4).

Budget committee A group of key management persons who are responsible for overall policy matters relating to the budget programme and for co-ordinating the preparation of the budget (p. 182).

Business process A series of steps that is followed in order to carry out some task in a business (p. 302).

Business process re-engineering involves mapping and then redesigning business processes in order to eliminate unnecessary steps, reduce opportunities for errors, and lower costs. (p. 313).

Capital budgeting The process of planning significant outlays on projects that have long-term implications, such as the purchase of new equipment or the introduction of a new product (p. 234).

Cash budget A detailed plan showing how cash resources will be acquired and used over some specific time period (p. 183).

Constrained management style A management approach that concentrates on easy to measure events and lacks flexibility (p. 195).

Constraint A limitation under which a company must operate, such as limited machine time available or limited raw materials available that restricts the company's ability to satisfy demand (p. 88).

Continuous or perpetual budget A 12-month budget that rolls forward one month as the current month is completed (p. 180).

Contribution approach A profit statement format that is geared to cost behaviour in that costs are separated into variable and fixed categories rather than being separated according to the functions of production, sales and administration (p. 25).

Contribution margin The amount remaining from sales revenue after all variable expenses have been deducted (p. 25).

Contribution margin method A method of computing the break-even point in which the fixed expenses are divided by the contribution margin per unit (p. 51).

Contribution margin ratio (CM ratio) The contribution margin as a percentage of total sales (p. 47).

Control The process of instituting procedures and then obtaining feedback to ensure that all parts of the organization are functioning effectively and moving towards overall company goals (p. 4).

Conversion cost Direct labour cost plus manufacturing overhead cost (p. 17).

Cost behaviour The way in which a cost reacts or responds to changes in the level of business activity (p. 22).

Cost centre A business segment whose manager has control over cost but has no control over revenue or the use of investment funds (p. 281).

Cost driver A factor, such as machine-hours, beds occupied, computer time, or flight-hours, that causes overhead costs (p. 108).

Cost leadership Aiming to be the lowest cost producer in an industry (p. 260).

Cost of capital The overall cost to an organization of obtaining investment funds, including the cost of both debt sources and equity sources (p. 238).

Cost-plus pricing A pricing method in which a predetermined mark-up is applied to a cost base to determine the target selling price (p. 150).

Cost–volume–profit (CVP) graph The relations between revenues, costs and level of activity in an organization presented in graphic form (p. 52).

Customer-level activities Activities that are carried out to support customers but that are not related to any specific product (p. 126).

Decentralized organization An organization in which decision making is not confined to a few top executives but rather is spread throughout the organization (p. 280).

Defender A company which concentrates on reducing costs and/or improving quality in existing markets/products (p. 260).

Degree of operating leverage A measure, at a given level of sales, of how a percentage change in sales volume will affect profits. The degree of operating leverage is computed by dividing contribution margin by profit (p. 57).

Delivery cycle time The amount of time required from receipt of an order from a customer to shipment of the completed goods (p. 268).

Differential cost Any cost that differs between alternatives in a decision-making situation. In managerial accounting, this term is synonymous with avoidable cost and relevant cost. Also see Incremental cost (p. 26).

Differential revenue The difference in revenue between any two alternatives (p. 26).

Direct labour Those factory labour costs that can easily be traced to individual units of product. Also called touch labour (p. 16).

Direct labour budget A detailed plan showing labour requirements over some specific time period (p. 186).

Direct materials Those materials that become an integral part of a finished product and can conveniently be traced into it (p. 16).

Direct materials budget A detailed plan showing the amount of raw materials that must be purchased during a period to meet both production and stock needs (p. 186).

Direct method The allocation of all of a service department's costs directly to operating departments without recognizing services provided to other service departments (p. 111).

Economic value added (EVA) A concept similar to residual profit (p. 288).

Environmental management accounting is the collection and analysis of physical and monetary information on environmental costs and benefits in order to make environmentally sensitive decisions (p. 9).

Executional drivers Cost factors such as work force involvement, quality management capacity utilization, plant lay-out efficiency, product configuration effectiveness, and exploitation of linkages (p. 261).

Feedback Accounting and other reports that help managers monitor performance and focus on problems and/or opportunities that might otherwise go unnoticed (p. 4).

Finished goods stock budget A budget showing the cost expected to appear on the balance sheet for unsold units at the end of a period (p. 189).

First-stage allocation The process by which overhead costs are assigned to activity cost pools in an activity-based costing system (p. 128).

Fixed cost A cost that remains constant, in total, regardless of changes in the level of activity within the relevant range. If a fixed cost is expressed on a per unit basis, it varies inversely with the level of activity (p. 23).

Full cost See Absorption costing (p. 107).

High-low method A technique for separating mixed costs into fixed and variable components (p. 61).

Ideal standards Standards that allow for no machine breakdowns or other work interruptions and that require peak efficiency at all times (p. 207).

Incremental analysis An analytical approach that focuses only on those items of revenue, cost and volume that will change as a result of a decision (p. 49)

Incremental cost An increase in cost between two alternatives. Also see Differential cost (p. 26).

Indirect labour The labour costs of caretakers, supervisors, materials handlers, and other factory workers that cannot conveniently be traced directly to particular products (p. 16).

Indirect materials Small items of material such as glue and nails. These items may become an integral part of a finished product but are traceable to the product only at great cost or inconvenience (p. 16).

Intermediate market A market in which a transferred product or service is sold in its present form to outside customers (p. 164).

Internal rate of return The discount rate at which the net present value of an investment project is zero; thus, the internal rate of return represents the interest yield promised by a project over its useful life. This term is synonymous with time-adjusted rate of return (p. 238).

Investment centre A business segment whose manager has control over cost and over revenue and that also has control over the use of investment funds (p. 281).

Job-order costing system A costing system used in situations where many different products, jobs or services are produced each period (p. 107)

Just-in-time A production system in which materials are purchased and produced only as needed to meet actual customer demand so that stocks are reduced to the minimum and in some cases to zero (p. 303).

Kaizen budgeting Rather than base budgets on historical standards, kaizen budgeting plans for incremental improvements in efficiency and reduction in costs (p. 158).

Kaizen costing The reduction of cost during production through continuous gradual improvements that reduce waste and increase efficiency (p. 158).

Labour efficiency variance A measure of the difference between the actual hours taken to complete a task and the standard hours allowed, multiplied by the standard hourly labour rate (p. 218).

Labour rate variance A measure of the difference between the actual hourly labour rate and the standard rate, multiplied by the number of hours worked during the period (p. 217).

Lean production The identification of a value stream and challenging all forms of waste or non-value adding activity (p. 303).

Life-cycle costing Analyses costs incurred throughout the life of a product from development through to full production (p. 260).

Make or buy decision A decision as to whether an item should be produced internally or purchased from an outside supplier (p. 85).

Management accounting The phase of accounting concerned with providing information to managers for use in planning and controlling operations and in decision making (p. 4).

Management by exception A system of management in which standards are set for various operating activities, with actual results then compared to these standards. Any differences that are deemed significant are brought to the attention of management as 'exceptions' (p. 206).

Manufacturing cycle efficiency (MCE) Process (value-added) time as a percentage of throughput time (p. 271).

Manufacturing overhead All costs associated with manufacturing except direct materials and direct labour (p. 16).

Manufacturing overhead budget A detailed plan showing the production costs, other than direct materials and direct labour, that will be incurred over a specified time period (p. 187).

Margin Net operating profit divided by sales (p. 284).

Margin of safety The excess of budgeted (or actual) sales over the break-even volume of sales (p. 54).

Market price The price being charged for an item on the open (intermediate) market (p. 164).

Marketing mix Price is one element in product competitiveness together with product, promotion and place (p. 260).

Marketing or selling costs All costs necessary to secure customer orders and get the finished product or service into the hands of the customer (p. 17).

Mark-up The difference between the selling price of a product or service and its cost. The mark-up is usually expressed as a percentage of cost (p. 150).

Master budget A summary of a company's plans in which specific targets are set for sales, production, distribution, and financing activities and that generally culminates in a cash budget, budgeted profit and loss account, and budgeted balance sheet (p. 183).

Materials price variance A measure of the difference between the actual unit price paid for an item and the standard price, multiplied by the quantity purchased (p. 214).

Materials quantity variance A measure of the difference between the actual quantity of materials used in production and the standard quantity allowed, multiplied by the standard price per unit of materials (p. 215).

Material requirements planning (MRP) An operations management tool that uses a computer to help manage materials and stocks (p. 186).

Multiple predetermined overhead rates A costing system in which there are multiple overhead cost pools with a different predetermined rate for each cost pool, rather than a single predetermined overhead rate for the entire company. Frequently, each production department is treated as a separate overhead cost pool (p. 109).

Negotiated transfer price A transfer price agreed on between buying and selling divisions (p. 159).

Net operating profit Profit before interest and profit taxes have been deducted (p. 283).

Net present value The difference between the present value of the cash inflows and the present value of the cash outflows associated with an investment project (p. 235).

Non-value-added activities are activities in an organization that do not add value to that organization's products or services. (p. 313).

Operating assets Cash, debtors, inventory, plant and equipment, and all other assets held for productive use in an organization (p. 283).

Operating department A department or similar unit in an organization within which the central purposes of the organization are carried out (p. 109).

Operating leverage A measure of how sensitive profit is to a given percentage change in sales. It is computed by dividing the contribution margin by profit (p. 57).

Opportunity cost The potential benefit that is given up when one alternative is selected over another (p. 27).

Organization-sustaining activities Activities that are carried out regardless of which customers are served, which products are produced, how many batches are run, or how many units are made (p. 126).

Overhead application The process of charging manufacturing overhead cost to job cost sheets and to the work in progress account (p. 108).

Participative budget *See* Self-imposed budget (p. 180).

Payback period The length of time that it takes for a project to recover its initial cost out of the cash receipts that it generates (p. 242).

Performance report A detailed report comparing budgeted data to actual data (p. 4).

Period costs Those costs that are taken directly to the profit and loss account as expenses in the period in which they are incurred or accrued; such costs consist of selling (marketing) and administrative expenses (p. 17).

Plan-do-check-act cycle is a systematic, fact-based approach to continuous improvement (p. 309).

Planning and control cycle The flow of management activities through planning, directing and motivating, and controlling, and then back to planning again (p. 5).

Plantwide overhead rate A single predetermined overhead rate that is used throughout a plant (p. 109).

Practical standards Standards that allow for normal machine downtime and other work interruptions and that can be attained through reasonable, though highly efficient, efforts by the average worker (p. 208).

Predetermined overhead rate A rate used to charge overhead cost to jobs in production; the rate is established in advance for each period by use of estimates of total manufacturing overhead cost and of the total allocation base for the period (p. 108).

Price elasticity of demand A measure of the degree to which the volume of unit sales for a product or service is affected by a change in price (p. 150).

Prime cost Direct materials cost plus direct labour cost (p. 17).

Product costs All costs that are involved in the purchase or manufacture of goods. In the case of manufactured goods, these costs consist of direct materials, direct labour, and manufacturing overhead. Also see Stock-related costs (p. 17).

Product differentiation Aims to maintain a price premium based on superior product quality (p. 261).

Product-level activities Activities that relate to specific products that must be carried out regardless of how many units are produced and sold or batches run (p. 126).

Production budget A detailed plan showing the number of units that must be produced during a period in order to meet both sales and stock needs (p. 185).

Profit centre A business segment whose manager has control over cost and revenue but has no control over the use of investment funds (p. 281).

Prospector A company that is continually searching for market opportunities (p. 260).

Range of acceptable transfer prices The range of transfer prices within which the profits of both the selling division and the purchasing division would increase as a result of a transfer (p. 160).

Raw materials Any materials that go into the final product (p. 16).

Relaxing (or elevating) the constraint Increasing the capacity of a bottleneck (p. 307).

Relevant cost A cost that differs between alternatives in a particular decision. In managerial accounting, this term is synonymous with avoidable cost and differential cost (p. 76).

Relevant range The range of activity within which assumptions about variable and fixed cost behaviour are valid (p. 23).

Required rate of return The minimum rate of return that an investment project must yield to be acceptable (p. 239).

Residual income The net operating profit that an investment centre earns above the required return on its operating assets (p. 288).

Responsibility centre Any business segment whose manager has control over cost, revenue or the use of investment funds (p. 281).

Return on investment (ROI) Net operating profit divided by average operating assets. It also equals margin multiplied by turnover (p. 283).

Sales budget A detailed schedule showing the expected sales for coming periods; these sales are typically expressed in both pounds and units (p. 183).

Sales mix The relative proportions in which a company's products are sold. Sales mix is computed by expressing the sales of each product as a percentage of total sales (p. 58).

Second-stage allocation The process by which activity rates are used to apply costs to products and customers in activity-based costing (p. 133).

Segment Any part or activity of an organization about which the manager seeks cost, revenue or profit data (p. 281).

Self-imposed budget A method of preparing budgets in which managers prepare their own budgets. These budgets are then reviewed by the manager's supervisor, and any issues are resolved by mutual agreement (p. 180).

Selling and administrative expense budget A detailed schedule of planned expenses that will be incurred in areas other than manufacturing during a budget period (p. 189).

Service department A department that provides support or assistance to operating departments and that does not engage directly in production or in other operating activities of an organization (p. 110).

Shared service centres Organizations which specialize in the delivery of the routine trans-actions of support services that are required by the operating units of large organizations (p. 314).

Simple rate of return The rate of return computed by dividing a project's annual accounting profit by the initial investment required (p. 243).

Six sigma An approach that focuses on the variation from the mean rather than average times (p. 311).

Special order A one-time order that is not considered part of the company's normal on-going business (p. 87).

Standard cost card A detailed listing of the standard amounts of materials, labour and overhead that should go into a unit of product, multiplied by the standard price or rate that has been set for each cost element (p. 206).

Standard cost per unit The standard cost of a unit of product as shown on the standard cost card; it is computed by multiplying the standard quantity or hours by the standard price or rate for each cost element (p. 210).

Standard hours allowed The time that should have been taken to complete the period's output as computed by multiplying the actual number of units produced by the standard hours per unit (p. 212).

Standard hours per unit The amount of labour time that should be required to complete a single unit of product, including allowances for breaks, machine downtime, cleanup, rejects, and other normal inefficiencies (p. 209).

Standard price per unit The price that should be paid for a single unit of materials, including allowances for quality, quantity purchased, shipping, receiving, and other such costs, net of any discounts allowed (p. 208).

Standard quantity allowed The amount of materials that should have been used to complete the period's output as computed by multiplying the actual number of units produced by the standard quantity per unit (p. 211).

Standard quantity per unit The amount of materials that should be required to complete a single unit of product, including allowances for normal waste spoilage, rejects and similar inefficiencies (p. 208).

Standard rate per hour The labour rate that should be incurred per hour of labour time, including employment taxes, fringe benefits and other such labour costs (p. 209).

Stock-related costs (also known as inventoriable costs) Synonym for product costs (p. 19).

Strategic choice Choosing not only which industries and products to compete in but also how a company plans to compete (p. 260).

Strategic management accounting The use of management accounting information to help managers choose where and how to compete (p. 260).

Structural drivers Factors such as scale, scope, experience, technology and complexity (p. 261).

Sub-optimization An overall level of profitability that is less than a segment or a company is capable of earning (p. 159).

Sunk cost Any cost that has already been incurred and that cannot be changed by any decision made now or in the future (p. 27).

Target costing The process of determining the maximum allowable cost for a new product and then developing a prototype that can be profitably manufactured and distributed for that maximum target cost figure (p. 157).

Theory of constraints (TOC) A management approach that emphasizes the importance of managing constraints (p. 307).

Throughput accounting (TA) Ranking products by calculating the throughput accounting ratio (p. 309).

Throughput time The amount of time required to turn raw materials into completed products (p. 270).

Time-adjusted rate of return This term is synonymous with internal rate of return (p. 238).

Total quality management An approach to quality that focuses on serving customers and using teams made up of frontline workers to aim for zero defects (p. 309).

Transfer price The price charged when one division or segment provides goods or services to another division or segment of an organization (p. 159).

Turnover The amount of sales generated in an investment centre for each pound invested in operating assets. It is computed by dividing sales by the average operating assets figure (p. 284).

Unit-level activities Activities that arise as a result of the total volume of goods and services that are produced, and that are performed each time a unit is produced (p. 126).

Value chain The major business functions that add value to a company's products and services (p. 261).

Variable cost A cost that varies, in total, in direct proportion to changes in the level of activity. A variable cost is constant per unit (p. 21).

Variable overhead efficiency variance The difference between the actual activity (direct labour-hours, machine-hours, or some other base) of a period and the standard activity allowed, multiplied by the variable part of the predetermined overhead rate (p. 220).

Variable overhead spending variance The difference between the actual variable overhead cost incurred during a period and the standard cost that should have been incurred based on the actual activity of the period (p. 219).

Variance The difference between standard prices and quantities on the one hand and actual prices and quantities on the other hand (p. 211).

Vertical integration The involvement by a company is more than one of the steps from production of basic raw materials to the manufacture and distribution of a finished product (p. 85).

Working capital The excess of current assets over current liabilities (p. 237).

Yield A term synonymous with internal rate of return and time-adjusted rate of return (p. 238).

Yield management A practice of achieving high capacity utilization through varying prices according to market segments and time of booking (p. 153).

Yield percentage A performance metric calculated by dividing actual revenue by the maximum potential revenue (p. 153).

Zero-based budgeting A method of budgeting in which managers are required to justify all costs as if the programmes involved were being proposed for the first time (p. 196).

Index

Note: **bold** page numbers indicate key terms definitions